Regional Connection under the Belt and Road Initiative

T0359072

China's Belt and Road Initiative (BRI) is intended to radically increase investment and integration along a series of land and maritime routes. As the initiative involves more than 100 countries or international organizations and huge amounts of infrastructure construction, cooperation between many different markets is essential to its success. Cheung and Hong have edited a collection of essays that, between them, examine a range of practical issues facing the BRI and how those issues are being addressed in a range of countries. Such challenges include managing financing and investment, ensuring infrastructure connectivity, and handling the necessary e-commerce and physical logistics.

Emphasizing the role of Hong Kong as an intermediary and enabler in the process, this book attempts to tackle the key practical challenges facing the BRI and anticipate how these challenges will affect the initiative's further development. The book provides a holistic and international approach to understanding the implementation of the BRI and its implications for the future economic integration of this huge region.

Fanny M. Cheung is Pro-Vice Chancellor of the Chinese University of Hong Kong (CUHK); Co-Director of the Hong Kong Institute of Asia-Pacific Studies, CUHK, Hong Kong; and Co-Convenor of the Global China Research Programme, CUHK, Hong Kong

Ying-yi Hong is Associate Director of the Hong Kong Institute of Asia-Pacific Studies, CUHK, Hong Kong and Co-Convenor of the Global China Research Programme, CUHK, Hong Kong.

Routledge Studies on Asia in the World

Routledge Studies on Asia in the World will be an authoritative source of knowledge on Asia studying a variety of cultural, economic, environmental, legal, political, religious, security, and social questions, addressed from an Asian perspective. We aim to foster a deeper understanding of the domestic and regional complexities which accompany the dynamic shifts in the global economic, political, and security landscape towards Asia and their repercussions for the world at large. We're looking for scholars and practitioners – Asian and Western alike – from various social science disciplines and fields to engage in testing existing models which explain such dramatic transformation and to formulate new theories that can accommodate the specific political, cultural, and developmental context of Asia's diverse societies. We welcome both monographs and collective volumes which explore the new roles, rights, and responsibilities of Asian nations in shaping today's interconnected and globalized world in their own right.

The Series is advised and edited by Matthias Vanhullebusch and Ji Weidong of Shanghai Jiao Tong University.

Sustainable Development Goals in the Republic of Korea
Edited by Tae Yong Jung

Access to Higher Education: Refugees' Stories from Malaysia
Lucy Bailey and Gül İnanç

The New International Relations of Sub-Regionalism
Asia and Europe
Edited by Hidetoshi Taga and Seiichi Igarashi

Regional Connection under the Belt and Road Initiative
The Prospects for Economic and Financial Cooperation
Edited by Fanny M. Cheung and Ying-yi Hong

Find the full list of books in the series here:
www.routledge.com/Routledge-Studies-on-Asia-in-the-World/book-series/RSOAW

Regional Connection under the Belt and Road Initiative

The Prospects for Economic and Financial Cooperation

Edited by Fanny M. Cheung
and Ying-yi Hong

Routledge
Taylor & Francis Group

LONDON AND NEW YORK

First published 2019
by Routledge
2 Park Square, Milton Park, Abingdon, Oxon OX14 4RN

and by Routledge
52 Vanderbilt Avenue, New York, NY 10017, USA

First issued in paperback 2020

Routledge is an imprint of the Taylor & Francis Group, an informa business

British Library Cataloguing-in-Publication Data
A catalogue record for this book is available from the British Library

Library of Congress Cataloging-in-Publication Data
A catalog record for this book has been requested

ISBN 13: 978-0-367-58354-5 (pbk)
ISBN 13: 978-1-138-60749-1 (hbk)

Typeset in Galliard
by Apex CoVantage, LLC

Contents

Preface

In September 2013, Chinese President Xi Jinping unveiled the Belt and Road Initiative (BRI) as a grand development strategy to promote regional connectivity, economic cooperation, cultural exchange, and mutual learning among countries along two ancient economic corridors. Participation in the BRI is open to all countries and international and regional organizations. The initiative is based on the Silk Road Economic Belt and the 21st-Century Maritime Silk Road for promoting cooperation and mutual growth in the regions along both routes. An action plan, *Vision and Actions on Jointly Building Silk Road Economic Belt and 21st-Century Maritime Silk Road*, was put forward in March 2015. The plan laid down strategies for regional integration through five proposed land and maritime routes and six new international development corridors. These are land bridges and maritime routes connecting the Asian and European continents. The initiative has involved more than 100 countries or international organizations.

Economic and financial cooperation is one of the major priorities for cooperation in the BRI, and the construction of infrastructure, the free flow of economic factors, the efficient allocation of resources, and the further integration of markets are important bases for strengthening such connectivity. Hong Kong enjoys various advantages in professional services, such as in accounting, investment environment and risk assessment, environmental consulting, and construction and project management. More importantly, Hong Kong also has a sound legal system based on common law and a well-developed financial system that can facilitate the efficient raising of capital and financing. Hence, Hong Kong can play a unique and active role in promoting economic and financial cooperation in the Belt and Road regions.

In order to promote research work for China's global engagement and to study the role Hong Kong can play in the process, The Chinese University of Hong Kong in 2015 set up a Global Research (GCR) Programme (www.gcr.cuhk.edu.hk/) which consolidated our institutional infrastructure and the research capacity of over 40 scholars, housed under the Hong Kong Institute of Asia-Pacific Studies (HKIAPS) as the secretariat. With the support of the Central Policy Unit (CPU) of the Hong Kong SAR government, HKIAPS successfully co-organized two academic international conferences on Hong Kong and the World under the Belt and Road Initiative. These took place on the campus of the Chinese

University of Hong Kong in 2015 and 2016. The conference in 2015 established a multidisciplinary network across the Belt and Road regions and assessed the opportunities for and challenges to the BRI. The conference in 2016 focused on economic and financial cooperation among the Belt and Road economies (especially Hong Kong). Each conference attracted more than 400 participants. These include prominent scholars, members of think tanks, and other stakeholders from Hong Kong, Mainland China, Belt and Road countries, and the world. Participants presented their research findings and observations in thematic discussion sessions and exchanged views during round-table discussions on the overall potentialities of economic and financial cooperation in the Belt and Road regions. The discussions further enhanced our understanding of various aspects of the implementation of the BRI.

In 2017, thanks to funding support from the University Grants Council of Hong Kong, the HKIAPS invited internationally renowned historians Gungwu Wang and Peter Frankopan to give two public speeches to examine the humanistic ramifications and interfaces of China's global outreach, with special reference to historical roots and intercultural exchanges. Prof Wang spoke on the silk road and the centrality of old world Eurasia in a history of the world. He sketched Belt and Road regions in 5,000 years of Eurasian history and explored the historical meaning of multidimensional exchanges and interactions. Prof Frankopan, an Oxford historian, spoke on the future of the BRI. He focused on the connections, opportunities, and challenges.

The aforementioned academic events organized by the HKIAPS not only brought together scholars, policymakers, and members of think tanks from around the globe to promote research on China's engagement with the world, but also led people from all walks of life to think more about the idea of a future of diversity, sustainability, and prosperity for all. This book is a quality selection of research observations presented in those public lectures and conferences. Authors have updated their ideas and arguments after conference exchanges and blinded reviews. Some have included the most recent evidence from observation and research.

Themes of this book include prospects, strategies, and policies of the BRI; finance and investment of the BRI; and infrastructure connectivity and e-commerce and logistics.

The first section on history and evaluation has two chapters. Gungwu Wang elaborates the relevance of the BRI to world history, and Wen Wang et al. assess the implementation of the BRI after four years.

The second section is on finance and investment. It discusses the role of Hong Kong as a financial centre and makes a comparison between China and Japan in investment strategies. Kevin C. K. Lam et al., set the recent financial crisis as the backdrop, examine opportunities for Hong Kong in investment and finance, and discuss the prospects for Hong Kong to be an equity financing centre. C. K. Law and Derek Yuen compare the investment strategies of China and Japan in infrastructure projects on ASEAN countries.

The third section is on infrastructure connectivity and compares specific projects in Central Asia, Cambodia, and Malaysia. Roman Vakulchuk and Indra

Overland introduce a possible role the BRI could play in the market integration of Central Asia. Lak Chansok illustrates the development of infrastructure connectivity in Cambodia through the BRI. Chow-bing Ngeow reviews the political economy of China's railway investment in Malaysia.

The fourth section is about e-commerce and logistics. It addresses the implications of the digital age on the implementation of the BRI and the prospects of maritime logistics in the BRI. Kam-Fai Wong et al. evaluate the use of information technologies to tackle language barriers, to bring about inclusive development, and to bridge the digital divide in BRI regions. Jai Acharya depicts the possibilities and challenges of maritime logistics in Asia Pacific regions from the perspective of the BRI.

The final section takes a forward-looking view to explore prospects that the BRI may face. Peter Frankopan plots some key areas of chances and challenges that may arise.

In sum, papers in this book not only focus on the implementation, challenges, and implications of specific development or investment project opportunities in the Belt and Road regions but also emphasize the special role, function, and contribution of Hong Kong in fostering and strengthening various linkages between China and the Belt and Road regions. This book is one of the first publications on economic and financial cooperation in the BRI from the perspectives of renowned scholars and experienced practitioners. More importantly, it is also a long-awaited book on the role that Hong Kong could play in the BRI. We hope this book will serve as both a milestone and a road sign for future academic and practical research on the BRI.

We are indebted to the generous funding support from the Central Policy Unit of Hong Kong SAR Government, University Grants Council of Hong Kong, and the Global China Research programme of the Chinese University of Hong Kong. We are also thankful to Dr Victor Zheng, Ms Posan Wan, Dr Shiru Wang, Dr Hua Guo, and Miss Tiffany Yu for their capable work in making this book possible.

Fanny M. Cheung
Ying-yi Hong

Notes on contributors

Jai Acharya is Managing Director of International Shipping Bureau (Singapore) Pte Ltd and Director of International Ocean Institute Singapore (Focal Point), Singapore.

Lak Chansok is Lecturer at the Department of International Studies, Institute of Foreign Languages, Royal University of Phnom Penh. He is also Researcher at the Cambodia 21st Century Maritime Silk Road Research Centre at the Royal University of Phnom Penh.

Chun-Hung Cheng is Associate Professor at the Department of Systems Engineering and Engineering Management, Chinese University of Hong Kong (CUHK). He also works for the Ministry of Education Key Laboratory of High Confidence Software Technologies (CUHK Sub-Lab) at CUHK.

Waiman Cheung is Professor at the Department of Decision Sciences and Managerial Economics, Chinese University of Hong Kong (CUHK). He is also Director of Asian Institute of Supply Chains and Logistics at the Chinese University of Hong Kong.

Peter Frankopan is Professor of Global History at the University of Oxford. He is also Director of the Oxford Centre for Byzantine Research and Senior Research Fellow at Worcester College, University of Oxford.

Jinjing Jia is Director of the Department of Macroeconomics, Chongyang Institute for Financial Studies, Renmin University of China.

Kevin C. K. Lam is Professor at the Department of Accountancy, Hang Seng Management College, Hong Kong.

Cheung-kwok Law is Senior Research Fellow, Global China Research Programme, Chinese University of Hong Kong (CUHK). He is also Director of Policy, Aviation Policy and Research Center at CUHK.

Heather M. F. Lee is Assistant Professor at the Department of Accountancy, Hang Seng Management College, Hong Kong.

Julia J. Liu is Assistant Professor at the Department of Accountancy, Hang Seng Management College, Hong Kong.

Ying Liu is Research Fellow at the Chongyang Institute for Financial Studies, Renmin University of China.

Chow-bing Ngeow is Deputy Director of the Institute of China Studies, University of Malaysia.

Indra Overland is Research Professor and Head of the Energy Programme, Norwegian Institute of International Affairs. He is also Professor at Nord University.

Roman Vakulchuk is Senior Researcher at the Norwegian Institute of International Affairs (NUPI).

Gungwu Wang is Chairman of the East Asian Institute at the National University of Singapore. He is also University Professor at the National University of Singapore.

Stacy Z. Wang is Assistant Professor at the Department of Accountancy, Hang Seng Management College, Hong Kong.

Wen Wang is Executive Dean, Chongyang Institute for Financial Studies, Renmin University of China.

Kam-Fai Wong is Director of the Centre for Innovation and Technology at the Chinese University of Hong Kong. He is also Associate Dean (External Affairs), Faculty of Engineering, Chinese University of Hong Kong.

Junyong Xiang is Deputy Director of the Department of Industrial Studies, Chongyang Institute for Financial Studies at Renmin University of China.

Derek Yuen is Lecturer on the Master of Social Science on the Global Political Economy Programme, at the Chinese University of Hong Kong.

Part I
Retrospect and evaluation

1 Silk roads and the centrality of Old World Eurasia

Gungwu Wang

China's One Belt One Road Initiative has attracted considerable interest since it was launched. Thousands of scholars, activists, businessmen, and government officials all over the world have been engaged in trying to understand its significance. Ultimately, the initiative is about what developments it can bring to those who take part. There are numerous studies about how it would work, and also much speculation about China's intentions. Underlying it all is an assumption that the Chinese have a strategic plan, and that each participating partner sees it as directly beneficial.

The literature available is so large that I am unable to keep up with most of it. People in Hong Kong along the frontline of the project would be more aware of what is involved than almost anybody else. So I shall fall back on being a historian and look for the way this initiative fits into the longer period of world history. Some of you know that I had a series of dialogues with my colleague Ooi Kee Beng on Eurasia in world history. There we examined the Old World where the three enduring world civilizations centred on the Mediterranean and southern and eastern Asia connected with one another through the Eurasian continent.

Eurasia the Old World

From a historian's point of view, this Eurasia has had 5,000 years of recorded history, longer and more continuous than any other part of the world. There were, of course, states and societies elsewhere but, if they did not record their history, we do not know much about them. For the Eurasian people, however, their thousands of years of recorded history provide us with a strong sense of the continuity of the human experience in a super-continent. Of course, this Eurasia is hard to define. In my book, Eurasia refers to Europe, North Africa, and what we call Asia today. We are still trying to reconstruct from fragments of archaeological and anthropological findings the history of some other parts of the world, but their earlier links with Eurasia have not been determined. What distinguishes Eurasia is that it was highly interconnected, often deeply interlocked, throughout that recorded history. I have tried to understand some of the consequences flowing from these links. The story is unevenly told and we know some parts of it better than others, but enough of the story was so closely tied together that it is possible to construct a meaningful picture.

This was the Old World before the discovery of the New World by Europeans when they crossed the Atlantic 500 years ago. What became global after that included the Americas and the course of human story began to change direction. Today, we may ask if that Old World Eurasia is still relevant. Is it merely a part of global history and there is no turning back? The records describing that Old World suggest that it still has a role to play. Clearly it was a world of contestations displaying a great deal of violence and brutality. But it was also one of continuous culture contacts that enhanced the development of several civilizations. At the same time, it was also a world in which relatively peaceful trading connections by seas also enriched many economies over millennia.

This Old World divided into four main parts. Three of them had distinctive and enduring civilizations while the fourth connected the other three during long periods of contact and competition. I shall not go into details about how they interacted with one another.

In brief, the civilization that arose in the Mediterranean was probably the most ancient. It started with the two rivers of Tigris and Euphrates and was followed by Egypt on the Nile. The Greco–Roman model of city-states developed separately but was subsequently integrated eastwards with the monotheistic Abrahamic religions. That led to struggles for dominance first within a Christian West and then also with an Islamic East, bitter struggles that continued for centuries. That competition for power included the ambition to control all trade with the wealthy realms of India and China on the other side of Eurasia. Eventually, that led the European west to cross the Atlantic and Indian Oceans and build the powerful navies that determined the shape of modern world history.

As for the Indian and Chinese civilizations, they were ancient and resilient and, when threatened by Western dominance, have fought to survive to the present. On the edges of Asia, one was centred on the Ganges River on the Indian sub-continent and the other on the Yellow and Yangzi rivers of China. Connecting these two with the Mediterranean were the realms of nomadic tribes and oasis-based towns across the vast region of continental Eurasia. For a long time, this was the untamed middle that helped the three civilizations to interact with one another. Those linkages did much to shape at least 2,000 years of recorded history before modern times.

Today's globalization, unlike the 5,000 years of Eurasia, has had a relatively short history. The developments arising from the extended contacts and settlements across the Atlantic and across the Indian Ocean, as well as those across the Pacific from the Atlantic, have created our maritime global world. The drive that enabled that to happen began in the 16th century primarily with economic goals, but soon led to political and strategic struggles for domination and empire. This second stage of political globalization has been particularly significant because it forced a new modernization process across the globe. While that process made us more alike and more connected, it also at the same time injected into each state and society deep disagreements and tensions that simply would not go away. This is the world that we have inherited, one that was created since the 18th century.

During the 20th century, economic dynamism shifted across the Atlantic, and at its centre was the United States of America. The United States carried the seeds of European civilization of the Mediterranean across the seas and opened up a new way of looking at global history from a perspective unknown in the past. For the last half century, that New World has dominated the rest of the world with its economic and military power. This is the reality we have lived with since the end of the Second World War. In this context, the world now observes with growing interest China's efforts to recover after a great fall. It is riveting to see how China is regaining a position that the world has not known for two centuries.

We know that China was the centre of a great civilization that kept meticulous and well-structured records of its history and that provided its people with a strong sense of continuity with their past. Their civilization had endured and survived many kinds of challenges during the past three millennia. Unlike ancient civilizations that disappeared after the fall of their states, China is a civilization-based state that had fallen and risen several times.

China's survival experiences

The Chinese have been changing throughout their history. This is something worth emphasizing. Chinese civilization did not stagnate the way some books have portrayed it. The portrait of an unchanging China through thousands of years of history was simply not true. The China before the Qin–Han unification was quite different from imperial China. The Qin–Han period was when identifiably Han peoples came to share similar values and beliefs. This marked a very important turning point in their history.

That was only the beginning. After the fall of the Han dynasty, what was "China" went through a very turbulent period of three centuries. The main catalysts for the changes were invading nomadic forces along its borders, particularly from the North and West. More than 200 years of political divisions followed and they were accompanied by religious and political transformations. There was considerable resistance to rule by the tribal leaders but there were also adaptations to new social and economic conditions. By the time the "Chinese" were brought together again following the empire's re-unification under the Sui–Tang regimes, they were a different body of peoples.

From the format of the official historical records, we may get the impression that there had not been any break in continuity. But if the records were read carefully, it would be clear that the Chinese peoples had undergone considerable change. The most striking example is the introduction of Buddhism from India and Central Asia. Its ideas and practices induced local Taoists to reinterpret their own traditions. The benefits of opening to the outside world were incalculable. There developed significant growth in relationships not only overland along what has come to be called the Silk Road, but also across the Silk Road by sea to the Indian Ocean. By the time of the Sui–Tang unification, we see a very different China. Those familiar with the development of South China would know that the

Yue peoples there identified themselves as Chinese only during the Tang dynasty. To them, being Chinese was becoming Tangren, people of the Tang.

There followed a period of cultural consolidation when the Song rulers defended and refined their heritage and brought considerable advances to Chinese society and economy. But it was also the time when a series of new rulers from Manchuria, Mongolia, and further west in Central Eurasia imposed their rule over much of northern China and eventually all of China. The Chinese fought back and reunited the country under the Ming. But, despite great efforts to teach the invaders to accept Chinese culture, it proved impossible not to absorb new influences from the foreign rulers. Notable were some of the scientific and technological ideas and skills that the Mongols brought to China, but there were also aspects of governance that were retained.

How the Chinese reacted and adapted to foreign ideas, not least among the Ming elites that had set out to restore Han and Tang political and cultural values, has aroused great interest. Modern studies show that the conquest dynasties did produce changes at various levels of society. This was even more obvious during Manchu rule after 1644. The Qing rulers skilfully merged the Confucian state structure with their Manchu institutions and created a mixed parallel system of governance that served them well for over 250 years.

With over 1,500 years of change in response to foreign power and ideas, the picture of a stagnant China waiting for the West to come and arouse it from slumber is totally misleading. China was often slow and reluctant and paid a heavy price for their sluggishness, but its people have always reacted to challenges and changes were taking place all the time. Of course, there was an inbuilt resilience that came from a core set of values and practices based on what was inherited from the Qin–Han "revolution". That core was supported by a set of classical texts and standard histories that embodied the sense of continuity and identity, thus enabling China and its governance ideals to survive.

The way Chinese elites, increasingly well-schooled to govern by Confucian principles, adapted new ideas and sought opportunities to make China stronger and more defensible is a fascinating story. They succeeded in learning from defeat and foreign conquest and, from time to time, enabled China to become larger and more integrated. People who compare the maps of the Ming and Qing dynasties are often astonished how much the borders of China have been extended. Certainly, the land area of China was doubled in the course of 200 years. Chinese leaders since 1912 are still learning how to deal with what the Manchu Qing had added to the country's historical borders.

But the greatest challenge China faced began during the second half of the 19th century. At the beginning of that century, China was still powerful and highly respected for its achievements. However, when it began to decline, it did so very quickly. This was largely because Chinese leaders underestimated the new kind of power that British and other European national empires brought to Asia, the central factor in the new globalization based on maritime dominance. It was accompanied by the economic system of capitalism that supported imperial expansion beyond the Americas to Africa and almost all of Asia. During that stage of momentous change, the Chinese found they had no answer to the challenge and had to go through more than a hundred years of turmoil in response. For the first time in Chinese history, the country faced powerful enemies who came overland and by sea at the same time.

In recent times, the Chinese people have rediscovered the Zheng He expeditions sent out when China was master of the seas and had the biggest navy in the world. Zheng He went out to the Indian Ocean seven times and confirmed that there were no enemies out there. The Ming court then decided that the voyages were not worth the immense cost. Enemies were threatening overland from the north, so they spent a fortune building the Great Wall instead. Thus, they decided to give up their maritime supremacy. The decision was not wrong. It was a realistic and practical response to the realities of the time. What were needed were coastal defence forces primarily to deal with piracy and enough to keep the trading classes honest. Four centuries later, they were helpless in the face of a modern navy backed by very efficient economic institutions. For a country that was essentially rural and agrarian, the challenge was too much to overcome without a total overhaul of everything they knew.

The much-studied Chinese decline need not detain us here. What does need stressing is that the enemies not only came by sea but also, in the form of Tsarist Russian expansion, arrived overland. The Russian response to West European imperialism was to expand deep into central and northern Asia to the borders of Qing China. It was significant that the first modern treaty signed between two equal states, the Treaty of Nerchinsk in 1689, was between the Chinese and Russians. The West saw that as extraordinary, but the Qing rulers viewed it as the normal way that China dealt with powerful overland enemies. Those who came by sea had not been enemies and were treated as trading entities that could be regulated and controlled. Thus, the Chinese were really surprised when the new naval power was turned against them.

The Chinese economy also declined rapidly after 1840. The answer to that challenge was to learn enough from the capitalist enterprises to compete. But the Chinese soon realized that the treaty concessions they had made had given so many advantages to the foreign companies that this was not enough. They would have to dismantle the whole treaty system to have any chance to succeed. Pushing back to the past was not the answer. A total restructuring that gave the Chinese a level playing field was essential. This was not exactly the China dream, but it was soon seen as a precondition in order that China could regain its position in the world. Generations of leaders subscribed to this vision of the future. It would have been, however, no more than a dream if the Chinese had remained divided. As long as they were, foreign powers could go on intervening to further their own interests. The Japanese went further to invade China in order to break the country up and keep each part under their control.

By that time, everybody knew that China could not become rich and powerful again unless the country was unified. Thus, the reunification of the country in 1949 was the first success after a century of what the Chinese continued to describe as years of humiliation. Restructuring could begin so that effective long-term programs could be devised. They were caught in the Cold War between the United States and USSR and Mao Zedong and his colleagues had no choice but to take sides. On ideological grounds, they had to accept Soviet leadership in the global struggle. They managed eventually to get out from under that umbrella after receiving Nixon and Kissinger and moving closer to America.

I offer the preceding summary to underline the Chinese capacity to endure and recover many times in their history. What are the challenges now? The leaders were committed to communist ideology, but recognized by the end of the Cultural Revolution that there was no future pursuing that path. Deng Xiaoping took the bold decision to adopt capitalism as a means towards the socialism he still wanted for China. His reforms were successful at the level of material wealth and enabled the recovery of military and political power for the central government. There is no question that Deng Xiaoping was correct in choosing to proceed as he did. But to the surprise of the Chinese and just about everyone else, the Soviet Union collapsed and communist ideology lost credibility. For those who had committed their lives to revolutions in order to build a communist world, that disaster was a shock from which they have not fully recovered. They have since learnt to cope with the global market economy and finding new roles for themselves. The Deng Xiaoping era of the past 40 years saw the use of economic weapons to ensure development and create the platform for the wealth and power that Chinese would need to fully restore their position in the world.

China under Xi Jinping

China has gained a position in the world that would have been hard to imagine a hundred years ago. The speed at which it recovered from the conditions of the 1970s was indeed surprising. I am old enough to remember what China was like when the war ended in 1945, the poverty and deprivation all around. It is incredible how much China has achieved since that time. Now that China is wealthier and stronger, President Xi Jinping could give a confident report to the 19th Party Congress that sees China in a position where it does not have to be as modest as it used to be. He believes that the country is now capable of leadership in many matters, something it has not been able to do for a long time. He can now say that China should play a more prominent part in world affairs. Coincidently, other things are happening that encourage the Chinese to believe that the world is changing and in many ways to China's advantage. And this mood is embedded in the 19th Party Congress message.

There are still many challenges ahead. Some are new and others remain salient from the recent past, and these will be of concern for a while yet. One of the new challenges is something that is much discussed in the West, particularly in the United States. I refer to the so-called Thucydides trap. It has attracted the attention of Chinese leaders who have made a point of denying that they will fall into that trap. The fact that they made such a denial suggests that they have taken the challenge seriously.

The Thucydides trap is drawn from the work of the ancient Greek historian Thucydides. He had concluded from the experience of Athens and Sparta that, when a rising power challenges the established power, they eventually would be in conflict and war will follow. Graham Allison, a well-known political scientist who knows his history well, has gone further to show how many times this happened in Europe and possibly also elsewhere. He found many examples of this occurring and has warned that the rising power almost unavoidably forces the established power to go to war to stop its challenger from rising.

What is most telling in modern times are the examples of Germany and Japan. When Germany became the rising power, Britain's response was to try to weaken or diminish its power. That led to a series of complex moves on both sides that were responsible for the two world wars. Japan was another case of a rising power, not as powerful as Germany, but nevertheless one that threatened Anglo-American interests in this part of the world. In the end, conflict became inevitable and it led the Japanese to the attack on Pearl Harbour that forced the Americans to go all out to defeat Japan.

The two cases have been used as analogies for China as the rising power and the United States as the established power. Therefore, the possibility that war between them is inevitable has to be taken seriously. The Chinese have carefully examined the arguments and examples used and seem to have concluded that what the Germans and Japanese did could not be applied to what they are doing for the development of their country. I do think that the Chinese have learnt enough about history to understand where the Germans and Japanese had gone wrong and believe that they would not make the same mistakes. One must hope that they are right and are doing the upmost to avoid the miscalculations that Germans and Japanese made and not give Americans reason to declare war. If they can do that, then the trap does not exist for them.

It is too early to say whether the Chinese can succeed because the trap can hang over both sides for a long time. In the meantime, another challenge that derives from more recent events is more serious. This challenge has not been called a trap but may be seen as a series of calculated risks between uneasy balance of power and aggressive containment. I refer to what had been in the minds of most strategists of the last century, and especially during the 40 years of the Cold War. Because this eventually ended with total victory on one side, it has not been described as any kind of trap. During that global Cold War, the plans and policies adopted by two new powers, the United State and the Soviet Union, dominated strategic thinking. They eventually led to the collapse of the Soviet Communist party and to a triumphant United States declaring total victory. Afterwards, American strategies have been diversified but the strategy of aggressive containment has remained on the table. At its simplest, the argument goes that what had worked well against the powerful Soviet Union could be successfully used against Communist China.

Analogies are never perfect. The Soviet response to the central balance of terror between the two superpowers was to concentrate on matching American power as much as possible. The Chinese have responded differently by focusing on economic development, including using the latest capitalist methods to support their socialist goals. It was noted when Xi Jinping came to power, one of the first things he did was to ask his party colleagues to study why the Soviet Union collapsed. He obviously took that very seriously. He also encouraged them to read de Tocqueville to help them understand what can go wrong after a successful revolution also what made the United States become the power it now is. Both are examples of how conscious he was of the lessons of history. Most of all, he paid close attention to the results of the Cold War. That was certainly a valuable lesson, as important as the trap that Deng Xiaoping was careful to avoid.

There are leaders in both the United States and China who do wish to avoid replicating the Cold War conditions that destroyed the Soviet Union. However, there is ample evidence that both in the Pentagon and in the defence centres in China, there are strategists who continue to think in Cold War terms. The clearest example of this may be found in the underlying American support of Taiwan independence and China's commitment to reunify the island with the mainland. If either side wants a war to break a stalemate, this is readymade for extreme provocation. On the US side, the fact that there had been a successful formula encourages some to believe that exerting pressure to contain China could enable them to destroy the CCP as they did the Soviet Communist Party. If the planners in China thought along the same lines and are ready to counter that strategy, that could be the trigger of the decisive conflict that both sides say they do not want. We thus cannot rule out the possibility that the Cold War might be the trap, one that is more real and urgent than the Thucydides trap.

There are obviously darker aspects of US–China relations that are behind the challenges that Chinese leaders face. One of China's imaginative responses today is the Belt Road Initiative (BRI). When Xi Jinping first talked about the Silk Roads, many took note but no one was sure how far he would go. It was now clear that he is thinking long-term and has a large picture framed in his mind. He does not expect this initiative to produce quick results. He knows it will take time, and that it is a great challenge to everyone, especially to neighbour states and not least to China as well.

What seems to be particularly interesting is that the BRI could help China avoid both the traps that I have just described. China has made clear that the initiative does not challenge the established power but is aimed at meeting local and regional needs and will be done with the cooperation and partnership of those concerned. By definition, it concentrates on Old World Eurasia. In this way, Xi Jinping is indicating that China does not want to encourage Cold War thinking and is seeking to avoid political and military confrontation with the United States. This represents a reaffirmation of the continuities of Old World history, the 5,000 years of recorded history mentioned earlier. That history is well known and can provide something of a roadmap for actions designed for the future.

This Eurasia is home to nearly three-quarters of the world's population. In addition, it is expected that the most dynamic economic developments will move from the Atlantic to the Indo-Pacific. The record shows that wars overland were the norm on the continent whereas the connective maritime polities traded operated openly and with minimal conflicts. The new emphasis looks to continue to depend on the global maritime economy as that economy shifts from the New World, having been centred for the past three centuries on the North Atlantic, to the Indian Ocean and the Western Pacific. That will at the same time also revive the idea of Eurasian centrality in world history. It is therefore important for those concerned to consider how realistic is this Old World response that seems to be what the BRI represents.

If it is, that has two advantages. I have already suggested how it can help avoid direct confrontations with the United States by focusing on developing, or restoring, the centrality of the historical Eurasia where the vast majority of people still live. The second advantage is that it opens up the wider use of the development toolbox of the past 200 years. It can draw together the practical skills that various parts of Eurasia have mastered, the modern technology, the knowledge of finance and infrastructural investment, that each has learnt from capitalist development. These countries now realize that they can use these modern instruments of interconnectivity to link up the Eurasian world, not merely in old ways but also by seeking new paths. These would include new kinds of linkages both continental and maritime that would give priority to urgent regional and local needs and not merely those devised to serve global goals. The Eurasian Old World is developing the capacity to establish new sets of relationships that will allow that region to develop more freely away from priorities determined elsewhere. I do not know whether China will succeed in this aim but think the Chinese see this Eurasia as central to their future and also as a way of helping them regain their position in the world.

The new Silk Roads

The BRI is a project for the long haul. Its success depends on the stability sustained by continued economic growth. That leads me to say that there are at least three conditions that China would need to fulfil for the initiative to succeed. The first is that China must remain unified. The second is that the CCP is connected with the whole of China's past and thus put its legitimacy beyond doubt. And the third is that China's future be defined so that that its people can fully believe in it.

Unification is what had enabled China to regain its sovereignty and confidence in its security, something that it has not had for more than a hundred years. That unity has allowed the modern state to reconnect with its past and give its people assurance that China has risen yet again. At its core is the stability of its distinctive party-state. I stress that this party-state, the *dangguo* 黨國, is not the same as a one-party state. In Western political science literature, much has been written about one-party states where one political party seeks to dominate the country, keep out other parties, and not allow any of them to succeed. The party-state, however, conceives itself as the state. That is to say, the state is the party.

This is not entirely new. In many ways, the Nationalist government in Nanjing between 1928 and 1949 often acted as if the Kuomintang was the state. In graphic terms, the association of the Kuomintang with the Chinese state was projected when outside government buildings and in their offices, the Kuomintang flag was crossed with the national flag of China. The CCP had begun differently, basing its state on the Soviet model. It now has reached the point when it sees China as dependent on the CCP for its survival and rebirth. The CCP saved China and the two are indistinguishable. The party-state therefore provides continuity with the emperor-state that had served China for two millennia. Of course, the two are not the same; it is the party as a whole and not its leader that replaced the emperor. This is why it is so vital for the Party to be united, dedicated, and incorruptible. And Xi Jinping has been determined to make the CCP healthy again.

One very difficult area for Xi Jinping to sort out is the CCP's relationship with the law. The traditional emperor was above the law, but the CCP today does not want to be seen as distant from the ruled. It also sees its position as one that carries new kinds of sacred responsibilities. It not only has the power but the duty to care for its people better than the old system. What is important are the strong appeals for continuity with Chinese history. We should not be surprised that Chinese leaders today identify with the eras beyond Deng Xiaoping and Mao Zedong and see themselves in the longer historic framework that connects them to the 1912 revolution of Sun Yat-sen as the successor to the Qing dynasty and thus back to all the legitimate rulers of China.

This continuity deserves closer attention. It draws from the Chinese tradition that all knowledge may be classified under the four categories of *Jingshi ziji* 经史子集. The most important has always been *jing* and *shi*, the Classics and the Records. The other two were supportive but not central the way *jing* and *shi* were. *Jing* provided the principles of government, almost always interpreted by the Confucians at the court, especially during the Ming and Qing. But *shi* was more deeply grounded. It goes way back to ancient records that traced the origins of the state. Ever since there were records, from the *Shangshu* 尚书 Book of Records to the *Chunqiu* 春秋 Chronology, to all the officially recognized collections of documents, there has been absolute respect for continuity. Certainly, it was the *Shiji* Records of Sima Qian and the *Hanshu* History of Ban Gu together with the successive sets of Standard Histories that created the authoritative sense of Chineseness. That continuity provides the anchor that reminded all rulers how to overcome the many threats from the deserts, the steppes, and the highlands, and also how to deal with internal disruptions. In that way, the condition of centralized unity was always the goal to be defended at all cost.

In Chinese eyes, whether Han or non-Han, the capacity to stay united was what made China strong and secure and the sense of continuity reinforced that unity of both the country and its civilization. When its people grew in numbers and accepted that civilization, the territory they occupied also grew. That continuity was passed down through the centuries by the *Shi* records that shaped and complemented the Confucian *Jing*. The party-state today still seeks to embody the continuity with the regimes of the past in order to ensure that its modernizing goals will be suffused with the country's rich heritage.

After the continuity legitimized the unified central state, the priority now is to find ways to consolidate what has been achieved. This has led its leaders to look further beyond the country's borders. The current Belt and Road Initiative is a striking example of enabling China to reconnect with the Old World with modern instruments. This begins with neighbours that had shared China's past in different ways. It is understood that what follows can never be the same because the world has radically changed. Nevertheless, it makes sense to reconnect with that world both maritime and overland. For that, there are ample experiences to help China rebuild the relationships that had existed in the past. Of course, this would not be limited to the happier and more peaceful relationships; some had been extremely violent, notably those on the continent that led to many destructive wars. China would have to draw on all that they have learnt from their records before it can hope to restore a new balance to the region, the stability and security it so desires.

Indeed, the Chinese know the need for balanced policies. In their relations with the outside world, they lost balance when Ming and Qing China paid too much attention to continental enemies and too little to possible enemies who came by sea. Only too late did they realize that maritime enemies could also be an existential threat. In responding to that challenge the past 100 years, they have now rediscovered that the sea could also be extremely beneficial to the country's economy. Deng Xiaoping's reforms since the 1980s set out to open the country's doors to maritime trade as well as to global investments. And it was those reforms that have enabled China to develop so successfully during the last 40 years.

That shows how much he and his colleagues recognize the need for balance, especially for greater attention to maritime affairs. Since the 1990s, they have devoted vast resources to the establishment of a truly modern navy together with investments in a number of port facilities that they hope can ensure access and safety across the South China Sea. They now have a credible force in their waters and one that can reach out to ports in the Indian Ocean. This is part of the balance that China believes they need to have. In that context, while it is too early to tell whether the BRI will receive the international support it needs to succeed, the initiative does represent the balance that China now seeks.

Finally, the believable Chinese future refers to what Xi Jinping describes as the new era for socialism with Chinese characteristics. On the surface, to call this a new era sounds banal. But underlying it is a hundred years of dreaming about having China restored to its original greatness. The past three generations of leaders and thinkers had all hoped for a revival that they could sustain. The Chinese now believe they have reached the point when it is possible to declare that they have found an alternative to the modernization model offered by the West. Their recent achievements have allowed them to build a political structure that enables them to restore continuity with key parts of their heritage that the party-state still values. They now believe that they have arrived at something that can lead them to greater heights. Therefore, they should no longer hesitate to tell the world where they want to go. Only time can tell whether the timing in doing so is right. But the confidence displayed in President Xi Jinping's speech about the new era for socialism with Chinese characteristics is clearly central to his China dream.

Many comparisons are now made of Xi Jinping and his powerful predecessors, Mao Zedong and Deng Xiaoping. Some comparisons are helpful but others can be misleading. For example, Mao Zedong and his generation faced enormous problems trying to bring unity to the country. He led the fight against the Kuomintang and the Japanese invaders and, after victory in 1949, he fought his own comrades and, by the end of the Cultural Revolution, almost destroyed his Communist party. It cannot be denied that he succeeded in what he did most of the time, but it is also clear that he left a damaged heritage. Xi Jinping does not face Mao's problems and his power draws from a high degree of respect for the institutions he inherited. And he is very focused on protecting the CCP's image and efficacy.

As for comparing him with Deng Xiaoping, there were also fundamental differences in what needed to be done. Deng Xiaoping had totally reversed the revolutionary Mao's calls for class struggle and opened the country to capitalist methods in most remarkable ways. He had urged the people to learn everything from capitalism that they thought would be useful in order to shape the kind of socialism for which China hoped. He had determined that China would be as modern and progressive as the best that could be found anywhere in the world. In comparison, Xi Jinping is bent on telling us that the time has come to define the country's new era. China has arrived, having learnt from Mao Zedong's mistakes and Deng Xiaoping's achievements. The changes that have made it possible to look afresh at "socialism with Chinese characteristics" are now in full display.

Why socialism?

The question reminds us that China has sought to be modern and progressive for more than a century. Xi Jinping's vision therefore needs a flag that represents that quest for progress for future generations to follow. He seems to have decided that the name of Karl Marx best stands for that future. Unlike the names of Lenin, Stalin, and even Mao, his is a name that China's party-state can accept without reservations. Chinese leaders today know that they cannot depend on the name of Confucius because it is not one that can represent the progress that most Chinese want. They also believe that the kinds of hero-figures that earlier generations had appealed to, for example, Locke or Rousseau, Darwin or Keynes, are no longer relevant to China's development model.

In comparison, Marx the activist scholar-philosopher was someone whose ideas served the cause of progress for several generations all over the world. It was, after all, Marx's analysis of stages of progress in history, whether accurate or not, that enabled the Chinese to think of progress in new and completely different ways. It can be said that the idea of progress was one of the most powerful ideas that the Chinese people embraced in the 20th century. That idea helped to take them out of the shadow of the golden past, away from the insistent exhortations to return to ancient values. In fact, progress was the ideal that inspired both the Nationalist and Communist parties. The CCP went further and identified it with the Marxist vision that each stage of historical change would ultimately advance the whole society to a higher stage. Thus, Marx would appear to be the best marker and therefore the flag on China's mast calling for future progress. Whether that leads to a Communist society or not, nobody at this stage knows and few really care. In the meantime, progress is something the Chinese can believe in and the socialism associated with Marx is for what China can now openly stand.

Deng Xiaoping has proved that there need be no contradiction between social-ism and capitalism. The wealth-creating and technologically inventive pillars of capitalism have provided socialism in China with the means to accumulate the wealth that can then be redistributed more fairly among the people. Socialism, I recall Deng Xiaoping saying very famously, is not much good if it is poor when there would be no surpluses for redistribution. Some must get rich first, then you can redistribute and practise socialism. Thus, capitalist technologies, methods, and innovation support a viable socialism. In any case, as Marx had said, this socialism was the stage that would come after capitalism.

Where do Chinese characteristics come from? It is difficult to pin that down because there seems to be, within China, many possibilities that are being dis-cussed and debated. I have followed some of the discussions, but cannot yet be certain where the debates will lead. The range of modern ideas and values is impressive and younger Chinese people seem to adopt them readily. Some are faddish and superficial and seem to offer too much too quickly. There are those who hope that China's values would someday include being free and democratic, but seems to accept that such changes could only come gradually. It would need people to internalize them and become part of a future heritage. Yet others argue that such values would not have staying power if they were copied wholesale from the West. The Chinese people do not reject the idea of universal values. Many believe that China can offer universal values of its own. But political ideas and institutions that threaten the party-state and the stability of China would always remain suspect.

It is instructive to look at what the Chinese are learning from the outside world and how quickly they are learning. On almost every front and every field of knowledge, the Chinese are competing, trying to be as good if not better than the people who had created the knowledge in the first place. That sense of want-ing to master everything they can is now prevalent throughout the country. It is the apex of the great transformation that sprang from Deng Xiaoping's reforms. That has made it possible for Xi Jinping to confidently proclaim a new era. The capacity and willingness to learn clearly encapsulates one of the Chinese charac-teristics that he can count on. Chinese historical records show that such a quest for the highest possible achievement had always been one of the admirable traits in China's past. What Deng Xiaoping did was to reopen the doors for his people to proceed to learn everything they can. That is not a characteristic common to every culture. The last 40 years of success now allow Chinese leaders to argue that this spirit has its roots in Confucian learning and is one that all Chinese should try to acquire.

Xi Jinping and his colleagues now believe that the people have the answer to the question of China's future. It is not necessary to follow the liberal development model that the United States and parts of the Western Europe have offered. There are modified forms of that model that other parts of Europe have developed to attain their socialist goals. While most Americans reject those goals as unsuitable for them, most Europeans have not. Several countries in Europe openly seek to be more or less socialist. The Chinese may not wish to follow those paths because of the reservations they have about how viable their political values are for China. But they now accept that socialism with capitalism does work.

In short, some of the Chinese leaders seem to eye the problem as one of getting right the relationship between socialism and capitalism. Whether it is socialism assisted by capitalist knowledge, innovation, and creativity, or capitalism modified and softened to enable some redistribution would be a matter of people's choice. Looked at closely, the differences between the two sets of choices are not unbridgeable. It may boil down to a question only of emphasis. If strong competitive impulses were needed to enable development to be dynamic, then capitalist methods would have priority. Eventually, however, society would benefit by doses of socialism that allow the state to be fair and satisfy the needs of more people. That way, capitalist ways would have enough freedom to develop while accompanied by publicly managed policies.

The socialist alternative, on the other hand, is to define a different goal and place the emphasis on the well-being of the majority of people. In order for that to be possible, using capitalist institutions and methods would allow the economy to acquire the wealth necessary for redistribution. Perhaps this difference will always divide nations and systems. I cannot predict what the future will bring. But Xi Jinping has affirmed that socialism with Chinese characteristics stands on the side of progress. Given that as the goal, the best capitalist methods that make the socialist alternative viable and creditable should be acceptable. The current Chinese commitment to revive Silk Roads and focus on the centrality of Old World Eurasia could then be seen as an effort to avoid confrontation with the capitalist global system that the Americans espouse. If that China initiative can be seen as a progressive way of achieving a fairer society for the Chinese people and their neighbours and not as a threat to the American system, that could make it a big step forward for countries concerned to work together for a more secure world.

2 Progress on the Belt and Road Initiative

A four-year evaluation

Wen Wang, Jinjing Jia, Junyong Xiang, and Ying Liu

The Belt and Road Initiative (BRI) has realized significant progress over the past four years. Now that an impressive array of key projects is underway, the commitment to achieving common development and shared growth through joint consultation is underscored.

President Xi intimated that more than 100 countries and international organizations are currently involved in the BRI, of which 30 have signed cooperation agreements with China, and China is working with more than 20 countries on capacity-building projects in the manufacturing sector. The United Nations and other international organizations view the BRI in a positive light.

In addition, financial cooperation within the framework of the Asian Infrastructure Investment Bank (AIIB) and Silk Road Fund (SRF) is gaining traction, and a number of signature projects have been launched. Cooperation between China and countries along the Belt and Road is gaining pace, stimulating growth in these economies and creating opportunities for shared development.

Built on an international consensus of fundamental principles of economic development, the BRI represents an emerging trend in global economic cooperation and offers a rosy outlook for development.

This chapter reviews the BRI's main achievements over the past four years from eight perspectives: top-level design, policy coordination, facilities connectivity, unimpeded trade, financial integration, people-to-people bond, China's domestic efforts, and suggestions for future growth. Actionable ideas for the further implementation of the BRI will be seen.

A strategic framework for top-level design

On 12 November 2013, the *Decision of the Central Committee of the Communist Party of China on Some Major Issues Concerning Comprehensively Deepening the Reform* was adopted at the Third Plenary Session of the 18th Central Committee of the CPC, heralding the official endorsement of the BRI from the highest organ of state power. On 4 November 2014, President Xi chaired the Eighth Meeting of the Central Leading Group for Financial and Economic Affairs, which examined the BRI in depth. From 9 to 11 December of the same year, the BRI was identified by the Central Economic Work Conference as a key 2015 strategy for promoting regional economic development.

Premier Li Keqiang enunciated the BRI's importance in government work reports released in 2014 and 2015. On 1 February 2015, a special group led by Vice Premier Zhang Gaoli was set up to oversee the implementation of the BRI. The Office of the Leading Group, placed at the National Development and Reform Commission (NDRC), has four departments: General Affairs, Silk Road, Maritime Silk Road, and International Cooperation. A comprehensive leadership and coordination mechanism for implementing the BRI was thus brought into being.

On 28 March 2015, the NDRC, the Ministry of Foreign Affairs, and the Ministry of Commerce jointly released the *Vision and Actions on Jointly Building Silk Road Economic Belt and 21st-Century Maritime Silk Road*, setting forth guiding principles, defining routes, and stipulating cooperation priorities for the BRI.

Principles

The BRI is fully cognizant of the interests and concerns of the participants. It strives to uphold the spirit of peace, cooperation, openness, inclusiveness, mutual learning, and mutual benefit. Whereof the following principles are accordingly promulgated:

1   The BRI accords with the spirit of the UN Charter.
2   The BRI is geared towards cooperation, with participation open to all countries and organizations, whether international or regional.
3   The BRI is harmonious and inclusive.
4   The BRI follows market rules.
5   The BRI seeks mutual benefit.

As will be evident, China's BRI is open, inclusive, and mutually beneficial. It seeks to realize development that is mutually beneficial and sustainable.

Two parallel roads

The Silk Road Economic Belt (SREB) and the 21st-Century Maritime Silk Road (MSR) are the two concrete manifestations of the BRI. The former focuses on bringing together China, Central Asia, Russia, and the Baltic states; linking China with the Persian Gulf and the Mediterranean Sea through Central Asia and West Asia; and connecting China with Southeast Asia, South Asia, and the Indian Ocean. The latter has two routes: one from China's ports along its coast to Europe via the South China Sea and the Indian Ocean, and another from China's ports along its coast through the South China Sea to the South Pacific.

On land, the BRI will focus on jointly building the New Eurasian Land Bridge and developing China–Mongolia–Russia, China–Central Asia–West Asia, China–Pakistan, Bangladesh–China–India–Myanmar, and the China–Indochina economic corridors by taking advantage of international transport routes, relying on hubs along the Belt and Road, and using key economic industrial parks as cooperation platforms. At sea, the BRI will focus on jointly building smooth, secure, and efficient transport routes connecting major seaports along the Belt and Road. Closer cooperation and connection between land and maritime routes is imperative if greater progress in realizing the BRI is to be made.

Policy coordination: a broad consensus

Policy coordination plays a critical role in supporting the BRI to bolster mutual political trust, reach consensus, coordinate development strategies, facilitate trade, and introduce mechanisms for multilateral cooperation.

Over the past four years, and on the basis of a broad consensus among all participants, China has been working with countries along the BRI to advance projects by leveraging the BRI's existing bilateral and multilateral mechanisms for regional and cross-regional cooperation.

Bilateral cooperation

China has signed many memoranda of understanding (MOU) on cooperation with countries along the Belt and Road. As of 30 June 2016, China had issued joint proposals and statements with 56 countries and regional organizations on bilateral cooperation with a view to implementing the BRI. The relevant MOU or agreements have been signed accordingly.

At the same time, China continued to introduce bilateral joint working mechanisms and improve existing ones, to better coordinate and promote the implementation of cooperation projects.

As of 30 June 2016, China had signed free trade agreements (FTAs) with 14 countries that cover 22 countries and regions, the partners geographically distributed across Asia, Latin America, Oceania, and Europe. Along the Belt and Road, China has signed FTAs with 11 countries and bilateral investment agreements with 56 countries, thus greatly promoting trade and investment cooperation.

Multilateral cooperation

China continues to promote multilateral cooperation mechanisms, making remarkable progress in implementing the BRI. Existing mechanisms are truly gaining traction. Some examples are the Shanghai Cooperation Organization (SCO), China–CEE Cooperation (16 + 1), ASEAN Plus China (10 + 1), Asia Pacific Economic Cooperation (APEC), Bo'ao Forum for Asia (BFA), Asia–Europe Meeting (ASEM), Asia Cooperation Dialogue (ACD), Conference on Interaction and Confidence-Building Measures in Asia (CICA), Forum on China–Africa Cooperation (FOCAC), China–Arab States Cooperation Forum (CASCF), China–Pacific Island Countries Economic Development and Cooperation Forum, Pan–Beibu Gulf Economic Cooperation Forum, Greater Mekong

Subregion (GMS) Economic Cooperation, Central Asia Regional Economic Cooperation (CAREC), Lancang–Mekong Cooperation Mechanism (LMCM) and China–Gulf Cooperation Council Strategic Dialogue. These have enticed more countries and regions to participate in the BRI.

High-level reciprocal visits

Reciprocal visits made by President Xi and Premier Li and their foreign counterparts played no small part in enhancing the political goodwill that is essential to cooperation between China and countries along the Belt and Road. Between September 2013 and August 2016, President Xi visited 37 countries (18 in Asia, nine in Europe, three in Africa, four in Latin America, and three in Oceania), where his promotion of the BRI was warmly received. Up to the end of 2016, more than 100 countries have expressed their support and willingness to participate in the initiative. China has signed 46 cooperation agreements with 39 countries and international organizations, covering a broad range of fields that include connectivity, production capacity, investment, economy and trade, finance, science and technology, society, humanities, quality of life, and marine issues. In addition, BRI has gained support from the UN. On 17 March 2017, the UN Security Council unanimously adopted Resolution 2344, calling on the international community to strengthen regional economic cooperation through the BRI.

Coordination of development strategies

Following the reciprocal state visits and leveraging of bilateral and multilateral mechanisms, China's BRI is echoed in development strategies adopted by many countries along the Belt and Road, including The Bright Road (Kazakhstan), Oil and Gas Program for Western Region (Saudi Arabia), Eurasian Economic Union (Russia), Prairie Road (Mongolia), Juncker Plan (EU), Northern Powerhouse (UK), Eurasia Initiative (South Korea), Two Corridors and One Ring (Vietnam), A Vision for Developing North Australia (Australia), Master Plan on ASEAN Connectivity (ASEAN; Association of Southeast Asian Nations), The Responsible Development Strategy (Poland), Global Maritime Fulcrum Strategy (Indonesia), Middle Corridor Initiative (Turkey), Reindustrialization Strategy (Serbia), Connectivity Blueprint for 2015–2025 (APEC), the Asia–Europe Connectivity Initiative, and the United Nations' 2030 Agenda for Sustainable Development. Through the coordination of their development strategies, these countries and international organizations will join hands in building the Silk Road Economic Belt and the 21st-Century Maritime Silk Road with a focus on the environment, health, intelligence, and peace.

The BRI and development strategies which have already been rolled out provide a foundation for regional or cross-regional development.

As stated, the BRI proposes a trade and transport network connecting Europe, Asia, and Africa. Of the six economic corridors concerned, the New Eurasian Land Bridge, the China–Mongolia–Russia Economic Corridor, and the China–Central

Asia–West Asia Economic Corridor are worth particular attention, for they will bring together the most economically vibrant East Asian states and the highly developed European economy while facilitating trade flows between the Persian Gulf and the Mediterranean Sea, thereby creating opportunities for countries in the Eurasian hinterland. The China–Pakistan Economic Corridor, the China–Indochina Peninsula Economic Corridor, and the Bangladesh–China–India–Myanmar Economic Corridor run through eastern and southern parts of Asia, the world's most densely populated areas, connecting major cities and population and industrial clusters along the Belt and Road. The Lancang–Mekong River international sealane and regional railways, highways, and oil and gas networks link the Silk Road Economic Belt with the 21st-Century Maritime Silk Road, whose economic radiation effects cover South Asia, Southeast Asia, the Indian Ocean, the South Pacific, and other regions. The transport network consisting of railways, highways, sea routes, and air routes, together with electric power transmission and telecommunication networks and oil and gas pipelines, creates a connectivity network that provides the physical infrastructure of the six economic corridors.[1]

New Eurasian Land Bridge Economic Corridor

This corridor extends westward from the eastern coast of China to Central and Eastern Europe, passing through the northwestern part of China, Central Asia, and Russia. Construction of this corridor is based on a modern international logistics system including China–Europe rail services, with a focus on economic and trade development and production capacity cooperation, expansion of cooperation in energy and other resources, and establishment of a highly efficient regional market. By the end of 2016, China had opened 39 China–Europe rail routes, entailing the operation of some 3,000 trains to 14 cities in nine European countries, making the railway an important platform for countries along the Belt and Road to promote connectivity and enhance economic and trade cooperation. The China–Kazakhstan international logistics cooperation project is progressing smoothly and has become an important window of cooperation for Kazakhstan in trade and cross-border transportation. The China–Kazakhstan Khorgos International Border Cooperation Centre project is advancing steadily. The Port of Piraeus project is running smoothly, contributing to the mutual benefit and win-win results of China and Greece.

China–Mongolia–Russia Economic Corridor

At his meeting on 11 September 2014 with the heads of state of Russia and Mongolia, President Xi proposed that the three neighbours dovetail the Silk Road Economic Belt with the Eurasian Economic Union proposal and Mongolia's Prairie Road programme, to build the China–Mongolia–Russia Economic Corridor. On 9 July 2015, relevant departments of the three countries signed the "Memorandum of Understanding on Compiling the Outline of the Plan on Establishing the China–Mongolia–Russia Economic Corridor". On 23 June 2016, the three heads of state witnessed the signing of the "Outline of the Plan on Establishing the China–Mongolia–Russia Economic Corridor", the first multilateral cooperation plan under the BRI. Through the combined efforts of the three countries, the outline has been put into practice.

China–Central Asia–West Asia Economic Corridor

This corridor extends westward from northwestern China via Central Asia to the Persian Gulf, the Arabian Peninsula, and the Mediterranean coast, involving Central Asia, West Asia, and North Africa. On 5 June 2014, at the sixth ministerial conference of the China–Arab States Cooperation Forum, President Xi proposed the China–Arab "1 + 2 + 3" cooperation network: take energy cooperation as the main axis, and infrastructure and trade and investment as the two wings, to make breakthroughs in the three high-tech areas of nuclear energy, aerospace satellites, and new energy. During the 2016 G20 Hangzhou Summit, the heads of China and Kazakhstan witnessed the signing of the "Cooperation Plan on Dovetailing the Silk Road Economic Belt and Nurly Zhol (Bright Road)". China also signed cooperation documents on building the Belt and Road with Tajikistan, Kyrgyzstan, Uzbekistan, and other countries, and MOUs on building the Belt and Road with Turkey, Iran, Saudi Arabia, Qatar, Kuwait, and other countries. China and Turkey have reached an important consensus on cooperation in Turkey's east-west high-speed rail project, and have started substantive talks.

China–Indochina Peninsula Economic Corridor

Starting from southwest China, the corridor connects China with countries on the Indochina Peninsula, thus serving as an important channel for wider and higher-level cooperation between China and ASEAN. On 26 May 2016, the Ninth Pan–Beibu Gulf Economic Cooperation Forum and China–Indochina Peninsula Economic Corridor Development Forum issued the "Initiative of the China–Indochina Peninsula Economic Corridor". China signed MOUs on Belt and Road cooperation with Laos, Cambodia, and other countries, launching preparation of bilateral cooperation plans. It has worked to promote cooperation between China and Vietnam on land infrastructure, and started early work on Phase II renovation of the Lancang–Mekong River channel and construction of the Sino–Laos Railway and the Sino–Thai Railway. It has also established the Mohan/Boten Economic Cooperation Zone between China and Laos in exploring new models for integrated development of the border economy.

China–Pakistan Economic Corridor

This corridor is a flagship programme of the BRI. The governments of both China and Pakistan attach great importance to it and have actively started preparation of long-term plans. On 20 April 2015, top leaders of the two countries held a groundbreaking ceremony for several China–Pakistan Economic Corridor projects, during which 51 cooperation agreements and MOUs were signed, of which almost 40 involve the corridor construction. Construction has started on the Karakoram Highway(KKH) Phase II (Thakot to Havellian Section), also known as the Friendship Highway, and the Peshawar–Karachi Motorway, the largest highway infrastructure project under the China–Pakistan Economic Corridor. Construction of the Gwadar Free Zone has been accelerated, and energy and power projects have been quickly launched along the corridor.

Bangladesh–China–India–Myanmar Economic Corridor

This corridor connects the three subregions of East Asia, South Asia, and Southeast Asia, and links the Pacific and Indian oceans. In December 2013, the first meeting of the Joint Working Group for the Bangladesh–China–India–Myanmar Economic Corridor took place in Kunming, China. The parties involved signed the minutes of the meeting and a plan on joint research on the corridor, formally launching intergovernmental cooperation for this programme. In December 2014, the second meeting of the Joint Working Group for the Bangladesh–China–India–Myanmar Economic Corridor took place, at which the four countries discussed the prospects, priorities, and development direction for the construction of the corridor.

Facilities connectivity: a solid foundation

Facilities connectivity has been identified as one of the BRI's priorities. China is working with countries and regions along the Belt and Road in coordinating infrastructure standards, connecting infrastructure networks, integrating energy infrastructure, and creating the Information Silk Road. An infrastructure network that links subregions in Asia and that extends into Asia, Europe, and Africa is coming into being.

Standard coordination

A series of conferences and workshops have been held to coordinate standards adopted in countries participating in the BRI. On 22 October 2015, the "Action Plan for the Belt and Road Standard Coordination 2015–2017" was released. The plan issued ten guidelines for developing procedures and mechanisms for mutual certification of standards adopted in countries along the Belt and Road. The top-level planning agreements and coordination plan cover 13 key areas: infrastructure construction and investment, trade, energy, finance, industrial sector, logistics and transport, standards and certifications, environmental protection, agriculture, culture, information, think tank collaboration, and local collaboration.

Transport connectivity

Over the past four years, China has promoted the construction of transport infrastructure in countries along the Belt and Road. Also, Chinese state-owned enterprises (SOEs) are expanding their presence in the transport infrastructure in these countries.

Making an endeavour to promote transport facilitation, China signed 16 agreements with 15 countries along the Belt and Road, and opened 356 international transport routes running through 73 land ports. China has also signed 38 bilateral or regional ocean shipment agreements with 47 Belt and Road countries, and bilateral intergovernmental aviation transport agreements with 62 countries. Direct civil flights now reach 43 countries.

Simultaneously, relevant projects have been running smoothly. As of 30 June 2016, 39 freight train lines between China and Europe were operational, contributing to a transport infrastructure network linking subregions in Asia and extending into Asia, Europe, and Africa. The construction of the China–Laos Railway, the Hungary–Serbia Railway, the China–Russia High-speed Railway, the Jakarta–Bandung High-speed Railway in Indonesia, the Peshawar–Karachi Motorway in Pakistan, the Karakoram Highway(KKH) Phase II (Thakot to Havellian Section), the ports of Piraeus, Hambantota, and Gwadar and other symbolic projects are well underway. The Addis Ababa–Djibouti Railway, the first transnational electrified railway in Africa, has been completed and come into service. With the reconstruction of the north-south TKU (Taldykorgan–Kalbatau–Ust–Kamenogorsk) Highway in Kazakhstan, the electrification of railways in Belarus, and the railway tunnels built by Chinese enterprises in Uzbekistan and Tajikistan, local transport capacity will be comprehensively improved.

Between the mooting of the BRI in 2013 and 30 June 30 2016, large SOEs such as China Railway Group Ltd and China Communications Construction Co Ltd signed construction contracts for 38 large showpiece projects of transport infrastructure, covering 26 countries and focusing on key routes, port cooperation, and the improvement of infrastructure in developing countries. In addition, China has launched 15 new airport projects and 28 airport expansion projects in provinces along the Belt and Road. According to China's Key Civil Aviation Projects 2015, released by the Civil Aviation Administration of China, the total investment in the 51 strategic projects launched under the BRI will reach ¥200 billion.

Energy connectivity

China increased its energy infrastructure exports to countries and regions along the Belt and Road. From October 2013 to 30 June 2016, Chinese SOEs participated in the construction of 40 overseas energy projects, including power plants, electricity transmission facilities, and oil and gas pipelines, covering 19 countries along the Belt and Road.

In 2014, work began on the Tajikistani part of the Central Asia–China Gas Pipeline (Line D) and the Russian part of the Russia–China Gas Pipeline (East Route).

The year 2015 saw a number of breakthroughs in major projects. Chinese nuclear power companies launched cooperation projects in Romania, the United Kingdom, Pakistan, and Argentina. Chinese hydroelectric companies worked on cooperation projects in Angola, Brazil, Nepal, Pakistan, Laos, and Argentina. In particular, the Karot Hydroelectric Project in Pakistan was the Silk Road Fund's first overseas investment. All these projects help alleviate local pressure on power supplies.

During the first half of 2016, China signed deals for 16 energy projects with countries along the Belt and Road.

Information connectivity

Chinese telecommunication service providers such as China Unicom, China Telecom, and China Mobile are speeding up cross-border transmission projects in countries along the Belt and Road to expand international telecommunication infrastructure.

So far, China is connected with North America, Northeast Asia, Southeast Asia, South Asia, Australia, the Middle East, North Africa, and Europe through submarine communication cables, and with Russia, Mongolia, Kazakhstan, Kyrgyzstan, Tajikistan, Vietnam, Laos, Myanmar, Nepal, India, and other countries through overland cables. Transmission coverage is further extended into Central Asia, Northern Europe, and Southeast Asia.

In addition, the China-led TD–LTE standard is being widely embraced. The Global TD–LTE Initiative, of which China is a founding partner, currently has 116 operator members and 97 vendors. 52 TD–LTE networks are operational in 30 countries, including China, the United States, Japan, India, Saudi Arabia, Russia, and Australia, and 83 TD–LTE networks are deployed in 55 countries.

China has signed MOUs on general aviation cooperation with 15 countries. China is working with France on marine satellites and Space Variable Objects Monitor (SVOM) satellites and is assisting in designing, manufacturing, assembling, testing, launching, and data-processing Venezuela's VRSS–2 satellite.

Unimpeded trade: a big step forward

Unimpeded trade is an important building block in the BRI. Over the past four years, China and the Belt and Road countries have been working together to facilitate trade and investment activities by negotiating bilateral agreements on investment protection and tax treaties to avoid double taxation, in order to remove trade and investment barriers and create a healthy business environment.

Trade facilitation

The negotiations on bilateral FTAs are making solid progress. As of 30 June 2016, China had signed 14 FTAs covering 22 countries and regions; eight more FTAs are under negotiation, and five are in the pipeline. Multilateral free trade frameworks are also taking shape. The China–ASEAN Free Trade Area has been upgraded, and the China–Georgia free trade talks have been completed. Real progress has been achieved in the talks on the Regional Comprehensive Economic Partnership, and breakthroughs have been made in the talks on the China–Maldives Free Trade Area. Talks on the China–Gulf Cooperation Council Free Trade Area, the China–Israel Free Trade Area, the China–Sri Lanka Free Trade Area, and Phase II of the China–Pakistan Free Trade Area are progressing. Joint research on the feasibility of the China–Nepal Free Trade Area, the China–Bangladesh Free Trade Area, and the China–Moldova Free Trade Agreement is making progress as well. China is actively promoting China–Japan–South Korea FTA negotiations, and strategic research on the FTA of Asia–Pacific. Existing regional and bilateral free trade mechanisms are being improved to create a sophisticated, periphery-based free trade network to support the BRI and serve global markets.

Integrated customs clearance

China has been pushing ahead with its customs clearance reform, launching pilot projects for one-stop international trade and customs services. The Forum for Heads of Customs Administrations of the countries along the Belt and Road was held to promote integrated customs clearance systems. Efforts are being made to extend freight train lines into countries along the Belt and Road to make customs clearance more convenient and international movement of goods more efficient. Collaborative efforts in securing and facilitating supply chains are being stepped up, and negotiations on tariff concession are in progress. As of 30 June 2016, China had signed Authorized Economic Operator arrangements with Singapore, South Korea, the European Union, and the Hong Kong Special Administrative Region (HKSAR) to provide better customs clearance for authorized Chinese companies.

Transformation and upgrading in trade structure

China has been broadening its trade ties with countries along the Belt and Road. It also continues to launch pilot projects for trade in services. From June 2013 to June 2016, China recorded US$3.1 trillion worth of commodity trade along the Belt and Road, which accounts for 26 percent of its total trade volume. As of 30 June 2016, China had signed contracts in services outsourcing with countries along the Belt and Road worth US$9.41 billion, up 33.5 percent from that of the previous year. Cross-border e-commerce as part of international trade is booming. Cross-border e-commerce pilot areas have been identified to encourage Chinese companies to open offshore warehouses as well as to optimize the distribution-supply structure and accelerate the trade-facilitation process.

Investment facilitation

Negotiations on bilateral investment treaties are making good progress. As of 30 June 2016, China had signed bilateral investment treaties with 104 countries along the Belt and Road and introduced a Joint Economic and Trade Commission, among other mechanisms, to promote investment cooperation and provide a legal and institutional basis for bilateral investment cooperation.

Against this backdrop, investment cooperation activities between China and countries along the Belt and Road are moving steadily forward, reflecting enormous growth potential. As of 30 June 2016, China had invested a total of US$51.1 billion in these countries, accounting for 12 percent of China's overseas direct investment (ODI) over the same period. In particular, China invested US$6.86 billion directly in countries along the Belt and Road during the first half of 2016, of which Singapore, Indonesia, India, Malaysia, Laos, and Russia were the main beneficiaries. This accounted for 7.7 percent of its total investments over the same period. Countries along the Belt and Road invested US$3.36 billion in China, accounting for 4.8 percent of the total foreign direct investment (FDI) in China over the same period.

As of 30 June 2016, China had signed tax treaties with 53 countries along the Belt and Road, creating a network that covers the major investment sources and foreign investment destinations with the aim of eliminating tax barriers to investment.

Platform cooperation

National border ports, border economic cooperation areas, and cross-border economic cooperation areas are important platforms for deepening cooperation with neighbouring countries and regions, for enabling a head start in implementing the BRI, and for supporting the construction of the economic corridors on land and at sea.

As of the end of 2016, seven pilot border opening-up and development zones, including Dongxing in Guangxi, Mongla (Mohan), and Ruili in Yunnan; Erenhot and Manzhouli in Inner Mongolia; Suifenhe (Heilongjiang), and Pingxiang (Guangxi), 17 border economic cooperation zones and one cross-border economic cooperation zone (China–Kazakhstan Horgos International Border Cooperation Centre) were functional, and another 11 cross-border economic cooperation areas were in progress.

Substantive results have been made in developing offshore trade and economic cooperation zones. China has developed a number of overseas industrial development zones with sound infrastructure, a clear industrial focus, and access to a panoply of public services. These zones give rise to a geographic concentration of interconnected businesses and stand out as important platforms not only for international cooperation but also for capacity building and equipment manufacturing under the BRI.

As of the end of 2016, China had launched 56 trade and economic cooperation zones in 20 countries along the Belt and Road, with a total investment of US$18.5 billion. Of the 13 trade and economic cooperation zones that were evaluated, the China–Belarus Industrial Park, the Thai–Chinese Rayong Industrial Zone, and Indonesia–China Integrated Industrial Parks are in full operation.

This positive result can only be attributed to the "going global" strategy of Chinese companies.

Financial integration and networking for cooperation

Financial integration is a condition sine qua non of the BRI's successful implementation. China vigorously advocates forward cross-border financial cooperation with countries along the Belt and Road as well as international financial institutions, to meet these countries' needs in financing and financial services in infrastructure development. China also persistently develops the RMB (renminbi) trade settlement, currency swap, investment credit, and other financial services between countries along the Belt and Road and other economies. In addition, it seeks to reinforce cooperation with these countries in building up efficient financial regulation and supervision mechanisms in the region.

Synergies with financial cooperation mechanism

China has close and growing cooperation with the financial sectors of ASEAN, Russia, Central Asia, and the EU. To facilitate the coordination of financial policies, we have brought into play the strengths of such cooperation platforms as ASEAN + China, Japan, the ROK (10 + 3) Framework, the Shanghai Cooperation Organization (SCO) Finance Ministers and Central Bank Governors Meeting, the SCO Interbank Association, Executives' Meeting of East Asia Pacific Central Banks, the China–ASEAN Interbank Association, and the Central Bank Governors' Club of Central Asia, Black Sea Region, and the Balkan Countries. Efforts have been made to promote the Chiang Mai Initiative Multilateralization and establish a US$240 billion regional foreign exchange reserve, to stabilize regional finance. In January 2016 China officially joined the European Bank for Reconstruction and Development (EBRD) and has been strengthening cooperation with the bank through high-level exchanges, joint financing, cooperation on trade and investment, and policy coordination.

Creation of innovative financing platforms

Belt and Road cross-border financial cooperation consists of several levels of cooperation and involves various participants. Of these, international and multilateral development financial institutions play a significant role.

The AIIB, an inter-governmental multilateral development institution for the Asian region, focuses on infrastructure development, with the aim of enhancing connectivity and economic integration among Asian regions. It also seeks to promote cooperation between China and other interested parties.

Founded on 25 December 2015 and headquartered in Beijing, the AIIB boasts an authorized capital of US$100 billion. Having BRI-related projects as one of its investment priorities, the AIIB approved US$509 million in investments for its first projects on 25 June 2016. These involved inter alia, power, transportation and urban development, covering Bangladesh, Indonesia, Pakistan, and Tajikistan. By the end of 2016, the AIIB had provided US$1.7 billion in loans to nine projects. Based on market rules, informed by international practice, and guided by professional standards, the SRF is a medium- and long-term development and investment fund established pursuant to the Company Law of the People's Republic of China on 29 December 2014, with an investment of ¥61.525 billion from the State Administration of Foreign Exchange, China Investment Corporation, Export–Import Bank of China, and China Development Bank. Its principal mandate is investment opportunities and the provision of investment and financing support under the BRI.

By the end of 2016, the fund had signed 15 projects, with an estimated investment value of US$6 billion. The projects cover such areas as infrastructure, energy utilization, and production capacity and finance cooperation in Russia, Mongolia, Central Asia, South Asia, and Southeast Asia. The fund also allocated US$2 billion to start the China–Kazakhstan Production Capacity Cooperation Fund. It had also signed a three-party cooperation framework agreement with Beijing Enterprises Holdings Limited and EEW Energy from Waste GmbH, an MOU with the European Bank for Reconstruction and Development, and an MOU with Serbia on joint development of renewable energy projects.

China also proposed the China–CEE Joint Investment and Financing Framework, including a US$10 billion special loan, the China–CEE Investment Cooperation Fund, and other mechanisms to provide financing support to Central and Eastern Europe. The Industrial and Commercial Bank of China took the lead in founding China–CEE Financial Holdings Ltd., which launched the China–CEE Fund.

As the first development financial institution established by BRICS states in the aftermath of the global financial crisis, the New Development Bank (NDB), centred on economic development in the Third World (with a particular emphasis on investments in infrastructure), is envisaged as a financial safety net offering a certain amount of foreign exchange with its currency reserve pool, should the next global financial crisis ever occur. Established on 21 July 2015 and headquartered in Shanghai, the NDB has an authorized capital of US$100 billion. It announced its first round of loans for clean energy projects in China, India, Brazil, and South Africa.

Deepening cooperation with domestic financial institutions

Domestic policy-based financial institutions serve as the backbone for financial cooperation. By 30 June 2016, the China Development Bank had set up a Belt and Road project pool involving over 900 projects from over 60 countries in such sectors as transportation, energy and resources. The Export–Import Bank of China holds an outstanding balance of over 1,000 projects involving roads, railways, ports, power resources, pipelines, communication, and industrial parks in the 49 countries along the Belt and Road. The Export–Import Bank of China also recently signed over 500 projects with countries along the Belt and Road. By 30 June 2016, China Export & Credit Insurance Corporation had supported export, domestic trade, and investment with a total value of US$2.3 trillion. Its policies cover thousands of exporters and hundreds of medium- and long-term projects concerning the export of high technology, large electro-machinery, and the export of complete equipment for overseas engineering contracts.

Domestic commercial banks serve as the follow-up driver for commercial cooperation. The business network of Chinese-funded banks, primarily China's Big Five (ICBC, CCB, BOC, ABC, and BOCOM), has taken shape among countries along the Belt and Road. As of 31 March 2016, nine Chinese-funded banks have set up 56 Level–A branches in 24 countries along the Belt and Road. In addition, 56 commercial banks from 20 Belt and Road countries have set up seven subsidiaries, 18 branches, and 42 representative offices in China.

At the same time, transnational banking cooperation mechanisms like the Shanghai Cooperation Organization Bank Union and China–ASEAN Bank Union have facilitated financial convenience towards the development of the BRI.

RMB regionalization and internationalization

The use of RMB in cross-border trade and investment has been expanding. By 30 June 2016, cross-border RMB settlements between China and countries and regions along the Belt and Road had exceeded ¥2.63 trillion.

The People's Bank of China has been strengthening currency cooperation with the central banks of other countries. As of 15 August 2016, it had signed bilateral currency swap agreements with an aggregate of more than ¥3.12 trillion (not including those already expired or terminated) with central banks or other currency authorities of 35 overseas countries and regions, 21 of which are countries or regions along the Belt and Road. As of 30 June 2016, the inter-bank foreign exchange market in China had launched direct trade among 11 currencies.

The establishment of cross-border RMB payment, clearing, and settlement has been gaining momentum. As of 20 August 2016, China had signed bilateral currency settlement on general trade with the central banks of countries such as Russia and Belarus, as well as bilateral currency settlement on border trade with the central banks of countries such as Kyrgyzstan and Kazakhstan. As of 30 June 2016, there were 20 RMB clearing banks in business, of which seven are located in countries and regions along the Belt and Road. The People's Bank of China signed MOUs with the Federal Reserve and Central Bank of the Russian Federation to build up bilateral currency settlement mechanisms in the United States and Russia, on 7 June and 25 June 2016 respectively.

Offshore RMB markets have sprung up in rapid succession. In addition to HKSAR, Taiwan, and Singapore as the major offshore RMB deposit and loan markets, the accelerated development of offshore RMB markets in Britain, Germany, and some other key European countries – expected to be the most important offshore RMB market outside Asia – are to be witnessed.

Cooperation on financial regulation and supervision

The People's Bank of China has been engaged in constructive operations of the Financial Stability Board, Basel Committee on Banking Supervision, and other international organizations and their affiliated working teams. It would, under the Executive Meeting of East Asia–Pacific Mechanism, further strengthen regional economic and financial monitoring and consistently improve crisis management and intervention framework.

By the end of 2016, the People's Bank of China had signed MOUs on financial intelligence communication and cooperation with 42 overseas anti-money-laundering organizations. The China Banking Regulatory Commission had signed MOUs or Exchange of Notes on bilateral regulation and supervision with financial authorities of 29 countries along the Belt and Road. The China Securities Regulatory Commission had signed 64 MOUs on regulation and supervision with securities authorities of 59 countries and regions. In addition, the China Insurance Regulatory Commission, by enhancing connection with the International Association of Insurance Supervisors, has been vigorously promoting cooperation on insurance regulation with countries along the Belt and Road. The Asian Forum of Insurance Regulators located its secretariat in China to strengthen exchanges and cooperation on insurance regulation and supervision in Asia.

People-to-people communication: steady progress

People-to-people communication provides public support for implementing the BRI. Since the launch of the initiative three years ago, China has been, by upholding the spirit of friendly cooperation of the Silk Road, energetically developing cooperation on culture and education, tourism, health care and medical service, science and technology as well as exchanges among youth, political parties, governments, and non-governmental individuals and organizations in countries and regions along the Belt and Road, thus winning public support for the implementation of the BRI.

Cooperation on culture and education

Thanks in no small part to the stunning success of the BRI, there is extensive potential for cooperation and development between China and countries along the Belt and Road. China will provide 10,000 government scholarships to students from countries along the Belt and Road as well as 120,000 training opportunities and 150,000 scholarships for citizens of other developing countries to receive education in China. Local governments in China have also launched programmes like the Silk Road Special Scholarship to encourage international cultural and educational exchanges. There are up to 33 educational cooperation and foreign aid programmes like China–ASEAN Education Cooperation Week, providing platforms for educational exchanges and cooperation among countries and regions along the Belt and Road.

As of 30 June 30 2016, China had worked with countries and regions along the Belt and Road for 19 sessions of the Year of the Country and set up 25 overseas Chinese culture centres and 500 Confucius Institutes in 125 countries. China had signed up to 41 MOUs on cultural cooperation with these countries and regions. The International Symposium on the Silk Road Economic Belt was held in Urumqi, Xinjiang Uyghur Autonomous Region, in June 2014, and the International Seminar on the 21st-Century Maritime Silk Road Initiative was held in Quanzhou, Fujian Province, in February 2015. By the end of 2016, China had built 30 Chinese culture centres and set up Confucius Institutes in countries along the Belt and Road. China has held important events such as the Silk Road (Dunhuang) International Cultural Expo, Silk Road International Arts Festival, and Maritime Silk Road International Arts Festival. China, Kazakhstan, and Kyrgyzstan jointly applied and succeeded in listing "Silk Roads: the Routes Network of Chang'an–Tianshan Corridor" on UNESCO's World Cultural Heritage. In foreign aid, China has restored cultural sites such as Ta Keo Temple of Angkor, Cambodia; Itchan Kala, the Ancient City of Khiva; Khorazm in Uzbekistan; and provided aid for postquake restoration of cultural relics in Nepal and Myanmar. It has also applied to have the Maritime Silk Road listed as an item of World Cultural Heritage, and promoted the Mazu marine culture. In short, there have been many cultural exchanges across the world, unprecedented in history, since the launch of the BRI.

Cooperation on tourism

The BRI is an initiative to drive the cooperation and development of countries along the Belt and Road, as well as a vision and a new way to develop tourism. As of 30 June 2016, 22 Chinese provinces (including Hainan) and the Xinjiang and Ningxia Autonomous Regions had established partnership programmes with countries along the Belt and Road. China had also worked with relevant countries to hold nine Tourism Year events with diversified features, and over 130 promotion events like Tourism Week, Tourism Promotion Week, and Tourism Month.

China has also endeavoured to facilitate visa procedures. As of 30 June 2016, 21 countries and regions had removed visa requirements for Chinese visitors, and 37 countries and regions had started to grant visas on arrival, greatly facilitating non-governmental exchanges among different peoples.

In addition, the China National Tourism Administration will help 150 million Chinese tourists to visit foreign lands along the Belt and Road, with a total expenditure of US$200 billion. In addition, China will attract 85,000,000 visitors from the area, with a total spending of US$110 billion in China.

Health and medical care

As of 30 June 2016, China had concluded a range of cooperation agreements on medical staff training, public health service, and traditional medicine with ministries of health, medical schools, and other organizations from Central and East Europe, ASEAN, the Arab League, and other regions and countries. In addition, it had signed 23 international agreements with these countries and regions. China had also been engaged in 29 cooperation projects including the Sino–African Cooperation Program on Poverty Reduction and Public Welfare and the Sino–African Cooperation Program on Public Health.

Within its 52-year engagement in international medical aid undertaking, China has sent more than 23,000 doctors abroad to 67 countries and regions. By 30 June 2016, China had dispatched 52 medical teams to 51 countries. Of these, 43 were sent to 42 African countries. The China International Search and Rescue Team, a UN-certified international heavy rescue team, was the first team at the earthquake area in Nepal. All this reflects the initiatives and responsibilities taken by China, an emerging power.

China has also promoted exchanges and cooperation on traditional medicine with countries along the Belt and Road, founded 16 overseas traditional Chinese medicine centres, including one in the Czech Republic, and signed Chinese medicine cooperation agreements with 15 countries. The Chinese government signed the "Memorandum of Understanding on Health Sector Cooperation Under the Belt and Road Initiative" with the World Health Organization, to build a healthy Silk Road. China has also set up a Medical Centre for the Silk Road Economic Belt in Xinjiang Uygur Autonomous Region to provide medical services to surrounding countries in Central Asia.

Cooperation on science and technology

China has been witnessing increasingly close scientific and technological cooperation with the Belt and Road countries, such as the Internet Plus Strategy in Eurasia, the inauguration of the Qamchiq Tunnel, the longest railway tunnel in Central Asia (a part of China's high-speed railway going global programme), and the release of the *Beijing Declaration on Global Collaboration in Earth Observation for Belt and Road*. By 30 June 2016, China had signed 56 MOUs on scientific and technological cooperation with countries along the Belt and Road, in sectors such as space, energy, and ecology. These encompass Asia, Europe, Latin America, and Africa. In addition, China had established 38 scientific and technological centres, ranging from Belt and Road smart industrial parks, joint labs, international technological transfer centres, to industrial cooperation centres and incubation centres, in conformity with its 13th Five-year Plan. This has enhanced bilateral and multilateral technological cooperation.

Youth exchanges

The youth of today carry a particularly heavy burden on their shoulders as cultural emissaries, as they seek to play their part in the construction of their countries' futures and that of the BRI. China has jointly held eight events of the Youth Exchange Year with relevant countries, such as the China–Russia Youth Friendly

Exchange Year and China–Germany Teenager Exchange Year, and launched nine youth talent training and development programmes, like African Talents Programme and Talented Young Scientists Programme, to develop young talents for relevant countries. China has also hosted innovation and entrepreneurship-themed forums and conferences, like the Belt and Road Innovation and Entrepreneurship Forum, to actively explore and promote China's cooperation with countries along the Belt and Road on youth education and employment, by integrating advantaged resources of relevant countries.

Cooperation among political parties and governments

Friendly exchanges with political parties and parliaments of different countries are of great significance for promoting friendship and consolidating current achievements. The Communist Party of China has always attached great importance to amicable exchanges with foreign political parties. China has established a range of political party exchange mechanisms including Asian Political Parties' Special Conference on the Silk Road and Economic and Trade Dialogue of the China–Europe High-level Political Parties Forum. For parliament exchanges, the National People's Congress, within the framework of the Asian Parliamentary Assembly, developed exchanges with legislatures from more than 42 countries on the Belt and Road. It is hoped that this initiative will play an important role in promoting international relations, strengthening mutual understanding of peoples, and boosting the development of the Belt and Road.

Non-governmental cooperation

As of 30 June 2016, China had held 63 events of exchange and cooperation with non-governmental organizations from countries along the Belt and Road, the scope and depth of which are increasing from year to year. For cultural and media cooperation, China has been engaged in 35 significant events, including the book launch ceremony of *Belt and Road: Opportunities and Challenges* at the 47th Cairo International Book Fair, and Chinese and Foreign Media Forum for the BRI. For public welfare, environmental protection, poverty reduction, and opening up, China has worked with countries along the Belt and Road to host 26 events such as World Day to Combat Desertification Global Observance and the Belt and Road Joint Action High-level Dialogue, Belt and Road International League for Peaceful and Friendly Development of Youth, and China–ASEAN Forum on Social Development and Poverty Reduction, interweaving a well--rounded cooperation network.

Cooperation among think tanks

Think tanks have functioned as policy coordinators, consultants, and advisers during the development course of the Belt and Road by drawing on the wisdom of the collective. Since the launch of the BRI, a great number of think tanks focusing on the Belt and Road have emerged one after another, whether affiliated with a particular entity (governments, enterprises, or universities) or an independent one. Each boasts diversified and distinctive advantages. To integrate the research resources of different sectors and build cross-disciplinary and multi-field research platforms, 11 unions and mechanisms have been established, like the Belt and Road Think Tank Association, the International Think Tank Association, the Silk Road Think Tank Network, the Belt and Road 100–Talent Forum, and the University Think–tank Union, with fruitful results. Chinese think tanks have been actively enhancing exchanges with those from countries along the Belt and Road and exerting great influence on the international arena by organizing up to 29 relevant events such as China–Iran Think Tank Dialogue, China–Turkey Think Tank Dialogue, China–Kazakhstan Think Tank Dialogue, and US–China South China Sea Dialogue.

Joint efforts to shape an all-dimensional strategy

China has been actively developing the BRI since its launch three years ago, injecting impetus into the development of an open economy by giving full play to the advantages of various parts of China, implementing more opening-up policies, and strengthening interaction and cooperation between the various regions of the country. As will be seen, regions across China have made great efforts.

Northwest and northeast China

The Xinjiang Uyghur Autonomous Region has been taking full advantage of its geographical location and rich resources in working with the BRI to seize opportunities in building the New Eurasian Land Bridge Economic Corridor, the China–Central Asia Economic Corridor, the China–Pakistan Economic Corridor, and the China–Mongolia–Russia Economic Corridor, achieving progress in connectivity, international capacity cooperation, open platforms construction, economic, trade, and technology exchanges, as well as cultural exchanges.

Shaanxi Province, Ningxia Hui Autonomous Region, Gansu Province, and Qinghai Province have been working proactively in accordance with the BRI to seize opportunities in developing the New Eurasian Land Bridge Economic Corridor, the China–Central Asia Economic Corridor, the China–Pakistan Economic Corridor, and the China–Mongolia–Russia Economic Corridor.

Remarkable accomplishments have been made in Belt and Road development programmes like the Euro–Asia Economic Forum, the Round Table Meeting of Cities along the Silk Road Economic Belt, the Ningxia Inland Opening-up Pilot Economic Zone, the China–Kazakhstan Horgos International Border Cooperation Centre, the China–Arab States Import & Export Trading Centre, Lanzhou New Area Free Trade Zone, Lanzhou International Trade and Logistic Park, Golden Port Qinghai International Bonded Shopping Centre, Chengdu Investment and Trade Fair, Investment and Trade Fair for Qinghai Enterprises Participating in Economic Restructure, Qinghai Halal Food Cultural Tourism

Festival, Dongchuan Railway Logistics Centre, Lanzhou Central Asia International Freight Train, and Lanzhou Central Europe International Freight Train. The Inner Mongolia Autonomous Region took the initiative to work according to the BRI and form a new type of cooperation mechanism with Russia and Mongolia by building on the China–Mongolia–Russia Economic Corridor.

The provinces of Heilongjiang, Jilin, and Liaoning have been making good use of their advantaged locations, strengthening sea–rail transportation cooperation with the Russian Far East, promoting the development of the Beijing–Moscow High-Speed Rail Corridor, and economic liaison with Japan, the Republic of Korea, and other relevant countries, while paying close attention to the connectivity with South China economic zones. Since the launch of the BRI, remarkable progress has been made in Belt and Road mechanisms and programmes like Heilongjiang Land-and-sea Silk Roads, Changchun–Siping Economic Belt, Baishan–Tonghua–Dandong Economic Belt, Hulun Buir China–Russia–Mongolia Cooperation Pilot Zone, Longjiang Silk Road Economic Belt, Harbin New Area, Shenyang Airport Economic Zone, China–Germany Equipment Manufacturing Industrial Park in Shenyang, Changchun Xinglong Comprehensive Free Trade Zone, and Shenyang–Manzhouli–Europe International Rail Line.

Southwest China

Guangxi Zhuang Autonomous Region, Yunnan Province, and Guizhou Province have been actively working in accordance with the BRI and giving overall consideration to the development both at home and abroad. They have been energetically developing Guangxi Beibu Gulf Economic Zone, Pearl River–West River Economic Belt, and China–Indochina Peninsula Economic Corridor, further accelerating the development of China Beibu Gulf Pilot Free Trade Zone and promoting the Pan–Beibu Gulf Economic Cooperation Mechanism. They have also been actively engaging in the economic cooperation of the Bangladesh–China–India–Myanmar Economic Corridor and Great Mekong Subregion, enhancing the China–ASEAN Cooperation Mechanism, launching a new cooperation mode of the China–Malaysia Joint Industrial Park, and setting up a range of national opening -up and cooperation platforms including Guangxi (Dongxing) Key Pilot Zone for Opening up and Development and China–Indonesia Economic and Trade Cooperation Zone.

A number of key Belt and Road mechanisms have settled in southwest China, including the approved Guizhou Inland Open Economy Pilot Area and Kunming Comprehensive Bonded Zone, the launch of Guian Comprehensive Bonded Zone and Honghe Comprehensive Bonded Zone, the approved Mengla (Mohan) Major Development and Opening Pilot Area as well as the starting operation of Guizhou–Shenzhen–Europe International Sea-Rail Freight Line, Guizhou–Chongqing–Xinjiang–Europe International Freight Line, and Yunnan–Central Europe Freight Train.

Notable progress has been made in the Ruili Key Development and Opening-up Experimental Zone, Lincang Border Economic Cooperation Zone, China–Laos

Economic Cooperation Zone, China–Myanmar Economic Cooperation Zone, and China–Vietnam Economic Cooperation Zone, thus enhancing bilateral and multilateral cooperation with surrounding countries. Southwest China has been expanding regional cooperation with Pan–Pearl River Delta Economic Zone, Yangtze River Delta Economic Zone, Circum–Bohai Sea Economic Zone, Beijing–Tianjin–Hebei Economic Zone, and Hong Kong, Macao, and Taiwan, as well as encouraging local enterprises going global. The Tibet Autonomous Region, by speeding up the vital route opening to South Asia, has been promoting the development of the Trans-Himalaya Economic Belt and Jilong Cross-order Economic Cooperation Zone and giving impetus to its open economy.

Inland China

Henan Province has been an active participant in the BRI. The China (Zhengzhou) Cross-border Pilot Comprehensive E-business Zone has been approved, and Phase III of Zhengzhou–Xinzheng Comprehensive Bonded Zone has been largely completed. Henan Province has launched integrated customs integration with nine customs districts and 11 quarantine districts. It has been promoting a range of cooperation with countries along the Belt and Road and strategic cooperation with Cargolux Airlines International of Luxemburg, CFL of Luxemburg, and PKP of Poland.

Shanxi Province has taken the initiative to join in Belt and Road construction, strengthen connections with Beijing, Tianjin, Hebei, and the Circum–Bohai area, promote the development of the Yellow River Golden Delta and Yangtze River Golden Delta, and encourage coal miners to go global to promote international capacity cooperation.

Jiangxi Province has made positive achievements in economic and trade exchanges and interaction with countries along the Belt and Road by pushing forward the development of Nanchang–Rotterdam International Rail, the accelerated completion and operation of Ganzhou Comprehensive Bonded Area, and the official launch of Jiujiang Chengxi Port. It strengthened domestic connectivity by enhancing opening up and cooperation with the Yangtze River Economic Belt, the Pan–Pearl River Delta, the Yangtze River Delta, and the Fujian Delta Economic Zone.

Sichuan Province and Chongqing Municipality have been proactive participants in Belt and Road construction and the Yangtze River Economic Belt by building the Yangtze River Economic Belt Comprehensive Transportation Corridor, reinforcing overall planning of riverside industries, and cooperation between the Upper and Middle Reaches of the Yangtze River Economic Belt, and Russian Volga Federal District (the Twin River Region). The China–Singapore (Chongqing) Demonstration Initiative on Strategic Connectivity has started, and significant achievements have been made in important China–Europe land transportation mechanisms like Chengdu–Europe Express Rail and Chongqing–Xinjiang–Europe Rail.

Hubei, Hunan, and Anhui provinces have been enthusiastic about the BRI, Beijing–Tianjin–Hebei Coordinated Development, and Yangtze River Economic

Belt, striving to build themselves into vital centres and hubs of the Belt and Road; actively organizing enterprises to explore markets in BRIC states, in countries along the Belt and Road, and to open up emerging markets and international exchange and cooperation channels; implementing and promoting development of BRI cooperation frameworks like the Wuhan New Port and Airport Comprehensive Bonded Zone, Xiangyang and Yichang Bonded Logistics Centres, South Hunan's Demonstration Area for Undertaking Industrial Transfer, and the mechanism of China–Germany Joint Commission for Economic Cooperation.

Coastal China

Beijing, Tianjin, and Hebei have been working at top speed on cooperation in key fields of Beijing–Tianjin–Hebei Coordinated Development, further engaging in the BRI and Circum–Bohai Sea Cooperation, vigorously exploring the international market, and in particular cooperating with business communities in Europe, the United States, Japan, South Korea, Southeast Asia, and Australia, driving forward the cooperation on international capacity and equipment manufacturing, and improving the collaboration mechanism with AIIB, Silk Road Fund, and other platforms.

Zhejiang Province, Jiangsu Province, and Shanghai Municipality have been actively engaging in the implementation of the Belt and Road, the Beijing–Tianjin–Hebei Coordinated Development, and the Yangtze River Economic Belt. They have been promoting the integrated development of the Yangtze River Delta and facilitating the construction of China (Shanghai) Pilot Free Trade Zone, Zhejiang Marine Economic Development Demonstration Area, and Zhoushan Archipelago New Area. They have also been building and pushing forward connectivity programmes concerning the Belt and Road, like Ningbo–Zhoushan Port Integration, Yiwu–Xinjiang–Europe Freight Train, Yangshan Bonded Port Expansion, and China–Kazakhstan (Lianyungang) Logistics Terminal, enhancing the development of the open economy and promoting a range of international capacity and equipment manufacturing projects as well as economic and trade cooperation with countries along the Belt and Road.

Shenzhen City, Guangdong Province, and Fujian Province have been taking the initiative to build the Belt and Road by strengthening in-depth cooperation with Hong Kong and Macao and building multilevel regular exchange platform and cooperation mechanisms. They have been promoting the coordinated development of both east and west banks of Pearl River Estuary and regional cooperation in the Pan–Pearl River Delta; strengthening under specific Belt and Road mechanisms opening up cooperation areas in Qianhai of Shenzhen, Nansha of Guangzhou, Hengqin of Zhuhai, and Pingtan of Fujian; steadily driving the construction of the Fujian Strait Pilot Blue Economic Zone, Guangdong–HK–Macao Bay Area, and Shenzhen, Dongguan, and Huizhou, plus Shanwei and Heyuan Economic Rim; and speeding up construction of the Dongguan Shilong Railway International Logistics Centre and China–Russia Trade Park.

Hainan Province has been taking the initiative to build the Belt and Road by enhancing exchange and cooperation with countries and regions along the Belt and Road, taking an active part in the construction of China–ASEAN Free Trade Zone, Pan–Pearl River Delta, and Boao Forum for Asia, propelling construction of Haikou Outsource Demonstration City and Yangpu International Energy Exchange, and exploring foreign trade and the emerging markets along the Belt and Road.

Hong Kong, Macao, and Taiwan

HKSAR is actively involved in the BRI by giving full play to its unique advantages and providing necessary platforms of fundraising and financing, trade and logistics, trade environment, specialized service and infrastructure, and people-to-people communication in the BRI. For fundraising and financing, Hong Kong will offer the capital needed in infrastructure and diversified financing channels to take in the fortunes along the Belt and Road and meet the needs of risk management, further promoting the establishment of RMB offshore centres.

For trade and logistics, Hong Kong has signed civil aviation transport services agreements or international civil aviation transit services agreements with 40 of the 60 countries along the Belt and Road, and it will continue to seek civil aviation transport agreements with other air service providers along the line to consolidate its position as the international aviation hub and build itself into a major trade and logistics platform along the Belt and Road.

For trade, Hong Kong will keep giving full play to its own advantages to strengthen economic and trade relationships with countries along the Belt and Road and sign even more FTAs and investment agreements. Hong Kong has established an economic and trade office in Singapore and in three in European countries along the Belt and Road. It will establish one in Indonesia in 2016 and another one in South Korea at the earliest possible date.

For specialized service and infrastructure, Hong Kong will provide consultation and participate in business operations for regions along the Belt and Road as well as specialized international legal and dispute settlement services for China inland, and assist in building and improving overseas business risk management.

For people-to-people communication, HKSAR will reinforce the Targeted Scholarship and Quality Education Fund mechanisms and encourage more students from Belt and Road countries to study in Hong Kong, while giving full play to its advantage of being multicultural, to enhance art and cultural exchanges with countries along the Belt and Road. HKSAR will establish a Belt and Road Office to coordinate central policies and local policies.

Macao SAR is actively involved in the BRI by giving full play to its unique advantages in traditional Chinese medicine and tourism, consolidating its position as a platform serving business and trade cooperation between China and Portuguese-speaking countries, and deepening exchanges and cooperation with ASEAN as well as Portuguese-speaking countries.

Mainland China has made well-organized arrangements for the participation of Taiwan in the BRI. The Taiwan Affairs Office of the State Council, PRC and China Development Bank proposed in *The Cross-Straits Economic Integration Development and Cooperation Agreement* that China would support ventures jointly established by enterprises from both sides of the straits to invest in a third site and support Taiwan enterprises in participating in BRI construction and participate in programmes including overseas manufacturing bases, economic and trade pilot zones, and infrastructure construction. China will support qualified and capable Mainland-funded enterprises to invest in Taiwan and enhance two-way investment and shareholding by way of capital, equity, and technology. China will also support the infrastructure of a cross-straits economic function area and financial innovation pilot programmes, and reinforce credit aid in Taiwan investment areas, Taiwan farmers entrepreneurial parks, a cross-straits agricultural cooperation pilot zone, bases for undertaking industrial transfer, cross-straits cultural exchange bases, and other infrastructure and associated projects.

Five suggestions for the future of the BRI

The BRI serves as a noble attempt for a community of shared interests, future, and responsibility, opening up a new mode of mutual benefits and reaching beyond the parochial zero-sum mindset. China will not only be the initiator but also a responsible and reliable practitioner for the steady, practical, and orderly construction of the Belt and Road. In such circumstances, we propose the following five suggestions:

Build an overall planning and coordination mechanism for efficient and integrated progress

The BRI is a long-term programme for which a highly efficient and powerful overall coordination mechanism is of vital importance. Currently, the overall coordination mechanism among ministries, provinces, and cities needs further reinforcement. The lack of coordination of Chinese enterprises' overseas investment has deleterious effects on the BRI's development that relies on market-oriented operation.

Therefore, great attention should be attached to institutional design as well as exploring and establishing an efficient and powerful nationwide coordination mechanism, in order to offer overall planning and coordination for the BRI. A "positive list" for the construction of the Belt and Road could be introduced to guide all sides to identify the trends in building the Belt and Road and promote more reasonable policy expectations to be formed at different levels of government. Also, a "negative list" for the construction of the Belt and Road should be issued to confirm forbidden fields and fully inspire the initiative and creativity of participants in building the Belt and Road.

Adhere to the principle of long-term consistent progress and encourage innovative mechanisms and platforms

In the process of building the Belt and Road, local authorities have high expectations of the development dividend of the BRI. Some consider the Belt and Road a new way to attract investment, whereas others, without practical measures for development, use the BRI as a slogan for local development.

Therefore, it should be made clear that the Belt and Road construction is a long-term, complex, and systematic programme, and blind adherence to construction should be prevented. There is no existing experience for reference, so efforts should be made to explore ways of innovative construction.

Tell BRI stories to boost cohesion among countries for the construction of the Belt and Road

The BRI serves as an important reflection of China's active participation in global governance and a vital practice in projecting China's image as a major power. The BRI advocates cooperation, mutual benefits, and common development, and aims to build a community of shared interests, future, and responsibility, featuring mutual political trust, economic integration, and cultural inclusiveness.

There are a great number of ethnic groups with diversified cultures, languages, and religious beliefs along the Belt and Road. It is of great importance to inherit the Silk Road spirit of "peace and cooperation, openness and inclusiveness, mutual learning and mutual benefit".

China should give full interpretation of the BRI's connotation and denotation and clearly show the positive effects of the BRI, which would facilitate the deepening of international cooperation. This would also help shape mainstream understanding of the BRI among the Chinese public and help reduce misunderstanding of the BRI abroad.

Utilize the global Chinese network to tap into international talent reserves

Overseas Chinese are important resources with unique advantages for China. Statistics show that there are over 60 million overseas Chinese in 198 countries and regions across the world. They are familiar with foreign culture, have a good command of the language, and have formed a network of communication with easy access to technology, capital, and information resources.

There are formal or informal unions among overseas Chinese, such as the World Chinese Entrepreneurs Convention and the World Federation of Overseas Chinese Associations. In building the Belt and Road, it is of great importance to strengthen institutional and cultural connection between China and countries along the Belt and Road. Overseas Chinese could serve as an important link to help reduce the gap between China and the countries where they reside. A productive network of global Chinese talent should be developed for the progress of the Belt and Road.

Establish a business support system to provide all-round and effective assistance

A comprehensive business service support system is urgently needed, as many Chinese enterprises going global lack specialized strategies on investment and international operation in countries and regions along the Belt and Road. Some companies fail to make good use of the Chinese and international financial markets, and lack effective risk management and response solutions.

As a result, comprehensive support for Chinese enterprises in investment banking services, business trust, administration, legal affairs, auditing, consulting, and investigation should be in place, to help Chinese enterprises prosper while going global. This would also offer powerful backup for the development of the BRI.

Conclusion

In the past four years, the Chinese government has been actively engaging in Belt and Road development. It has been strengthening communication and consultation with countries along the Belt and Road, promoting practical cooperation, and implementing a range of policies and measures. All these activities have contributed to the current progress in the BRI's development.

The Belt and Road entails all-dimensional cooperation to build a new international economic and trade relationship. Traditional international economic and trade relationships tend to be horizontally organized, which carries out "horizontal" trade negotiations based on tariffs. In contrast, in the wake of the release of *Visions and Actions on Jointly Building the Silk Road Economic Belt and 21st-Century Maritime Silk Road* in March 2015, all China's provinces and regions as well as government ministries have accomplished BRI-related policy planning and implementation. The BRI has opened up an all-dimensional cooperation mode integrating both governments and enterprises at home and abroad. The Silk Road spirit and core principles of "peace and cooperation, openness and inclusiveness, mutual learning and mutual benefit" have been rooted as an important consensus of the Chinese and international communities.

The BRI requires long-term cooperation to create new and sustainable international economic and trade relationships. In this era featured by sustainable development, the BRI integrates long-term infrastructure interconnectivity into bilateral relations, rather than narrowly focusing on short-term commodity trade. This enriches economic and trade relations according to their time dimensions.

The BRI also means inclusive cooperation and adds new connotations to diversified international economic and trade relations. The economy and trade in China have been witnessing new trends. Capacity building and economic and trade cooperation, based on overseas economic and trade cooperation zones, have given birth to new interdependence in international economic and trade business. Overseas economic and trade cooperation zones have been functioning as important carriers for the Belt and Road, along with the increasingly institutionalized international capacity-building cooperation, investment and trade facilitation, and accelerated two-way investment.

The BRI signals innovative cooperation, aiming to create new and interactive patterns of international economic and trade relationships. As a result of the development of globalization, all countries and regions are closely connected and have merged into a community with shared interests. Through policy coordination, facilities connectivity, unimpeded trade, financial integration, and people-to-people communication, the BRI will be jointly built through consultation to meet the interests of all. Efforts should be made to integrate the development strategies of the countries along the Belt and Road. The BRI represents a new trend in global economic cooperation and has become a global consensus. It also offers a very promising view for the international economy.

In conclusion, the BRI is of strategic significance for strengthening cooperation among countries and building a community of a shared future, featuring mutual political trust, economic integration, and cultural inclusiveness. It will soon be a new engine for world economic growth and write a new chapter in invigorating the Silk Road Economic Belt and the 21st-Century Maritime Silk Road.

Note

1 The information on the progress of the six economic corridors is from 'Building the Belt and Road: Concept, Practice and China's Contribution', Office of the Leading Group for the Belt and Road Initiative, May 2017.

Bibliography

Chongyang Institute for Financial Studies, Renmin University of China (RDCY) 2015, *International trade pivot cities under the Belt and Road initiative* [《一带一路"国际贸易支点城市研究》]. China CITIC Press, Beijing.

Chongyang Institute for Financial Studies, Renmin University of China (RDCY) 2016, *RDCY report: adhering to the planning, orderly and pragmatically build the 'Belt and Road'*. The Belt and Road Progress Research Team. Available from: http://en.rdcy.org/displaynews.php?id=25582. [26 March 2017].

Chongyang Institute for Financial Studies, Renmin University of China (RDCY) 2017, *RDCY think tank series: Belt and Road series*. Foreign Languages Press, Beijing.

Joint Communiqué of the Leaders Roundtable of the Belt and Road Forum for International Cooperation 16 May 2017. Available from: www.beltandroadforum.org/english/n100/2017/0516/c22-423.html. [15 July 2017].

Liu Wei (ed) 2017, *Understanding 'the Belt and Road' blueprint* [《读懂' 一带一路'蓝图》]. The Commercial Press, Beijing.

The National Development and Reform Commission, Ministry of Foreign Affairs, and Ministry of Commerce of the People's Republic of China 2015, *Vision and actions on jointly building Belt and Road Economic Belt and 21st century Maritime Silk Road*, March. Available from: http://en.ndrc.gov.cn/newsrelease/201503/t20150330_669367.html. [27 September 2017].

Office of the Leading Group for the Belt and Road Initiative 2017, *Building the Belt and Road: concept, practice and China's contribution*. Foreign Languages Press, Beijing.

Wang Wen 2017a, ' "Belt and Road": shaping a new open world' ('一带一路'塑造新的开放世界'), *The Silk Road review* [《丝路瞭望》], July, pp. 20–23.

Wang Wen 2017b, ' "Belt and Road": reshaping Chinese people's world view' ['一带一路'重构中国人的世界观], *Journal of Central Institute of Socialism* [《中央社会主义学院学报》], August, pp. 33–38.

Wang Yiwei 2015, *Belt and Road: opportunities and challenges* [《一带一路机遇与挑战》]. People's Publishing House, Beijing.

Xi Jinping 2017, 'Work together to build the Silk Road Economic Belt and the 21st Century Maritime Silk Road', Speech at the opening ceremony of The Belt and Road Forum for International Cooperation, 14 May. Available from: http://news. xinhuanet.com/english/2017-05/14/c_136282982.htm. [27 September 2017].

Part II
Finance and investment

3 Hong Kong as an equity financing centre for the Belt and Road nations

Kevin C. K. Lam, Heather M. F. Lee, Julia J. Liu, and Stacy Z. Wang

Economists, most notably David Ricardo, have long argued that more open international trade will enhance the economic welfare for all participating countries and allow them to specialize in what they can do best.[1] Luft (2016) argues that the Belt and Road Initiative (BRI) can bring prosperity to the many developing Asian countries that lack the capacity to undertake major infrastructure projects on their own, by connecting them through a web of airports, deepwater ports, fibre-optic networks, highways, railways, and oil and gas pipelines. Although it is too early to say that the intention of the BRI is to establish a free trade zone similar to the European Union (EU) and the North American Free Trade Agreement (NAFTA), the initiative will have beneficial economic effects for the countries involved.

The Belt and Road countries: economic and social background

In this section, we review the institutional details of the Belt and Road countries. Because numerous countries are involved, we focus on those in Asia, including those in Southeast, South, and Central Asia. These countries are closer to China and are probably less susceptible to influence or coercion by other powerful nations. Thus, we have 27 economies to analyse under such classification: 11 in Southeast Asia, seven in South Asia, and nine in Central Asia. We choose not to cover the remaining Belt and Road jurisdictions and do not believe that our insights or conclusions will differ had those jurisdictions in the BRI been included.

Table 3.1 shows the general social and economic conditions of these Asian Belt and Road countries and regions. The data reflect the condition at the end of 2016. The countries have very different populations (Population), ranging from 1.3 billion in India and China to about 0.42 million in Brunei and Maldives. All Belt and Road countries and regions surveyed in this paper account for 52 percent of the world's total population. The economic significance of each country in GDP also varies. There are economic giants such as China (US$11.2 trillion) and India (US$2.2 trillion) and many small economies such as Bhutan ($2,240 million). Two of the world's top ten economies (China and India) are in

Table 3.1 Economic conditions of the Belt and Road countries and regions

		Population	GDP	GDP Per Capita	GDP Growth
	China	1,378.67	11,199.15	8,123.18	6.70
	HKSAR	7.35	320.91	43,681.14	2.05
Belt and Road Countries					
Southeast Asia	Brunei	0.42	11.40	26,938.50	−2.47
	Cambodia	15.76	20.02	1,269.91	6.88
	Indonesia	261.12	932.26	3,570.29	5.02
	Laos	6.76	15.90	2,353.15	7.02
	Malaysia	31.19	296.36	9,502.57	4.24
	Myanmar	52.89	67.43	1,275.02	6.50
	Philippines	103.32	304.91	2,951.07	6.92
	Singapore	5.61	296.97	52,960.71	2.00
	Thailand	68.86	406.84	5,907.91	3.23
	Timor-Leste	1.27	..	..	..
	Vietnam	92.70	202.62	2,185.69	6.21
South Asia	Bangladesh	162.95	221.42	1,358.78	7.11
	Bhutan	0.80	2.24	2,804.00	6.17
	India	1,324.17	2,263.52	1,709.39	7.11
	Maldives	0.42	3.59	8,601.63	4.09
	Nepal	28.98	21.14	729.53	0.56
	Pakistan	193.20	283.66	1,468.19	5.74
	Sri Lanka	21.20	81.32	3,835.39	4.38
Central Asia	Afghanistan	34.66	19.47	561.78	2.23
	Armenia	2.92	10.55	3,606.15	0.20
	Azerbaijan	9.76	37.85	3,876.94	−3.10
	Georgia	3.72	14.33	3,853.65	2.74
	Kazakhstan	17.80	133.66	7,510.08	1.00
	Kyrgyzstan	6.08	6.55	1,077.04	3.83
	Tajikistan	8.73	6.95	795.84	6.90
	Turkmenistan	5.66	36.18	6,389.33	6.20
	Uzbekistan	31.85	67.22	2,110.65	7.80
Northeast Asia	Mongolia	3.03	11.16	3,686.45	0.98
	Republic of Korea	51.25	1,411.25	27,538.81	2.83
Central and Eastern Europe	Albania	2.88	11.93	4,146.90	3.46
	Belarus	9.51	47.43	4,989.25	−2.65
	Bosnia and Herzegovina	3.52	16.56	4,708.72	1.99
	Bulgaria	7.13	52.40	7,350.80	3.44
	Croatia	4.17	50.43	12,090.67	2.93
	Czech	10.56	192.92	18,266.55	2.43
	Estonia	1.32	23.14	17,574.69	1.57
	Hungary	9.82	124.34	12,664.85	1.95
	Latvia	1.96	27.68	14,118.06	1.95
	Lithuania	2.87	42.74	14,879.68	2.30
	Macedonia	2.08	10.90	5,237.15	2.41
	Moldova	3.55	6.75	1,900.20	4.10
	Montenegro	0.62	4.17	6,701.00	2.50
	Poland	37.95	469.51	12,372.42	2.68
	Romania	19.71	186.69	9,474.13	4.82

		Population	*GDP*	*GDP Per Capita*	*GDP Growth*
	Russia	144.34	1,283.16	8,748.36	−0.22
	Serbia	7.06	37.75	5,348.29	2.78
	Slovakia	5.43	89.55	16,495.99	3.29
	Slovenia	2.06	43.99	21,304.57	2.49
	Turkey	79.51	857.75	10,787.61	2.88
	Ukraine	45.00	93.27	2,185.73	2.31
Africa	Ethiopia	102.40	72.37	706.76	7.56
	South Africa	55.91	294.84	5,273.59	0.28
Australasia	New Zealand	4.69	185.02	39,426.62	3.95
Middle East	Bahrain	1.43	31.86	22,354.17	..
	Egypt	95.69	336.30	3,514.49	4.30
	Iran	80.28	..	..	..
	Iraq	37.20	171.49	4,609.60	11.00
	Israel	8.55	318.74	37,292.61	4.04
	Jordan	9.46	38.65	4,087.94	2.00
	Kuwait	4.05	..	..	..
	Lebanon	6.01	47.54	7,914.00	1.76
	Oman	4.42	66.29	14,982.36	..
	Palestine	..	..	..	..
	Qatar	2.57	152.47	59,330.86	2.23
	Saudi Arabia	32.28	646.44	20,028.65	1.74
	Syria	18.43	..	..	..
	United Arab Emirates	9.27	348.74	37,622.21	3.04
	Yemen	27.58	27.32	990.33	−9.78

Source: World Development Indicators 2016, compiled by the World Bank.

Notes: Population (in millions) is based on the de facto definition of population, which counts all residents regardless of legal status or citizenship. The world total population at the end of 2016 was 7.442 billion. Available from: https://data.worldbank.org/indicator/SP.POP. TOTL?view=chart [21 September 2017].

GDP (in US$ thousand millions) is the sum of gross value added by all resident producers in the economy plus any product taxes and minus any subsidies not included in the value of the products. Available from: https://data.worldbank.org/indicator/NY.GDP.MKTP. CD?view=chart [21 September 2017].

GDP Per Capita (in US$) is gross domestic product (GDP) divided by Population. Available from: https://data.worldbank.org/indicator/NY.GDP.PCAP.CD?view=chart [21 September 2017].

GDP Growth (in percentage) is the annual growth rate of GDP at market prices based on constant local currency. The world average for 2016 was 2.438. Available from: https://data. worldbank.org/indicator/NY.GDP.MKTP.KD.ZG?view=chart [21 September 2017].

our sample. Singapore is the most developed economy here, with per capita GDP of US$52,960, and Hong Kong is the next with $43,681. Interestingly, there are many countries with very high GDP growth rates (GDP Growth), even higher than that of China (6.7 percent). These countries include Uzbekistan (7.8 percent), India (7.11 percent), Bangladesh (7.11 percent), Laos (7.02 percent), Philippines (6.92 percent), Tajikistan (6.90 percent), and Cambodia (6.88 percent). It is clear that the potential opportunities offered by this Belt and Road vision are enormous, as the growth rates of most membership countries are significantly higher than the world average of 2.4 percent.

Table 3.2 outlines the capital market infrastructure of these Asian Belt and Road countries and regions as of 2016. India has the largest number (5,820)

Table 3.2 Capital market development and institutions of the Belt and Road countries and regions

		#Listed Co	Market Capitalization of Listed Co	Value of Stocks as percentage of GDP	Ease of Doing Business
China		3,052	7,320.74	163.3612	78
HKSAR		1,872	3,193.24	421.0177	4
Belt and Road Countries					
Southeast Asia	Brunei	..	..	..	72
	Cambodia	..	..	..	131
	Indonesia	537	425.77	9.697585	91
	Laos	..	..	..	139
	Malaysia	893	359.79	33.1643	23
	Myanmar	..	..	..	170
	Philippines	262	239.74	11.75821	99
	Singapore	479	640.43	63.32463	2
	Thailand	656	432.96	79.88374	46
	Timor-Leste	..	..	..	175
	Vietnam	320	66.40	10.99205	82
South Asia	Bangladesh	557	..	..	176
	Bhutan	..	..	..	73
	India	5,820	1,566.68	34.98968	130
	Maldives	..	..	..	135
	Nepal	..	..	..	107
	Pakistan	..	..	..	144
	Sri Lanka	295	18.68	1.480294	110
Central Asia	Afghanistan	..	..	..	183
	Armenia	..	..	..	38
	Azerbaijan	..	..	..	65
	Georgia	..	..	..	16
	Kazakhstan	85	40.16	0.55491	35
	Kyrgyzstan	..	..	..	75
	Tajikistan	..	..	..	128
	Turkmenistan	..	..	..	..
	Uzbekistan	..	..	..	87
Northeast Asia	Mongolia	..	..	..	64
	Republic of Korea	..	..	..	..
Central and Eastern Europe	Albania	..	..	..	58
	Belarus	55	..	..	37
	Bosnia and Herzegovina	..	..	..	81
	Bulgaria	..	..	..	39
	Croatia	160	..	..	43
	Czech	..	..	..	27

		#Listed Co	Market Capitalization of Listed Co	Value of Stocks as percentage of GDP	Ease of Doing Business
	Estonia	..	..	..	12
	Hungary	43	22.55	6.282961	41
	Latvia	..	..	..	14
	Lithuania	..	..	..	21
	Macedonia	..	..	..	10
	Moldova	..	..	..	44
	Montenegro	..	..	..	51
	Poland	861	138.69	9.720708	24
	Romania	84	..	..	36
	Russia	242	622.05	10.87769	40
	Serbia	..	..	..	47
	Slovakia	..	..	..	33
	Slovenia	38	5.26	0.695081	30
	Turkey	380	171.76	32.85434	69
	Ukraine	121	..	..	80
Africa	Ethiopia	..	..	..	159
	South Africa	303	951.32	136.4936	74
Australasia	New Zealand	173	80.05	5.910529	1
Middle East	Bahrain	43	19.39	1.044977	63
	Egypt	251	33.32	2.9974	122
	Iran	325	108.79	..	120
	Iraq	..	..	..	165
	Israel	427	213.98	16.25879	52
	Jordan	224	24.57	6.686178	118
	Kuwait	..	..	..	102
	Lebanon	10	12.12	..	126
	Oman	113	23.29	3.709341	66
	Palestine	..	..	..	..
	Qatar	44	154.82	12.43281	83
	Saudi Arabia	176	448.83	47.39515	94
	Syria	..	..	..	173
	United Arab Emirates	125	213.21	14.19346	26
	Yemen	..	..	..	179

Source: World Development Indicators 2016, compiled by the World Bank.

Notes: #Listed Co, including foreign companies which are exclusively listed, is the number of companies who have shares listed on an exchange at the end of 2016. Available from: https://data.worldbank.org/indicator/CM.MKT.LDOM.NO?view=chart [15 September 2017].

Market Capitalization of Listed Co (in US$ thousand millions) is the share price times the number of shares outstanding (including their several classes) for listed domestic companies. Data are end of 2016 values converted to US dollars using corresponding year-end foreign exchange rates. Available from: https://data.worldbank.org/indicator/CM.MKT.LCAP.GD.ZS [15 September 2017].

Value of Stocks as percentage of GDP is the total number of shares traded, both domestic and foreign, multiplied by their respective matching prices, expressed as a percentage of GDP. Data are end of 2016 values. Available from: https://data.worldbank.org/indicator/CM.MKT.TRAD.GD.ZS?view=chart [15 September 2017].

Ease of doing business ranks economies from 1 to 190, 1 being the friendliest. The higher the number, the less friendly the business environment. Available from: https://data.worldbank.org/indicator/IC.BUS.EASE.XQ?view=chart [15 September 2017].

of listed companies (#Listed Co), followed by China (3,052) and Hong Kong (1,872). However, in market capitalization (Market Capitalization of Listed Co), China is the largest (US$7.3 trillion), followed by Hong Kong (US$3.1 trillion) and then India (US$1.5 trillion). Some countries in the table have missing data, mostly because their stock markets do not exist or are inactive. Hong Kong has the most active stock market, with annual turnover 412 percent of its GDP (Value of Stocks as percentage of GDP). That is followed by China (163 percent), Thailand (79 percent), and Singapore (63 percent). Singapore has the friendliest business climate (Ease of Doing Business) in Asia, ranking number one among the countries surveyed in our study and number two worldwide, followed by Hong Kong, which ranks number four worldwide. However, there are countries in the Belt and Road lists that are regarded as not business friendly, with a ranking after 150 out of the 190 countries and regions surveyed, such as Afghanistan, Bangladesh, Myanmar, and Timor–Leste.

BRI opportunities for Hong Kong as an equity financing centre

Funding gaps

Based on the data presented previously, it is not surprising to see the Belt and Road countries are mostly in the developing stage in their infrastructure development, particularly those relating to transportation, energy, and telecommunication facilities. However, many of them have high economic growth rates. Their economic growths can only be sustained with investment in their economic infrastructure. Interestingly, China had more than 40 years of infrastructure development and has gradually acquired competitive advantages in completing the development projects efficiently. Table 3.3 shows the projects under construction, with collaboration from China, in some of the Belt and Road countries as of May 2017. The financing of massive infrastructure projects is critical before China's industrial know-how can spread across Asia and Africa, which will, in turn will create new markets for Chinese construction companies. For example, an initial investment of US$1.4 billion and further investment of US$13 billion are needed to develop the Colombo Port City in Sri Lanka; Africa's first transnational electric railway, which opened in 2017 and runs for 466 miles from Djibouti to Addis Ababa, the capital of Ethiopia, requires US$4 billion; and US$6 billion investment is needed to build the 260-mile rail line from northern Laos to the capital, Vientiane (Perlez & Huang 2017). The Asian Development Bank expects emerging Asian economies to need infrastructure investment totalling US$1.7 trillion a year to maintain economic growth, but only about half that would be available (Law 2017).

So far, more than 90 percent of Asian infrastructure investment comes from public sectors. The Export–Import Bank of China, a Chinese state-funded and state-owned policy bank, lent more than US$80 billion in 2015 and has financed more than 1,000 projects in 49 Belt and Road countries. The Asia Infrastructure

Table 3.3 Projects underway with collaboration from China under the Belt and Road Initiative as of May 2017

Countries	Infrastructure	Details
Belarus	Industrial Park	Occupying an area of 91.5 square kilometres, this industrial park will be the largest one China has built overseas.
Pakistan	Gwadar Port Free Zone	The free zone will be modelled after the Shekou Industrial Zone in Shenzhen, China, comprising a port, an industrial park, and residential and business areas.
	Karot Hydropower Project	Started at the end of 2015, it is scheduled to be operational by 2020. An investment of US$1.65 billion, the power station will have an installed capacity of 720MW and an average annual output of 3.2GWh.
Sri Lanka	Colombo Port City	The Port City will involve a combined floor area of over 5.3 million square metres, with an initial direct investment of US$1.4 billion. It is expected to attract further development investment of US$13 billion and create 83,000 long-term jobs.
Eurasia	China Railway Express to Europe	The "Belt and Road on rail" helps boost connectivity between China and the rest of Eurasia.
Indonesia	Jakarta-Bandung Railway	The rail link is expected to stimulate growth in such sectors as metallurgy, manufacturing, infrastructure, power generation, and logistics; create jobs; and promote structural transformation in Indonesia.
Laos	China–Laos Railway	China's first overseas railway project to provide a direct link to China's internal rail network. It will also be an important section of the pan-Asia railway network.
Thailand	China–Thailand Railway	The 900-kilometre railway is the first standard-gauge railway in Thailand. Serving Thailand's northeastern regions and covering major cities, it will boost economic development and standards of living in those regions.
Kenya	Mombasa-Nairobi Railway	The 471-kilometre-long Mombasa-Nairobi railway is the first section of a planned East Africa railway network, connecting Nairobi, the capital city of Kenya, with Mombasa, the largest port in East Africa. It will also be the first new rail line in Kenya in a century.
Ethiopia	Addis Ababa-Adama Expressway	The first expressway in Ethiopia and East Africa. The road was built with financing support from the Chinese government and using Chinese technology and standards. In addition to extensive use of local labour, the project's Chinese contractor brought technical and managerial expertise to Ethiopia, contributing to its capability in infrastructure development.

Source: Xinhuanet. The information was published by the New World Press under the China Foreign Languages Publishing Administration. Available from: http://news.xinhuanet.com/english/2017-05/10/c_136271092.htm [15 September 2017].

Investment Bank (AIIB), a China-led multilateral institution with 57 member countries, is part of the potential solution. Nevertheless, it plans to increase operations gradually, investing US$3 billion – US$5 billion in 2017 and US$10 billion in 2018 (Kynge 2016). Due to limited room for increased public involvement, the Asian Development Bank has estimated an annual funding shortfall for Asian infrastructure projects of US$750 billion between 2010 and 2020 (Asian Development Bank 2009). Although China would provide the seed capital for many of these infrastructure projects, Wong (2016) estimated the funding gap could amount to US$8 trillion. In addition, the funding provided by China could kick-start these projects, but Belt and Road countries should seek continuous financing by recycling capital from the savings glut in China and along the Belt and Road regions (Mak 2016). In light of this, there is a need for a sustainable source of funding to which these countries can resort. Funds from private sectors could fill the financing gap (Qu 2017). Equity financing, by raising capital from a broader range of global private investors, is surely one such probable source. Hong Kong, one of the most important equity financing centres in the world, may have a role to play.

Advantages of Hong Kong as a financial centre

Table 3.4 summarizes the advantages of Hong Kong as a financial centre. Hong Kong, as an international financial centre with strong networks with China and worldwide, is ideally positioned to connect investors and BRI investment projects. Hong Kong has been the freest economy in the world for 23 years in a row, ranked by the Heritage Foundation in the United States (Yau 2017) and consistently ranked number one in economic freedom by the Fraser Institute in Canada. It also has a free flow of information and a simple and efficient tax system with low tax rates. Its fundraising and financing capabilities enable a smooth and efficient flow of capital. Hong Kong's financial markets have a high degree of liquidity and operate under effective and transparent regulations.

Furthermore, Hong Kong occupies a nodal point on the 21st-Century Maritime Silk Road, which, along with the Silk Road Economic Belt, make up the BRI. It is located in the time zone of GMT + 8 to form a seamless link to US and European markets. Its banking system is effective and stable. It is closely connected with the world at the heart of Asia; five hours' flight from half the global population and four hours away from all Asia's key markets. The robust transportation network and efficient telecommunication systems also facilitate Hong Kong in being a very efficient financial centre. Finally, one thing unique in Hong Kong is its China advantage. Being close to China, the second-largest world economy, and with China's per capita GDP growing consistently, high savings rate, and recent initiative of stock connections (Shanghai–Hong Kong and Shenzhen–Hong Kong), Hong Kong will also play an increasing role as a centre where China's citizens can park their savings.

In addition, Hong Kong has a highly educated labour force and a rich pool of professional talents and scores high on the human development index (United Nations 2013). Hong Kong provides world-class services in accounting, law, and

Table 3.4 Hong Kong's financial infrastructure

* People
  A rich pool of professional talents and educated workforce
* Environment
  Freest economy in the world (Heritage Foundation, Fraser Institute)
  Free flow of information and capital
  Open and competitive business environment
  Sound judiciary framework: common law system
  Simple and efficient tax system with low tax rates
  Consistently, top rank in Global Financial Centre, Financial Development, Best
     to Do Business, World Competitiveness Indices, Freest Economy, Easiest to
     do Business
* Market access
  Located in a time zone with seamless link to the US and European markets
  Ready access to international financial markets and business capital
  Mature and vibrant stock market
  Effective and stable banking system
* Infrastructure
  Sophisticated and extensive business infrastructure
  Five hours' flying time from half the global population
  Robust transport network and efficient telecommunications systems
* China advantages
  China, the second-largest world economy, per capita GDP consistently growing
  Citizens with very high saving rates looking for good investment opportunities
  Developing banking, securities, and pension systems
  Stock-Connect initiatives widen the pool of investors:
     Shanghai–Hong Kong Stock Connect
     Shenzhen–Hong Kong Stock Connect

Source: InvestHK. Available from: www.investhk.gov.hk/zh-hk/files/2012/11/2012.11-fs-pitch book-en.pdf [28 February 2018].

management consultancy through both international and local firms along the process of equity financing. In relation to Belt and Road business opportunities, Hong Kong is by far the most popular offshore centre for seeking professional services, providing 50 percent of professional services related to Belt and Road business (Morrow 2017). The highly educated labour force and the rich pool of professional talents have accumulated their years of experience in providing equity-financing-related services in China and Asia. These professionals can advise on tax, legal, and risk management and can assist in dispute resolution, particularly in arbitration. The largest international accounting firms and law firms have a presence in Hong Kong. Hong Kong local firms also have a wealth of experience in raising capital for Chinese and other Asian companies and infrastructure finance.

Equity financing in Hong Kong

The Hong Kong Stock Exchange (HKEX) operates two markets, the Main Board and the Growth Enterprise Market (GEM). The Main Board caters to companies with a profitable operating track record or those that can meet alternative financial standards. GEM caters for smaller growth companies and has lower admission criteria. GEM also acts as a stepping stone to Main Board listing and provides a streamlined procedure for transfer to the Main Board once a company meets the Main Board admission criteria.

Starting in the 1990s, HKEX became the primary stock market for mainland Chinese companies to list and raise capital. Also, worldwide investors have gained access to China's leading companies through investing in their Hong Kong-listed shares. More recently, an increasing number of overseas companies have been looking to invest in infrastructure projects in China, and that trend will accelerate under the BRI. In 2016, mainland Chinese companies dominated new listings on the HKEX by accounting for 80.5 percent of all funds raised through Initial Public Offering (IPO) (Yiu 2016b). Hong Kong also plays host to some of the world's largest IPOs by Chinese companies. The Postal Savings Bank of China, for example, raised US$7.4 billion in its September 2016 IPO in Hong Kong, the world's largest IPO in 2016 (Lau & Barreto 2016).

However, it is crucial for Hong Kong to make sure its listing policies and listing rules evolve with the transforming listing needs associated with the BRI. Hong Kong faces keen competition from other stock exchanges as a listing host. In the first quarter of 2017, Hong Kong lost out to New York, Shanghai, and Shenzhen on the value of funds raised via IPO (Yiu 2017). Although proximity to China is believed to be the number one reason many Chinese companies choose to list in Hong Kong, Singapore, a Belt and Road participating country, provides an alternative by being the gateway to Southeast Asia, where many BRI projects are initiated (Samtani 2017). However, existing listing regulations in Hong Kong were designed decades ago for property developers, banks, financiers, and traditional retailers. As a result, the current equity securities listed on the HKEX are largely financial companies, retailers, and consumer services companies. Table 3.5 shows the market capitalization of Hong Kong-listed companies from 2014 to 2016 by industries. Financial institutions occupy about 30 percent market capitalization on the Main Board (Panel A), and consumer goods and consumer services constitute around 23 percent and 16 percent market capitalization on the GEM (Panel B). It is questionable whether BRI-related companies, particularly those in infrastructure, energy, and technology, find Hong Kong an appealing listing destination. Recently, Hong Kong has fought with London and New York to host the Saudi Aramco IPO, which is expected to become the largest ever in 2018, valuing the oil giant at US$2 trillion (Yiu 2017).

A major initiative of the Chinese and Hong Kong market regulators in the last two years is the establishment of channels for mainland Chinese investors to invest in the Hong Kong equity market and for Hong Kong and international investors to invest in the Chinese equity market through Hong Kong. The first step was the launch of the Shanghai–Hong Kong Stock Connect scheme in November 2014, followed by the launch of the Shenzhen–Hong Kong Stock Connect scheme in December 2016. The two schemes provide Hong Kong and international investors with direct trading access to Shanghai- and Shenzhen-listed shares for the first time, while mainland Chinese investors gained direct

Table 3.5 Market capitalization of Hong Kong listed companies by industries

Panel A: Main Board (in HK$ thousand millions)

Industry Classification	2014		2015		2016	
Energy	1,170.24	4.70%	863.91	3.54%	991.65	4.06%
Materials	528.77	2.12%	430.57	1.76%	504.70	2.06%
Industrials	1,053.16	4.23%	1,140.25	4.67%	879.44	3.60%
Consumer Goods	2,753.06	11.06%	2,793.12	11.44%	2,744.32	11.22%
Consumer Services	1,961.30	7.88%	1,527.83	6.26%	1,729.38	7.07%
Telecommunications	2,331.55	9.37%	2,257.39	9.24%	2,124.89	8.69%
Utilities	1,500.94	6.03%	1,459.61	5.98%	1,356.82	5.55%
Financials	7,457.46	29.96%	7,180.57	29.40%	7,229.79	29.57%
Properties & Construction	3,454.25	13.88%	3,520.00	14.41%	3,420.40	13.99%
Information Technology	1,629.89	6.55%	2,101.79	8.60%	2,488.20	10.18%
Conglomerates	1,051.80	4.23%	1,150.53	4.71%	980.85	4.01%
Equity Total	24,892.42	100.00%	24,425.55	100.00%	24,450.43	100.00%

Panel B: GEM (in HK$ thousand millions)

Industry Classification	2014		2015		2016	
Energy	1.58	0.88%	1.64	0.64%	1.35	0.43%
Materials	11.67	6.50%	8.56	3.32%	4.88	1.57%
Industrials	8.30	4.63%	21.07	8.16%	26.63	8.57%
Consumer Goods	34.34	19.14%	49.52	19.18%	49.22	15.83%
Consumer Services	40.36	22.50%	57.50	22.27%	71.84	23.11%
Telecommunications	4.19	2.33%	8.46	3.28%	2.99	0.96%
Utilities	1.79	1.00%	3.41	1.32%	5.13	1.65%
Financials	21.83	12.17%	32.68	12.66%	44.94	14.45%
Properties & Construction	5.61	3.13%	17.96	6.96%	58.16	18.71%
Information Technology	49.75	27.73%	57.27	22.18%	45.64	14.68%
Conglomerates	0.00	0.00%	0.11	0.04%	0.09	0.03%
Equity Total	179.41	100.00%	258.18	100.00%	310.87	100.00%

Source: HKEX. Main Board. Available from: www.hkex.com.hk/eng/stat/statrpt/factbook/factbook2016/Documents/23.pdf [15 September 2017].
GEM. Available from: www.hkex.com.hk/eng/stat/statrpt/factbook/factbook2016/Documents/06.pdf [15 September 2017].

Notes: Industry Classification refers to the Hang Seng Industry Classification System, provided by Hang Seng Indexes Company Limited.

access to Hong Kong-listed shares. The Hong Kong and Chinese regulators plan to launch "Primary Equity Connect", a scheme to allow investors to subscribe for IPO shares through the Stock Connect schemes which are not currently allowed. Such schemes would provide the BRI-involved Chinese companies a simple and direct approach to raise equity capital in Hong Kong from worldwide investors and provide a gateway for the foreign companies in Belt and Road countries to gain access to capital funding in China through Hong Kong.

The reality of Hong Kong as an equity financing centre for Belt and Road countries

Although Hong Kong has a huge potential as an equity financing centre for the Belt and Road countries, this has not happened. To be eligible for listing in Hong Kong, a company is required to have incorporated in either a "Recognized Jurisdiction" or an "Acceptable Jurisdiction". Listing Rules of Hong Kong recognize only four jurisdictions as the recognized jurisdictions as companies' places of incorporation for listing on the HKEX: Hong Kong, the People's Republic of China, the Cayman Islands, and Bermuda. Overseas companies, for which the places of incorporation are not in the recognized jurisdiction, are expected to show that the jurisdiction in which they are incorporated offers standards of stockholder protection that are at least equivalent to those provided in Hong Kong, in accordance with Listing Rule 19.05(1)(b). To foster overseas companies to list in Hong Kong, after having reviewed the shareholder protection standards of respective jurisdictions, additional jurisdictions are approved as jurisdictions acceptable as a company's place of incorporation, the acceptable jurisdictions. The number of acceptable jurisdictions has been increasing steadily but slowly from three jurisdictions in 2007 to 21 in 2017 (Securities and Futures Commission (SFC) & Hong Kong Exchanges and Clearing Limited (HKEX) 2013; JPS 2013, p. 1). Table 3.6 shows the acceptable overseas jurisdictions under the current listing policy of the HKEX. It also presents the names of the companies in a particular jurisdiction listed in Hong Kong. Only two Belt and Road countries, Singapore and India, are acceptable jurisdictions under this list. Eleven companies from Singapore are currently listed or cross-listed in Hong Kong. Although India is now an acceptable overseas jurisdiction, none of the Indian companies are listed in Hong Kong as of August 2017. Moreover, it can be seen that several companies from Australia, Brazil, Germany, Singapore, and Japan previously listed or cross-listed in Hong Kong have since chosen to be delisted. Such delisting may signal the issues relating to their trading liquidity and possibly the level of support made available to them. Unless Hong Kong can overcome these issues, companies may not want to be listed in Hong Kong.

Table 3.7 shows the distribution by domicile of the listed firms on the HKEX in 2016 and 2011. Most Hong Kong-listed companies are incorporated in the Cayman Islands and Bermuda, followed by China and Hong Kong. In aggregate, companies incorporated in these four recognized jurisdictions represent about

Table 3.6 List of acceptable overseas jurisdictions

Jurisdictions	Actual Listing: Primary or Secondary
Australia	Sino Gold Mining Ltd. (Delisted in December 2009; Old Stock Code: 01862)
Brazil	Vale S.A. (Delisted in July 2016; Old Stock Code: 06210/ 06230)
British Virgin Islands	Winsway Coking Coal Holdings Ltd. (01733); China New Town Development Company Ltd. (01278); Grand Concord International Holdings Ltd. (00844); Termbray Petro-king Oilfield Services Ltd. (02178); Feishang Anthracite Resources Ltd. (01738); Tianhe Chemicals Group Ltd. (01619); Tianyun International Holdings Ltd. (06836); Sundart Holdings Ltd. (01568); Pantronics Holdings Ltd. (01611)
Canada – Alberta	Sunshine Oilsands Ltd. (02012); Persta Resources Inc. (03395)
Canada – British Columbia	SouthGobi Energy Resources Ltd. (01878); China Gold International Resources Corp. Ltd. (02099)
Canada – Ontario	Manulife Financial Corp. (00945)
Cyprus	
England and Wales	HSBC Holdings Plc (00005); Prudential Plc (02378); Standard Chartered Plc (02888); Kazakhmys Plc (00847)
France	
Germany	Schramm Holding AG (Delisted in March 2012; Old Stock Code: 00955)
Guernsey	
India	
Isle of Man	
Israel	
Italy	Prada S.p.A. (01913)
Japan	SBI Holdings, Inc. (Delisted in June 2014; Old Stock Code: 06488); Dynam Japan Holdings Co., Ltd. (06889); Fast Retailing Co., Ltd. (06288); Niraku GC Holdings, Inc. (01245)
Jersey	United Company Rusal Ltd. (00486); West China Cement Ltd. (02233); Glencore International Plc (00805)
Korea	
Labuan	
Luxembourg	L'Occitane International S.A. (00973); Samsonite International S.A. (01910)
Russia	
Singapore	China XLX Fertiliser Ltd. (01866); Sound Global Ltd. (00967); Novo Group Ltd. (01048); Hengxin Technology Ltd. (01085); Midas Holdings Ltd. (01021); Elec & Eltek International Company Limited (01151); CapitaMalls Asia Ltd (Delisted in July 2014; Old Stock Code: 06813); Technovator International Limited (01206); Anacle Systems Limited (08353); BOC Aviation Limited (02588); Weiye Holdings Limited (01570)
US – State of California	
US – State of Delaware	
US – State of Nevada	

Source: HKEX. Available from: www.hkex.com.hk/eng/rulesreg/listrules/listsptop/listoc/ list_of_aoj.htm [16 September 2017].

Table 3.7 Jurisdictions of incorporation for Hong Kong listed companies in 2016 and 2011

	2016		2011	
Cayman Islands	781	45.59%	504	38.01%
Bermuda	474	27.67%	456	34.39%
China	218	12.73%	139	10.48%
Hong Kong	204	11.91%	199	15.01%
	1,677	97.90%	1,298	97.89%
British Virgin Islands	9	0.53%	3	0.23%
Singapore	9	0.53%	8	0.60%
Canada	4	0.23%	3	0.23%
England	4	0.23%	4	0.30%
Japan	3	0.17%	1	0.08%
Jersey	3	0.17%	3	0.23%
Luxemburg	2	0.12%	2	0.15%
Italy	1	0.06%	1	0.08%
US	1	0.06%	1	0.08%
Brazil	0	0.00%	1	0.08%
Germany	0	0.00%	1	0.08%
	36	2.10%	28	2.11%
Total	1,713	100.00%	1,326	100.00%

Source: HKEX. *HKEX Fact Book 2016: Trading statistics and analysis.* Available from: www.hkex.com.hk/eng/stat/statrpt/factbook/factbook2016/fb2016.htm and *HKEX Fact Book 2011: Trading statistics and analysis.* Available from: www.hkex.com.hk/eng/stat/statrpt/factbook/factbook2011/Documents/07.pdf [16 September 2017].

98 percent of the companies listed. Companies from other jurisdictions represent only about 2 percent of the total numbers listed. Singapore is the only Belt and Road country with companies listed on the HKEX. Moreover, from 2011 to 2016, there was an increase of only eight companies from other jurisdictions that are listed in Hong Kong, making a total of 36 in 2016.

It is clear that Hong Kong has yet to play the role of financing capital of these Belt and Road countries. Table 3.8 shows the listing of companies from Belt and Road countries on the New York Stock Exchange (NYSE) in the US and the London Stock Exchange (LSE) in the UK as of 31 December 2016. Although there are a number of companies from Bangladesh, India, Indonesia, Malaysia, Pakistan, Philippines, and even Kazakhstan listed or cross-listed on the NYSE and on the LSE, there are no companies from the Belt and Road countries listed or cross-listed in Hong Kong, except for several Singaporean companies. Moreover, some companies from Belt and Road countries have been listed on the NYSE and the LSE for a considerable time, as early as in 1994 (Philippine Long Distance Telephone Company from Philippines) on the NYSE and in 2005 (Beximco Pharmaceuticals Limited from Bangladesh) on the LSE. This

Table 3.8 Belt and Road companies listed on NYSE
and LSE as of 31 December 2016

	NYSE	*LSE*
Bangladesh	0	1
India	11	23
Indonesia	1	0
Kazakhstan	0	4
Malaysia	0	1
Pakistan	0	4
Philippines	1	2
Singapore	2	4
Total	15	39

Source: NYSE. Available from: www.nyse.com/publicdocs/ nyse/data/Non-US_Monthly_2016_12.xlsx. LSE. Available from: www.londonstockexchange.com/statistics/historic/ company-files/company-files.htm [16 September 2017].

shows that there are healthy and robust companies from Belt and Road countries. It also shows that major stock exchanges are willing to provide listings to companies from developing countries. These companies generate tax and other revenue for the country of listing and create employment opportunities for their professionals.

There are many potential reasons for the absence of the Belt and Road countries listed in Hong Kong. One such reason may be the relatively safe and conservative approach regarding the permission of firms from the developing countries to be listed in Hong Kong. As mentioned, according to Listing Rule 19.05(1)(b), overseas issuers not incorporated in one of the recognized jurisdictions are required to satisfy the standards of stockholder protection. Therefore, companies incorporated in other countries which seek to have primary listing in Hong Kong have to prove that their country of domicile meets the standards of shareholder protection equivalent to Hong Kong. As reported in Table 3.6, these acceptable jurisdictions typically include countries such as Australia, the UK, the United States, Germany, Korea, Japan, Singapore, and Brazil. India has been lately included as one of the acceptable domiciles, but there is no Indian firm listed in Hong Kong. Nonetheless, this is a good start. For those who want to seek secondary listings in Hong Kong, an issuer listed on another stock exchange must satisfy the HKEX requirement that its primary listing is on an exchange where the standards of shareholder protection are at least equivalent to those provided in Hong Kong (Listing Rule 19.30(1)(b)). As shown in Table 3.9, these exchanges typically include those from the developed countries and located in London, New York, Australia, Tokyo, Toronto, Frankfurt, Paris, Stockholm, Switzerland, the Netherlands (Amsterdam), Italy, Spain (Madrid), Singapore, and Brazil.

Table 3.9 Recognized stock exchange for secondary listing in Hong Kong

Waivers from the Main Board Listing Rules are likely to be granted to applicants seeking secondary listing on the HKEX that have a primary listing on the main market on one of the following stock exchanges:

1 The Amsterdam Stock Exchange
2 The Australian Securities Exchange
3 The Brazilian Securities, Commodities and Futures Exchange
4 The Frankfurt Stock Exchange
5 The Italian Stock Exchange
6 The London Stock Exchange
7 The Madrid Stock Exchange
8 NASDAQ OMX
9 The New York Stock Exchange
10 The Paris Stock Exchange
11 The Singapore Exchange
12 The Stockholm Exchange
13 The Swiss Exchange
14 The Tokyo Stock Exchange
15 The Toronto Stock Exchange

Source: Paragraph 91, "Joint Policy Statement Regarding the Listing of Overseas Companies", issued by the Securities and Futures Commission and the Hong Kong Exchange and Clearing Limited, 27 September 2013 (JPS 2013).

Challenges and policy implications for Hong Kong

Place of incorporation

The requirement for the designated place of incorporation may create barriers for overseas companies to list in Hong Kong. As mentioned, companies listed in Hong Kong are required to incorporate in the recognized jurisdictions. The place of incorporation represents the place of establishment of a company, and the core shareholder rights are stipulated under the company law of the company's place of incorporation. However, a company's principal place of business where the business is carried out can be located in a jurisdiction different from the place of incorporation. If this is the case, the principal place of business plays a crucial role for legal enforcement and tax purposes. In practice, both place of incorporation and place of principal business of a company are considered for listing. Previously, if a company's place of principal business was different from the place of incorporation, this would trigger the scrutiny of the regulators or the listing application might even be considered unsuitable (FSDC 2014, p. 41; SFC & HKEX 2017; JPS 2007, p. 3).[2] Designating recognized jurisdictions and acceptable jurisdictions may cause listing applicants to think that place of incorporation is the dominant factor for listing purposes. This practice may also inadvertently lead investors to view negatively jurisdictions that fall outside the designated jurisdictions. This is not the practice of the major international exchanges like the LSE, where every issuer should have a level playing field for fair and equal treatment, enabling these exchanges to accommodate the capital needs of overseas companies.

We need to debate whether such a long-standing conservative policy of cross-country listings should be allowed to remain unchanged. More importantly, exchanges in the United States and London do allow companies in developing countries to list their shares in their stock exchanges, and they are promoting their advantages to the developing countries. The questions we need to ask are: (1) Do we need to strictly adhere to "hierarchical thinking", i.e. pass the country screen first and then only let companies from allowable countries to be considered for listing? (2) Will we allow good companies to list or cross-list even when they come from countries that are not from recognized jurisdictions and acceptable jurisdictions and regarded as having poor investor protection? There are bad companies even in very good jurisdictions (e.g. Enron was listed on the NYSE), and companies with very good potential from less affluent jurisdictions. Similar to the idea that we should not discriminate against promising youth to enter reputable universities, we should not discriminate against any promising companies from the yet-to-be acceptable jurisdiction. Also, these countries have high growth rates, in particular with the implementation of the BRI. With a higher potential for growth and in turn a greater opportunity for return, there should be markets for mature and successful companies from these jurisdictions to cater for their capital needs and for investors with different appetites for risks. An open-minded approach is needed to re-evaluate their suitability for listing in Hong Kong. In fact, as shown in Table 3.8, the NYSE and the LSE are allowing companies from Third World countries to list shares in their stock exchanges as long as they meet the admission requirements. With reference to the practices of leading international exchanges, the regulators of Hong Kong may consider lifting the jurisdiction requirement for overseas companies to list in Hong Kong. Moreover, as a result of the recent Stock Connect initiatives, more investors from China are allowed to invest their money in the shares listed in Hong Kong, so a wider return-risk spectrum will be welcomed by investors too.

Shareholder protection standards

Other than the requirement for the designated place of incorporation, the conformity of shareholder protection standards of Hong Kong may create barriers for overseas companies to list in Hong Kong. As mentioned, overseas companies are not prohibited from listing in Hong Kong according to the Listing Rules, even if they are not under recognized jurisdictions, as long as they can show there are in place in their home jurisdictions equivalent shareholder protection standards of Hong Kong. These are shareholder protection provisions of the Companies Ordinance of Hong Kong (COHK) and the requirements of the Listing Rules. Otherwise, they may need to amend their constitutional documents to include the relevant shareholder protection standards. However, different countries have different legal systems on shareholder protection standards, and no two sets of legal standards on shareholder protection are identical. The legal system in Hong

Kong is inherited from the common law system of the UK, yet there are differences in certain provisions between the shareholder protection standards of these two jurisdictions. It may be even difficult for a company incorporated in a jurisdiction to adopt the civil law system to comply with the shareholder protection standards equivalent to those of a common law system. Additional resources in both time and money will be incurred for compliance purposes, at least for professional costs incurred for reviewing the shareholder protection standards, revising the constitutional documents of the company, not to mention the procedural complexity of the revising process and the uncertainty of the result of the listing application. In certain situations, the amendments may even violate the laws and regulations of the home jurisdiction. Only a handful of overseas companies listed in Hong Kong means there is room for improvement for these listing rules.

The advantages of restricting listing to companies domiciled in countries with strong investor protection is that the investment risk of equity investors can be controlled. However, this philosophy is incompatible with the envisioned role of Hong Kong as an equity financing centre for Belt and Road countries. There is also no reason to believe that the Hong Kong shareholder protection system is necessarily superior. Fong and Lam (2014), for instance, explore some of the shareholder protection issues in the Hong Kong stock markets. Table 3.10 shows some indices on shareholder protection standards – disclosure, director liability, shareholder rights, and corporate transparency – based on the World Development Indicators in 2016 (compiled by the World Bank). As seen from Table 3.10, not all Belt and Road countries have unacceptable investor protection standards. Some even compare favourably to India, one of the acceptable jurisdictions and the Belt and Road jurisdictions. For instance, according to Table 3.10, Georgia, Kazakhstan, Malaysia, Tajikistan, and Thailand have disclosure, director liability, and corporate transparency indices equal to or even better than does India. The implications are clear. These Belt and Road countries have been actively reforming their governance and investor protection systems.

In addition to the above, under the Listing Rules there is no specific elaboration regarding with what and how shareholder protection standards should be complied. Some policy statements giving clearer guidelines for the compliance of the shareholder protection standards have been issued to clarify the uncertainty only since 2007 (JPS 2007, 2013). This explains why the number of listed overseas companies in HKEX has been minimal. The latest policy statement issued in 2013 detailed the requirements on shareholder protection standards and other disclosure issues for primary listing as well as some other requirements for secondary listing (JPS 2013). Also, country guides on each acceptable jurisdiction were issued setting out guidance on how companies incorporated there can meet the requirements for equivalent shareholder protection standards of Hong Kong.

The policy statement and the country guides issued show that the HKEX in recent years appears to apply a more liberal approach to implement the shareholder protection requirement. Companies are not required to comply exactly with the shareholder protection standards of Hong Kong, allowing more variations in the standards as long as the shareholder protection standards of the overseas

Table 3.10 Quality of disclosure, director liability, shareholder rights, and corporate transparency in Belt and Road jurisdictions as of 1 June 2016

	DISCL	DIR LIAB	SH RIGHTS	CORP TRANSP
Hong Kong	10	8	9	8
China	10	1	1	9
Afghanistan	1	1	0	2
Armenia	5	6	8	7
Azerbaijan	10	5	7	6
Bangladesh	6	7	4	6
Bhutan	4	4	6	5
Brunei	4	8	5	5
Cambodia	5	10	1	5
Georgia	9	6	7	8
India	7	6	10	6
Indonesia	10	5	6	5
Kazakhstan	10	6	9	8
Kyrgyzstan	7	5	4	7
Laos	6	1	5	1
Malaysia	10	9	8	7
Maldives	0	8	4	5
Myanmar	3	0	5	3
Nepal	6	1	8	5
Pakistan	6	6	8	5
Philippines	2	3	1	7
Singapore	10	9	8	8
Sri Lanka	8	5	6	6
Tajikistan	8	6	9	7
Thailand	10	7	4	7
Timor-Leste	5	4	8	5
Turkmenistan	..	..	..	..
Uzbekistan	8	3	6	5
Vietnam	7	4	7	7

Source: World Bank Group 2016, *Doing Business 2017: Equal Opportunity for All.*

Notes: DISCL = disclosure; DIR LIAB = director liability; SH RIGHTS = shareholder rights; CORP TRANSP = corporate transparency. The index ranges from 1 to 10. The higher the index, the better the quality.

jurisdiction are not materially different from those of Hong Kong and the main legal principles are achieved. For instance, a super majority vote is interpreted as three-quarters majority of votes by members as stipulated in accordance with the COHK, but now other versions of a super majority vote are explicitly discussed and allowed (JPS 2013). The regulators also clarify how the overseas companies disclose certain discrepancies instead of amending the constitutional documents to reduce the procedural complexity involved in varying the constitutional documents. The adoption of more a disclosure-led approach is in line with the trend that there is a drop of unsophisticated retail investors and an increase of more sophisticated institutional and professional investors (HKEX 2017b, p. 20).[3] Moreover, in case the compliance with the shareholder protection standards in

Hong Kong contravenes the law of the home jurisdiction, to facilitate listing of overseas companies and at the same time to maintain the quality of the listed company, the regulators may grant a waiver to the company from strict compliance (HKEX 2015). With clearer guidelines and a more transparent system, it is expected that there will be an increasing trend for companies in acceptable jurisdictions to list in Hong Kong. For companies, at least for the first issuers, from jurisdictions not in the list of the acceptable jurisdictions, including most of the Belt and Road countries, although a more liberal approach is adopted by the regulators, they are under uncertainty regarding the additional costs incurred for amending their constitutional documents and the results of their listing applications. As mentioned, an open-minded approach is needed to re-evaluate their suitability for listing in Hong Kong.

Regulatory cooperation agreement

For listing in Hong Kong, one of the major concerns for regulators is whether there is any cooperation arrangement with the regulator of the overseas jurisdiction for access to and exchange of information for regulatory investigation and enforcement purposes. Without access to a company's information, the regulator may have difficulty pursuing legal action against wrongdoers. The only possible action is to suspend trading or delist a stock, as in the accounting failure cases of Chinese-listed companies in the United States in the early 2010s (Lee 2016). The SFC, the equity market regulator in Hong Kong, and the HKEX issued a policy statement and required that the statutory securities regulator in an overseas company's jurisdiction of incorporation and place of central management and control must either (1) be a full signatory of the International Organisation of Securities Commission's Multilateral Memorandum of Understanding Concerning Consultation and Cooperation and the Exchange of Information (IOSCO MMOU), or (2) have entered into a bilateral agreement with the SFC for mutual assistance and exchange of information for the purpose of enforcing and securing compliance with the laws and regulations of that home jurisdiction and Hong Kong (JPS 2013). To be designated as acceptable jurisdictions, it is important to meet the first criterion, as all statutory regulators of the 21 acceptable jurisdictions fulfilled the first criterion and are full signatories of the IOSCO MMOU (HKEX 2017c).[4] No acceptable jurisdiction meets only the second criterion. Instead, there are a number of acceptable jurisdictions, other than being signatories of the IOSCO MMOU, that signed various bilateral arrangements for investigatory assistance and exchange of information with the SFC (HKEX 2017c).[5]

The IOSCO MMOU is the first global information-sharing arrangement for securities regulators for cooperation in fighting breaches of securities-related laws. In addition to the SFC, there are more than 100 signatories to the IOSCO MMOU from other jurisdictions, as of June 2017, including ten (Bangladesh, Brunei, India, Indonesia, Malaysia, Pakistan, Singapore, Sri Lanka, Thailand, and Vietnam) out of the 27 Belt and Road countries and regions surveyed in this chapter (SFC 2017). As most Belt and Road countries (17 out of 27) are not signatories to the IOSCO MMOU, the companies from these jurisdictions cannot meet the regulatory cooperation requirement and are likely not able to list in Hong Kong, unless with the explicit consent of the SFC (JPS 2013). Other than India and Singapore, the two out of the above ten signatories, which are currently the acceptable jurisdictions, more efforts may be expected to collaborate with other Belt and Road countries as acceptable jurisdictions for listing purposes, at least to consider collaborating with the remaining eight jurisdictions which are also full signatories of the IOSCO MMOU. Moreover, the regulators may consider signing bilateral agreements with securities authorities from the jurisdictions which are not signatories to the IOSCO MMOU. Alternatively, the regulators may launch some specific measures for BRI companies, discussed in later sections.

Listing requirements: financial tests and "centre of gravity"

To list in Hong Kong, companies must meet the requirements of both the designated place of incorporation and equivalent shareholder protection standards. In addition, they are required to meet certain financial tests.

- *Profit test of main board*

To list on the Main Board, a new applicant must have a trading record of at least three financial years and fulfil one of the following three financial tests (Listing Rule 8.05(1) to (3)). (1) Profit/market capitalization test: profit of at least HK$50 million in the last three financial years (with profits of at least HK$20 million in the most recent year, and at least in aggregate HK$30 million recorded in the two preceding years), and a market capitalization of at least HK$200 million at the time of listing. (2) Market capitalization/revenue/cash flow test: at least HK$2 billion in market capitalization with HK$500 million of revenue in the latest financial year and positive cash flow from operating activities of at least HK$100 million in aggregate for the three preceding financial years. (3) Market capitalization/revenue test: at least HK$4 billion of market capitalization with HK$500 million in revenue in the latest financial year. It is clear that, at the very minimum, an applicant must have aggregate profits of HK$50 million in the three most recent financial years and a market capitalization of HK$200 million at the time of listing. In the view of HKEX, the profit requirement serves as an effective indicator of the past performance of an applicant's management during the track record period and generally a good indicator of an applicant's future profitability (HKEX 2017a). If an applicant is not profitable, it is allowed to meet alternative tests which require at least HK$500 million of revenue in the latest financial year. The HKEX's statistics shows that 92 percent of applicants to the Main Board from 2010 to 2015 chose to meet the profit test (HKEX 2017a).

The profit requirement of the HKEX is higher than most competitors in overseas markets. Table 3.11 presents the minimum profit requirements of the HKEX Main Board and its overseas competitors. In terms of the aggregated profit over

Table 3.11 Comparison of minimum profit requirements of the main board of HKEX and overseas competitor markets (in HK$ millions)

Markets	Three-Year Aggregate Profit	Final Year Profit
HKEX Main Board	50	20
Australian Stock Exchange	5.8	2.9
FCA (UK)	No profit test	No profit test
NASDAQ (US)	85	17
NYSE (US)	77.6	15.5
Singapore Exchange	Not required	169
Shanghai Stock Exchange	35	Not required

Source: HKEX June 2017, 'Consultation Paper: Review of the Growth Enterprise Market (GEM) and Changes to the GEM and Main Board Listing Rules', Table 7.

Notes: For purposes of comparison, the profit required is aggregated over three years and converted to Hong Kong dollars.

all three years of a track record period, the minimum HK$50 million requirement is higher than that of the Australian Stock Exchange and the Shanghai Stock Exchange but lower than NASDAQ and NYSE. The Singapore Exchange (SGX) only tests the profit made in the last year of the three-year track record. The Financial Conduct Authority (FCA), a financial regulatory body in the UK, does not have a profit test. In terms of the profit for the final year of a listing applicant's track record period, the minimum HK$20 million requirement is higher than that of the Australian Stock Exchange, NASDAQ, and NYSE, but lower than SGX. The Shanghai Stock Exchange does not test the final year profit, and FCA in the UK does not have a profit test. However, except for the Shanghai Stock Exchange, other overseas Main Markets in Table 3.11 test a listing applicant's pre-tax profit, whereas the HKEX Main Board tests the net profit attributable to shareholders (i.e. after tax profit). To meet the profit test, an applicant must exclude any associated companies and other entities whose results are recorded in the applicant's financial statements using the equity method of accounting. The profit should also exclude any income or loss generated by activities outside the ordinary and usual course of the listing applicant's business. Therefore, the profit requirement is more stringent than that of most competitor markets.

- *Cash flow test of GEM*

The GEM is primarily a market for small and mid-sized companies. It was designed to have less stringent admission requirements than the Main Board, which is for larger companies. GEM Listing Rule 11.12A(1) requires a listing applicant to have a trading record of at least two financial years and aggregate operating cash flow of HK$20 million in the two years prior to listing, subject to a minimum market capitalization of HK$100 million. Similar to the requirements of the Main Board, to meet the cash flow test, an applicant must exclude any associated companies, joint ventures, and other entities whose results are recorded in the applicant's financial statements using the equity method of accounting or proportionate consolidation. The cash flow refers to the applicant's cash flow generated from operating activities in the ordinary and usual course of business before changes in working capital and taxes paid.

The HKEX views cash flow as an appropriate indicator of business viability for small to mid-sized companies as compared to the profit and revenue tests for Main Board applicants. In practice, about 95 percent of the companies listing on GEM from 2010 to 2016 were profitable at the time of listing (HKEX 2017b). However, the minimum cash flow requirement implies that a GEM listing applicant must have revenues. Start-up companies in certain high-growth sectors, such as technology and biotechnology, are at the early stage of development. They raise capital for the specific purpose of research and development of products that have not yet reached the commercialization stage, and therefore they do not have adequate revenue or positive operating cash flow to meet the listing criteria on the GEM.

Due to the stringent admission requirements, companies seeking a Hong Kong listing are held to a higher financial standard. According to the HKEX statistics (HKEX 2017b), in the past ten years, over 6,000 mainland companies that did not meet the Main Board profitability test or the GEM cash flow test have listed on National Equity Exchange and Quotations[6] (NEEQ), NYSE, and NASDAQ. The number of those with a minimum market capitalization of at least HK$200 million (the minimum for the Main Board) amounted to 1,502. Of these, 42 listed on NYSE or NASDAQ, and 1,460 listed on NEEQ. In addition to mainland companies, there are a notable number of overseas companies with significant revenue from mainland China that have not met the financial eligibility requirements of the HKEX and have been attracted to list in overseas competitor markets.

- *"Centre of gravity" test of secondary listing*

If a company already has a primary listing on another exchange, it can apply for a secondary listing in Hong Kong. The same listing requirements apply to both primary and secondary listing applicants. However, in practice, the HKEX may grant waivers from the Listing Rules to an applicant seeking a secondary listing on the Main Board, provided that it is a company that (JPS 2013): (1) has a market capitalization in excess of US$400 million and has been listed for at least five years on the primary market (which track record may be waived if the applicant is well established and has a market capitalization significantly larger than US$400 million), normally with a long track record of clean legal and regulatory compliance on the primary market; (2) has a primary listing on one of the 15 accepted exchanges (provided that the applicant has not been waived or exempted from compliance with the laws or rules of the primary market); and (3) has a "centre of gravity" outside China. This concept of centre of gravity is not defined in the joint statement. The HKEX has indicated a number of factors that will be taken into account when determining the issue, e.g. the location of the applicant's headquarters, its central management and control, its main business operations and assets, its corporate and tax registration, the nationality and country of residence of its management and controlling shareholders (FSDC 2014).

Currently, companies with a centre of gravity in Greater China are prohibited from pursuing a secondary listing in Hong Kong. The intention of this prohibition is to discourage such companies from seeking to avoid the more stringent rules that apply to primary listings by listing via an overseas listed shell (refer to as "regulatory arbitrage") (HKEX 2017b). As mentioned, a number of large mainland Chinese companies have already sought listings elsewhere. Because of this centre of gravity restriction, mainland Chinese companies that have listed on overseas markets, principally the United States, for reasons other than regulatory arbitrage are prevented from accessing the HKEX via a secondary listing.

Despite the HKEX's efforts in promoting itself as an equity financing centre for secondary listings, there are only seven secondary-listed companies on the HKEX (see Table 3.12). Some reputable companies (e.g. Peninsular and Oriental System Navigation Company) obtained and subsequently withdrew their secondary listings in Hong Kong. In the three most recent years, three companies have delisted: Vale S.A. delisted in July 2016, CapitaMalls Asia Limited in July 2014, and SBI Holdings in June 2014. Generally speaking, trading in these stocks has not been very active since listing.

In order to provide more opportunities for companies targeting Belt and Road countries to raise capital in Hong Kong, the HKEX may need to incorporate more flexibility in the eligibility criteria, as well as remove the requirement for geographical centre of gravity outside China for mainland companies already listed elsewhere but wishing to secondary list in Hong Kong. At the same time, however, the HKEX has to ensure that Hong Kong's robust regulatory framework is maintained.

Table 3.12 Secondary listing companies in Hong Kong

Stock Code	Stock Name	Jurisdiction of Incorporation	Primary Markets
06288	Fast Retail-DRS	Japan	Tokyo Stock Exchange
06388	Coach-DRS-RS	Maryland, US	New York Stock Exchange
00805	Glencore-S	Jersey	London Stock Exchange
00847	Kazakhmys-S	UK	London Stock Exchange and Kazakhstan Stock Exchange
00945	Manulife	Canada – Ontario	Toronto Stock Exchange
01021	Midas Hldgs-S	Singapore	Singapore Exchange
01878	SouthGobi-S	Canada – British Columbia	Toronto Stock Exchange

Source: HKEX. Available from: www.hkex.com.hk/eng/rulesreg/listrules/listsptop/listoc/co_inf.htm [21 September 2017].

Market segmentation

Compared with its overseas competitors that use several listing boards (e.g. NYSE and NASDAQ in the United States) or differentiate segments within listing boards (e.g. premium listing segment, standard listing segment, and high growth segment on the Main Market of the LSE) to better accommodate different needs of issuers and investors, the HKEX lacks diversity in its market segments available for issuers and investors. As mentioned, there are only two platforms on the HKEX, the Main Board and the GEM, for companies raising capital. However, these two platforms take quite a conservative approach which is not able to keep pace with the diverse needs of issuers with different profiles. Currently, other than the barriers as mentioned in the preceding sections, companies with non-standard governance structures, pre-profit companies, i.e. those without track records of profits or revenue, and mainland Chinese companies that wish to secondarily list, are not allowed to list in Hong Kong, whereas they are accepted by other leading stock exchanges. For instance, the listing application of the e-commerce giant, Alibaba Group Holding (Alibaba), was rejected in Hong Kong due to its non-standard governance structure, i.e. the dual-class share (DCS) structure which grants the founding partners more rights than other shareholders have (Yiu 2016a), which was contrary to the listed governance structure in Hong Kong that required having the voting rights of the shares in proportion to the relative interests of those shares, e.g. the one-share-one-vote governance structure.[7] Even though companies are allowed to establish a DCS structure in Hong Kong according to the COHK,[8] they are not allowed to list on the HKEX, which requires fair and equal treatment of all shareholders. Alibaba then raised a record US$25 billion by going public on the NYSE in 2014, the world's biggest IPO to date (Egan 2015). Currently, the use of the DCS structure is permitted under the listing rules of NYSE, NASDAQ, LSE (only on the standard listing segment), and Toronto Stock Exchange.

The regulators of the leading stock exchanges can also react fast to the evolving needs of issuers by making adjustments to their well-established regulatory frameworks. Singapore has recently proposed allowing companies with a DCS structure to list on the SGX (Singapore Exchange 2017). The FCA in the UK has recently reviewed the effectiveness of its listing regime and proposed having a distinct international segment for large overseas companies (Financial Conduct Authority 2017). The FCA also varies listing rules in order to allow the listing of Saudi Aramco, a national oil company of Saudi Arabia. Saudi Aramco plans to go public for an estimated US$100 billion in 2018, which will surpass Alibaba and become the biggest IPO in history, leading the major stock exchanges, e.g. NYSE, LSE, Tokyo Stock Exchange, SGX, and HKEX, to compete for this IPO. To attract the oil giant to choose LSE for its IPO, the FCA proposed creating a new category within the listing rules for companies controlled by sovereign entities with less onerous disclosure and regulatory requirements (Binham & McCrum 2017).

Hong Kong is now considering opening a New Board to accommodate the various needs of the issuers and investors. However, the proposed New Board, including two segments, the New Board PRO and the New Board Premium, may not be able to entertain the needs of the companies from Belt and Road countries. Although it is proposed that companies are no longer required to provide equivalent shareholder protection standards (for companies to list on the New Board PRO and for companies listed on NYSE and NASDAQ to seek secondary listing on the New Board Premium), they are still required to locate in jurisdictions where regulatory cooperation agreements are in place. As mentioned, most Belt and Road countries are not signatories of the IOSCO MMOU and thus do not have these regulatory cooperation agreements. The New Board may still not be able to fill the gap for capital funding for these companies.

To keep pace with international legal development, to give companies with various profiles greater flexibility in raising capital, especially for BRI projects, as well as to provide investors a wider range of investment opportunities, particularly in view of more sophisticated institutional and professional investors in the markets, the regulators of Hong Kong may consider further differentiating market segments and expanding the listing eligibility criteria while at the same time maintaining the quality of the regulatory framework for listing.

Cross-border supervisory collaboration

It is understandable that the regulators of Hong Kong may have concerns for the listing applicants from Belt and Road countries. Economically, as mentioned, these countries are comparatively less affluent in GDP and per capita GDP. Companies from these countries may inevitably have difficulties meeting certain existing admission requirements of the HKEX, e.g. the profitability test or the cash flow test, for listing purposes, not to mention the recent proposal to raise the admission requirements by the HKEX (discussed in the next section) (HKEX 2017a). Combined with political instabilities of some of these Belt and Road countries where intermittent political upheavals and repeated conflicts with neighbouring countries are common, this creates uncertainty about the investment plan and may adversely affect the performance of the companies. Moreover, the political uncertainty adds to the concerns regarding the enforcement of regulatory supervision and the possibility of effective communication. Due to a conservative risk appetite and a small range of acceptable jurisdictions, the SFC may also have limited experience in anomalies related to political risk, cultural differences, and operating uncertainty, which are likely to appear in BRI involved companies.

It is important for the SFC to boost collaboration with overseas regulators or regulators of Belt and Road countries in specific when more companies from overseas jurisdictions are listed in Hong Kong. Special attention should be paid to innovative and complex products and transactions. For instance, there was a recent collaboration between the SFC and the China Securities Regulatory Commission (CSRC), the financial market regulator of China. As mentioned, the launch of the Shanghai–Hong Kong Connect scheme and the Shenzhen–Hong Kong Connect scheme provides equity investors in Hong Kong a direct channel to invest in China-listed companies which seek equity financing for BRI projects. However, the enhanced connectivity between Hong Kong and China markets could induce manipulative trading and other opportunist behaviours. The SFC and the CSRC could join forces in preventing, identifying, and fighting those criminals. On 10 March 2017, the CSRC and the SFC published their first joint enforcement by sanctioning two individuals for the manipulative trading of securities committed through the Shanghai–Hong Kong Stock Connect since the launch of the connect scheme in 2014 (ONC Lawyers 2017). The two individuals controlled four securities accounts in Hong Kong and China to repeatedly conduct price building, price maintenance, overweighting, and selling off shares of Zhejiang China Commodities City Group, listed in Shanghai and traded on the Shanghai–Hong Kong Stock Connect during the period 4 February to 23 June 2016. It is imperative that the SFC have regular and timely collaboration with overseas regulators.

A hub for infrastructure project companies under the BRI

Although China has pledged to inject US$124 billion into Belt and Road countries, a huge amount of capital will be needed from private financing (Reuters 2017). One platform Hong Kong offers BRI infrastructure project companies to raise capital is by listing on the stock exchange. As discussed, all companies seeking a listing in Hong Kong must comply with certain basic listing requirements, unless waivers are granted by the HKEX. The SFC also has powers to object to a proposed listing under section 6 of the Securities and Futures (Stock Market Listing) Rules. The HKEX and the SFC have been making efforts to boost Hong Kong's profile as an equity financing centre for infrastructure project companies, particularly BRI-related companies.

• *Waiver conditions*

To qualify for a listing on the Main Board, an applicant must have a minimum trading record of three years and meet certain minimum profit requirements. GEM applicants must have a positive cash flow of at least HK$20 million for the two preceding years. However, newly formed infrastructure project companies[9] intend to raise capital for the specific purpose of the creation and construction of major infrastructure projects. They are therefore, in many instances, in the pre-construction or construction stage, without a track record of revenue, let alone profits or positive cash flows. It is hard for these companies to qualify for a listing in Hong Kong.

To facilitate newly formed infrastructure project companies to raise capital in Hong Kong, the HKEX grants a waiver to these companies and allows them to proceed with their proposed listing if certain conditions are satisfied (Main Board Listing Rule 8.05B(2) and GEM Listing Rule 11.14(1)). The key waiver condition is that the project company, at the time of listing, must be a "pure" infrastructure project company, having the right to build the project and operate the completed project, and not engaged in any other businesses. These requirements would exclude building and construction companies or other service providers. Moreover, the project must be carried out under a long-term (at least 15 years) concession or mandate awarded by a government and be of a substantial size (the company's share of the total capital cost of the project is at least HK$1 billion). Other waiver conditions, such as restrictions from change of business in the first three years post-listing, expertise and experience requirements of directors and management, and enhanced disclosure must also be met.

Particularly, for Main Board applicants, the HKEX may accept a shorter trading record period and may vary or waive the profit test if a newly formed infrastructure project company is able to demonstrate that:

1   it is a party to and has the right to build and operate (or participate in the results from the operation of) a particular infrastructure project(s). The project(s) may be carried out by the applicant company directly or through subsidiaries or joint venture companies. Companies which finance, but do not undertake the development of the project(s), will not be considered under rule 8.05B(2);

2   at the time of listing, it is not engaged in any businesses other than those stipulated in the infrastructure project mandate(s) or contract(s);

3   the infrastructure project(s) must be carried out under a long-term concession or mandate (there should normally be at least 15 years remaining in each concession or mandate at the time of listing) awarded by government and be of a substantial size (i.e. the applicant company's share of the total capital cost of the projects should normally be at least HK$1 billion);

4   where it is involved in more than one project, the majority of its projects are in the pre-construction or construction stage;

5   the bulk of the proceeds of the offering will be used to finance the construction of the project(s) and not principally to repay indebtedness or to acquire other non-infrastructure assets;

6   it will not and will procure its subsidiaries or joint venture companies not to acquire any other type of assets or engage in such activity which will result in a change of business from those stipulated in the infrastructure project mandates(s) or contract(s) in the first three years after listing;

7   its substantial shareholders and management have the necessary experience, technical expertise, track record and financial strength to carry out the project(s) to completion and to operate it/them thereafter. In particular, its directors and management must have sufficient and satisfactory experience of at least three years in the line of business and industry of the new applicant. Details of such expertise and experience must be disclosed in the listing document of the new applicant; and

8   such additional disclosure of matters and documents, including business valuations, feasibility studies, sensitivity analyses and cash flow projections, as the Exchange may at its discretion require, will be included in the listing document of the new applicant.

For GEM applicants, even with all the preceding conditions satisfied, the HKEX only accepts a trading record of less than two years, but the company must still meet the cash flow requirement of HK$20 million for that shorter trading record period.

- *Risk-mitigation factors*

The SFC and the HKEX have recognized that infrastructure project companies can give rise to special investment risks that reflect the nature of the project or its location, and thus these companies are under greater levels of scrutiny during the listing application process. Prominent disclosure of such risks is required in the prospectus. However, disclosure alone is not enough to address the regulators' concern about whether the risky issuer is suitable for listing in Hong Kong. On 11 April 2017, the SFC announced (SFC 2017) that it is willing to take a more flexible approach to infrastructure project companies seeking a listing on the Main Board. Despite the risks associated with such projects, if there are sufficient risk-mitigation factors, the SFC will take those into account when reviewing the proposed listing. These factors are particularly relevant for many Belt and Road infrastructure projects.

In the announcement, the SFC set out a list of factors which, if one or more are present, will improve the risk profile of an infrastructure project company and reduce the likelihood of the SFC disapproving the proposed listing. These risk-mitigation factors include, for example:

1   a large shareholding by a relevant Chinese SOE, sovereign wealth fund, a substantial listed company or a substantial and globally active institutional investor;
2   a sizeable Chinese, development or international bank committed to providing ongoing project finance;
3   a direct involvement or shareholding by the relevant state government;
4   the project located in a jurisdiction that is an IOSCO MMOU signatory, or if this is not the case, there is sufficient comfort that the SFC can obtain relevant public and non-public information about the activities of the company in the jurisdictions in which it operates. This comfort could be based on a bilateral memorandum of understanding between the SFC and the overseas securities regulator; on whether the listed holding company is incorporated in Hong Kong; on whether books and records are kept in Hong Kong, or on whether there are Hong Kong resident director(s).

The SFC recognizes that the list of factors is not exclusive and other factors may be proposed in substitution and that not all of these factors may be applicable in any one case. However, the SFC has also stated that the more of these factors are present, the lower the level of potential risk is perceived by the investing public, and thus the lower the chance of the listing application being rejected.

- *The need for regulators' further efforts*

It is clear from the SFC's statement and the HKEX's listing rules that, placing a high priority on protecting the interests of retail investors, the regulators have a low risk appetite for the "risky" issuers and accordingly adopt a relatively safe and conservative approach regarding the permission of infrastructure project companies seeking to list in Hong Kong. Despite the SFC's willingness to relax certain listing requirements, many existing infrastructure project companies find they are still unable to meet the SFC's or HKEX's existing admission criteria unless there is a major change in the ownership structure, nature of the project, or funding arrangements (Yee 2017). For BRI infrastructure project companies seeking a listing in Hong Kong, the regulatory requirements of HKEX and SFC must be taken into consideration at a very early stage. To achieve listing, it is important to find the qualifying project partners, obtain the appropriate financial and governmental support for the project, and have the acceptable corporate governance structure in place.

Considering the current stringent requirements for listing infrastructure project companies, the proposed New Board is highly anticipated. The New Board is planned to target earlier stage companies that do not meet the track record or financial test criteria for the Main Board or the GEM. Due to more flexible rules for listings of start-ups or pre-profit companies, it is expected that there will be greater numbers of infrastructure project companies seeking listings in Hong Kong, especially those under the BRI. However, questions arise about whether the listing rules for infrastructure companies will be relaxed to create a more favourable listing environment and to what extent, whether the New Board will be open to institutional investors only or also open to retail investors, and whether the SFC will revisit its risk-mitigation factors in light of such listings on the New Board (Yee 2017). Although the New Board may not cater for infrastructure project companies incorporated in the Belt and Road countries that are not signatories of the IOSCO MMOU (as discussed), it is expected to attract the BRI infrastructure project companies incorporated in the recognized or acceptable jurisdictions as well as the BRI-related Chinese companies listing on overseas markets but seeking a secondary listing in Hong Kong. It is hoped that the introduction of the New Board and the proposed market segmentation could lead to Hong Kong becoming an attractive equity financing centre for infrastructure projects in Belt and Road countries and in Hong Kong playing a key role in bridging the infrastructure funding gap.

Summary and conclusion

Under the current system, most Belt and Road countries do not have the shareholder protection standards regarded as acceptable for listing in Hong Kong. If the intention is to develop Hong Kong as an equity financing centre of the Belt and Road countries, we need to revisit our policy regarding the listing of overseas companies, the financial admission criteria, the secondary listing of mainland

Chinese companies, and the listing requirements of infrastructure projects. There are always risk and return trade-offs in such decisions. Developing Hong Kong as an equity financing centre of the Belt and Road countries may not only help to open a source of financing for the Belt and Road projects but may also create the need for many jobs.

An interesting phenomenon is that, recently, Hong Kong's own operator of railway networks and a listed company in the Main Board, MTR Corporation, is partnering with China Railway Group, a Chinese SOE, to bid for the contract of building a 350-kilometre high-speed rail line between Kuala Lumpur and Singapore. If successful, it would be the MTR's first project related to the BRI (Zhen & Sun 2017). The move by MTR could be followed by other Hong Kong companies in port and airport operations, which are in high demand for infrastructure projects in BRI countries. These Hong Kong-based companies could certainly raise capital, if necessary, at home.

Notes

1 See, for example, Maneschi (1998), who surveyed the theory of comparative advantage in international trade.
2 JPS 2007 was updated and replaced by JPS 2013.
3 The proportion of retail participation in the HKEX has declined from 39 percent of the secondary trading turnover in 2001 to 27 percent in 2015.
4 See respective Country Guides of Acceptable Overseas Jurisdictions.
5 See respective Country Guides of Acceptable Overseas Jurisdictions.
6 National Equity Exchange and Quotations (NEEQ) is a Chinese over-the-counter system for trading shares of public limited companies that are not listed in the two stock exchanges in Shenzhen and Shanghai. The exchange was also nicknamed 'The New Third Board' in China, as there was an old trading system that NEEQ replaced.
7 Main Board Listing Rule 8.11 and GEM Listing Rule 11.25.
8 COHK, s.588.
9 See Main Board Listing Rule 8.05B(2) for definitions. A newly formed project company refers to a company formed to construct a major infrastructure project. Infrastructure projects are projects that create the basic physical structures or foundations for the delivery of essential public goods and services that are necessary for the economic development of a territory or country. Examples of such projects are the construction of roads, bridges, tunnels, railways, mass transit systems, water and sewage systems, power plants, telecommunication systems, seaports, and airports.

Bibliography

Asian Development Bank 2009, *Infrastructure for a seamless Asia*. Asian Development Bank Institute, Tokyo.
Binham, C & McCrum, D 2017, 'New FCA rules open door to London Saudi Aramco listing', *Financial Times*. Available from: www.ft.com/content/43-3bffef-be26-3801-b9b6-67605a206560. [16 September 2017].
Egan, M 2015, 'Jack Ma wishes Alibaba never went public', *CNN Money*. Available from: http://money.cnn.com/2015/06/09/investing/jack-ma-alibaba-ipo-china/index.html. [15 September 2017].

Financial Conduct Authority (FCA) 2017, 'Review of the effectiveness of primary markets: the UK primary markets landscape', Discussion Paper 17/2, pp. 22–23. Available from: www.fca.org.uk/publication/discussion/dp17-02.pdf. [4 March 2018].

Financial Services Development Council (FSDC) 2014, 'Positioning Hong Kong as an international IPO centre of choice'. Available from: www.fsdc.org.hk/sites/default/files/IPO4-2%20%28Final%2017-6-2014%29.pdf. [28 February 2018].

Fong, WM & Lam, K 2014, 'Rights offerings and expropriation by controlling shareholders', *Journal of Business Finance and Accounting*, vol. 41, no. 5–6, pp. 773–790.

HKEX 2015, 'Country guide on India', November, p. 8. Available from: www.hkex.com.hk/listing/rules-and-guidance/other-resources/listing-of-overseas-companies/list-of-acceptable-overseas-jurisdictions?sc_lang=en. [4 March 2018].

HKEX 2017a, 'Review of the Growth Enterprise Market (GEM) and changes to the GEM and main board listing rules', Consultation Paper, June. Available from: www.hkex.com.hk/eng/newsconsul/mktconsul/Documents/cp2017062.pdf. [28 February 2018].

HKEX 2017b, 'New Board', Consultation Paper, June. Available from: www.hkex.com.hk/eng/newsconsul/mktconsul/Documents/cp2017061.pdf. [28 February 2018].

HKEX 2017c, 'Country Guides', 17 March. Available from: www.hkex.com.hk/listing/rules-and-guidance/other-resources/listing-of-overseas-companies/list-of-acceptable-overseas-jurisdictions?sc_lang=en. [4 March 2018].

Kynge, J 2016, 'How the Silk Road plans will be financed', *Financial Times*, 10 May. Available from: www.ft.com/content/e83ced94-0bd8-11e6-9456-444ab5211a2f. [28 February 2018].

Lau, F & Barreto, E 2016, 'Postal savings bank of China IPO raises $7.4 billion after pricing at low end', *Thomson Reuters*, 21 September. Available from: www.reuters.com/article/us-china-post-bank-ipo/postal-savings-bank-of-china-ipo-raises-7-4-billion-after-pricing-at-low-end-idUSKCN11R08G. [28 February 2018].

Law, LJ 2017, 'How Hong Kong can be a key pillar for Belt and Road infrastructure', *The South China Morning Post*, 8 June. Available from: www.scmp.com/comment/insight-opinion/article/2097338/how-hong-kong-can-be-key-pillar-belt-and-road-infrastructure. [28 February 2018].

Lee, H 2016, 'Financial reporting and audit failures in transition economy: examples of auditors in China's financial market', *Law and Financial Market Review*, vol. 10, no. 1, pp. 4–15.

Luft, G 2016, 'China's infrastructure play: why Washington should accept the New Silk Road', *Foreign Affairs*, September–October, pp. 68–75.

Mak, L 2016, 'Hong Kong banking on a big role in financing China's One Belt, One Road plan linking Asia to Europe and the Middle East', *South China Morning Post*, 19 January. Available from: www.scmp.com/business/global-economy/article/1902826/hong-kong-banking-big-role-financing-chinas-one-belt-one. [28 February 2018].

Maneschi, A 1998, *Comparative advantage in international trade: a historical perspective*. Edward Elgar Publishing, Cheltenham.

Morrow, C 2017, 'One Belt One Road and Hong Kong. Corporate go global strategy and legal risks prevention summit forum', *Charltons Law Firm*, 16 January. Available from: www.charltonslaw.com/hong-kong-law/belt-and-road-initiative-and-hong-kong/. [28 February 2018].

ONC Lawyers 2017, 'Join forces: SFC co-operated with CSRC to sanction against manipulative trading', *ONC Lawyers Newsletter*, May. Available from: www.onc. hk/en_US/join-forces-sfc-co-operated-csrc-sanction-manipulative-trading/. [28 February 2018].

Perlez, J & Huang, Y 2017, 'Behind China's $1 trillion plan to shake up the economic order', *New York Times*, 13 May. Available from: www.nytimes.com/2017/ 05/13/business/china-railway-one-belt-one-road-1-trillion-plan.html. [28 February 2018].

Qu, H 2017, 'Financing China's Belt & Road initiative – private capital is essential to fund this huge trading network', *HSBC website*, 31 May. Available from: www.gbm.hsbc.com/insights/rmb/financing-china-belt-and-road-initiative. [28 February 2018].

Reuters 2017, 'Xi Jinping says the rejection of protectionism is part of what One Belt One Road is about', *Reuters*, 15 May. Available from: http://fortune. com/2017/05/15/china-xi-jinping-belt-road-summit-protectionism/. [6 March 2018].

Samtani, R 2017, 'Hong Kong vs. Singapore: weighing Asia's financial hubs', *CNBC*, 24 April. Available from: www.cnbc.com/2017/04/24/hong-kong-vs-singapore-weighing-asias-financial-hubs.html. [28 February 2018].

Securities and Futures Commission (SFC) 2017a, 'The international organization of securities commissionsmultilateral memorandum of understanding'. Available from: www.sfc.hk/web/EN/about-the-sfc/collaboration/overseas/iosco-mmou. html. [16 September 2017].

Securities and Futures Commission (SFC) 2017b, 'Statement on the SFC's approach to certain project companies seeking a listing in Hong Kong and the exercise of powers under the securities and futures (stock market listing) rules'. Available from: www.sfc.hk/web/EN/news-and-announcements/policy-statements-and-announcements/statement-on-the-sfcs-approach-to-certain-project-companies-seeking-a-listing.html. [6 March 2018].

Securities and Futures Commission (SFC) and Hong Kong Exchanges and Clearing Limited (HKEX) 2007, 'Joint policy statement regarding the listing of overseas companies' (JPS 2007). Available from: www.sfc.hk/web/doc/EN/general/gen eral/press_release/07/07pr31_statement.pdf. [4 March 2018].

Securities and Futures Commission (SFC) and Hong Kong Exchanges and Clearing Limited (HKEX) 2013, 'Joint policy statement regarding the listing of overseas companies' (JPS 2013). Available from: www.hkex.com.hk/-/media/HKEX-Market/ Listing/Rules-and-Guidance/Other-Resources/Listing-of-Overseas-Companies/ Joint-Policy-Statement-20130927/new_jps_0927.pdf. [6 March 2018].

Singapore Exchange (SGX) 2017, 'Possible listing framework for dual class share structure', Consultation Paper, p. 1. Available from: www.rajahtannasia.com/ media/2716/sgx_dcs_consultation_paper_-sgx_20170216-final.pdf. [4 March 2018].

United Nations 2013, *Human development report 2013*. United Nations Development Programme. Available from: http://hdr.undp.org/en/2013-report. [28 February 2018].

Wong, TSP 2016, 'Hong Kong should further develop debt market to facilitate OBOR', *Hong Kong Economic Journal*, 1 March. Available from: www.ejinsight. com/20160305-hong-kong-should-further-develop-debt-market-to-facilitate-obor/. [6 March 2018].

Yau, C 2017, 'Hong Kong pips Singapore to be ranked world's freest economy for 23rd consecutive year', *South China Morning Post*, 16 February. Available from: www.scmp.com/news/hong-kong/economy/article/2071423/hong-kong-pips-singapore-be-ranked-worlds-freest-economy-23rd. [28 February 2018].

Yee, E 2017, 'Infrastructure listings in Hong Kong – easier times to come?' *Norton Rose Fulbright Law Firm*. Available from: www.nortonrosefulbright.com/knowl edge/publications/149426/infrastructure-listings-in-hong-kong-easier-times-to-come. [28 February 2018].

Yiu, E 2016a, 'Hong Kong SFC plans to get off regulatory back seat to attract new economy startups', *South China Morning Post*, 8 November. Available from: www.scmp.com/business/money/markets-investing/article/2043976/hong-kong-sfc-plans-get-regulatory-back-seat. [28 February 2018].

Yiu, E 2016b, 'Hong Kong tops global IPO markets despite total funds raised sliding to eight-year low', *South China Morning Post*, 27 December. Available from: www.scmp.com/business/companies/article/2057428/hong-kong-tops-global-ipo-markets-despite-total-funds-raised. [28 February 2018].

Yiu, E 2017, 'SFC to ease Hong Kong listing conditions for firms linked to Belt and Road', *South China Morning Post*, 11 April. Available from: www.scmp.com/busi ness/banking-finance/article/2086776/sfc-ease-hong-kong-listing-conditions-firms-linked-belt-and. [28 February 2018].

Zhen, S & Sun, N 2017, 'China Railway plans to team up with MTR to jointly develop rail projects along the new Silk Road', *South China Morning Post*, 11 September. Available from: www.scmp.com/business/article/2110704/china-railway-plans-team-mtr-jointly-develop-rail-projects-along-new-silk. [28 February 2018].

4 A comparison of investment strategies of China and Japan in infrastructure projects in ASEAN

*Cheung-kwok Law and Derek Yuen**

Across the ASEAN (Association of Southeast Asian Nations) region, the governments of China and Japan are promising hundreds of billions of dollars in spending to upgrade and construct roads, ports, railways, and other infrastructures. It is true that, in the infrastructure sector, China carries comparative advantages in funding and technologies. "High-speed rail diplomacy" is a prominent illustration of China's aggressive expansion into the overseas infrastructure sector (Chan 2016; Yu 2014). Notwithstanding China's notable achievements in the past decade, it remains a latecomer compared to Japan: the year 2014 marked the sixtieth anniversary of Japan's official development assistance (ODA). Japan, through the Japan International Cooperation Agency (JICA), has been the biggest source of ODA to many ASEAN countries (Ministry of Foreign Affairs of Japan 2015b). This includes grants, technical cooperation, and loans, not to mention Japan has the Asian Development Bank (ADB) as its investment vehicle. However, the newly established China-led Asian Infrastructure Investment Bank (AIIB) helps China embrace many of the norms and standards that the United States defined for the Multilateral Development Banks (MDBs) (Morris 2016) and could assist China in offsetting certain disadvantages in its overseas investment practices in the longer term.

This chapter consists of three parts. The first part offers a historical overview and examines the reasons facilitating China's rise as a key infrastructure investor in ASEAN as well as Japan's relative decline from the 1990s onward. It accounts for Japan's return as a dominant infrastructure exporter from 2010 and its renewed model for ODA and foreign infrastructure investment. The second part further analyzes the overseas infrastructure investment models of China and Japan. The two models have different orientations, goals, and results. This could largely explain why the return of more Japanese investment in recent years has received great enthusiasm in the ASEAN region (Jennings 2017; Lamb & Dao 2015; Mezza 2015; Strafford 2016). In order to review the major differences in China's and Japan's infrastructure projects in ASEAN, the third part provides three sets of railway projects involving both China and Japan simultaneously for comparative purposes.

China's rise in infrastructure investment in ASEAN

China's foreign economic cooperation includes foreign direct investment, foreign contract engineering, foreign labour service, foreign economic aid, and recipient aid. Foreign contract engineering is one of the major modes in China's "Going Out (Go Global) Strategy". It began in the late 1970s on the basis of foreign economic-assisted projects. As a new form of foreign economic cooperation, foreign contract engineering has increasingly developed during the period of China's reform and opening-up process over the past 30 years. Foreign contract engineering is an outcome and result of China's reform and opening up and has become a mature form of business operation in China's foreign economic cooperation. This operation has increasingly played an important role in the development of China's national economy (Zhu 2010). By the end of 2007, about 3,000 Chinese enterprises obtained the right of operation for foreign contract engineering, of which 51 companies were ranked among the top 225 contractors in the world (Zhu 2010).

There were two developments in the 1990s that have greatly enhanced China's position as an infrastructure investor and exporter in ASEAN. One was Western sanctions imposed on, and subsequently Japan's suspension of ODA to, Myanmar. The other one was the Greater Mekong Subregion (GMS) Economic Cooperation Programme initiated by the ADB in 1992.

Western sanctions and Japan's suspension of ODA to Myanmar

Japanese economic assistance to Myanmar began in the form of war reparations in 1955. Japan's ODA to Myanmar rapidly increased from the latter half of the 1970s, when the Ne Win government opened up to more official overseas assistance in order to overcome the country's economic and political crisis during the mid-1970s. The Burma Aid Group of the international community met for the first time in Tokyo in 1970. Following the donors' meeting, official inflows to Myanmar increased sharply. Between 1978 and 1988, Myanmar received US$3,712.3 million in assistance, a sum equivalent to 15.1 percent of the country's total imports for the same period. It is widely believed that, without such huge aid, the Ne Win regime could not have survived the economic crises in the 1970s and 1980s (Kudo 2007, p. 270).

The rise of the military government in 1988 almost coincided with the end of the Cold War, which dramatically changed the international and regional political landscape surrounding Myanmar. The United States ceased to support authoritarian governments in developing countries even if they were allies. Accordingly, Japan also started to change its ODA policy. Japan adopted its first ODA Charter in 1992, which placed greater emphasis on human rights and democracy (Kudo 2007, p. 272). The suspension of Japanese ODA to Myanmar was one of the earliest applications of the ODA Charter (Kudo 2007, p. 275) and meant that the Japanese government lost one of its most effective diplomatic tools towards Myanmar.

As a result, China filled the vacuum that was created by Western sanctions and Japan's suspension of ODA. Soon after the border trade was opened in 1988, China became a major trading partner of Myanmar. China also replaced Japan as a major donor of economic assistance to Myanmar.

China's economic cooperation with Myanmar seems to have expanded about 1997, when the United States imposed the first economic sanctions that banned new foreign investments by American firms. Moreover, Senior General Than Shwe's state visit to Beijing in January 2003 marked another significant development, when China offered Myanmar a preferential loan amounting to US$200 million and an RMB50 million grant (equivalent to US$6.3 million). Shortly after that, the United States imposed the second round of sanctions in July 2003 on all Myanmar's exports.

Having been enhanced and promoted by China's economic cooperation programmes, Chinese enterprises became heavily involved in Myanmar's industrial, infrastructure, and energy development. By March 2009, China had signed numerous foreign contract engineering agreements with Myanmar, totalling US$5.8 billion (Zhu 2010, pp. 91–92).

Greater Mekong Sub-region (GMS) Economic Cooperation Programme

The ADB initiated the GMS Economic Cooperation Programme in 1992. The GMS consists of Cambodia, Laos, Myanmar, Thailand, Vietnam, and Yunnan Province of China. The subregion is rich in natural resources. Along with its strong agricultural base, it contains extensive timber and fisheries resources, considerable mineral potential, and some of Asia's best potential for hydropower projects and large coal and petroleum reserves. The GMS programme has launched more than 100 cooperative projects since 1992, covering infrastructure, energy resources, trade and investment, telecommunications, environment, tourism, agriculture, and human resources development (Zhu 2009, p. 86).

The Chinese government takes a positive attitude towards GMS and actively participates in this cooperative mechanism. In addition to the implementation of projects, China provided US$30 million for the construction of the Laos section of the Kunming–Bangkok highway; US$5 million for the navigation channel improvement project on the Upper Mekong River; and training programmes on agriculture, customs affairs, telecommunications, etc. In 2004, China set up a special fund totalling US$20 million under the ADB for human resources development and poverty alleviation. In 2005, China decided to expand the range of products eligible for preferential tariff from Laos, Cambodia, and Myanmar, aiming at raising intra-regional trade. Chinese leaders pledged additional financial support to GMS cooperation (Zhu 2009, p. 92).

In short, the economic and geopolitical development has greatly promoted China's relations with Cambodia, Laos, Myanmar, Vietnam, and Thailand since 1990. China's overall national strength has been substantially increased, as has the economic expansion into Southeast Asia. These factors created favourable conditions for the expansion of China's infrastructure investment into the region.

Principles of China's foreign economic aid and development cooperation

Following the expansion of China's foreign economic aid, China has been gradually substantiating its own principles of foreign economic aid and cooperation. This started with the "Eight Principles of China's Foreign Economic Aid and Technical Assistance", as promulgated by former Prime Minister Zhou Enlai when he visited 14 countries in Asia and Africa in 1964. The core content included equality, mutual benefit, and non-interference in internal affairs (State Council of People's Republic of China 2011).

In May 1996, former President Jiang Zemin further declared five principles about China's cooperation with African countries: (1) true friendship, (2) equal treatment and non-interference in each other's internal affairs, (3) mutual benefit and common development, (4) close consultation and cooperation, and (5) future orientation. Indeed, these principles are not only aimed at economic cooperation with African countries but would also apply to all developing countries (Zhu 2009, p. 73).

In the latest White Paper on China's Foreign Aids (State Council of People's Republic of China 2011), the basic features of China's foreign aid policy are expressed in the following terms:

1   unremittingly helping recipient countries build up their capacity for sustainable development,
2   imposing no political conditions,
3   adhering to equality,
4   remaining realistic while striving for the best, and
5   paying attention to reform and innovation.

Concerns about Chinese infrastructure investment

The new international and regional reality after the Cold War and China's reform and opening up have created the conditions for the rapid development of Chinese contract engineering and investment in ASEAN. Indeed, these countries lack funds and technology for infrastructure projects. China's national enterprises are often supported by concessionary loans to bid for construction contracts and BOT (build, operate, transfer) schemes in these countries.

There are a number of concerns regarding the negative impacts of Chinese national enterprises investing in infrastructure projects overseas. The Chinese projects are prone to inefficiency and corruption and are undertaken with little transparency and concern for their impacts on local communities. From time to time, this results in serious backlash as these enterprises fail to deal with sensitive issues relating to local labour, the environment, social responsibility, and human rights (McDonald, Bosshard & Brewer 2009; Yu 2014). In some cases, it has caused irreversible damage to the reputation of Chinese enterprises and of the Chinese government. Anti-Chinese sentiments have come to the surface as a result. Yu (2014) recently concluded that China was facing serious challenges to implementing its plan for ASEAN. Political trust had been relatively low due to ongoing maritime disputes in the South China Sea and China's growing military power. Moreover, China's promise of "non-interference in domestic affairs" tends to give the impression that China is willing to fund projects that would benefit governments known to repress their citizens and are corrupt.

Many Chinese companies have not been successfully adapting to the international competitive environment, paying little attention to environmental issues, employing illegal labour, using substandard construction materials, monopolizing all the economic benefits, intensifying problems of relocation of affected residents, and being involved in corruption. Chinese government officials often justify their approach to overseas investments by asserting that developing countries should not be held to the same standards as are developed nations (McDonald, Bosshard & Brewer 2009).

As China's overseas direct foreign investment (ODFI) is increasing rapidly and encountering many problems, the Ministry of Commerce of China issued several important documents to provide guidance to Chinese companies for overseas investments: (1) "Industrial Guidance Catalogue for ODI in Countries" (2004); (2) "Outward Investment: Guidance by Nations/Regions" (2015b, the first report published in 2009); and (3) "The Notice of Security Early Warning and Information Notification System for ODFI and Cooperation" (2010). Concurrently, the Ministry of Foreign Affairs also has a warning system for overseas political development.

In September 2005, China's Ministry of Commerce suggested that the OECD (Organisation for Economic Co-operation and Development) and China would need to cooperate on issues of corporate social responsibility. In August 2006, the Ministry of Commerce issued recommendations for improving the safety of workers in Chinese overseas investments, which urged Chinese companies to hire local workers, respect local customs, and adhere to international safety standards in their projects. Furthermore, there was a special chapter on "Social Responsibility" highlighted in the Ministry of Commerce of PRC's report (2015a), which was a serious attempt by the Chinese government to warn Chinese companies investing overseas.

Japan's ODA retrenchment and a strong comeback

There is in fact one more important factor attributing to China's rising dominance in infrastructure investment in ASEAN until recent years: the decline of Japan's ODA since the 1990s.

During the 1990s, Japan established itself as the world's top donor. However, the fiscal and financial deterioration that followed the collapse of the bubble economy caused the country's ODA to enter a period of retrenchment. Over a period of 14 years, the initial ODA budget declined continually, so that by 2013 it represented just 48 percent of its peak amount in 1997. By 2007 Japan had slid to fifth place on the list of major donors compiled by the Development Assistance Committee (DAC)[1] of OECD. Public opinion turned inwards, and the proportion of the general public that indicated strong support for Japan's foreign aid and economic cooperation declined sharply between 2002 and 2004. To exacerbate the situation, the Great East Japan Earthquake struck in March 2011, causing devastation and suffering. The reconstruction placed a further heavy fiscal burden upon the government's budget (Ohno 2014, pp. 2–3).

From 2010 onwards, however, a new wave of internationalization began. Many small and medium-sized enterprises (SMEs) in the manufacturing sector showed strong interest in pursuing new opportunities abroad. These SMEs have demonstrated not only a willingness to take on new risks but also have started to move their production overseas without the support of a conglomerate, which was rarely the case in the past. Consequently, the government adopted a new policy to provide active support to these pioneers (Ohno 2014, p. 5).

In response to the accelerated OFDI of Japanese firms, which was partly triggered by the global financial crisis, the Japanese government began strengthening partnerships with the private sector within its ODA activities. The primary target was Japanese firms active in developing countries. Economic cooperation agencies like the Ministry of Economy, Trade and Industry (METI), the Japan External Trade Organization (JETRO), and the Overseas Human Resources and Industry Development Association (HIDA) have long supported Japanese businesses and are forging public-private partnerships as the core part of their operations. Even JICA and the Ministry of Foreign Affairs, which had previously demonstrated reluctance to support individual firms and rarely became involved in any business proposals presented to them, have started to use ODA budgets to support new private sector partnership activities overseas.

When the Liberal Democratic Party (LDP) came into power at the end of 2012, Prime Minister Shinzo Abe unveiled the Japan Revitalization Strategy "Japan is Back", which would advance Japan's global outreach as one of its three action plans. The global outreach action plan set specific numerical targets for infrastructure exports and the overseas expansion of SMEs (Ohno 2014, p. 6). In 2013, Prime Minister Abe visited ten Southeast Asian countries. This was unprecedented not only for a Japanese prime minister but for all non-ASEAN leaders (Nobuhiro 2014, p. 2).

In May 2015, Prime Minister Abe announced a new strategy on "Promoting High-Quality Infrastructure Investment in Asia". The plan is to invest US$110 billion in Asia between 2016 and 2020 (30 percent higher than that in the previous five years). For example, Japan has been a major sponsor to Philippine projects in recent years. By the end of July 2016, JICA's assistance to the Philippines covered 20 ongoing project loans amounting to about US$2.8 billion.

Japan's partnership with its private sector within development cooperation coincides with a change in the international trends in developmental assistance. The international trend in aid has recently been moving towards the establishment of common goals by the international community. Various countries and organizations would implement aid in coordination with each other to achieve these common goals. This objective has been documented in the United Nations' Millennium Development Goals.[2] Compared with aid coordination in the past, which emphasized cooperation and coordination on an individual project basis, development assistance in recent years has placed greater emphasis on ownership by partner countries, in which donor countries and aid agencies jointly support developing countries' own development plans and priorities (Japan International Cooperation Agency 2016).

The utilization of ODA by the Japanese government to foster partnership with the private sector has turned the qualities of the Japanese private business into Japan's strength in overseas investment, including infrastructure projects. Japan has a vibrant manufacturing industry, and their companies demand high standards of "Quality, Cost and Delivery" from every partner at every stage of the implementation and production process. Japanese companies, once decided on overseas investment, will remain committed for the long term. They will develop local supporting industries, train the local workforce, and transfer technology to local counterparts (Ohno 2014, p. 14).

Indeed, there are developing country leaders and government officials who clearly recognize the potential benefits of these operational features of Japanese firms. On a visit to Japan during the Fifth Tokyo International Conference on African Development (TICAD V), Ethiopian Prime Minister Hailemariam Desalegn strongly expressed an interest in inviting Japanese companies, in particular the manufacturing sector, to invest in Ethiopia. He was obviously looking for "quality", not "quantity", in investment from foreign countries. The values, labour ethics, and the culture for excellence as implemented by Japanese companies have been increasingly recognized by developing countries. Top local government officials from Vietnam also remarked that, although FDI had been pouring into the country from around the world, only Japan committed to enhance local capacity while pursuing commercial benefit (Ohno 2014).

The China model for infrastructure investment in ASEAN

Starting from the Eight Principles declared by the former Prime Minster Zhou Enlai in 1964, China's foreign aid and economic cooperation model has been a "developing country to developing country" model, emphasizing mutual benefit and non-interference (Kobayashi 2008; State Council of People's Republic of China 2011; Trinidad 2016). Unlike DAC aid donors, which adopted a common definition and scope of development assistance, China aid is a broad concept encompassing securing more overseas contracts, expanding trade and investment, exporting labour, consulting services, and promoting other foreign direct investment (Foster et al. 2009, p. 9). As a non-DAC member, China has some flexibility to pursue short-term national interests through aid programmes (Sato et al. 2011).

In China, the foreign aid programme has been administrated by the Ministry of Commerce of the State Council (Kobayashi 2008; State Council of People's Republic of China 2011; Trinidad 2016). According to the State Council of the People's Republic of China (2011), the Ministry of Commerce's responsibility comprised "formulation of foreign aid policies, regulations, overall and annual plans, examinations and approval of foreign aid projects and management of project execution". Other official institutions involved include the Ministry of Foreign Affairs, Ministry of Finance, China EximBank, Executive Bureau of International Economic Cooperation, and China International Centre for Economic and Technical Exchanges. Although China's SOEs (state-owned enterprises) are not officially part of the aid system, Cheng, Fang and Lien (2012) noted that they had become increasing influential in shaping foreign aid policy, particularly in construction, mining, and information technology.

China faced little direct competition in infrastructure investment from Japan in the ASEAN region before 2010. As a result, China has had the privilege of setting up the infrastructure investment model more in accordance with its interest. When compared to the Japan model, which is foreign policy and development based (discussed in the following section), the China model is rather more of investment and corporate based, while obviously taking China's national interest into account. The development of this approach has been significantly shaped by the Going Out Strategy since 2001.

In 2000, the Fifth Plenary Session of the 15th Congress of the Chinese Communist Party issued the "Suggestions to Develop the 11th Five-Year Plan for National Economic and Social Development". It decided to initiate the Going Out Strategy. The suggestions listed four main investment types that were to be encouraged (processing, trade, resources extraction, and project contracting) and proposed to give overseas investments policy support through credit, insurance, and other facilitative services (Huang & Wikes 2011, p. 9).

In 2001, the strategy was incorporated into the "Outline of the 11th Five Year Plan for National Economic and Social Development". This document marked the birth of China's Going Out Strategy and the comprehensive development of China's overseas investments. It also set the trend for policies in the succeeding ten years and began a new chapter for overseas investment by China. Supported by this new strategy, overseas investment grew significantly and attracted great international attention (Huang & Wikes 2011, p. 10).

Although overseas investments have always been an important part of Chinese foreign policy, the Going Out Strategy has, to some extent, decentralized the existing policymaking mechanism. This has made the major business corporations, including SOEs, export-oriented companies, financial institutions, energy companies, and local governments new foreign policy actors (Jakobson & Knox 2010). As the course was set, further reforms, credit support, new policies, supervision, and regulatory measures would be required to encourage and refine Chinese investment activities abroad.

Chinese ODFI increased to nearly US$120 billion in 2015, seeking to acquire foreign technology, expand the market, and diversify energy supply. China now is the third-largest investing economy. Despite the rapid development, China's ODFI is still relatively small compared with its GDP (Ministry of Commerce of PRC 2015b).

In contrast, ASEAN's FDI increased for the third consecutive year to US$136.2 billion in 2014, two-thirds coming from the EU, intra-ASEAN, Japan, the United States, and Hong Kong (ASEAN & UNCTAD 2015). This amount exceeded FDI inflows to China. Though China ranked sixth on the list, a substantial proportion of Hong Kong's investment may originate from China as well. ASEAN companies showed strong interest in expanding their regional presence, and resulting infra-ASEAN investment increased rapidly by 26 percent to US$24.4 billion in 2014. Furthermore, if we combine the four types of investment item of infrastructure projects into ASEAN, Japan and China contributed about US$450 million each in 2014 (see Table 4.1).

Because ODFI is increasing rapidly and Chinese companies are encountering new issues overseas, the Ministry of Commerce of PRC has issued several important documents to provide guidance for overseas investment to Chinese companies. The ministry has also published a set of investment guidelines through its webpage for outward direct investment in 2015 (Ministry of Commerce of PRC 2015b). The guidelines were first published in 2009 and now cover 171 countries. It advises the way investors should carry out survey and analysis to evaluate risks before making any investment. Indeed, a new working group on "Security under BRI" was set up under the leadership of Vice Premier Zhang Gaoli in 2016. This is a monitoring, assessing, warning, and protecting mechanism.

Table 4.1 Top FDI sources to ASEAN and breakdown by infrastructure types (2014, US$, million)

	(a) Electricity & Gas Supply	(b) Water Supply; Sewerage & Waste Mgt.	(c) Trans. & Storage	(d) Info. & Comm.	Total (a to d)	Total FDI Flows to ASEAN
EU	243.6	84.6	495	491.4	1,314.6	29,269 (21.5%)
Intra-ASEAN	−53.9	8.9	418.4	435.7	809.1	24,377 (17.9%)
Japan	18.7	4.4	326.2	94	443.3	13,381 (9.8%)
US	0.9	1.3	−17.3	28.5	13.4	13,042 (9.6%)
Hong Kong	−18	1	12.7	1,001.70	997.4	9,505 (7.0%)
China	387.5	2.5	57.9	−5.6	442.3	8,869 (6.5%)
Australia	0.7	0.2	306.2	−137.1	170	5,703 (4.2%)

Source: Association of Southeast Asian Nations (ASEAN) and United Nations Conference on Trade and Development (UNCTAD), 2015.

The guidance documents also address the environmental and social dimensions of investment, outlining the country's environmental laws and providing tips for establishing good relationships with the recipient country. In addition, guidelines for environmental and social impacts have been issued by China EximBank and China Development Bank (CDB) to outline environmental and social responsibility requirements for loans and to ensure the projects fulfil the related requirements in host countries (Ministry of Commerce of PRC 2015b, pp. 17–18).

Putting this under the context of ASEAN and China's Belt and Road Initiative (BRI), such an approach has been translated to infrastructure investment strategy that emphasizes enhancing the region's connectivity. This could fulfil China's domestic economic needs and geopolitical design. The China model is essentially geared to these very goals that could effectively utilize China's high-speed rail technology and its engineering capacity, of which SOEs play a dominant role. Although this approach stressing hardware seems straightforward, local problems created can only be alleviated through enhancing its soft power capabilities over time.

The Japan model for infrastructure investment in ASEAN

Despite 2014 marking the sixtieth anniversary of Japan's ODA, Japan's ODA to ASEAN had been at low tide from the end of the Cold War to 2010, while China was dominating the scene. In the changing geopolitical landscape in Asia, Japan urgently needs to reassert its role in the region, by offering a better model for infrastructure development to serve the need of ASEAN.

Japan, as a member of OECD, has for years adopted the DAC principles in providing official development assistance, based on a developed-country-to-developing-country model to alleviate poverty. Japan's efforts in enhancing its investment model began with a review of its 2003 ODA Charter. In February 2015, Shinzo Abe's government abandoned the term ODA in the new Development Cooperation Charter that would emphasize aid as a catalyst for development partnerships. The new aid programme is grounded on "human security" perspectives, which stress protecting and empowering individuals. Aid will be mainly given to support the self- help efforts of developing countries to alleviate poverty. The basic requirement will be the creation of a foundation for human capital, socio-economic infrastructure, the private sector, institutions, and regulations. Japan aims to leverage its own experience, expertise, and technology to help developing countries realize quality development (Dugay 2015). It is also necessary to promote "quality infrastructure investment" to bridge the infrastructure gap, which has become a bottleneck in regional and global economic growth.

Further applications of Japan's new Development Cooperation Charter in the ASEAN region can be clearly identified in the "New Tokyo Strategy 2015 for Mekong–Japan Cooperation" (Ministry of Foreign Affairs of Japan 2015c). This strategy specifies the four main pillars: industrial infrastructure development, soft infrastructure, sustainable development, and the coordination with various stakeholders (Ministry of Foreign Affairs of Japan 2015b). Tokyo is prioritizing both hard and soft infrastructure.

Sustainable development is clearly a focus. It places priority on disaster risk reduction, climate change, conservation, and water resource management. It also commits to address environmental and social concerns. This is particularly important for the hydropower development in the Mekong subregion.

Integration and coordination are at the heart of Japan's new Mekong strategy. An entire pillar is devoted to coordination with various stakeholders, including recipient countries, international organizations, NGOs, and the private sector (Ministry of Foreign Affairs of Japan 2015b). JICA's leading and integrating role will further be enhanced under the new charter.

The "New Tokyo Strategy 2015" distinguishes the Japan model from the China model. These pillars of action could outperform China's existing infrastructure investment programmes by offering better "quality infrastructure investment" and a comprehensive approach for development. Japan, in pursuit of "quality as well as quantity", emphasizes sustainable development, full collaboration with other countries, and international organizations.

In particular, the highlight of the strategy lies in its second pillar: soft infrastructure. The "soft efforts" centre on advancing industrial structures and human resources development. This is the initiative to strengthen "soft" connectivity (institutional, economic, and people-to-people) that best characterizes the Japan model and differentiates it from the China model.

Unlike the China model, which has a dominant infrastructure focus and whose main purpose is to enhance the "hard" connectivity of the region, the "soft efforts" of the Japan model focus on laying the groundwork for the region's institutions and developing its "institutional connectivity" with Japan. Strengthening "institutional connectivity" involves support for the development of the legal system and intellectual property rights system, education, modernization of customs and postal systems, and streamlining of port procedures. In particular, Japan will attempt to assume an important role in the development of the legal and judicial systems of the Mekong region.

Similarly, strengthening "people-to-people connectivity" prepares for the consolidation of democratization, the rule of law, and the protection of basic human rights in the region. Japan's strategy aims at empowering both the people and the government of the developing countries through development cooperation. As indicated in the outline of the Development Cooperation Charter, Japan will continue to emphasize the developing countries' *own* initiatives and *self-help* efforts and support their efforts for *self-reliant development*. Obviously, the development of human resources, socio-economic infrastructure, regulations, and institutions is part of Japan's plan to build the foundation for self-reliant development. Correspondingly, Japan takes full account of international development goals such as the Millennium Development Goals (MDGs) and the Post-2015 Development Agenda of the United Nations (UN) for legitimacy. Japan's foreign policy provides the main driver for its infrastructure investment overseas, which will not be diluted by other secondary considerations.

Three sets of railway projects in ASEAN by China and Japan

In order to analyze the differences between the China model and the Japan model by infrastructure investment projects in ASEAN (as theorized in the previous sections), we would like to refer to the actual implementation and development of three sets of railway projects (in the Philippines, Thailand, and Indonesia) involving both China and Japan simultaneously for comparative purposes. They are:

1   The Philippines: Malolos to Caloocan Rail by China (starting 2003) and Malolos to Tutuban Rail by Japan (starting 2015) (Table 4.2);
2   Thailand: Bangkok to Nong Khai Rail by China (starting 2014) and Bangkok to Chiang Mai Rail by Japan (starting 2015); and
3   Indonesia: Jakarta to Bandung Rail by China (starting 2015) and Jakarta to Surabaya Rail by Japan (starting 2016).

This analysis is still at the preliminary stage, mainly because of the lack of comprehensive information. Ideally, we need the original contracts, company records, and official policy documents for the analysis. Currently, much of the

Table 4.2 A comparison of rail projects in the Philippines

	Rail Project by China	*Rail Project by Japan*
Nature of project	Malolos/Caloocan (32 km), construction only	Malolos/Caloocan + Tutuban (37 km), construction only
Contractor involved	China National Machinery and Equipment Corporation	Not decided yet
Philippines' companies involved	North Luzon Railways Corporation	Not decided yet
Terms of external financing	Other US$20m to US$200m supported by Philippine Government	Other 20% supported by Philippine Government
i institution involved	China Exim Bank	Japan International Cooperation Agency
ii total loan	US$400m	US$2b (Yen $242b)
iii interest rates	3%	0.1%
iv loan period	20 years	40 years
v grace period	5 years	10 years
Total project cost	US$421m to US$594b	US$2.4b (Yen$288b)
Time for construction	4 years	6 years (11/2015 to 11/2021)
Procurement policy	No bidding	Bidding

Source: Various official and news reports, compiled by the authors.

scattered information is obtained from literature reviews, press reports, and official websites.

The Northrail project to Malolos in the Philippines

The first set of rail projects chosen for analysis is the Malolos to Caloocan Project (32 kilometres), awarded to China (starting in 2003), and the Malolos to Tutuban Project (37 kilometres), awarded to Japan (starting in 2015) (Figure 4.1). Malolos is the capital city of the Province of Bulacan, located north of metro Manila. The China rail project was eventually cancelled by the Philippine government

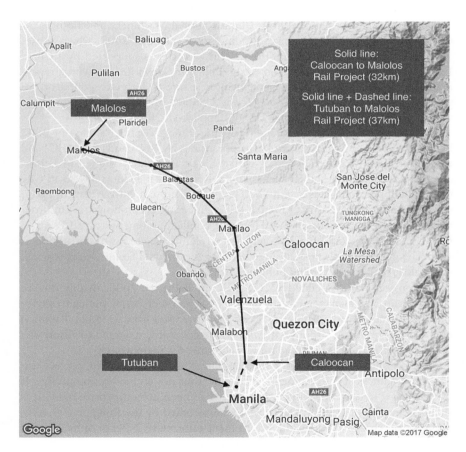

Figure 4.1 Illustrative routes of the Malolos to Caloocan and Tutuban to Malolos Rail Projects

Source: Map compiled by authors using Google Map data (2017).

in 2012, and an extended version of the failed Chinese project was awarded to Japan in 2015.

The Caloocan to Malolos Rail project by China

The Caloocan to Malolos Rail Project (32 kilometres) was Phase 1 of the Northrail Project. The plan was prepared by the Arroyo government, and the project was expected to be financed by the Japan Bank of International Cooperation (JBIC) under JICA. But as the resettlement issues for about 40,000 families along the route had not been resolved prior to construction, JICA decided to cancel the funding.

The Chinese interest moved in to fund the project in a relatively short time despite the outstanding resettlement issues. The construction contract was awarded to a Chinese national firm, China National Machinery and Equipment Corporation (CNMEC), by the Philippine government in 2003, which subsequently changed its name to Sinomach. This project was supported by a China EximBank loan of US$400 million to the Philippine government, with a repayment period of 20 years, at a 3 percent interest rate and a grace period of five years. The estimated cost of Phase 2 was US$600 million, against which the China EximBank pledged another US$600 million in 2007.

The project soon ran into difficulties. The original contract signed in 2003 between North Luzon Railways Corporation (NLRC) and CNMEC and the Buyer Credit Loan Agreement with China's EximBank (signed in February 2004) were subjected to challenge in the Regional Trial Court in Makati City of the Philippines in February 2006. The project subsequently engaged a consultant firm in 2007 (Systra, a French rail engineering consulting firm) in order to improve the construction work. However, conflicts among Systra, NLRC, and CNMEC delayed work on the project further, amid allegations of corruption as well. The government's poor arrangement for the affected families along the rail route also resulted in very bad publicity for the project.

The project was suspended by CNMEC in February 2008, mainly due to cost overrun and management problems. In September 2009, the contract for Phase 1 was amended and the total cost was increased from US$421.1 million to US$593.9 million. Although the Philippine government agreed to absorb the cost increase, no additional funding was allocated for the purpose.

After several lawsuits, in 2012 the supreme court ruled that the project was not a government-to-government agreement (thus not entitled to immunity). It was therefore declared invalid because there had been no competitive bidding as required by Philippine law. The project was cancelled by the Philippine government in March 2012. When the government informed CNMEC of its inability to service the loan, China EximBank declared a loan default.

Concurrently, the Philippine Audit Commission undertook an official audit on the project in 2012 (Avila et al. 2013). It was found that NLRC had already paid US$210.5 million to CNMEG. Also, China EximBank disbursed US$180.8 million of the loan to the Philippine government. However, the audit commission concluded that the value of construction was worth only US$81.5 million and NLRC had overpaid CNMEC by US$129 million. By September 2012, the Philippine government repaid US$46.1 million of the loan to China EximBank. In 2013, the Philippine government initiated arbitration in the International Arbitration Centre in Hong Kong (Robbies 2013; Toh 2013). So far, no information about the case has been made publicly available.

According to Philippine law, the project was apparently involved in many legal irregularities, including the following:

1   As the project involved funds contributed by the Philippine government, the project should undergo a public bidding process according to Philippine law. However, the project was awarded to CNMEC without the prior competitive bidding process.
2   CNMEC was even not a licensed foreign contractor in the Philippines.
3   NLRC had agreed on a supply agreement with CNMEC that lacked detailed technical specifications and performance criteria.

According to a recent study by Trinidad (2016, p. 307), "the subsequent termination of Chinese assistance for Northrail was mainly due to legal and political controversies that arose from mismatch of aid institutions between donor and recipient". The author highlighted that the Philippines was accustomed to DAC-based rules and practices governing the development aid process. However, Chinese aid is a broader concept encompassing the securing of overseas contracts, providing material supplies, labour exports, consulting services, and different types of foreign direct investment (Foster et al. 2009; Trinidad 2016).

The Tutuban to Malolos Rail Project by Japan

In May 2015, Prime Minister Abe announced a new strategy, "Promoting High-Quality Infrastructure Investment in Asia". The plan is to invest US$110 billion in Asia between 2016 and 2020 (30 percent higher than that in the previous five years). Japan has been a major sponsor of Philippine projects in recent years. By the end of July 2016, JICA's assistance to the Philippines covered 20 ongoing project loans amounting to about US$2.8 billion. Using the investment opportunity in the Philippine railway as a test case, similar investment projects would be undertaken in Thailand, Vietnam, Myanmar, etc. in the future (Leyco 2016). JICA has undertaken several detailed studies on the project (Japan International Cooperation Agency 2015a, 2015b; Japan International Cooperation Agency (JICA), Oriental Consultants Global Co., Ltd, Almec Cooperation, Katahira and Engineers International, and Tostems, Inc., 2015d).

Under this initiative, JICA and the Philippine government concluded a US$2 billion loan agreement in November 2015 for the construction of the North–South Commuter Project (Tutuban to Malolos). This is an extended version of the failed Chinese project (extended from Caloocan to Tutuban, 32 kilometres to 37 kilometres). The loan, JICA's largest assistance to the Philippine government so far, carried an interest rate of 0.10 percent per annum for the project and a maturity of 40 years inclusive of a ten-year grace period (JICA 2015c).[3] This loan would account for 80 percent of the total construction cost; the other 20 percent would be funded by the Philippine government. Current negotiations are ongoing and focusing on whether only Japanese companies would be qualified as the procurement source.

The Thai–Chinese Bangkok–Nong Khai Rail Project

Thailand has initiated two long-distance rail projects in recent years (Figure 4.2). The Bangkok – Nong Khai Project (with four phases) mid-speed rail project was awarded to China Railway Construction Corporation in November 2014. The

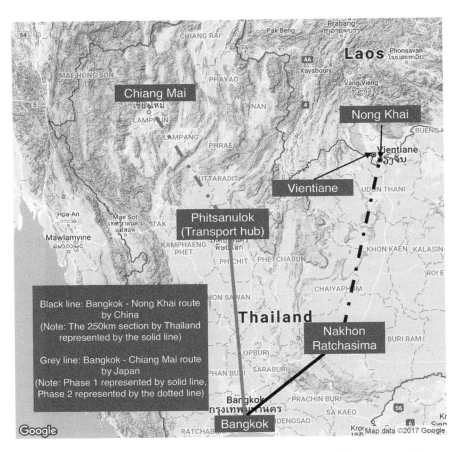

Figure 4.2 Illustrative routes of the Bangkok to Nong Khai and Bangkok to Chiang Mai Rail Projects

Source: Map compiled by the authors using Google Map data, Google (2017).

Bangkok–Chang Mai high-speed rail project (with two phases) was awarded to Japan in May 2015.

In 2010, when the high-speed rail project to Nong Khai was conceptually agreed under the Democrat Party-led Thai government, Beijing indicated it would provide most of the investment. China wanted to accelerate regional trade under the ASEAN Free Trade Agreement and to demonstrate its bullet-train-building capabilities to the region. The first memorandum was signed between two governments in November 2014, and a groundbreaking ceremony for the project was held in December 2015. This is basically a government-to-government construction contract, mostly funded by China without open bidding.

Under this framework, a joint venture would be established to implement the project. China would conduct feasibility studies, design the system, construct tunnels and bridges, and lay tracks. Thailand would conduct social and environmental impact studies, expropriate land for construction, handle general civil engineering and power supply, and supply of construction materials. Once the project is completed, China would operate and maintain the system for the first three years. Both countries would share responsibility between the third and seventh years. Subsequently, Thailand would take over the responsibility, China as the advisor.

For the 867-kilometre mid-speed (160–180 kilometres/hour) Bangkok–Nong Khai Rail Project, the initial estimated cost by the Thai government was US$12billion.The focus is on the linkage of trade and services in ASEAN. It would connect to a 417-kilometre line from Vientiane to the northern Lao border and a 520-kilometre line from the Lao border to Kunming. This is a core part of the grant railway project linking Kunming to Singapore (3,000 kilometres), via Laos, Thailand, and Malaysia.

The project would be supported by a Chinese loan, at a 2.5 percent interest rate. The Thai government wanted to reduce the interest charge. A part of the total cost of the project would be raised through a public–private partnership (PPP) scheme and other infrastructure funds; 70 percent of the civic works would be reserved for Thai construction companies.

After nearly two years of bilateral negotiations, neither side has agreed on several major terms and conditions of the project: equity structure, total cost, interest rates on concessional loans, and land development rights (Table 4.3).

Table 4.3 Major terms of negotiation for Bangkok–Nong Khai Rail

	Thailand's Position	*China's Position*
Construction cost estimation	US$12billion	US$16.5 billion
Interest rate charged	2.0%	2.5%
Equity shares of joint venture	China investors: 60–70%	Not available
Land development rights along the rail route	Denied	Strongly demanded

Source: Various official and news reports, compiled by the authors.

Indeed, Chinese officials from the state-run China Railway Construction Corporation (CRCC) pressed for the rights to develop commercial property at the stations and along the railway route. The Thai government considered this an unacceptable demand (Zhou 2016).[4] Thailand would like to treat China as a co-investor and to share cost and risk. But CRCC has been perceived as aiming at maximizing profit on this project (Crispin 2016).

In March 2016, the Thai government decided to invest in a shorter rail by itself instead (Jiang 2016). Only the Bangkok–Nakhon Ratchasima Section (250 kilometres) of the original plan will continue to be built, and the estimated cost is about US$5 billion. The Thai government will resort to debt financing. The ten-year notes by state-linked investment funds were trading at 1.8 percent in early 2017, and the market estimated that the Thai government's total cost for the project would be much higher. Again, there were comments that the official cost figure had been grossly underestimated. Until July 2017, the Thai government approved US$5.5 billion to construct this first phase of a high-speed rail that would link to China in the longer term (Linder 2017). This rail would be completed in 2021.

Under the new arrangement, Thailand will provide the funding, and China will supply the technology and oversee procurement, on the condition that Thai contractors would be used. In fact, China was given the construction contract without competitive bidding. This may be a cause of dispute in the future (Crispin 2016; Zhou 2016).

Other than all these financial terms and commercial considerations, the political development in Thailand since 2010 has played a very important role. The high-speed rail was conceptually agreed between the Democrat Party-led Thai government and the Chinese government in 2010. This plan encountered new issues when Yingluck Shinawatra's party defeated the Democrat Party in 2011. There was another change in the government due to the military coup in May 2014. The Thai military government turned to Beijing for diplomatic and strategic support at a time when the United States and EU had criticized the suspension of democracy by the military government. The joint railway would be a symbol of economic and diplomatic achievements. If China fails to respond to the development in time, it is likely that the project will again face other complications, when a civilian government returns to power in the future (Zhou 2016).

The Thai–Japanese Bangkok–Chiang Mai Rail Project

Japan proposed Thailand adopt Shinkansen technology for constructing a high-speed rail link between Bangkok and Chiang Mai in recent years. The railway is part of Thailand's strategic plan for transport connectivity that links the mass transit systems of big cities to small towns along the rail as well as the neighbouring countries. Japan and Thailand signed the first memorandum for the 715-kilometre high-speed (250 kilometres/hour) Bangkok–Chiang Mai Rail Project in May 2015. The estimated investment cost is US$12 billion. The original plan was to commence rail operation in 2019 (Ongdee 2015; Thaicharoen 2015).

Japan's Transport Minister, Keiichi Ishii, and Thai counterpart, Arkhom Term-pittayapaisith, signed the second memorandum in August 2016 (JICA Thailand Office 2016). The memorandum stated that the 380-kilometre section between Bangkok and Phitsanulok be built first, because the traffic demand on this major transport hub is expected to be heavy. Japan will also provide technical assistance to promote city development along the railway, which would also increase passenger flow. The two countries will formulate a basic plan in 2017, after JICA releases the final feasibility study sometime in early 2017.

The Japanese government will provide a soft loan. This project will adopt the government-to-government model on engineering, procurement, and construction system, instead of opening bidding. A joint Thai–Japanese steering committee will be set up to manage the project.

The Jakarta–Bandung link in the Indonesian railway development

The Jakarta–Bandung High Speed Railway (HSR) project is underpinned by two important policy documents. The first one is the "Master Plan of National Railway" (RencanaInduk Perkereta–apian Nasional) published in 2011, whose aim was to boost the railway network to 12,100 kilometres on all major islands by 2030 (Table 4.4).

According to the Directorate General of Railways (2013), the existing railway network was about 3,464 kilometres in length in Java and about 1,352 kilometres on Sumatera Island. As of the date of writing, an urban railway system does not exist in Jakarta, let alone in other cities. The Jakarta Mass Rapid Transit (Phase 1) is currently under construction and expected operational in 2019.

At the same time, the Coordinating Ministry for Economic Affairs released the "Master Plan for Acceleration and Expansion of Indonesian Economic Development" (MP3EI) in 2011, which advocated building an economic corridor stretching from Jabodetabek (Jakarta Metropolitan Area) and Gerbangkertosusila (Surabaya Metropolitan Area) through the development of a trans-Java high-speed railway and toll road. The Jakarta–Bandung link is often seen as part of an ambitious railway project that links the Indonesian capital to other major cities in Java.

Table 4.4 Targets in National Railway Master Plan 2030 of Indonesia

Region	Passengers (millions)	Freight (million tons)	Length of tracks (km)
Java	595.0	4,031.5	6,800
Sumatera	27.5	281.5	2,900
Kalimantan	6.5	20.5	1,400
Sulawesi	16.0	31.5	500
Papua	15.5	2.0	500
Total	660.5	4,367.0	12,100

Source: Adapted from Dikun, S 2011, p 2.

Japan participated in the railway project in 2009. JICA took more than one year to conduct the feasibility study (and that was already after several studies carried out by METI of the Japanese government and various other Japanese institutions), whereas China's feasibility study was completed in less than five months (Table 4.5).

Table 4.5 Competition between China and Japan for Jakarta–Bandung Rail Project

Time	Japan	China
Mar 2009	Japan External Trade Organization prepared a project study for a HSR system for Jakarta – Surabaya	
Mar 2012	Ministry of Land, Infrastructure, Transport and Tourism prepared a study for a HSR line between Jakarta and Bandung	
Nov 2012	Ministry of Economy, Trade and Industry prepared a study investigating how to implement an HSR between Jakarta and Bandung	
Jan 2014	Feasibility study phase 1 started with a grant from Japan International Cooperation Agency worth US$3.5 million	
Mar 2015		Indonesia's SOE Minister Rini Soemarno and Chinese National Development and Reform Committee Chairman Xu Shaoshi (徐绍史) sign MOU on feasibility study with a grant worth US$5 million
Apr 2015	JICA submitted feasibility study to the Coordinating Ministry for Economic Affairs	
Aug 2015		China submitted feasibility study
Sep 2015	**President Jokowi turned down both proposals, citing they were not technically or financially feasible**	
Oct 2015		Presidential Regulation No.107/2015 enacted and assigned Jakarta–Bandung high-speed railway to PT Kereta Cepat Indonesia China (PT KCIC), a joint venture of 4 Indonesian SOEs and China Railway International.

Source: Japan International Consultants for Transportation 2013; S Dikun 2011, Table 4.1; and 'Government goes ahead with high-speed railway', *The Jakarta Post*, 21 January 2016. Compiled by the authors.

The proposals from China and Japan were initially turned down by the Jokowi administration in September 2015. In a sudden turn of events, the Indonesia government put forward Presidential Regulation No.107/2015, targeted at speeding up the development of supporting facilities and facility procurement for the Jakarta–Bandung HSR. The project was assigned to PT Kereta Cepat Indonesia China (PT KCIC), a joint venture of four Indonesian SOEs (the construction firm Wijaya Karya, the toll operator Jasa Marga, the railway operator Kereta Api Indonesia, and the plantation firm Perkebunan Nusantara VIII) and China Railway International (CRI) in October 2015. These four Indonesian SOEs jointly hold 60 percent of PT KCIC; the remaining 40 percent are owned by CRI.

China's proposal was very competitive in the total cost and construction time, but the loan they offered was seemingly more expensive than was Japan's proposal (Table 4.6). China, via the Chinese Development Bank, offered a loan denominated in both US dollars and renminbi, and charged an interest rate of 2 percent and 3.46 percent respectively. Japan proposed an all-yen loan at 0.1 percent interest.

The fundamental difference between these two proposals lies with the perception of the nature of the project. Japan viewed the project as a government-to-government deal and required a guarantee from the Indonesian government, whereas China structured it as a business-to-government deal (adopting the BOT structure, assuming all investment risk) and did not require a government guarantee or involve state funds. This made the Chinese proposal much more appealing to the Indonesian government, which has been working under a tight budgetary and credit environment.

In March 2016, PT KCIC was offered a concession period of 50 years with a fixed starting date on 19 May 2016, in lieu of any state resources and guarantees. The concession agreement also required PT KCIC to keep the construction period within three years from the issuance of the construction permit. Although explicit penalty terms for construction delays were not present in the agreement, such delays would still penalize PT KCIC in a shorter period for obtaining revenues.

China has also pledged to develop train cars locally and invest in an aluminium plant in Indonesia. The construction of the railway is expected to create 40,000 new jobs, and supporting infrastructure in nearby areas is expected to bring an additional 48,000 new jobs in the coming 15 years after the train is operational.

The Jakarta–Bandung HSR project has hardly been smooth sailing for China since it was awarded in October 2015. The major obstacle was getting all the permits required for the railway construction. Many permits were crammed in at the last minute before the groundbreaking ceremony on 21 January 2016.

AMDAL approval came just one day before the groundbreaking ceremony despite incomplete paper work, including the Environment Management Plan (RKL) and the Environment Monitoring Plan (RPL). Officials from the Environment and Forestry Ministry criticized the issuance process as *irregular*, citing the time given to gathering information for the analysis was reduced from the usual six months to one week ('Govt goes ahead with high – speed railway 2016').

Table 4.6 A comparison of proposals from China and Japan

	China		Japan
	First Proposal	*Revised Proposal*	
(1) Project description			
Scope of project	Gambir–Gedebage	Halim-Karawing–Walini–Tegalluar	DukuhAtas–Gedebage
Railway track (km)	150.5	142.3	140.14
Number of stations	8	4	5
Speed	350–380 km/h	250 km/h*	320 km/h
Total cost	US$5.5b	US$5.1b*	US$6.2b
Time frame	Begin construction 2016 Complete 2018 Operational 2019		Begin construction 2017 Complete 2019 Operational 2021
Construction (years)	3		4
(2) Financing Arrangement			
Institutions involved	China Development Bank, PT Kereta Cepat Indonesia China (PT KCIC): a joint venture of four Indonesian SOEs and China Railway International.		Japan International Cooperation Agency (JICA), Indonesian government
Financing	25% Equity, 75% Loans from CDB		25% State Budget, 75% Loans from JICA
Loan terms	60% US$, 40% RMB		100% yen
Interest rates	2% on US$, 3.46% on RMB		0.1%
Loan period	40 years		40 years
Grace period	10 years		10 years
Government guarantee	No		Yes
(3) Construction			
Excavation (km)	16.6	52.6	24.2
Landfill (km)	40.5		34.58
Raised (km)	70.5	73.8	39.2
Tunnels (km)	22.9	16.8	42.14

Source: Adapted from Salim & Negara 2016, Table 4.1. Data updated using various news reports.

Note: *Cost escalation very likely after last-minute design change in July 2016, when rail tracks were widened from 4.6 m to 5 m, which would boost speed from 250 km/h to 350 km/h. (See 'RIs first high-speed railway may be costlier on design change', *The Jakarta Post*, 11 July 2016.)

Various scholars also warned that the railway ran through earthquake-prone areas and that an absence of a natural disaster test would threaten the safety of passengers ('High-speed railway surrounded by four quake sources' 2016).

The Ministry of Transportation issued a construction permit covering merely the first five kilometres of the 142.3-kilometre railway tracks in March 2016, i.e. two months after the groundbreaking ceremony. It then took another five months for the construction permit to be extended to 56.8 kilometres (about

40 percent). In late August 2016, PT KCIC finally obtained the construction permit for the entire route. This resulted in a delay of construction of seven months, or equivalent to 30 percent of the expected construction time.

As of June 2016, PT KCIC was reported to have acquired 60 percent of the land. KCIC intended to build a terminal in Halim as the first stop of the Jakarta end of the route. But this would cut into Indonesia's air force base at the Halim Perdanakusuma Airport. The military has not yet approved this arrangement, and the negotiation between PT KCIC and the military is ongoing. There were also media reports saying that the Chinese Development Bank, which funds 75 percent of the project, was reluctant to disburse the loan, citing slow progress in the land acquisition ('Jakarta–Bandung high-speed rail project stalls' 2016).

China's win over Japan in the Jakarta–Bandung HSR project is often claimed as one of the recent successes of Chinese diplomacy since the launch of the Belt and Road Initiative. Japan's early involvement obviously put China in a disadvantage in the competition for this HSR project, but China counteracted that disadvantage by showing its quick decision and willingness to shoulder most of the project risk.

Surabaya rail section in Indonesia awarded to Japan

However, the Jakarta–Bandung route is only part of the planned Jakarta–Bandung–Cirebon–Surabaya railway project – one that stretches some 750 kilometres across three provinces (Figure 4.3).

Amid the various issues surrounding the Jakarta–Bandung route, Indonesia offered the Jakarta–Surabaya project to Japan without a competitive tendering, in October 2016 ('Indonesia offers Japan Jakarta–Surabaya rail project' 2016; 'Indonesia asks Japan to build its new Jakarta–Surabaya railway' 2016). During a state visit to Indonesia in January 2017, Japan's Prime Minster Abe and Indonesia's President Jokowi also carried out follow-up discussions about this project.

Figure 4.3 Illustrative routes of the Jakarta to Bandung and Jakarta to Surabaya projects
Source: Map compiled by the authors using Google Map data, Google (2017).

The plan is to upgrade the existing railway connecting Jakarta and Surabaya from about 90 kilometres per hour to a semi high-speed railway running at about 150–200 kilometres per hour (see 'Japan rehabilitates Jakarta – Surabaya railway 2016). This decision highlights the close economic and diplomatic ties between Indonesia and Japan. Moreover, this would signal Indonesia's doubts about China's ability to deliver large-scale infrastructure projects. According to the latest report (Susanty 2017), the ongoing feasibility study would provide a cost reassessment, which would determine whether the train is to be powered by electricity or diesel. The escalation in cost will result in new uncertainties for the project.

Conclusion

Although it is not possible for us to come to a precise conclusion about the differences in the investment strategy of China and Japan in ASEAN's infrastructure projects (using only three rail projects as examples, ones that are in progress), we are able to suggest the following observations for further deliberation (Table 4.7).

1 ASEAN countries usually take a balanced approach towards investment offers by China and Japan, such that they get the best infrastructure deals and maintain diplomatic neutrality.
2 Japan has been a core member of OECD and observes DAC-based rules and practices closely. Such rules are the foundation of a developed-country-to-developing-country model for alleviating poverty and sustainable development. In recent years, Japan has attempted to take full account of international development goals such as the Post-2015 Development Agenda of the United Nations. All Japan's ODAs are put under the administration and control of one dedicated JICA, whose role has recently been enhanced under the new Development Cooperation Charter.
3 China is not a member of OECD and thus not bound by DAC-based rules. China's bilateral practices in overseas infrastructure investment permit greater flexibility in their terms of cooperation with other developing countries. This is a developing-country-to-developing-country model based on mutual benefit and non-interference. The Ministry of Commerce (MOFCOM) is the main administrative agency authorized by China's State Council to oversee foreign aid. In reality, MOFCOM is more a coordinator for aid and development projects rather than a dedicated single aid and development agency. Infrastructure projects serve both political and economic objectives for China.
4 China's SOEs are becoming an important player in the supply chain of these infrastructure projects, and the profit motive is an important element. China's Thai rail project seemed to fail, at least partially, due to the hard bargain struck by the China Railway Construction Corporation for the land development rights along the route and the higher interest charged.
5 The three Japanese rail projects are centrally administered by JICA, under the same set of rules and guidelines. In particular, all the yen loans are charged

Table 4.7 A comparison of characteristics of China's and Japan's Railway Projects in ASEAN

	China	Japan
Relevance to host country	China's interest is an important factor, aiming at mutual benefits	Projects closely aligned with development priority of recipient country
Nature	Projects with profit motives and on commercial principle	Development and aid projects
Main administrative agency	Ministry of Commerce (more as a coordinator)	JICA (one agency in-charge)
Multilateral framework	AIIB starting to follow MDB rules, filtering through China Model in long term	Adopting OECD DAC-based, MDB rules
Planning and preparation	Hasty, without comprehensive consideration	"Quality" approach, with detailed studies, soft infrastructure included
Main players	National enterprises	Private companies
Financing sources	Multiple sources: China Exim Banks, China Development Bank, etc.	Japan Bank for International Cooperation, under JICA
Financing charges	Different terms and rates for different projects	JBIC offering same terms for every project
Project nature	Mostly tied, no bidding	Moving towards untied, bidding
Risk assessment	Incomplete	Down to meticulous details
Technology transfer	Grossly mentioned in official documents	Explicitly stated in JICA's documents
Outcome	Prone to controversies but competitive in terms of cost and construction time	Aligned with visions of host countries, more problem-solving, supported by soft infrastructure

Source: Compiled by the authors.

at 0.1 percent interest rate per annum. For the Chinese rail projects, different interest rates were charged by China EximBank and CDB. In particular, CDB is operating on the commercial principle.

6   For the selected rail projects for comparison, the Japanese government and related institutions have been involved in the planning process of the rail projects for a much longer time than have the Chinese. This has gained the significant confidence of the host countries.

7   The Japanese have been undertaking feasibility studies and risk-assessment exercises in much greater detail with a huge budget and patience, i.e. Japan's quality approach to overseas infrastructure investment. The Chinese counterparts might have taken decisions without comprehensive consideration. Such a strategy may permit the Chinese to gain the rail contract by offering

some special concessions and taking more risks. But the long-term cost and risk elements might eventually defeat the Chinese venture.

8   China's rail project in the Philippines ran into legal and political controversies. These controversies were exploited by political opposition parties, the media, and NGOs. The Philippine government's poor arrangement for relocated families along the route also aroused bad publicity for the project. The Chinese government and the company involved did not have sufficient experience and soft power to mitigate the situation.

9   Another controversial aspect of China's ASEAN rail projects is that the required supplies for the project were typically procured from Chinese companies, and contracts were awarded to Chinese SOEs. Thus, the benefit to the host would be reduced. As the three corresponding rail projects of the Japanese are still at the inception stage, how far the Japanese would do this differently has yet to be seen.

10 Fundamentally, the soft power of Japanese in ASEAN has been much stronger than that of the Chinese. Japanese assistance programmes and infrastructure projects would align more closely with the social and economic visions of the host countries. They are more problem-solving for the host countries. Their people usually have a warmer perception of Japanese investment and involvement than of the Chinese. This will have a direct bearing on the decisions of the respective host government.

11 In response to the intensifying competition for infrastructure projects in ASEAN and changing geopolitical environment, both Chinese and Japanese governments have been enhancing their investment strategies. The Ministry of Commerce of China has issued many guidelines to assist Chinese firms going overseas. Japan issued a new Development Cooperation Charter, emphasizing quality infrastructure investment and institutional connectivity.

The China model clearly lacks the same dimension of transparency and environmental and social standards as characterized by Japan's infrastructure investment. It also lacks sophistication in the development of soft power. Moreover, the recent high-profile development of AIIB as initiated by China deserves greater attention.

The China-led AIIB, with 58 founding members, has decided to adopt the core values and standards of the MDBs. The institution's first Chinese president is himself a veteran of the World Bank and ADB. A close look at the rules of AIIB reveals no departures from the norms and practices of the existing MDBs. Similarly, China's trust funds vested with the MDBs adhere to the same standards (Morris 2016). This could help make up the disparity between the China and Japan models. Apparently, AIIB and other Chinese trust funds under MDBs would only support a very small number of infrastructure projects in the short to medium term. The impact of the AIIB model may take a long time to filter through the China model, which is mainly bilateral.

For the three cited railway examples, the Chinese encountered different difficulties at different stages of project implementation. Moreover, the Chinese are learning and adapting. The Japanese have ventured into similar projects in recent years, by adopting rather different approaches. At this stage, it would be premature to conclude that the Japan model would definitely lead to a higher probability of success for implementing infrastructure projects in ASEAN. As the details of the Japanese projects are still unfolding and geopolitics in ASEAN remain fluid, how the cost and benefit of these infrastructure projects would be shared among various stakeholders is still uncertain. The ultimate question is: will China and Japan establish high-level cooperation to invest in infrastructure projects in ASEAN, such that every stakeholder could be a winner?

Notes

* The authors express their deepest gratitude to the research support provided by Ting-hin Yan, Wai-ying Chan, and Hong-lam Wong of the Hong Kong Institute of Asia – Pacific Studies of the Chinese University of Hong Kong.
1 Under the DAC definition, ODA must meet these criteria: (1) it is undertaken by governments or government agencies, (2) its main objective is the promotion of economic development and welfare of developing countries, and (3) it is concessional in character, with a grant element of at least 25 percent.
2 According to the United Nations (n.d.), "The Millennium Development Goals (MDGs) are the world's time-bound and quantified targets for addressing extreme poverty in its many dimensions – income poverty, hunger, disease, lack of adequate shelter, and exclusion – while promoting gender equality, education, and environmental sustainability. They are also basic human rights – the rights of each person on the planet to health, education, shelter, and security".
3 'Special Terms for Economic Partnership' were applied to this project. See press release of JICA on 25 November 2015 (Japan International Cooperation Agency (JICA) 2015c).
4 See also Thailand rebuffs railway deal with China, *The Straits Times*, 5 May 2016.

Bibliography

Agcaoili, L 2012, 'PHL forming legal team for North Rail arbitration', *The Philippine Star*, 28 October. Available from: www.philstar.com/business/2012/10/28/860936/phl-forming-legal-team-north-rail-arbitration. [26 September 2016].
Association of Southeast Asian Nations (ASEAN) & United Nations Conference on Trade and Development (UNCTAD) 2015, *ASEAN investment report 2015: infrastructure investment and connectivity*, ASEAN Secretariat, Jakarta.
Avila, F, Florentino, A, Olavere, G, Ong, BJ, Sy, F, Mercado, C & Dejeto, D 2013, *Northrail project phase 1, section 1: North Luzon railways corporation*. Republic of the Philippines, Commission on Audit, Quezon City, Philippines. Report number: 2012–002, Special Audit.
Cabuenas J 2015, 'PHL, Japan sign loan agreement for P93-B Tutuban – Malolos railway', *GMA News Online*. Available from: www.gmanetwork.com/news/story/546028/money/economy/phl-japan-sign-loan-agreement-for-p93-b-tutuban-malolos-railway. [11 November 2016].
Camus, MR 2016, 'Japan seals P97-B commuter rail project', *Philippine Daily Inquirer*, 29 January. Available from: http://business.inquirer.net/206288/ph-japan-seal-p97-b-commuter-rail-project. [18 November 2016].

Chan, G 2016, *China's high-speed rail diplomacy: global impacts and East Asian responses*. East Asia Institute, National University of Singapore, Singapore.

Chanco, B 2015, 'Northrail gets new life from Japan', *The Philippines Star*, 25 November. Available from: www.philstar.com/business/2015/11/25/1525529/northrail-gets-new-life-japan. [7 October 2016].

Cheng, S, Fang, T & Lien, H-T 2012, 'China's international aid policy and its implications for global governance', Working Paper No. 29, June. RRCCPB, Bloomington, IN (Indiana University Research Center for Chinese Politics and Business).

Crispin, S 2016, 'China – Thailand railway project gets untracked', *The Diplomat*, 1 April. Available from: http://thediplomat.com/2016/04/china-thailand-railway-project-gets-untracked/. [13 October 2016].

Department of Transportation and Communications and Philippine National Railways, Republic of the Philippines 2015, 'North – South railway project – South line (Project Information Memorandum (Aug 2015))', Department of Transportation and Communications and Philippine National Railways, Republic of the Philippines. Available from: https://ppp.gov.ph/wp-content/uploads/2015/08/NSRP_PIM_FINAL.pdf. [7 August 2016].

Dikun, S 2011, 'Indonesia railway reform', paper presented to Indonesia Infrastructure Initiative Wrap-up Conference. Jakarta, Indonesia, 14 June.

Directorate General of Railways 2013, *Indonesia railways development*. Ministry of Transportation, Jakarta, Indonesia.

Dugay, C 2015, 'What does Japan's new charter mean for development?' *Devex*. Available from: www.devex.com/news/what-does-japan-s-new-charter-mean-for-development-85595. [9 September 2016].

Foster, V, Butterfield, W, Chen, C & Pushak, N 2009, *Building bridges: China's growing role as infrastructure financier for sub-Saharan Africa*, No. 5. World Bank Publications, Washington, DC.

'Govt goes ahead with high-speed railway' 2016, *The Jakarta Post*, 21 January. Available from: www.thejakartapost.com/news/2016/01/21/govt-goes-ahead-with-high-speed-railway.html. [20 April 2016].

'High-speed railway surrounded by four quake sources' 2016, *Kompas*, 27 January. Available from: http://print.kompas.com/baca/english/2016/01/27/High-Speed-Railway-Surrounded-by-Four-Quake-Source. [6 March 2016].

'High-speed train gets go ahead' 2014, *Bangkok Post*, 30 July. Available from: www.bangkokpost.com/archive/high-speed-train-gets-go-ahead/423129. [22 January 2017].

Huang, W & Wikes, A 2011, 'Analysis of China's overseas investments policies', Working Paper, No. 79. Bogor, Indonesia: Center for International Forestry Research (CIFOR).

'Indonesia asks Japan to build its new Jakarta-Surabaya railway' 2016, *Global Construction Review*, 12 October. Available from: www.globalconstructionreview.com/news/indonesia-asks-japan-build-it7s-n7ew-jak7arta/. [11 January 2017].

'Indonesia offers Japan Jakarta-Surabaya rail project' 2016, *The Jakarta Post*, 8 October. Available from: www.thejakartapost.com/news/2016/10/08/indonesia-offers-japan-jakarta-surabaya-rail-project.html. [12 December 2016].

'Jakarta-Bandung high-speed rail project stalls' 2016, *Nikkei Asian Review*, 28 July. Available from: http://asia.nikkei.com/Politics-Economy/International-Relations/Jakarta-Bandung-high-speed-rail-project-stalls. [5 November 2016].

Jakobson, L & Knox, D 2010, *New foreign policy actors in China*. Stockholm International Peach Research Institute, Solna, Sweden.

Japan International Consultants for Transportation 2013, *JICA* 「インドネシアジ ャワ高速鉄道開発事業準備調査（フェーズ I ）」の受注・契約について. Available from: www.jictransport.co.jp/admin/news/pdf/201312JICA_%20Indonesia %20_HSR.pdf. [10 January 2017].

Japan International Cooperation Agency 2015a, 'Draft resettlement action plan for north – south commuter rail project (Malolos to Tutuban)' Tokyo, Japan.

Japan International Cooperation Agency (JICA) 2015b, 'Ex-ante evaluation: north – south commuter railway project (Malolos – Tutuban)'. Available from: www. jica.go.jp/english/our_work/evaluation/oda_loan/economic_cooperation/ c8h0vm000001rdjt-att/philippines_151127_01.pdf. [4 February 2017].

Japan International Cooperation Agency (JICA) 2015c, 'Signing of Japanese ODA loan agreement with the Philippines: using Japanese technology and urban planning models to construct a landmark commuter railway system connecting Metro Manila and outlying areas'. Available from: www.jica.go.jp/english/news/ press/2015/151127_01.html. [10 February 2017].

Japan International Cooperation Agency (JICA) 2016, *Annual report, 2016*. Japan.

Japan International Cooperation Agency (JICA) Oriental Consultants Global Co., Ltd, Almec Cooperation, Katahira and Engineers International, & Tostems, Inc. 2015d, *The supplementary survey on north – south commuter rail project (Phase II-A) in the Republic of the Philippines – pre-final report*. Available from: http:// open_jicareport.jica.go.jp/pdf/12245890_01.pdf and http://open_jicareport. jica.go.jp/pdf/12245890_02.pdf. [10 February 2017].

'Japan rehabilitates Jakarta-Surabaya railway' 2016, *Tempo*, 20 October. Available from: https://en.tempo.co/read/news/2016/10/20/056813909/Japan-Reha bilitates-Jakarta-Surabaya-Railway. [10 November 2016].

Jennings, R 2017, 'China vs. Japan on giving foreign aid: 3 things other country should know', *Forbes*, 15 January. Available from: www.forbes.com/sites/ralphjen nings/2017/01/15/china-and-japan-ramping-up-checkbook-diplomacy-in-asia/#4d250ecf5e7b. [15 April 2017].

Jiang, S 2016, 'Not taking no for an answer, China Railway Group says – speed project in Thailand "still on"', *South China Morning Post*, 7 April. Available from: www.scmp.com/business/companies/article/193424/not-taking-no-answer-china-railway-group-says-high-speed-project. [27 October 2016].

JICA Thailand Office 2016, 'Signing of Japanese ODA loan agreement with Thailand for the mass transit system project in Bangkok (Red Line) (III)'. Available from: www.jica.go.jp/thailand/english/office/topics/160930.html. [11 October 2016].

Kobayashi, T 2008, 'Evolution of China's aid policy', Japan Bank for International Cooperation Institution, Working Paper, No. 27. Japan Bank for International Cooperation, Tokyo.

Kudo, T 2007, 'Myanmar and Japan: how close friends become estranged'. IDE Disscussion Paper, No. 118.

Lamb, V & Dao, N 2015, 'Perceptions and practices of investment: China's hydropower investments in mainland Southeast Asia', paper presented to the International Academic Conference organized by Chiang Mai University. Chiang Mai, Thailand, 5–6 June.

Leyco, C 2016, 'JICA backs Manila subway, railway project', *Manila Bulletin*, 11 September. Available from: https://ppp.gov.ph/?in_the_news=jica-backs-manila-subway-railway-projects. [8 December 2016].

Linder, A 2017, 'Thailand finally approved first stage of high-speed-railway to China'. Available from: Shanghaist.com/2017/07/12/thailand-China-railway approved. php. [17 September 2017].

McDonald, K, Bosshard, P & Brewer, N 2009, 'Exporting dams: China's hydro-power industry goes global', *Journal of Environmental Management*, vol. 90, pp. S294–S302.

Mezza, M 2015, *China and Japan battle for influence in Southeast Asia*, AEI. The National Interest, Washington DC.

Ministry of Commerce of PRC (中華人民共和國商務部) 2004, *Industrial guidance catalogue for ODI in countries* (商务部、外交部关于发布《对外投资国别产业导向目录》的通知). Ministry of Commerce of PRC, Beijing.

Ministry of Commerce of PRC (中華人民共和國商務部) 2010, *The ministry of commerce on the issuance of the notice of security early warning and information notification system for outward foreign direct investment and cooperation* (商务部印发《对外投资合作境外安全风险预警和信息通报制度》). Ministry of Commerce of PRC, Beijing.

Ministry of Commerce of PRC (中華人民共和國商務部) 2015a, *2015 report on development of China's outward investment and economic cooperation* (中國對外投資合作發展報告). Ministry of Commerce of PRC, Beijing.

Ministry of Commerce of PRC (中華人民共和國商務部) 2015b, *Public platform for outward investment: guidance by nations/regions* (走出去公共平台：國別 (地區) 指南). Ministry of Commerce of PRC, Beijing.

Ministry of Foreign Affairs of Japan 2015a, 'Cabinet decision on the development cooperation charter'. Available from: www.mofa.go.jp/files/000067701.pdf. [15 December 2016].

Ministry of Foreign Affairs of Japan 2015b, 'Quality infrastructure investment casebook'. Available from: www.mofa.go.jp/files/000095681.pdf. [15 December 2016].

Ministry of Foreign Affairs of Japan 2015c, 'New Tokyo strategy 2015 for Mekong-Japan cooperation'. Available from: www.mofa.go.jp/s_sa/sea1/page/e_000044. html. [15 December 2016].

Morris, S 2016, 'Responding to AIIB: U.S. leadership at the multilateral development banks in a new era', CFR Discussion Paper in September 2016. Washington, DC: Council on Foreign Relations.

Nobuhiro, A 2014, 'Japan's strategy toward Southeast Asia and the Japan – U.S. alliance'. Strategic Japan Working Paper. Center for Strategic and International Studies (CSIS), Tokyo.

Ohno, I 2014, 'Japanese development cooperation in a new era: recommendations for network-based cooperation', FRIPS Discussion Paper 14–15. National Graduate Institute for Policy Studies, Tokyo.

Ongdee, S 2015, 'Thai – Japanese rail link to Chiang Mai follows China model', *The Nation*, 18 May. Available from: www.nationmultimedia.com/news/national/aec/30260325. [17 December 2016].

'RIs first high-speed railway may be costlier on design change' 2016, *Jakarta Post*, 11 July. Available from: www.thejakartapost.com/news/2016/07/11/ri-s-first-high-speed-railway-may-be-costlier-design-change.html. [22 October 2016].

Robbies, R 2013, 'Manila, China inked rail loan payment deal amid row over contract's legality', *South China Morning Post*, 1 February. Available from: www.scmp.com/news/asia/article/1140575/manila-china-inked-rail-loan-payment-deal-amid-row-over-contracts-legality. [3 December 2016].

Salim, W & Negara, SD 2016, 'Why is the high-speed rail project so important to Indonesia', *ISEAS Perspective, 2016(16)*. ISEAS-Yusof Ishak Institute.

Sato, J, Shiga, H, Kobayashi, T & Kondoh, H 2011, '"Emerging donors" from a recipient perspective: an institutional analysis of foreign aid in Cambodia', *World Development*, vol. 39, no. 12, pp. 2091–2104.

State Council of People's Republic of China 2011, 'China's principles for economic aid and technical assistance to other countries', April 21. Available from: http://english.gov.cn/official/2011-04/21/content_1849913_10.htm. [7 November 2016].

Strafford, P 2016, 'Japan set to reap returns on investment in Myanmar', *East Asia Forum*, 26 August. Available from: www.eastasiaforum.org. [7 October 2016].

Susanty, F 2017, 'Japan train project at risk', *The Jakarta Post*, 26 July. Available from: www.pressreader.com/indonesia/the-jakarta-post/20170706/281479276441998. [6 October 2017].

Thaicharoen, K 2015, 'Thailand to approve $12 bn Japan railway scheme', *Reuters*, 20 May. Available from: www.reuters.com/article/thailand-railway-idUSL3N0YB3IJ20150520. [26 October 2016].

'Thailand rebuffs railway deal with China' 2016, *The Strait Times*, 5 May. Available from: www.straittimes.com/asia/se-asia/thailand-rebuffs-railway-deal-with china. [15 September 2016].

Toh, HS 2013, 'Arbitration hearing in Hong Kong in row over US$500m railway contract', *South China Morning Post*, 30 January. Available from: www.scmp.com/business/companies/article/1138893/arbitration-hearing-hong-kong-row-over-us500m-railway-contract. [13 October 2016].

Trinidad, D 2016, 'Institutional mismatch and Chinese aid in the Philippines: challenges and implications', *Asian Perspective*, vol. 40, no. 2, pp. 299–328.

United Nations. (n.d.) 'UN millennium project'. Available from: www.unmillennium project.org/goals/index.htm. [7 February 2017].

Yu, H 2014, 'China's eagerness to export its high-speed rail expertise to ASEAN members', *The Copenhagan Journal of Asian Studies*, vol. 32, no. 2, pp. 13–36.

Zhou, F 2016, 'China should avoid high-speed rail predicament', *Global Times*, 15 August. Available from: www.globaltimes.cn/content/1000668.shtml. [15 September 2016].

Zhu, ZM 2009, 'China's economic aid to CLMV and its economic cooperation with them. A China-Japan comparison of economic relationships with the Mekong River Basin countries'. Bangkok Research Centre, Research Report, No. 1. Bangkok, Thailand.

Zhu, ZM 2010, 'China's foreign economic cooperation for CLMV: contract engineering in CLMV', in M Kagami (ed), *Economic relations of China, Japan and Korea with the Mekong River Basin countries*, pp. 84–120. Bangkok Research Centre. Research Report, No. 3. IDE-JETRO, Bangkok, Thailand.

Part III
Infrastructure connectivity

5 China's Belt and Road Initiative through the lens of Central Asia

Roman Vakulchuk and Indra Overland

Introduction: a new Silk Road for Central Asia

The Belt and Road Initiative (BRI), aimed at connecting China, Europe and countries located along routes between China and Europe, was suggested by Xi Jinping in September 2013. This Chinese initiative envisages the completion of more than 100 small- and large-scale infrastructure projects that would improve China's connectivity with Western Europe via Central Asia and Russia, including roads, railroads, pipelines, industrial parks, and special economic zones. The five Central Asian states – Kazakhstan, Kyrgyzstan, Tajikistan, Turkmenistan, and Uzbekistan – are an important geographical focus of the project.

BRI encompasses nearly half the world's population, vast resources and 40 percent of global GDP (gross domestic product). As of 2017, 68 countries – including the Central Asian states – had expressed an interest in joining BRI. The plan is that the infrastructure will be accompanied by large-scale investment from Chinese companies and institutions such as the Silk Road Foundation with funds of US$40 billion, and the Asian Infrastructure Investment Bank (AIIB) with funds of US$100 billion. In addition, Beijing plans to provide development aid to the countries that participate in BRI.

There has been a steady increase in the influence of China in Central Asia since the early 1990s (Indeo 2017, p. 37). The total trade turnover between China and Central Asia grew 60-fold between 1991 and 2016, from US$500,000 million to 30 billion, excluding significant informal trade by small-scale entrepreneurs. Currently, 23,000 students from Central Asia study in China and more than 700,000 people travelled between Central Asia and China in 2015 (*Forbes* 2017a). Because of BRI, China is likely to remain the biggest investor in the region in the future, far exceeding the potential economic footprint of Russia and the West (Laruelle 2018, p. xii). China has also become one of the biggest importers of Central Asian energy resources. After BRI was launched, Beijing rapidly scaled up its public diplomacy and strengthened its soft power presence, especially in education and culture, thus increasingly becoming a norm-setter in Central Asia (Dave 2018, p. 99).

But how have Central Asian actors come to view China since BRI was launched? To what extent is the population aware of the risks and opportunities brought by

BRI? The fact that China made a promise to Central Asia concerning BRI should in theory improve the perception of China in the region. This should presumably also help project Beijing's image as source of economic opportunity for Central Asia's stagnant economies.

There is a growing body of scholarly literature on BRI and its implications for different parts of the world, including Central Asia (e.g. Amighini 2017; Ehteshami & Horesh 2018; Lim et al. 2016; Yilmaz & Changming 2018). However, less attention has been paid to the study and perception of BRI in Central Asia from the point of view of local actors (e.g. Laruelle 2018; Sternberg, Ahearn & McConnell 2017). This chapter makes an empirical contribution by studying whether the launch of BRI has led to a shift in Central Asian attitudes towards and perceptions of China. We discuss the interaction between China and each of the five Central Asian states, highlighting local attitudes towards and perceptions of the big neighbour. We focus on economic interaction, infrastructure and education initiatives as they are among the main pillars of the BRI agenda, while acknowledging that cooperation on political, diplomatic, and security issues has been no less important for shaping perceptions of China in Central Asia.

One limitation of our analysis should be mentioned. It is difficult to separate BRI analytically from other ongoing projects within the bilateral cooperation between China and the Central Asian countries, "as many bilateral agreements are now being brought under the Silk Road and BRI umbrella" (Dave 2018, p. 100). We attempt to overcome this limitation by tracing changes in attitudes towards and perception of China in general since 2013, when BRI was announced, and whether the change can be attributed to the promotion of BRI.

Central Asia and great powers

Especially during the decade from 2008 to 2018, China became one of the most important players in Central Asia, a region that remains largely unintegrated. In fact, Central Asia, while a culturally and historically homogenous region, remains one of the least integrated regions in the world. Apart from a zone free of nuclear weapons established in 2006,[1] which is the only region-wide organization, there are no regional platforms that bring together all five Central Asian states on a regular basis. All other organizations, such as the Commonwealth of Independent States (CIS), the Collective Security Treaty Organization (CSTO), the Eurasian Economic Union (EAEU), the Organization of Islamic Cooperation (OIC) and the Shanghai Cooperation Organization (SCO) include third states, among which are Afghanistan, China, Pakistan and Russia. Third parties often have their own priorities and promote and sometimes impose their own agendas that only strengthen the disintegration processes. Central Asia was once also considered to be a part of the so-called Great Game,[2] and major powers continue to play a role in the region (Xin 2016, p. 124). Some scholars even argue that the Great Game contest resumed after the terrorist attack of 9/11 and continues to influence the policies of the great powers towards Central Asia (Cooley 2012; Kim & Indeo 2013).

China realized how internally disconnected the region is and pursued a bilateral approach in its relations with Central Asian governments from the late 1990s onwards. The Chinese have acted patiently and pragmatically and over time have managed to build working relations with each of the five countries, including Turkmenistan, where the construction of the Turkmenistan–China gas pipeline can be viewed as a major Chinese success story in a country where both Russia and the United States have struggled to maintain a foothold. Despite the fact that BRI is a regional project, it is likely that, in the short and medium term, the collaboration between China and Central Asia will be based primarily on bilateral relations. Following China's example, Russia, the United States and international donors have taken an increasingly bilateral approach rather than a regional one, as the former is more pragmatic and brings more practical benefits in dealings with Central Asian countries.

Central Asia is a complex region characterized by both dynamism and stagnation and requires new approaches and tools for better comprehension by external actors. China needs an adequate understanding of these changing dynamics while also being an important source that feeds this dynamism through the BRI agenda. The region has many internal problems and conflicts, which explains persisting non-integration. Among the factors that contribute to these problems are regional competition for leadership, corruption, weak governance and economic stagnation, tensions over water resources, ageing infrastructure, and high costs of cross-border trade. For instance, Central Asia performs weakly on the Ease of Trading across Borders Index, where out of 189 countries Kyrgyzstan is ranked number 84, Kazakhstan 123, Tajikistan 149 and Uzbekistan 168 (World Bank 2018). In fact, informal barriers to trade limit cross-border cooperation and raise trade costs in Central Asia (Vakulchuk & Irnazarov 2014; Vakulchuk, Irnazarov & Libman 2012). If they are not eliminated, these informal barriers pose a risk to China's grand strategy of improving regional connectivity through BRI.

China in Central Asia: soft power and knowledge gaps

To make BRI a success, it is important for China to understand how it is perceived in Central Asia. Despite the region's lack of integration, perceptions of and attitudes towards China are similar across all five Central Asian countries. There are mixed perceptions of China, ranging from negative to positive. Several scholars agree that there is a significant difference in the perception of China by the ruling elites and by the broader public. Elites tend to be pro-China, while the public is sceptical of Chinese economic and cultural expansion (e.g. Y – W Chen 2015; Kassenova 2017; Laruelle & Peyrouse 2012; Peyrouse 2016; Toktomushev 2018; Burkhanov 2018). And yet, there is also a perception shared by the local elites that it is risky to rely excessively on China as a source of foreign investment (Lain 2018, p. 3). Although perceptions of China are similar, there is little consensus among the Central Asian states about the degree of Chinese influence in the region (Shahbazov 2016).

Peyrouse (2016, p. 18) notes that the main message from numerous China-related surveys conducted in Central Asia is that "China remains a *challenge* for Central Asia". The region's sinophobia is viewed as one of the major stumbling blocks for BRI (Farchy 2016; Kassenova 2017). Four factors can explain sinophobic attitudes towards China among the broader public. First, during the Soviet period China was presented and perceived as a threat, and these ideas linger on. Second, the population of Central Asia remains under-informed about China's activities in general and BRI in particular (Dave 2018). This in turn feeds into the notion that China is a threat. Third, the influx of Chinese immigrants constitutes a major concern for the population (Jochec & Kyzy 2018; Garibov 2018). Fourth, religion plays a role in Central Asian attitudes towards China, as Central Asia's Muslim population is concerned about Chinese government policy in the Xinjiang Uyghur Autonomous Region.

Another stumbling block for China–Central Asia relations is that both sides have limited knowledge of each other (Peyrouse 2016). This relates both to professional ties and people-to-people relations, the latter being one of the main objectives of BRI. There are only a few think tanks and research centres in Central Asia that specialize in China studies (e.g. the China Studies Centre in the Library of the First President of Kazakhstan in Astana and the China and Central Asia Studies Centre (CCASC) at the KIMEP University in Almaty – both opened in 2017). Also, China has only started building its knowledge about the region after 2014, as part of BRI public diplomacy effort (Dave 2018). New think tanks were established in China after 2013 in order to study countries that are part of BRI (D Chen 2015). China also opened 11 Confucius Institutes across Central Asia to promote language and culture. Most of them, however, were set up prior to the launch of BRI (see Table 5.1). And yet, as Zhao Huasheng, director of the Centre for Russia and Central Asian Studies at Fudan University, notes, "I do not think China has done enough. They have work to do to create a favourable image" (Zhao cited in Farchy 2016). There is scepticism among foreign partners when China's government promotes its ideas, values and visions, as they are perceived "as pure propaganda" (D Chen 2015). Thus, there is a persistent imbalance between China's economic and soft power presence in the region.

Table 5.1 Number of Confucius Institutes in Central Asia by country

Kazakhstan	4
Kyrgyzstan	3
Tajikistan	2
Uzbekistan	2
Turkmenistan	0
Total	11

Kazakhstan and China: facts and perceptions

Kazakhstan is rich in natural resources and an important transit partner for Beijing. China has overtaken Russia to become Kazakhstan's main trade partner; however, the relationship has received much less attention than that between China and Russia (e.g. Overland & Kubayeva 2018; Lo 2008; Braekhus & Overland 2007). China stands for 16 percent of Kazakhstan's total trade, and external debt to China amounts to US$12.3 billion. Major Chinese banks such as the Bank of China and the Industrial and Commercial Bank of China operate in Kazakhstan. Chinese companies invest in Kazakhstan's extractive industries. Sinopec invested US$1.4 billion, and China International Trust and Investment Corporation (CITIC) and China Investment Corporation (CIC) recently invested US$0.95 billion. China National Petroleum Corporation (CNPC) invested more than US$12 billion in petroleum production and provided US$6.2 billion to build oil and gas pipelines in Kazakhstan to facilitate the supply of energy resources from Central Asia to China (International Centre for Trade and Sustainable Development 2016). Chinese firms control nearly a quarter of Kazakhstan's oil production (Wilson 2016). During the years 2006–2009, the Kazakhstan–China oil pipeline was built and launched. In addition, the gas pipeline Beineu–Bozoi–Shymkent helps connect small gas pipelines in Kazakhstan into one system; this in turn expands gas exports to China.

In the long run, BRI may help make Kazakhstan a major logistical hub in Central Eurasia. Kazakhstan's Nurly Zhol development programme has many of the same objectives as BRI but at a domestic Kazakh level, and the Kazakhs have agreed to coordinate it with BRI. Similar to Kyrgyzstan, Kazakhstan seeks to strengthen its mediation role in China's trade relations with the entire region through BRI. The Western Europe–Western China international transport corridor crosses the territory of Kazakhstan and is intended to play an important role in boosting Chinese trade transit through the country. Furthermore, Khorgos, an international dry port and border cooperation centre, was constructed on the Kazakh border in 2015, providing Kazakhstan with the possibility of connecting to the Chinese port of Lianyungang. Its aim is to boost cross-border trade and cooperation and reach a capacity of 500,000 cargo containers by 2020, thus becoming the world's largest dry port (*The Astana Times* 2016). The centre, ambitiously referred to as New Dubai, allows for duty-free trade and has an industrial logistics hub. The Khorgos hub can be viewed as a flagship and game-changing project of BRI, on a level with the China–Pakistan Economic Corridor (CPEC) and the Hambantota port in Sri Lanka (Dave 2018, p. 99).

In 2015–2016, five agreements were signed, aimed at creating cluster cooperation zones in transport infrastructure, trade, processing industries, construction, agriculture and other areas. Moreover, the volume of Chinese investment has increased nearly sevenfold over the last five years (*Forbes* 2017b). In 2015, China announced the transfer of 51 industrial production sites from China to Kazakhstan, a milestone in the growing Chinese engagement with Kazakhstan. As of 2017, 12 sites, mainly from the processing industry, have been transferred.

In terms of soft power, China plays a more visible role in Kazakhstan than in any other Central Asian state. Four Confucius Institutes operate in the country in collaboration with local institutions and China also became an attractive destination for outbound Kazakh students from 2008 onwards. It is ranked second after Russia as the most popular destination for Kazakh students, and in 2007, about 3,000 Kazakhs studied in China (Kaukenova 2017). In 2016, the China Scholarship Council, a government agency that assists foreign students in China, reported that the number of Kazakh students had increased nearly fourfold, to 12,000 (Farchy 2016). The share of Kazakhs who study using student loans from the Chinese government was 32.7 percent, whereas those receiving student loans from the government of Kazakhstan was only 2.7 percent (Kaukenova 2017). These statistics show a clear trend towards rising popularity for China since 2007, and yet it lags far behind Russia, which hosted 73,000 Kazakh students in 2016 (Rakhman Alshanov in *Today.kz* 2017).

In Kazakhstan it is possible to distinguish between two rough groups, which can be referred to as sinophobes and sinophiles (Peyrouse 2016, pp. 17–18). The former is represented by the political and economic elite, whereas the latter is represented mainly by the political opposition, Uyghur associations and small business representatives. These two camps can be found in all five states of Central Asia. The dynamics behind the simple duality of these two categories are much more complex (Exnerova 2018, p. 134).

Kazakhstan's political elite has been supportive of close economic ties with China (Kassenova 2017), and the government has referred to and learnt from China's economic model in the post-communist reform process (Vakulchuk 2014, p. 181). Despite China's increased economic engagement with Kazakhstan and the growing interest in studying in China among the young, the overall attitude towards China in society can be viewed as the least positive in the region. In a survey conducted by the Eurasian Development Bank, only one in six people in Kazakhstan views the big neighbour as a friend, and China is ranked among the top three unfriendliest countries (Farchy 2016).

Compared to Kazakhstan's political leaders, the expert community tends to take a more critical view of China's increasing economic expansion, and yet their analyses and views are mixed and highlight the complexity of issues involved in the bilateral relationship (Laruelle & Peyrouse 2012). According to Dosym Satpayev (cited in Farchy 2016), a Kazakh political scientist and expert,

> [s]tatistically China is a very important trade partner of Kazakhstan. But a lot of people in Kazakhstan don't think of China as a big investor. They think of China as a big problem – people here believe China tries to increase its economic influence without any benefit to our countries.

Not only society but also the expert community remains under-informed about the scope and extent of Chinese–Kazakh relations. Konstantin Syroezhkin (cited in Razumov 2016), a local sinologist, notes that "there is informational reticence [*'informacionnaja zakrytost'*] in financial and economic cooperation between

Kazakhstan and China. No contracts are published or terms for obtaining loans are disclosed . . . the official statistics fail to separate between Chinese FDI and credits". Regarding BRI in particular, Dave (2018, p. 100) quotes a local expert who noted that "everyone talks about them [BRI projects], but nobody has seen them". Kassenova (2017, p. 113) emphasizes that there is no detailed information about BRI projects in Kazakhstan and this erodes trust in the government and strengthens the perception of China as a threat.

Society also remains sensitive to other sides of Chinese expansion. In 2016, protests took place in several parts of Kazakhstan (including Atyrau, Aktobe, Semey) against new amendments in the land code pertaining to the sale of land to foreigners. Many Kazakhs raised concerns about China's purchase of land. Furthermore, disputes and clashes take place regularly between Kazakh and Chinese workers at joint ventures. The Chinese workforce is usually better paid than the local one and this causes discontent on the part of the Kazakh workforce.

Moreover, in January 2017, there was a public protest in Astana against marriages between Kazakh women and Chinese men where the protesters requested the withdrawal of the Kazakh citizenship of women who marry Chinese men. Also, the activists suggested charging Chinese men a one-time tax of US$50,000 for marrying a local woman (*Lenta* 2017). However, Svetlana Kozhirova, a local sinologist, noted that the number of Chinese marrying local women is in fact small and that local mass media tend to distort perceptions about China (Kozhirova 2017). Beate Eschment, a Central Asia expert, notes that there is a paradox: the anti-China sentiment is strong in the country, and yet it is China that can help the country fight the economic crisis by attracting finance and investment (Volkov 2016). And yet, some experts argue that there has also been a gradual positive shift in the perception of China in Kazakhstan in recent years (Razumov 2016).

Kyrgyzstan and China: facts and perceptions

In the early 1990s, Kyrgyzstan lost many of its economic ties to the other former Soviet republics. To recover from the difficult early years of independence, the country found a new niche and became a transit hub for trade between China, Kazakhstan and Russia. The latter was also facilitated by Kyrgyzstan's accession to the World Trade Organization (WTO) in 1998 and China's accession in 2001. However, Kyrgyzstan has largely lost this status, and its capacity for re-exports has been limited since it joined the Eurasian Economic Union in 2015 and adopted stricter trade rules.

Unlike Kazakhstan, where China's presence is big due to natural resources and convenient logistics, Kyrgyzstan is of less interest to China due to the small size of its market and its geographic location. Nonetheless, the Chinese presence in the country has had significant repercussions due to the economic projects promoted by Beijing. Chinese companies are involved in the construction of major roads in Kyrgyzstan; the construction of the Datka Kemin electricity transmission line worth US$389 million provided by the Chinese partner was completed in 2015;

and Chinese companies built two petrol stations in Tokmak and Kara-Balta. Chinese firms also participate in natural resource extraction (e.g. gold mining).

The major opportunity for Kyrgyzstan lies in the construction of the China–Kyrgyzstan–Uzbekistan railway, which commenced before BRI, and the Turkmenistan–China gas pipeline, both of which cross Kyrgyz territory. In particular, the railway project is seen with great hope, as it can potentially provide annual fees of US$200 million for freight transit. Moreover, if the project is implemented, it should boost transport connectivity in Kyrgyzstan and Central Asia. Kyrgyzstan and Uzbekistan seek to include the railway project under the BRI umbrella (Putz 2017). However, there are several issues that can pose a risk to this project and explain why the project has not moved forward for many years: difficulties in the adoption of technical standards and norms; the gauge width difference (1,435 mm vs. 1,520 mm);[3] sources of funding; and the Chinese requirement to provide a deposit in the form of access to natural resources in Kyrgyzstan.

While for China the bilateral projects in Kyrgyzstan are small, they are significant for Kyrgyzstan. From 2012 onwards, China became Kyrgyzstan's biggest bilateral creditor: out of US$3.7 billion external debt, US$1.4 billion was issued by the Export–Import Bank of China (Abdrisaev 2016). Through its participation in BRI, Kyrgyzstan risks getting caught in a "debt trap" (see Figure 5.1). As Fernholz (2018) notes,

> [i]n the past, China has responded to the debtors inconsistently and hasn't followed best practices adopted by international lenders working with poor countries. Sometimes, the debt has been forgiven; other times, disputed territory or control of infrastructure has been demanded as recompense.

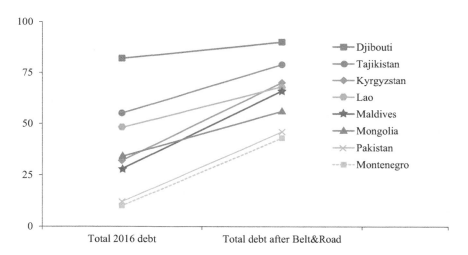

Figure 5.1 Countries at risk from BRI debt (vertical axis showing percentage of GDP)
Source: Center for Global Development in Fernholz (2018).

Debt dependency and the risk of loss of sovereignty are generally of concern for the Kyrgyz population (Jochec & Kyzy 2018). A further rise in debt due to BRI can only reinforce this concern.

China's soft power projections have had only limited influence in the country. Beijing has been mainly engaged in promoting culture-oriented and educational projects in Kyrgyzstan. In 2013, almost 2,000 students from Kyrgyzstan studied in China, while 1,000 Chinese students studied in Kyrgyzstan (*Kabar* 2013). Three Confucius Institutes have been opened on the premises of local universities.

Most of Kyrgyz society views China's cultural expansion rather negatively. A potential influx of Chinese immigrants is viewed as the most significant risk of continued Chinese investment in Kyrgyzstan (Jochec & Kyzy 2018). This has been fuelled also by clashes between local and Chinese workers at the TBEA Company, which builds electricity transmission lines.

And yet, the Chinese policy of soft power catch-up shows some positive dynamics. According to the 2017 survey of the Baltic Surveys/Gallup, about 60 percent of those surveyed assessed relations between Kyrgyzstan and China positively, and 32 percent viewed China as an economic partner. In contrast, the 2016 results showed lower numbers: 54 percent and 21 percent respectively (Siar – Consult 2017). Over time, China's soft power and public diplomacy efforts in Kyrgyzstan are likely to increase and can improve China's image in the country.

Tajikistan and China: facts and perceptions

China is one of Tajikistan's main economic partners. In 2016, the total trade turnover between the two countries amounted to US$885 million. The trade balance was largely in favour of China; more than 90 percent was Chinese imports to Tajikistan. In 2015, US$238 million or 81.2 percent of the total FDI that the country managed to attract was from China (Ulmasov 2016). Similarly to Kyrgyzstan, there is a debt trap risk for Tajikistan in case of deeper cooperation within BRI that may negatively affect the way China is perceived (see Figure 5.1).

In Tajikistan, AIIB plans to construct and expand the roads in the country, including the road that connects Tajikistan and neighbouring Uzbekistan. In 2016, AIIB and EBRD provided a direct loan worth US$55 million (US$27.5 million each) to modernize some parts of this road (EBRD 2016). This project is aimed at facilitating China's access to the markets of Central Asia, also stimulating the export of Chinese goods to the region. China has a common border with Tajikistan, and over the last several years Beijing has provided Dushanbe with a number of loans to construct roads and tunnels and modernize energy infrastructure. There are also plans for one of the branches of the Turkmenistan–China pipeline to cross Tajikistan. In 2014, CNPC and Tajiktransgas signed an agreement to start construction.

Several issues can complicate relations between the two countries and affect how China is perceived in Tajik society. The two countries have a territorial dispute in the eastern Pamirs. The first agreement on disputed territories was signed in 1999, when Tajikistan retained one piece of land but conceded another to China. In 2011, the dispute about another contentious territory was resolved: out of 28,000 square kilometres that China had initially claimed, it received 1,000 square kilometres (3% of Tajikistan's territory) in the eastern Pamirs, while Tajikistan got a partial debt write-off (Smirnov 2011; Eurasianet 2016). In 2017, the Tajik scientific community raised concerns about another possible territorial claim of China to Tajikistan: China's "policy is far beyond the goal of reaching historical fairness: the disputed land claimed by China is rich in gold and other precious metals and minerals" (*Eureporter* 2017).

As for education, two Confucius Institutes operate in the country, and about 5,000 Tajik students study in China, 400 with study loans from the Chinese government (Ulmasov 2016). Learning Chinese has become increasingly popular over the last years, especially in small towns that depend economically on Chinese companies (Tiido 2018). However, as in the other Central Asian republics, there is a degree of distrust of Beijing in Tajik society.

In general, local political elites are loyal to and supportive of China. It is commonly agreed that China can strengthen the region's stability and Beijing has also established military cooperation with Tajikistan (Shahbazov 2016). Beijing is viewed as a neighbour who is increasingly becoming an ally. At the same time, there is some indication that local entrepreneurs are unhappy about the growing Chinese economic presence (Peyrouse 2016).

The sociological surveys of 2008 and 2016 carried out by the Institute of Oriental Studies under the Academy of Sciences of the Republic of Tajikistan show a generally positive attitude of the local population towards China. According to a poll carried out in spring 2016, more than 90 percent of the respondents view Chinese engagement with Tajikistan positively (see *Central Asia Monitor* 2016). The population of Tajikistan considers China the second most attractive political and cultural partner after Russia. A comparison of attitudes in 2008 and 2016 indicates that China has gradually replaced Iran in the public eye even though Russia is still perceived as the most important partner. In 2008, only 8 percent of the surveyed people regarded China as the country projecting the biggest influence, but in 2016 this number rose to 12.5 percent. Russia's position declined from 89 percent in 2008 to 75.4 percent in 2016. Iran was seen as most influential by 9 percent in 2008 and by only 5.3 percent in 2016.

However, there is little evidence that BRI has changed the perception of China among the Tajiks much after 2013. Unlike Kazakhstan, where the BRI has spurred an active discussion of the role of China, BRI has gained less attention in Tajik society. Even though China is perceived more positively than before, this change has not been significant and Chinese–Tajik cooperation has not been widely discussed by the media or the expert community since 2013. The population remains poorly informed about BRI. The form of interaction between the governments of two countries has remained largely unaltered: closed high-level political meetings with little disclosure of information to the broader public.

Turkmenistan and China: facts and perceptions

Turkmenistan is known for being a reclusive state and one of the least accessible countries in the world. Despite this, the country has continuously developed its relations with China since 1991. Official status as a non-aligned state helps Turkmenistan remain autonomous in its foreign policy and so the close relations with China have been an exception in Ashgabat's largely isolationist foreign policy.

Energy in general and the supply of natural gas from Turkmenistan to China in particular are at the core of bilateral relations between the two states. At present, China absorbs more than half of Turkmenistan's natural gas exports. By May 2016, Turkmenistan had cumulatively supplied China with 138.6 billion cubic metres of natural gas (*Neftegaz* 2016). The Turkmenistan–China pipeline has three pipes and a fourth pipe is planned, which would bring the total capacity to 74–80 billion cubic metres. Turkmenistan is expected to play an important role in China's energy supply and energy security in the next decade, in line with BRI objectives and China's economic development goals. By 2030, China seeks to import 270 billion cubic metres of natural gas, up from 53 billion in 2015 (Solovieva 2016).

We should note the high degree of economic dependence of Turkmenistan on China. For Turkmenistan there is a risk of financial over-dependence on China (Lain 2018, p. 3). Turkmen natural gas exports to China can be viewed as compensation for the millions of credits it has received from Beijing. In 2011, China provided credit worth US$8 billion and issued another one in 2013. The trade turnover between China and Turkmenistan reached US$10 billion in 2013 but dropped to US$5.9 billion in 2016 (*Chronicles of Turkmenistan* 2017). Currently, more than 40 Chinese companies operate in Turkmenistan.

Turkmenistan is the only country in the region that has no Confucius Institute; however, a Turkmenistan Centre was established at the Oil University in Xi'an, China, in May 2017 (*Turkmenistan Today* 2017). This is the second study centre, as the first one was established in China in 2014. In 2014, about 1,500 students from Turkmenistan studied at Chinese universities (Izimov 2016). Given the limited information available, it is difficult to identify the perceptions and views of China by the local population.

Uzbekistan and China: facts and perceptions

Along with Kazakhstan, Uzbekistan is one of the economic locomotives of Central Asia. Even during the years of isolationist policy under former president Islam Karimov, Uzbekistan sought to deepen its trade and economic ties with China. In 2015, the trade volume reached nearly US$3 billion, higher than Tashkent's overall trade with Russia. In 2016, the trade volume reached US$4.2 billion. The two countries agreed to increase their bilateral trade by US$10 billion by 2020 (*Sputnik Uzbekistan* 2017a). Energy is an important part of bilateral cooperation, and in 2013 the two countries signed deals worth US$15 billion for the development of oil, gas, and uranium fields in Uzbekistan (*South China Morning Post* 2013).

Uzbekistan is an attractive economic partner for China, as it has one of the most diversified economies in Central Asia. In total, Chinese firms have invested about US$8 billion in the Uzbek economy since 1991. China also acted as donor, providing grants amounting to US$285 million for the implementation of more than 40 projects in the areas of health care, education, agriculture, water resources and labour. More than 700 companies, both Chinese and joint ventures, are engaged in oil and gas exploration, pipeline construction, transport infrastructure, telecommunications, textiles, irrigation, and new sources of energy in Uzbekistan.

According to the Uzbek National News Agency (*Uza* 2016), several big investment projects are being developed. One of them is a high-technology park in the Jizzakh special industrial zone formed in 2013. Uzbekistan also plays an important role as part of BRI, in particular in joint transport and logistics projects. The completion of the electrified Angren–Pap Railway in 2016 connected the Ferghana valley with central parts of the country. This railway will also be an important part of regional BRI-related connectivity plans. Using this railway, China should also gain easier access to Central Asia and ultimately South and Western Asia and Europe.

As for culture and education, the Chinese Central University for Nationalities opened an Uzbek Language Department. The Uzbek language is also taught at Beijing University, and an Uzbekistan Center and education-related exchange programme were launched at Shanghai University (*Central Asia Monitor* 2016). Two Confucius Institutes operate in Uzbekistan. The first opened in Tashkent in 2004 and was the first to be established in Central Asia.[4] In 2014–2015, the Chinese government provided a grant to 120 Uzbek students and interns as part of a bilateral agreement under the auspices of the Shanghai Cooperation Organization (SCO). In addition, 50 Uzbek students studied at the Lanzhou University as part of the Confucius Institute programme (*Sputnik Uzbekistan* 2017b).

There is still a gap between economy and culture when it comes to China's presence in Uzbekistan. Uzbek society has a vague understanding of China. The isolationist policy of Karimov's government contributed to this. Also, since 1991, South Korea more than China has been the role model for the Uzbek government. Chen and Günther (2016) found that the perception of China at the individual level has not been affected by BRI. They analyzed statistics from Google Trends and the Yandex search engine and found that there has not been a significant change in Uzbeks' interest in China since 2013. Chen and Günther (2016) concluded that "[l]ocal Uzbekistanis' perception of China varies depending on the issue. Respondents seem to have some impression of China's increasing cultural, economic and political influences. However, they do not necessarily know details of projects, such as the OBOR". There is a lack of think tanks and research centres that specialize in Chinese issues and systematically inform the public about the country.

Has BRI changed China's image in Central Asia?

Since BRI was announced as China's grand strategy in 2013 and the first BRI projects were launched, there has not been a major change in the perception of

China in Central Asia. Beijing's ties with the region have political and economic roots dating back to the early 1990s, and BRI has not yet become a game changer for local attitudes towards the big neighbour. The current perceptions of China, although mixed, were largely formed within the framework of bilateral relations that started in 1991. However, the announcement of BRI has expanded the discussion of China and its role in the region among Central Asians.

Analysing the region's perceptions of China and BRI, we can see similar patterns across all five Central Asia countries. There are some differences, but they are not significant. Each country is attracted by Chinese economic projects and educational opportunities; but there is also a persistent anti-Chinese sentiment across Central Asia related to potential Chinese demographic and cultural expansion and increased financial debt dependence that may follow economic expansion.

In the long run, BRI can boost infrastructure development among Central Asian countries and facilitate trade among them and with third countries. This can pave the way for a more positive attitude towards China. However, without more transparency, the more China is involved economically in the region through BRI, the more likely it will face resistance from the broader public (Sternberg, Ahearn, McConnell 2017; Dave 2018). Chen and Günther (2016) note that local perceptions of China in Uzbekistan are unlikely to change if the population remains poorly connected to the high-level political interaction on BRI. This also applies to other countries of Central Asia.

The local authorities have been passive and unsystematic in informing the public about ongoing projects with China. The expert community in Central Asia has also been critical of the general lack of information and transparency of Chinese investment and business activities in the region. Therefore, while the broader public expects more economic opportunities from BRI, it remains under-informed and concerned about the consequences of further Chinese economic expansion.

Chinese actors need to carry out more proactive information campaigns that reach not only to the local elites but also to the broader public. This is easier said than done. First, Chinese businesses have been criticized for their lack of transparent approach as well as corrupt practices when doing business in other parts of the world (e.g. in Africa; see Geerts, Xinwa, Rossouw 2014). Second, there is also a challenge of limited policy coordination between the Chinese central government and regional authorities (Stokke, Vakulchuk & Overland 2018). Regional Chinese authorities in the border regions often pursue their own agenda, which may differ from that of the central government. Therefore, the official Beijing position may be at odds with the day-to-day practices of local Chinese authorities as well as Chinese entrepreneurs. Regular practices are what shape perceptions; the official position is viewed more as propaganda if practices do not support it.

The Confucius Institutes have so far been ineffective as soft power instruments and do not appear to have improved China's image in Central Asia (Nursha 2018, p. 142). The increasing number of Central Asian students in China is unlikely to have an immediate effect and drastically change local perceptions of China.

However, in the long term the Confucius Institutes and especially the Central Asians studying in China may become game changers. As growing numbers of Central Asians learn to speak and read Chinese and/or have positive personal experiences of living in Chinese society, perceptions may shift on a larger scale.

The region's continuing internal challenges and lack of integration can threaten the BRI's sustainability. However, the replacement of Islam Karimov by Shavkat Mirziyoyev as President of Uzbekistan may change this picture. Uzbekistan is the most populous and most centrally located country in the region. The far more positive stance of Mirziyoyev towards trade and cooperation with the neighbouring countries is highly convenient for China's BRI initiative and may lay the ground for its acceleration.

Last but not least, a concern shared by many in Central Asia is that "the economic benefits felt by local populations in Central Asia will not be as substantive as the Chinese BRI vision suggests – namely, if projects and investments are not managed properly" (Lain 2018, p. 2). Some Chinese entrepreneurs have also questioned the success of BRI and complained about widespread corruption, weak governance, and limited local capacity to manage large-scale investment projects. As Laruelle (2018, p. xi) points out, "like all foreign investors, they are evidently not immune to the region's ills". Moreover, a rapid increase in BRI-related investment in the region may strengthen bad governance and corruption, provoke rent-seeking behaviour and competition among various interest groups (Cooley & Heathershaw 2017; Toktomushev 2018). Therefore, the success of BRI in Central Asia depends on the region's ability to tackle internal challenges as well as China's ability and preparedness to assist the countries in meeting their development goals and overcoming internal weaknesses.

Notes

1 The Central Asian Nuclear–Weapon-Free Zone (CANWFZ) treaty is a legally binding commitment by Kazakhstan, Kyrgyzstan, Tajikistan, Turkmenistan, and Uzbekistan not to produce, acquire, test, or possess nuclear weapons.
2 The Great Game is the analytical concept used to portray a contest among big powers such as the United States, Russia, and China for influence in Central Asia. The concept dates to the 19th century, when the Russian and British Empires were competing for the region that is today's Central Asia and Afghanistan.
3 A solution to gauge width difference was found at the dry port of Khorgos in Kazakhstan, where both the Chinese and the Kazakh gauge width standards apply. In Khorgos, goods delivered by Chinese trains are reloaded on to local Kazakh trains before they can be transported further.
4 Moreover, it is the only institute in the world that was opened according to the agreement signed during a visit to a foreign country by the President of People's Republic of China.

Bibliography

Abdrisaev, E 2016, 'Госдолг Кыргызстана и ситуация зарубежных стран' (Kyrgyzstan's external debt and the situation in foreign countries), *Kabar*, 17 October. Available from: www.kabar.kg/kabar/full/112595. [22 March 2018].

Amighini, A 2017. *China's Belt and Road: a game changer?* The Italian Institute for International Political Studies (ISPI), Milan.

Arduino, A 2017. 'China's energy interests in Central Asia and Russia' in F Wu & H Zhang (eds), *China's global quest for resources: Energy, food and water*, pp. 119–138. Routledge, Abingdon.

The Astana Times 2016. 'Economy news in brief', 9 November. Available from: https://astanatimes.com/wp-content/uploads/2016/11/111.pdf. [22 March 2018].

Braekhus, K & Overland, I 2007. 'A match made in heaven? Strategic convergence between China and Russia', *China and Eurasia Forum Quarterly*, vol. 5, no. 2, pp. 41–61. Available from: www.researchgate.net/publication/265455681.

Burkhanov, A 2018. 'The impact of Chinese Silk Road strategy on national identity issues in Central Asia. A media review', in M Laruelle (ed), *China's Belt and Road initiative and its impact in Central Asia*, pp. 153–161. The George Washington University, Washington, DC.

Central Asia Monitor 2016, 'Эксперты: "Китай вызывает чувство восхищения и страха в Азии"' (Experts: 'China inspires fascination and causes fear in Asia'), 12 August. Available from: https://camonitor.kz/24846-eksperty-kitay-vyzyvaet-chuvstvo-voshischeniya-i-straha-v-azii.html. [22 March 2018].

Chen, D 2015. 'The rise of China's new soft power', *The Diplomat*, 9 June. Available from: https://thediplomat.com/2015/06/the-rise-of-chinas-new-soft-power/. [22 March 2018].

Chen, D & Günther, O 2016, 'China's influence in Uzbekistan: model neighbor or indifferent partner?' Jamestown Foundation. *China Brief*, vol. 16, no. 17, pp. 11–14.

Chen, Y-W 2015, 'A research note on Central Asian perspectives on the rise of China: the example of Kazakhstan', *Issues & Studies*, vol. 51, no. 3, pp. 63–87.

Chronicles of Turkmenistan 2017. 'Товарооборот Туркменистана с Китаем в денежном эквиваленте значительно сократился' (Trade turnover in value between Turkmenistan and China has decreased), 6 January. Available from: www.chrono-tm.org/2017/01/tovarooborot-turkmenistana-s-kitaem-v-denezhnom-ekvivalente/. [22 March 2018].

Cooley, A 2012, *Great games, local rules*. Oxford University Press, Oxford.

Cooley, A & Heathershaw, J 2017, *Dictators without borders: power and money in Central Asia*. Yale University Press, New Haven, CT.

Dave, B 2018, 'Silk Road economic belt: effects of China's soft power diplomacy in Kazakhstan', in M Laruelle (ed), *China's Belt and Road initiative and its impact in Central Asia*, pp. 97–108. The George Washington University, Washington, DC.

EBRD 2016, 'Road project in Tajikistan becomes first joint EBRD-AIIB investment', *European Bank for Reconstruction and Development (EBRD)*, 24 June. Available from: www.ebrd.com/news/2016/road-project-in-tajikistan-becomes-first-joint-ebrdaiib-investment.html. [22 March 2018].

Ehteshami, A & Horesh, N 2018. *China's presence in the Middle East. The implications of the One Belt, One Road initiative.* Routledge, Abingdon.

Eurasianet 2016, 'Tajikistan, Turkmenistan submit to Chinese capture', 24 June. Available from: https://eurasianet.org/node/79401. [22 March 2018].

Eureporter 2017, 'China territorial claims cause unease in Tajikistan', 23 April. Available from: www.eureporter.co/frontpage/2017/04/23/china-territorial-claims-cause-unease-in-tajikistan/. [22 March 2018].

Exnerova, V 2018. 'Transnational ties and local society's role in improving the PRC's image in Central Asia', in M Laruelle (ed), *China's Belt and Road initiative and its impact in Central Asia*, pp. 126–134. The George Washington University, Washington, DC.

Farchy, J 2016, 'Kazakh language schools shift from English to Chinese', *Financial Times*, 9 May. Available from: www.ft.com/content/6ce4a6ac-0c85-11e6-9456-444ab5211a2f. [22 March 2018].

Fernholz, T 2018, 'Eight countries in danger of falling into China's "debt trap"', *Quartz*, 7 March. Available from: https://qz.com/1223768/china-debt-trap-these-eight-countries-are-in-danger-of-debt-overloads-from-chinas-belt-and-road-plans/. [22 March 2018].

Forbes 2017a, 'За 25 лет товарооборот Китая со странами ЦА вырос в 60 раз' (Over 25 years' trade turnover between China and Central Asian countries has grown up to 60 times), 11 January. Available from: https://forbes.kz/news/2017/01/11/newsid_132050. [22 March 2018].

Forbes 2017b. 'Объем китайских инвестиций в Казахстан вырос в 7 раз' (The volume of Chinese investment has risen seven times), 26 January. Available from: https://forbes.kz/news/2017/01/26/newsid_133690. [22 March 2018].

Garibov, A 2018. 'Contemporary Chinese labor migration and its public perception in Kazakhstan and Kyrgyzstan', in M Laruelle (ed), *China's Belt and Road initiative and its impact in Central Asia*, pp. 143–152. The George Washington University, Washington, DC.

Geerts, S, Xinwa, N & Rossouw, D 2014. *African's perception of Chinese business in Africa: a survey*. Ethics Institute of South Africa, Pretoria.

Indeo, F 2017. 'A comprehensive strategy to strengthening China's relations with Central Asia', in A Amighini (ed), *China's Belt and Road: a game changer?* pp. 35–51. The Italian Institute for International Political Studies (ISPI), Milan.

International Centre for Trade and Sustainable Development 2016, 'Китай наращивает инвестиции в Казахстан' (China augments investment in Kazakhstan), 28 January. Available from: www.ictsd.org/bridges-news/мосты/news/китай-наращивает-инвестиции-в-казахстан. [22 March 2018].

Izimov, R 2016, 'Руслан Изимов: Китай и Туркменистан: региональное измерение' (Ruslan Izimov: China and Turkmenistan: regional dimension), Central Asian Bureau for Analytical Reporting,17 August. Available from: http://cabar.asia/ru/ruslan-izimov-kitaj-i-turkmenistan-regionalnoe-izmerenie/. [22 March 2018].

Jochec, M & Kyzy, JJ 2018, 'China's BRI investments, risks, and opportunities in Kazakhstan and Kyrgyzstan', in M Laruelle (ed), *China's Belt and Road initiative and its impact in Central Asia*, pp. 67–76. The George Washington University, Washington, DC.

Kabar 2013, 'Интервью Посла КНР в Кыргызстане' (The interview of the ambassador of PRC in Kyrgyzstan), 6 September. Available from: http://old.kabar.kg/rus/kabar/full/62269. [22 March 2018].

Kassenova, N 2017, 'China's Silk Road and Kazakhstan's bright path: linking dreams of prosperity. *Asia Policy*, vol. 24, pp. 110–116.

Kaukenova, T 2017, 'Учеба в Китае: чего хотят и что получают наши студенты' (Studying in China: what do our students want and what do they get), *Zakon*, 2 March. Available from: www.zakon.kz/4846930-ucheba-v-kitae-chego-khotjat-i-chto.html. [22 March 2018].

Kim, Y & Indeo, F 2013, 'The new great game in Central Asia post 2014: the US "New Silk Road" strategy and Sino-Russian rivalry', *Communist and Post-Communist Studies*, vol. 46, no. 2, pp. 275–286.

Kozhirova, S 2017, 'Светлана Кожирова: Миф о том, что китайские женихи мечтают увезти из Казахстана казашек – это глупость' (Svetlana Kozhirova: the myth that Chinese men dream to take Kazakh ladies away from Kazakhstan – is foolishness), *IA-Centre*, 15 May. Available from: http://new.ia-centr.ru/experts/valeriy-surganov/svetlana-kozhirova-mif-o-tom-chto-kitayskie-zhenikhi-mechtayut-uvezti-iz-kazakhstana-kazashek-eto-gl/. [22 March 2018].

Lain, S 2018. 'The potential and pitfalls of connectivity along the Silk Road Economic Belt', in M Laruelle (ed), *China's Belt and Road initiative and its impact in Central Asia*, pp. 1–10. The George Washington University, Washington, DC.

Laruelle, M 2018. 'Introduction. China's Belt and Road initiative. Quo Vadis?', in M Laruelle (ed), *China's Belt and Road initiative and its impact in Central Asia*, pp. x–xii. The George Washington University, Washington, DC.

Laruelle, M & Peyrouse, S 2012. *The Chinese question in Central Asia: domestic order, social change, and the Chinese factor*. Columbia University Press, New York.

Lenta 2017, 'В Астане прошел митинг против браков казахских девушек с китайцами' (The protest against the marriages between Kazakh women and Chinese men took place in Astana), 11 January. Available from: https://lenta.ru/news/2017/01/11/astana/. [22 March 2018].

Lim, TW, Chan, H, Tseng, K & Lim, WX 2016. *China's One Belt One Road initiative*. Imperial College Press, London.

Lo, B 2008, *Axis of convenience: Moscow, Beijing, and the new geopolitics*. Brookings Institution, Washington, DC.

Neftegaz 2016, 'Китай получил 138,6 млрд м3 газа из Туркменистана по сети газопроводов Центральная Азия – Китай' (China received 138.6 billion cubic metres of gas from Turkmenistan through the Central Asia-China network of gas pipelines), 26 May. Available from: https://neftegaz.ru/news/view/149466-Kitay-poluchil-1386-mlrd-m3-gaza-iz-Turkmenistana-po-seti-gazoprovodov-Tsentralnaya-Aziya-Kitay. [22 March 2018].

Nursha, G 2018. 'Chinese soft power in Kazakhstan and Kyrgyzstan: a Confucius Institutes case study', in M Laruelle (ed), *China's Belt and Road initiative and its impact in Central Asia*, pp. 135–142. The George Washington University, Washington, DC.

Overland, I & Kubayeva, G 2018, 'Did China bankroll Russia's annexation of Crimea? The role of Sino-Russian energy relations', in Helge Blakkisrud & Elana Wilson Rowe (eds), *Russia's turn to the East: Domestic policymaking and regional cooperation*. Palgrave, Cham, pp. 95–118. Available from: www.researchgate.net/publication/322158372.

Owen, C 2016, 'Chinese expansion in Central Asia: problems and perspectives', *The Foreign Policy Centre (FPC)*. Available from: https://fpc.org.uk/chinese-expansion-in-central-asia-problems-and-perspectives/. [22 March 2018].

Peyrouse, S 2016, 'Discussing China: sinophilia and sinophobia in Central Asia', *Journal of Eurasian Studies*, vol. 7, pp. 14–23.

Putz, C 2017, 'What's next for the Belt and Road in Central Asia?' *The Diplomat*, 17 May. Available from: https://thediplomat.com/2017/05/whats-next-for-the-belt-and-road-in-central-asia/. [22 March 2018].

Razumov, Y 2016, 'Казахстан и Китай – сближение или имитация?' (Kazakhstan and China – rapprochement or imitation?), *Global Affairs*, 31 May. Available from: www.globala airs.ru/global-processes/Kazakhstan-i-Kitai – sblizhenie-ili-imitatciya-18190. [22 March 2018].

Shahbazov, F 2016. 'China's economic and military expansion in Tajikistan', *The Diplomat*, 23 November. Available from: https://thediplomat.com/2016/11/chinas-economic-and-military-expansion-in-tajikistan/. [22 March 2018].

Siar-Consult 2017, 'Public opinion survey. Residents of Kyrgyzstan, February 15 – March 2, 2017'. Baltic Surveys, The Gallup Organization, SIAR Research and Consulting, 2 May. Available from: http://siar-consult.com/wp-content/uploads/2017/04/Kyrgyzstan-Poll-Winter-2017-Public.pdf. [22 March 2018].

Smirnov, S 2011, 'Китай отщепил часть Таджикистана' (China nibbled part of Tajikistan), *Gazeta*, 13 January. Available from: www.gazeta.ru/politics/2011/01/12_kz_3489206.shtml. [22 March 2018].

Solovieva, O 2016, 'В Китае российский газ не ждут' (China does not expect Russian gas), *Nezavisimaya Gazeta*, 12 August. Available from: www.ng.ru/economics/2016-08-12/1_gas.html. [22 March 2018].

South China Morning Post 2013, 'Xi Jinping signs deals worth USD 15b in Uzbekistan', 9 September. Available from: www.scmp.com/news/china/article/1307127/china-uzbekistan-sign-agreements-worth-us15-billion. [22 March 2018].

Sputnik Uzbekistan 2017a, 'Узбекистан и Китай намерены довести товарооборот до $10 млрд' (Uzbekistan and China seek to expand trade turnover to USD 10 billion), 24 March. Available from: http://ru.sputniknews-uz.com/economy/20170324/5043655/Uzbekistan-i-Kitai-dovedut-tovarooborot-do-10-mlrd.html. [22 March 2018].

Sputnik Uzbekistan 2017b, 'У Узбекистана и Китая схожие позиции по многим вопросам' (Uzbekistan and China have similar takes on many issues), 21 June. Available from: http://ru.sputniknews-uz.com/politics/20160621/3082694.html. [22 March 2018].

Sternberg, T, Ahearn, A & McConnell, F 2017, 'Central Asian "characteristics" on China's New Silk Road: the role of landscape and the politics of infrastructure', *Land*, vol. 6, no. 55, pp. 1–16.

Stokke, K, Vakulchuk, R & Overland, I 2018. *Myanmar: A political economy analysis*. Norwegian Institute of International Affairs (NUPI) Report. Available from: www.researchgate.net/publication/323018961 [22 March 2018].

Tiido, A 2018, 'Language as a soft power tool in Central Asia', *Intersection*, 23 February. Available from: http://intersectionproject.eu/article/russia-world/language-soft-power-tool-central-asia. [22 March 2018].

Today.kz 2017, 'Каждый пятый казахстанский студент учится за границей' (Every fifth Kazakh student studies abroad), 23 August. Available from: http://today.kz/news/kazakhstan/2017-08-23/748787-kazhdyij-pyatyij-kazahstanskij-student-uchitsya-za-granitsej/. [22 March 2018].

Toktomushev, K 2018. 'One Belt, One Road: a new source of rent for ruling elites in Central Asia?', in M Laruelle (ed), *China's Belt and Road initiative and its impact in Central Asia*, pp. 77–85. The George Washington University, Washington, DC.

Turkmenistan Today 2017, 'Turkmenistan's center was opened in Xi'an city of the people's Republic of China', 26 May. Available from: http://tdh.gov.tm/news/en/articles.aspx&article7217&cat30 [22 March 2018].

Ulmasov, D 2016, 'Интервью посла Китая в Таджикистане Юе Бинь' (The interview of Yue Bin, the Ambassador of China to Tajikistan), *Ariana*, 7 September. Available from: www.ariana.su/?S=5.1609071136. [22 March 2018].

Uza 2016, 'Uzbekistan – China: new stage of cooperation – comprehensive strategic partnership', 23 June. Available from: www.uza.uz/en/politics/uzbekistan-china-new-stage-of-cooperation-comprehensive-stra-23-06-2016. [22 March 2018].

Vakulchuk, R 2014, *Kazakhstan's emerging economy: between state and market.* Peter Lang, Frankfurt/Main. Available from: www.researchgate.net/publication/299731455.

Vakulchuk, R & Irnazarov, F 2014, 'Analysis of informal obstacles to cross-border economic activity in Kazakhstan and Uzbekistan', ADB Working Paper, Series on Regional Economic Integration, No. 130. Asian Development Bank, Manila. Available from: www.researchgate.net/publication/323143800.

Vakulchuk, R, Irnazarov, F & Libman, A 2012, 'Liberalization of trade in services in Kazakhstan and Uzbekistan: analysis of formal and informal barriers'. Economic Education and Research Consortium (EERC), Working Paper No 12/06E. Available from: www.researchgate.net/publication/265008696.

Volkov, V 2016, 'Волна протестов в Казахстане: земельный вопрос как повод?' (The wave of protests in Kazakhstan: the land issue as a pretext?), *Deutsche Welle*, 6 May. Available from: www.dw.com/ru/волна-протестов-в-казахстане-земельный-вопрос-как-повод/a-19239492. [22 March 2018].

Wilson, WT 2016, 'China's huge "One Belt, One Road" initiative is sweeping Central Asia', *The National Interest*, 27 July. Available from: http://nationalinterest.org/feature/chinas-huge-one-belt-one-road-initiative-sweeping-central-17150. [22 March 2018].

World Bank 2018, *Trading across borders.* Available from: www.doingbusiness.org/data/exploretopics/trading-across-borders. [22 March 2018].

Xin, WL 2016. 'China's One Belt One Road initiative: a literature review', in TW Lim, H Chan, K Tseng & WL Xim (eds), *China's One Belt One Road initiative*, pp. 113–132. Imperial College Press, London.

Yilmaz, S & Changming, L 2018, 'China's "Belt and Road" strategy in Eurasia and Euro-Atlanticism', *Europe-Asia Studies*, vol. 70, no. 2, pp. 252–276.

6 The Belt and Road Initiative and Cambodia's infrastructure connectivity development

A Cambodian perspective

Lak Chansok

Introduction

Cambodia and China have always had a close relationship. The late Cambodian King Father Norodom Sihanouk was a close friend of China's Prime Minister Zhou Enlai, who provided him a place stay in Beijing after he was deposed from power by General Lon Nol and Prince Sirikmatak in 1970 (Zhai 2000). Zhou Enlai facilitated Sihanouk's return to Cambodia afterwards. After the Khmer Rouge period, China continued to be a close friend of, and ally to, Cambodia by being one of the 19 key signatories of the 1991 Paris Peace Accords. These were agreements on a comprehensive political settlement to Cambodia's prolonged conflicts, which returned both peace and political stability to Cambodia after decades of civil war. Many scholars refer to Cambodia's post1990s period as the "renaissance" of "Chineseness" in Cambodia, due to the swift rise of the Sino–Khmer economic and cultural activities there (Verver 2012; Nyiri & Tan 2017). China became even closer friends with Cambodia in this period, as is evident through the increasing military and development assistance and private investment. From 2006 to 2010 alone, it was reported that Cambodia had approved US$6 billion of Chinese investment, and at least another US$2 billion in grant aids and loans were approved by China (Chap 2010). Since 2010, China has been the top investor in Cambodia, contributing 29.92 percent of US$3.6 billion of the total investment in Cambodia in 2016 (The Council for the Development of Cambodia 2017). In 2017, it was estimated that bilateral trade between the countries would increase by 5 percent annually (Open Development Cambodia 2016).

This close Sino–Cambodia relationship has recently been enhanced to a strategic level, offering both countries the possibility of benefitting diplomatically, economically, and politically. In 2013, Chinese President Xi Jinping kicked off a grand and ambitious initiative to establish the land-based Silk Road Economic Belt and the sea-based 21st-Century Maritime Silk Road, together called the Belt and Road Initiative (BRI) (Xi 2013). Both initiatives primarily aim to promote regional connectivity, facilitate economic cooperation, enhance cultural exchanges, deepen mutual understanding, and establish mutually beneficial ties between China, Europe, and Africa with Southeast Asia as a crucial strategic partner not merely in providing port facilities but also in importing and exporting goods to the growing markets, specifically across the sea-based 21st-Century Maritime Silk Road.

With the establishment of the BRI, Cambodia, as a fast-growing member of the Association of Southeast Asian Nations (ASEAN), stands at a very critical juncture in the linkage of Asian connectivity. It is believed that the materialized BRI will provide Cambodia with a golden opportunity to develop its infrastructure and strengthen its economic competitiveness.

Sino–Cambodia relations in the context of the BRI

The bilateral relations of Cambodia and China go back 2,000 years when Chinese envoy Zhou Daguan came to visit Angkor of the Khmer Empire and recorded the prosperous Khmer history (Chandler & Harris 2007). The bilateral relations of these two countries became diplomatically and politically closer starting in the 1950s, when Norodom Sihanouk approached Chinese Prime Minister Zhou Enlai for assistance, especially after the coup d'état in Cambodia in 1970 (Zhai 2000). After the 1991 Paris Peace Accords, and especially after the 1997 clashes, Cambodia and China cultivated their close diplomatic, political, and economic ties. In 2006, China and Cambodia reached an agreement on a Comprehensive Partnership for Cooperation and upgraded it to a Comprehensive Strategic Partnership of Cooperation in 2010, seen as a milestone of deep, comprehensive, and all- round cooperation between the countries. Since the 2000s, China has increasingly become Cambodia's major investor. In this connection, Hong Kong, a Special Autonomous Region (SAR), has also been Cambodia's crucial export market, followed by mainland China and Macao. China has become the most significant import market for Cambodia (Figures 6.1 and 6.2). Bilateral trade is expected to rise gradually, especially when the BRI development projects are successfully materialized to promote and enhance regional infrastructure connectivity, which will benefit regional economic transactions.

Since 2011, China has been the top investor in Cambodia, followed by Japan, Thailand, South Korea, the United States, Australia, Singapore, Malaysia, and other countries (Table 6.1). China's investment capital alone accounted for 29.92 percent of the total investment in Cambodia in 2016, 2.37 percent more than the investment of Cambodia (Table 6.1). In addition, of the 6,321 registered companies in Cambodia in 2015, China has always ranked first with its 1,055 registered companies legally operating their businesses nationwide in Cambodia both inside and outside the Special Economic Zones (SEZs), attractive special areas for the development of various economic sectors bringing together industrial and other related economic activities. These were specifically established by the Cambodian government in December 2005, in order to attract more foreign direct investment, create more local job opportunities, and increase Cambodia's long-term economic development (Figures 6.3–6.6).

In addition to the economic relationship, since the late 1990s, China has been one of Cambodia's major donors. In 2014, Chinese President Xi Jinping

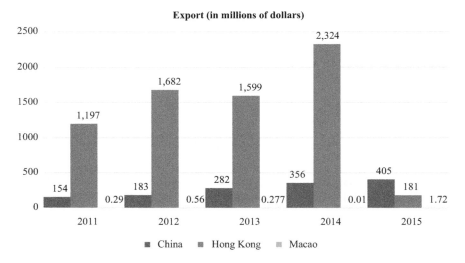

Figure 6.1 China–Cambodia trade (export)
Source: Suon (2016).

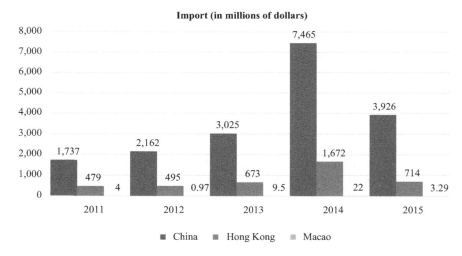

Figure 6.2 China–Cambodia trade (import)
Source: Suon (2016).

pledged to provide Cambodia with generous assistance between US$500 million and US$700 million (Radio Free Asia 2014). China's aid and assistance is not confined exclusively to financial aid packages. Since 2009, about 200 Cambodian cadets have been admitted to four-year courses provided by both

Table 6.1 Investment trend in Cambodia

Investment Capital by Country

Year	2012		2013		2014		2015		2016	
Total	$2.9 Billion		$4.9 Billion		$3.9 Billion		$4.6 Billion		$3.6 Billion	
Rank	Country	%	Country	%	Country	%	Country	%	Country	%
1	Cambodia	42.08	Cambodia	66.80	Cambodia	64.00	Cambodia	69.28	China	29.92
2	China	20.69	China	15.68	China	24.44	China	18.62	Cambodia	27.55
3	Korea	9.89	Vietnam	6.10	Malaysia	2.18	U.K	3.0	Japan	22.78
4	Japan	9.15	Thailand	4.37	Japan	1.72	Singapore	2.18	Thailand	4.61
5	Malaysia	6.04	Korea	1.76	Korea	1.66	Vietnam	1.92	Korea	4.59
6	Thailand	4.53	Japan	1.59	Vietnam	1.26	Malaysia	1.61	US	3.38
7	Vietnam	2.89	Malaysia	1.04	UK	1.13	Japan	1.28	Singapore	3.03
8	Singapore	2.59	Singapore	1.03	Singapore	0.89	Thailand	1.18	Vietnam	2.45
9	UK	0.51	UK	0.43	Thailand	0.88	Korea	0.21	Korea	0.21
10	US	0.42	France	0.27	Australia	0.51	Canada	0.19	India	0.55
11	Others	1.21	Others	0.93	Others	1.33	Other	0.53	Others	0.54

Source: The Council for the Development of Cambodia (2017).

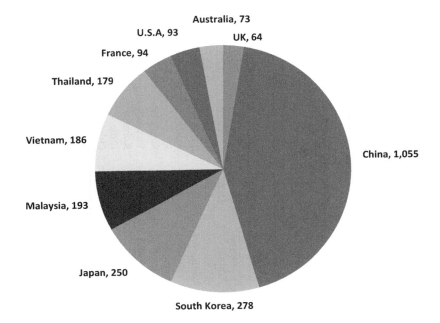

Figure 6.3 Registered companies in Cambodia in 2015
Source: Suon (2016).

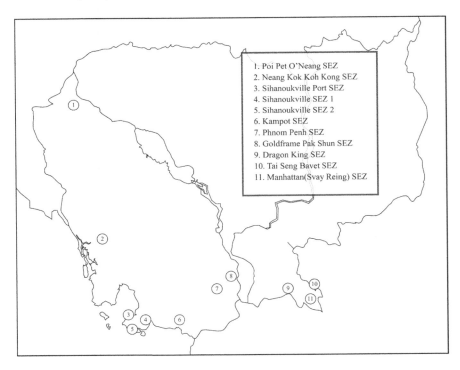

Figure 6.4 Cambodia's Special Economic Zones (SEZs)
Source: Compiled by author.

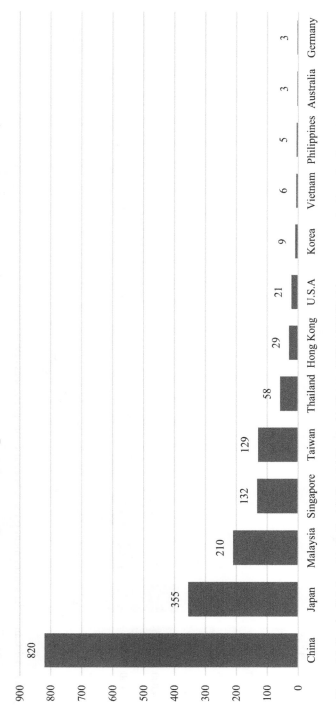

Total QIPs inside Special Economic Zone (1994–1st half of 2016)

Figure 6.5 Cambodia's investment inside Special Economic Zones (1994–2016)

Source: Suon (2016).

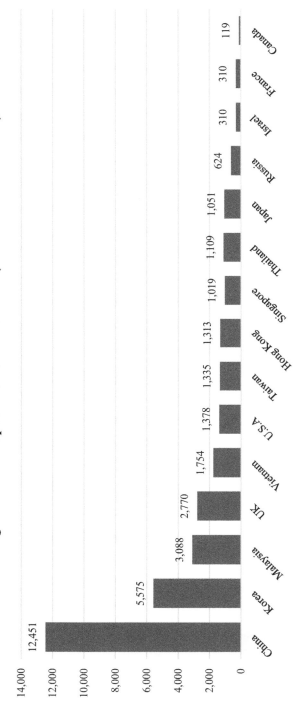

Figure 6.6 Cambodia's investment outside Special Economic Zones (1994–2016)
Source: Suon (2016).

China's Defence Ministry and advisors, of which compulsory six-month military training is conducted at military academies in China (Belford & Prak 2015). In 2013, China provided Cambodia with twelve military-grade helicopters worth US$195 million in loans. In 2014, China offered 26 trucks and 30,000 military uniforms to Cambodia's Defence Ministry. Moreover, a military training facility in Kampong Speu Province and a few joint military exercises between the two countries even in the South China Sea were technically and financially supported by China (Open Development Cambodia 2016). Since November 2015, China has pledged to increase its already substantial military support for Cambodia. Due to this immense non-conditional assistance, Cambodian Prime Minister Hun Sen used to describe China as "the most trustworthy friend" for Cambodia, and Chinese President Xi described Cambodia as a "good neighbour, like a brother" and "good friend with sincerity" in the Southeast Asian region (Var 2016).

In 2014, during the bilateral meeting with Chinese President Xi Jinping in Shanghai, Cambodian Prime Minister Hun Sen voiced strong support for China's BRI projects in order to promote and enhance more Sino–Cambodia economic and socio-cultural cooperation (China Ministry of Foreign Affairs 2014). Moreover, many other Cambodian senior officials, political and economic analysts, and academics have sceptically supported this initiative in the hope that it will strengthen exchange and mutual learning between different cultures and civilizations, as well as promote world peace and development.

Cambodia's engagement in the Belt and Road Initiative

Since 2014, the Royal Government of Cambodia has strongly supported and engaged in China's BRI development projects in three important ways. First, Cambodia has supported the BRI and Lancang–Mekong Cooperation (LMC) at both national and regional levels, particularly in the context of ASEAN and the Greater Mekong Subregion (GMS). At the 2nd Mekong–Lancang Cooperation (MLC) Leaders' Meeting under the theme "Our River of Peace and Sustainable Development" on 10 January 2018 in Phnom Penh, Cambodia and China as the co-chairs along with other member countries agreed on the Phnom Penh Declaration, a five-year plan of the MLC, to further promote high-level exchanges and dialogue among political parties; combine the MLC with other important development strategies, especially the BRI; and support the existing international financial institutions such as the Asian Infrastructure Investment Bank (AIIB) and the Silk Road Fund (SRF) to finance quality infrastructure expansion along the Mekong–Lancang countries (Phnom Penh Declaration 2018).

Second, Cambodia is one of the 57 founding members of the China-backed AIIB, a multilateral development bank based in Beijing, in addition to other existing financial institutions such as World Bank Group, International Monetary Fund (IMF), and Asian Development Bank (ADB). After the commencement of the operations of the AIIB in January 2016, the National Assembly of Cambodia passed legislation ratifying Cambodia's membership in the AIIB and its US$62.3 million investment to acquire 623 shares in this new development bank ('Assembly approves Cambodia's stake in AIIB' 2016). Cambodia's initial investment was US$12.4 million; the remaining investment money will be given in stages over the next ten years. The primary aims of this investment will benefit Cambodia in the long run because the country is enabled to access to more available loans from the AIIB for its infrastructure development and to earn more profit. It was estimated by the ADB that developing Asia would need US$750 billion to construct massive regional infrastructure connectivity (ADB 2010). In early 2017, the ADB also predicted that the infrastructure needs in Asia and the Pacific would double and exceed at least US$22.6 trillion through 2030 or roughly US$1.5 trillion annually (ADB 2017).

Third, Cambodia has continued strengthening its physical infrastructure, broken during decades of civil war, and enhancing its logistics effectiveness conducive to Cambodia's economic growth in the context of the BRI. According to the Council for the Development of Cambodia (CDC) (2010), the total coverage of road networks in Cambodia is roughly 30,268 kilometres. It is composed of (1) 4,695 kilometres of national roads (1 – digit National Roads: 2,052 kilometres; 2 – digit National Roads: 2,643 kilometres); (2) 6,615 kilometres of provincial roads; and (3) approximately 18,958 kilometres of rural roads. In addition, according to Cambodia's Ministry of Public Works and Transportation, it is estimated that Cambodia would need about US$9 billion in the next two years to build 850 kilometres of expressways and another US$26 billion to construct 2,230 kilometres of expressways by 2040 ('Cambodia – China talk expressway' 2016). Several bridges, including the China-funded Cambodia–China Friendship Bridge across the Mekong River and the recent Stung Trang–Krauch Chmar Bridge, were also built to facilitate and enhance domestic and regional economic transactions.

Moreover, according the CDC (2010), two crucial railway lines in Cambodia have been in operation. They include the 386-kilometre Northern Line and the 264-kilometre Southern Line, commencing from Phnom Penh station. In addition to the existing railway lines, China initiated several railway development projects, such as (1) the 405-kilometre railway from Preah Vihear Province through three southern provinces: Kampong Thom, Kampong Chhnang, and Kampong Speu to coastal Koh Kong Province; (2) the key railway between Phnom Penh and Preah Sihanouk Province; (3) the railway between Phnom Penh and Poipet and Thailand; (4) the railway between Phnom Penh and Snoul and Vietnam; and (5) the railway line between Phnom Penh and Phnom Penh Autonomous Port ('Lack of funds delays railway' 2014; Rose 2017). Moreover, the total number of regular flights and cargo into Cambodia has steadily risen in recent years. According to the official website of Cambodia's Phnom Penh Airport (2017), there were more than 830,000 passengers and 8,000 flights movements in January 2017, a significant increase of 19.7 percent and 15.5 percent respectively over the numbers in 2016. Also, the import and export tonnages in both Phnom Penh and Siem Reap Cargo Terminals grew by 28.5 percent to 4,156 tons in early 2017 (Figures 6.7–6.9).

Fourth, Cambodia has promoted an attractive investment policy for all investors by adopting the Open Door Policy, providing tax incentives, and improving its investment facilitation (Table 6.2). Since the implementation of the 1994 Law on Investment, the Cambodian government has adopted a more liberal foreign investment policy to promote its long-term economic growth. In order to

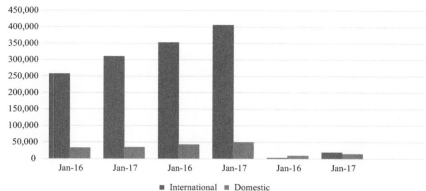

	Phnom Penh		Siem Reap		Preah Sihanouk	
	Jan-2016	Jan-2017	Jan-2016	Jan-2017	Jan-2016	Jan-2017
International	256,769	310,486	352,795	405,605	2,650	18,771
Domestic	32,705	34,385	42,194	49,587	9,018	14,269

Figure 6.7 Passengers at Cambodia's airports

Source: Cambodia Airports (2017).

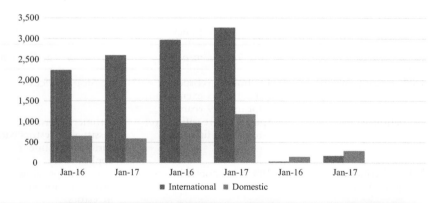

	Phnom Penh		Siem Reap		Preah Sihanouk	
	Jan-2016	Jan-2017	Jan-2016	Jan-2017	Jan-2016	Jan-2017
International	2,237	2,600	2,971	3,261	27	165
Domestic	651	588	966	1,178	141	285

Figure 6.8 Movements at Cambodia's airports

Source: Cambodia Airports (2017).

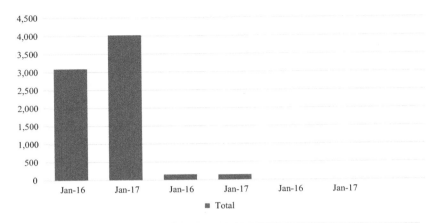

	Phnom Penh		Siem Reap		Preah Sihanouk	
	Jan-2016	Jan-2017	Jan-2016	Jan-2017	Jan-2016	Jan-2017
Total	3,085	4,016	149	140		

Figure 6.9 Cargo at Cambodia's airports

Source: Cambodia Airports (2017).

Table 6.2 Cambodia's attractive investment policy

Open Door Policy	Tax Incentives	Investment Facilitation
100% foreign ownership	Tax holiday (corporate income tax exemption) for up to 9 years	One-Stop Services
No nationalization	Special Depreciation up to 40% in first year	Customer Approach (assist all investors with various investment applications)
No local content requirements	20% of corporate income tax	Easing and speeding procedure for all investors
No export requirements	Import duty exemptions for machinery and equipment	Aftercare Services
No restriction on foreign exchange and no capital control	Import duty exemptions for production inputs/ raw materials	Investment Tracking System
No price controls on products or services	Consider to introduce a SMART Incentive Scheme	Consider for automated system

Source: Suon (2016).

effectively and efficiently facilitate both public- and private-sector investments, the Cambodian government also established the CDC, which is the highest one-stop decision-making body. The CDC has two important bodies, the Cambodian Investment Board (CIB) and the Cambodian Special Economic Zone Board (CSEZB), to deal with the investments outside and inside the SEZs respectively. One of the attractive policies for promoting foreign investment in Cambodia is the Open Door Policy. According to the policy, 100 percent ownership is granted to foreign investors with few restrictions. In addition, there is no nationalization, no local content requirements, no export requirements, no restriction on foreign exchange, no capital control, and no price control on both products and services (Suon 2016) despite few restrictions according to the laws and regulations.

Moreover, the Cambodian government has offered foreign direct investors (FDIs) more tax incentives in addition to other advantages such as potentially abundant natural resources and a relatively inexpensive labour force. A tax holiday up to nine years and special depreciation up to 40 percent in the first year and other investment incentives are specifically given to different types of Qualified Investment Projects (QIPs) with different amounts of their investment required for those incentives (Tables 6.3 and 6.4). Also, other tax incentives for the QIPs inside and outside the SEZs include 20 percent of corporate income tax, import duty exemptions for machinery and equipment, and import duty exemptions for production inputs and raw materials (Tables 6.2 and 6.5. Also, the CDC is considering introducing a SMART Incentive Scheme for the QIPs.

Furthermore, the Cambodian government offers FDIs investment facilitation. The CDC is the highest one-stop service government body in charge of the

Table 6.3 Types of qualified investment project and incentives

Type of QIP	Commodities to be imported free of duty
Domestically oriented QIPs	Production equipment, construction materials, and production input to be used in the production of exports goods
Export-oriented QIPs (except those which elect or which have elected to use the Customs Manufacturing Bonded Warehouse mechanism)	Production equipment, construction materials, raw materials, intermediate goods, and accessories
Supporting Industry QIPs	Production equipment, construction materials, raw materials, intermediate goods, and production input accessories. If the Supporting Industry QIP fails to supply 100% of its manufactured products to the export industry or directly export its products, the QIP shall pay the customs duties and taxes on production inputs for the quantity that has not been supplied to the export industry or directly exported

Source: The Council for the Development of Cambodia (n.d.).

Table 6.4 Minimum conditions required for the provision of incentives

Fields of Investment	Requirement for Investment
Supporting industry, which has its entire production (100%) supplying export industry	US$100,000 or more
Production of animal feed	US$200,000 or more
Production of leather products and related products	US$300,000 or more
Production of all kinds of metal products	
Production of electrical and electronic appliances and office materials	
Production of toys and sporting goods	
Production of motor vehicles, parts, and accessories	
Production of ceramic products	
Production of food products and beverages	US$500,000 or more
Production of products for textile industry	
Production of garments, textiles, footwear, and hats	
Production of furniture and fixtures that do not use natural wood	
Production of paper and paper products	
Production of rubber products and plastic products	
Clean water supplies	
Production of traditional medicines	
Freezing and processing of aquatic products for export	
Processing of any kind of cereal and crop products for export	
Production of chemicals, cement, agriculture fertilizer, and petrochemicals	US$1,000,000 or more
Production of modern medicines	
Construction of modern market or trade centre	US$2,000,000 or more More than 10,000 square metres Adequate space for car park
Training and educational institutes that provide training for skill development, technology or poly technology that serves industries, agriculture, tourism, infrastructure, environment, engineering, sciences, and other services.	US$4,000,000 or more
International trade exhibition centre and convention halls	US$8,000,000 or more

Source: The Council for the Development of Cambodia (n.d.).

rehabilitation, development, and oversight of investment activities in Cambodia. The one-stop services are very important for FDIs to reduce red tape and application costs, and speed up the investment process. In addition, a useful custom approach and "easing and speeding procedure" have been introduced to assist FDIs in various investment applications. Aftercare services and an investment tracking system are also provided for the FDIs to ensure that their investments are properly handled in Cambodia.

Table 6.5 Incentives in Special Economic Zones (SEZs)

Beneficiary	Incentives
Zone developers	• The exemption period for the Tax on Profit shall be provided for a maximum period of 9 years, in compliance with article 14.1 of the Law on the Amendment to the Law on Investment. • The import of equipment and construction materials to be used for infrastructure construction in the zone shall be allowed and exempted from import duties and other taxes. • The Zone Developer shall receive customs duty exemption on the import of machinery, equipment for the construction of the road connecting the town to the zone, and other public services infrastructure for the public interest as well as for the interests of the zone. • The Zone Developer may request, under the form of a temporary admission (AT), the import of means of transport and machineries used for the construction of the infrastructures in accordance with the laws and regulations in force. • The Zone Developer may obtain a land concession from the state for establishing the SEZ in areas along the border or isolated regions in accordance with the Land Law and may lease this land to the Zone Investors.
Zone investors	• The same incentives on customs duty and tax as other QIP shall be given. • The Zone Investor entitled to the incentive* on Value Added Tax (VAT) at the rate of 0% shall record the amount of tax exemption for its every import. The said record shall be disregarded if the Production Outputs are re-exported. If the Production Outputs are imported into the domestic market, the Zone Investor shall refund the amount of VAT as recorded in comparison with the quantity of export. • Note: Zone Investors entitled to incentives: investors such as garment and footwear manufacturers, their supporting industries or contractor.
Common	• Zone Developers, investors or foreign employees have the right to transfer all the income derived from the investment and salaries received in the zone to banks located in other countries after payment of tax. • The Zone Developer and the Zone Investor are entitled to obtain the investment guarantees as stated in Article 8, Article 9, and Article 10 of the Law on Investment in the Kingdom of Cambodia and other relevant regulations. • Non-discriminatory treatment as foreigners, non-nationalization, and no-fixing price.

Source: The Council for the Development of Cambodia (n.d.).

Cambodia's rationale to support the BRI

Since 2014, Cambodia has strongly supported the China-led BRI development projects at all levels, in accordance with its economic, political-security, and socio-cultural rationale, explained as follows.

Economic rationale

Geographically speaking, it is clear that the Belt and Road (B&R) region is a huge, potential, and very important market linking Asia to Africa and Europe through the Silk Road Economic Belt and the 21st-Century Maritime Silk Road. It includes 66 countries with roughly 4.4 billion people, or 70 percent of the global population and about 40 percent of the global GDP (gross domestic product) (Hofman 2015). It is also worth noting that the B&R region is not limited to Asia, Europe, and Africa, but potentially extending to South America or Latin America and stretching through the Artic, the Polar Silk Road, according to China's White Paper on Arctic Policy ('China publishes Arctic policy, eyeing vision of "Polar Silk Road"' 2018). The BRI is aimed not merely at promoting regional infrastructure connectivity but also at promoting inter-regional economic cooperation. Therefore, the B&R region is a potentially massive market for Cambodia and other relevant countries along the route to accelerate regional economic integration for their mutual economic benefits. Cambodia is geographically situated at a very important and strategic connecting point along the new silk routes between China and Southeast Asia and other countries, to assist in achieving the BRI objectives.

Second, under the BRI development framework, there are available financing sources in addition to World Bank Group and ADB. Those sources include the AIIB which has a current capital of US$45 billion, the Silk Road Fund (SRF) with US$40 billion, and the BRICs Development Bank (Lim et al. 2016) for building and reconstructing Cambodia's hard infrastructure connectivity. According to Cambodia's Ministry of Public Works and Transportation, Cambodia needs roughly US$9 billion in 2020 to build 850 kilometres of expressways and US$ 26 billion to construct 2,230 kilometres of expressways by 2040 ('Cambodia – China talk expressway' 2016). In addition, Cambodia needs more aid and available loans to strengthen and improve other physical infrastructures including airports, railways, bridges, and ports.

Third, the BRI is properly complementary to the existing connectivity cooperation frameworks and strategies, such as the Master Plan of ASEAN Connectivity 2025 (MPAC – 2025), Initiative for ASEAN Integration (IAI) Work Plan III, the United Nations 2030 Agenda for Sustainable Development, and the Greater Mekong Subregion Infrastructure Connectivity 2015–2020 and its corridors (Figures 6.10 and 6.11). Of all GMS corridors, central corridors and southern coastal ones are more important for Cambodia, linking Cambodia's southern coastal areas along the 21st-Century Maritime Silk Road to the other GMS countries including China. The southern corridor links Phnom Penh to Cambodia's neighbouring economic poles, Bangkok and Ho Chi Minh City. These three key GMS corridors across Cambodia are also consistent with Cambodia's Industrial Development Plan (2015–2025).

Last but not least, the BRI development strategies are compatible with the Royal Government of Cambodia's National Strategic Development Plan (NSDP 2014–2018) (the Royal Government of Cambodia 2014) and its Industrial Development Policy (IDP 2015–2025) (the Royal Government of Cambodia

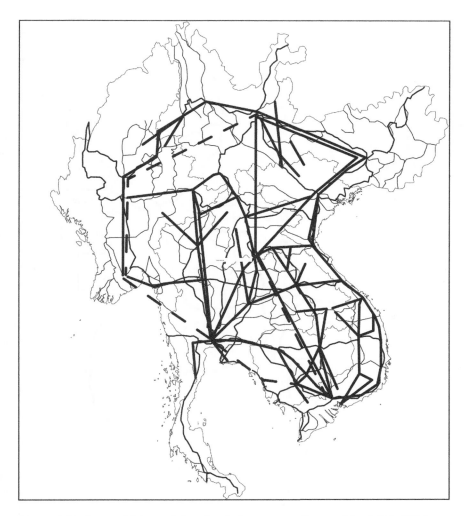

Figure 6.10 Greater Mekong Subregion Infrastructure Connectivity 2015–2020
Source: Compiled by author.

2015), according to which Cambodia's economic growth and development are prioritized and can be achieved through enhancing infrastructure connectivity. The NSDP 2014–2018 outlines the significance of infrastructure development, including both rehabilitation and construction as key driving factors for supporting Cambodia's economic growth, strengthening economic efficiency, improving economic competitiveness, and promoting Cambodia's economic diversification.

Cambodia's IDP 2015–2025 also points out the significance of infrastructure development as a key prerequisite to Cambodia's long-term industrial

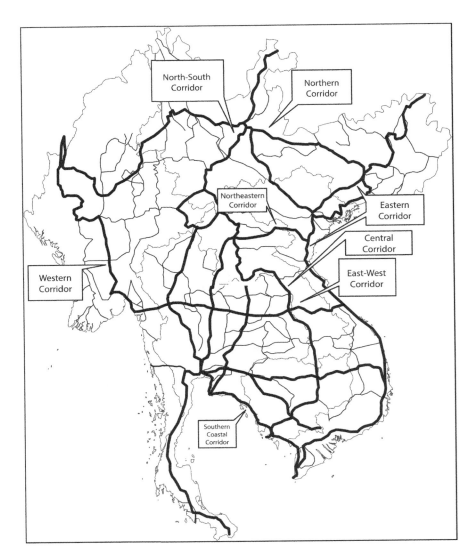

Figure 6.11 Greater Mekong Subregion Corridors
Source: Compiled by author.

development and economic growth. According to the IDP, Cambodia is favourably located geographically between two potential industrial regions, Bangkok and
Ho Chi Minh City, as well as close to huge Asian economies such as China, South
Korea, and Japan. Thus, Cambodia's infrastructure rehabilitation and construction need to take more geographical advantages. In short, the BRI development

projects, the new AIIB development bank, and the SRF are significant for Cambodia's infrastructure development and therefore compatible with both Cambodia's NSDP 2014–2018 and IDP 2015–2025.

Political security rationale

Cambodia has significantly enhanced its bilateral political relationship with China since signing the Comprehensive Strategic Partnership of Cooperation in 2010 and strictly adhering to the One-China Policy based on the key principles of mutual interests, mutual respect, and equal partnership. Since 2000, Cambodian Prime Minister Hun Sen reiterated continuing its One–China Policy and stated that "Cambodia will never change its One–China Policy, which is always adhered by our King Norodom Sihanouk [. . .] As the inheritor of the policy, I [Prime Minister Hun Sen] will continue to pursue it" ('Prime minister reiterates "One – China" policy' 2010). Cambodia's strict adherence to the One–China Policy implies its strong support of China's foreign policies including the BRI and the AIIB.

In addition, the upgraded version of Sino–Cambodia bilateral relationship has so far promoted mutual confidence and support for deeper and more comprehensive economic, socio-cultural, and particularly political-security cooperation. Cambodian Prime Minister Hun Sen regarded China as the most trustworthy partner for Cambodia, and Chinese President Xi Jinping described Cambodia as one of sincere friends and good neighbours in Southeast Asia (Var 2016). On 5 January 2018, during the Chinese foreign minister's press conference on Chinese Premier Li Keqiang's upcoming visit to Cambodia, China's foreign ministry spokesperson, Geng Shuang, reiterated the Sino–Cambodia relationship as a good model of a state-to-state exchange and stated that

> China and Cambodia are good neighbours, good friends, good partners and good brothers [. . .] China–Cambodia relations have brought tangible benefits to the two countries and two peoples, made positive contributions to peace and development of this region and the world at large and become a model for state – to – state exchanges. China is satisfied with the substantial progress in our bilateral relations.
>
> (Foreign Ministry Spokesperson Geng Shuang's
> Regular Press Conference 2018)

Therefore, this close bilateral political-security relationship serves as a core driving factor for Cambodia to support the China-proposed BRI development projects and the AIIB at regional and global levels.

Furthermore, this BRI is complementary to and compatible with the existing regional multilateral arrangements such as ASEAN Regional Forum (ARF), East Asia Summit (EAS), ASEAN Defence Ministers Meeting Plus (ADMM+), ASEAN Plus Three (APT), and other ASEAN+ forums in order to build strategic trust and confidence for regional peace, security, and development. The BRI also primarily aims to promote not only regional economic cooperation but also mutual understanding of different cultures and civilizations in Asia, Europe, and Africa, which are conducive to promoting and maintaining regional peace and security. Therefore, the BRI is also assisting the existing regional multilateral arrangements in reshaping regional political-security environment favourable for regional economic cooperation.

Socio-cultural rationale

The BRI is aimed at promoting people-to-people connectivity and cultural awareness and understanding of cultures and civilizations of all countries along the route. The BRI enables Cambodia to link its historical, natural, and cultural heritage sites to the other B&R countries in order to promote Cambodia's culture and tourist industrial development. Moreover, since 2013, the Chinese government under President Xi Jinping has invested significant resources to promote Chinese culture and its socialist ideology with Chinese characteristics by establishing museums, expos, research centres, festivals, and countless heritage initiatives (Winter 2018). All these initiatives are also important for promoting Cambodian culture, education through China-funded scholarships, and BRI-related research papers as crucial input to shape the policymaking of the Cambodian government.

For these three important reasons, there is no doubt that Cambodia's strong support for the China-backed BRI also serves Cambodia's political-security, economic, and social-cultural interests.

Mapping and remapping the 21st-Century Maritime Silk Road

Figure 6.12 shows that the sea-based 21st-Century Maritime Silk Road connects China's eastern parts to some key economic hubs in most maritime Southeast Asian countries, including the Philippines, Singapore, Indonesia, and Malaysia, as well as some countries in Africa and Europe. Therefore, this map is less relevant to Cambodia. Figure 6.13 reflects the reality that this Maritime Silk Road also connects to other potential economic hubs in Southeast Asia, including Cambodia, where massive physical infrastructure connectivity is required for materializing China's ambitious BRI development projects across the continents.

Cambodia's infrastructure connectivity development

Due to Cambodia's rationale and the significance of the BRI, the Royal Government of Cambodia has adopted and implemented its IDP (2015–2025) for Cambodia's infrastructure connectivity development in order to boost Cambodia's economic competitiveness and growth. According to the IDP, there are four important reasons. First, the BRI can further promote the development of the GMS economic corridors, linking Cambodia's southern and northern regions and up to Thailand and Laos. Second, under the IDP, the Cambodian government

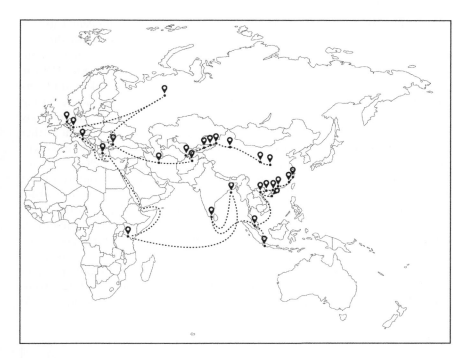

Figure 6.12 Mapping of the 21st-Century Maritime Silk Road

Source: Compiled by author.

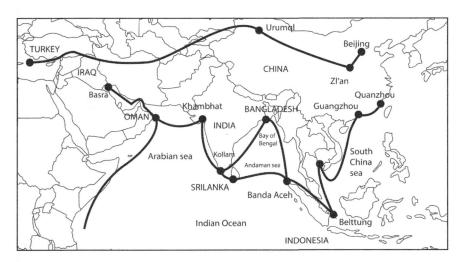

Figure 6.13 Remapping of the Belt and Road Initiative

Source: Compiled by author.

plans to strengthen and upgrade its crucial economic poles: Phnom Penh City, the capital city of Cambodia, as well as Sihanoukville and Koh Kong Province through roads, rails, and ports linking to the 21st-Century Maritime Silk Road to promote Cambodia's industries and trade with other countries. Third, under the IDP, the government also aims to connect its hard infrastructure nationwide and link its economic poles, especially from Sihanoukville and Koh Kong to neighbouring industrial centres, Bangkok and Ho Chi Minh City, two potential and relatively important markets for Cambodia. Last, the Cambodian government will further develop and upgrade Cambodia's physical infrastructures connecting to its potential SEZs and potential industrial zones along (1) coastal areas including Sihanoukville, Koh Kong, and Kompot provinces linking all concerned countries along the 21st-Century Maritime Silk Road; and (2) land-based borders with Thailand and Vietnam as Cambodia's neighbouring industrial centres (Figure 6.14).

According to the IDP (2015–2025), the Royal Government of Cambodia is also constructing and upgrading three key economic corridors for export, agricultural processing, and historical and cultural tourism. These are: (1) Sihanoukville–Phnom Penh Corridor for the export of goods from Cambodia to other countries and vice versa along the 21st-Century Maritime Silk Road; (2) Kompong Cham–North–West Industrial Corridor for agricultural processing; and (3)

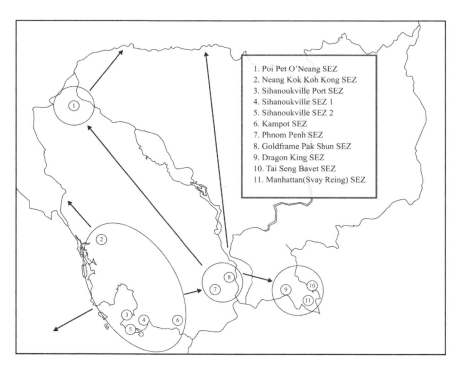

Figure 6.14 Cambodia's Special Economic Zones (SEZs) linked to Potential Areas
Source: Compiled by author.

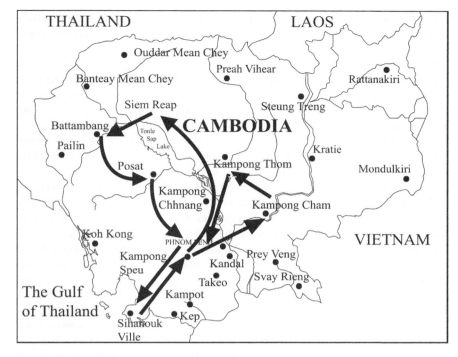

Figure 6.15 Cambodia's key economic corridors
Source: Compiled by author.

Sihanoukville and Phnom Penh–Siem Reap Corridors for cultural and historical tourism, which has been one of Cambodia's most competitive sectors to promote its economic growth (Figure 6.15).

Therefore, according to the IDP (2015–2025), constructing the GMS economic corridors, strengthening the infrastructure of Cambodia's potential economic poles, linking those economic poles to its neighbouring industrial centres, upgrading its hard infrastructures to its SEZs and potential industrial zones, and enhancing Cambodia's key economic corridors for exports, agricultural processing, and tourism are significant for Cambodia's economic competitiveness in the context of the BRI.

Cambodia's economic competitiveness

Many previous studies have argued that the success of the 21st-Century Maritime Silk Road is relevant and conducive to Cambodia's economic competitiveness in the region. There are seven reasons to support this argument. First, the Royal Government of Cambodia has implemented attractive investment and trade policies and strategies (Table 6.2) in order to promote more FDIs and create more local jobs for relatively inexpensive Cambodian labour. These attractive policies and strategies include the Open Door Policy with few restrictions, tax incentives, and investment facilitation, hugely contributing to Cambodia's economic competitiveness in the region.

Second, Cambodia has so far improved and strengthened its legal and regulatory frameworks and other procedures for trade facilitation and investment climate, mobilization, allocation of resources, etc. For instance, the Law on Investment adopted in 1994 was amended (or the Law on the amendment of the Law on Investment), the Labour Law of Cambodia, CDC's one-stop services, easing and speeding up of investment procedures, numerous investment-related sub-decrees, and other regulations were properly enhanced to provide all FDIs with a favourable investment environment in Cambodia.

Third, Cambodia continues to develop its physical infrastructure connectivity and strengthen its logistics system and effectiveness. According to Cambodia's Ministry of Public Works and Transportation, Cambodia plans to rehabilitate and construct its hard infrastructures including roads, bridges, railways, airports, and ports. For the expressways, Cambodia needs a total of US$35 billion to build 3,080 kilometres of expressways by 2040 ('Cambodia – China talk expressway' 2016). Currently upgraded and rehabilitated railways to Sihanoukville (254 kilometres), Poipet (388 kilometres), and Sisophon (48 kilometres) by Toll Royal Railways holding a 30-year exclusive concession to operate Cambodia's rail network (Chea 2016); its newly established rail lines to Phnom Penh International Airport; planned construction of more airports in Kandal Province and Sihanoukville; as well as the expansion and construction of seaports are all important for Cambodia's economic competitiveness.

Fourth, Cambodia has strived to develop its human resources and skills orientation in response to market needs through various programmes of national agencies and local and international civil society organizations. According to Madhur (2014), Cambodia's human resource base remains relatively low skilled in comparison to other countries in the region. Therefore, both quantity and quality of education in Cambodia have been enhanced to address the current and future skills gaps in recent years. In addition, the technical and vocational education and training (TVET) provided by Cambodia's Ministry of Labour and Vocational Training help to provide Cambodian people, especially young dropouts, with necessary skills in accordance with market demands to promote more skilled labour in Cambodia.

Fifth, Cambodia is developing and advancing its technological standard, innovation, creativity, and research and development (R&D) for its long-term economic competitiveness and growth. Moreover, Cambodia has promoted environmental management in the country to ensure sustainable economic growth and contribute to its economic competitiveness. And finally, according to the Suon (2016), Cambodia has provided raw material inputs, including public utilities, agricultural inputs, minerals, and land; as well as facilitated and promoted more foreign indirect investments with not only China but also other countries, particularly in the context of the BRI.

Remarkably, from 2011, the investment inflow in Cambodia reached US$24.1 billion (Figure 6.16). It is believed that the trend in Cambodia's investment

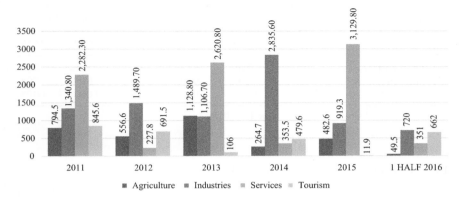

Figure 6.16 Cambodia's investment trend (2011–2016)

Source: Suon (2016).

Table 6.6 Distribution of GDP by sectors

Sector	1962	1988	2008	2013	2015	2020	2025
Agriculture	49%	44.5%	32.8%	31.6%	**29.0%**	**25%**	**23%**
Industry	19%	16.7%	22.4%	24.1%	**26.2%**	**28%**	**30%**
Manufacturing	–	12.7%	15.3%	15.5%	**16.0%**	**18%**	**20%**
Service	32%	34.8%	38.8%	38.5%	**39.4%**	**40%**	**40%**
Taxes on products less subsidies	0%	4%	6%	5.8%	**5.4%**	**7%**	**7%**

Source: The Royal Government of Cambodia (2015).

Table 6.7 Share of export products

Sector	1988	2008	2013	2015	2020	2025
Export of processed agricultural products	10%	10%	7.9%	**8%**	**10%**	**12%**
Manufacturing						
Garment and footwear	80%	70%	77%	**60%**	**55%**	**50%**
Non-garment and footwear	0.1%	0.5%	1%	**5%**	**10%**	**15%**

Source: The Royal Government of Cambodia (2015).

inflow will further increase when the BRI, especially the 21st-Century Maritime Silk Road, is fully implemented to link Cambodia to others along the route.

In this connection, Cambodia has clear plans to promote its priority development sectors up to the year 2025 including agro-industries/processing, tourism, manufacturing, automotive parts industries, electrical and electronic industries, and high value-added manufacturing. Cambodia also strongly encourages the rise of small and medium enterprises and large enterprises in Cambodia in Tables 6.6–6.8.

Table 6.8 Percentage of officially registered enterprises with proper balance sheet

Size/Type of enterprises	Officially Registered			Having balanced Sheet		
	2010	2020	2025	2010	2020	2025
Small enterprises	37%	70%	80%	4%	30%	50%
Medium enterprises	72%	80%	95%	24%	50%	70%
Large enterprises	93%	100%	100%	66%	100%	100%

Source: The Royal Government of Cambodia (2015).

Potential challenges for Cambodia

Despite huge economic benefits from the BRI, Cambodia is still lagging behind the realistic plans and should be more cautious of China's intention in the region. First and foremost, the lack of finances is a critical concern for Cambodia to develop quality and number of ports, railways, and roads connecting the 21st-Century Maritime Silk Road to other provinces in Cambodia in order to strengthen Cambodia's economic performance and growth. Compared to China and other ASEAN member countries, Cambodia's physical infrastructure is neither sufficient nor efficient enough to facilitate all huge economic activities.

Second, so far Cambodia has had two major international ports in Phnom Penh and Sihanoukville, two coastal ports in Kampot and Koh Kong, and many river ports in Kampong Cham, Kratie, Stung Treng, Kampong Chhnang, and Siem Reap in the Tonle Sap. The first major Phnom Penh international port, which remains a crucial port for foreign commerce and domestic communications, and the second major Sihanoukville Autonomous Port has had low capacity and efficiency for huge cargo. Moreover, the port handles over only 70 percent of the country's surface cargo and plans to be further extended in both length and depth so that the port could allow more than 90 percent of larger cargo ships in the region, up from 20 percent now, to anchor (Kawase, 2018).

Third, despite Cambodia's potential tourist sector along the 21st-Century Maritime Silk Road, the quality and number of services and sanitation have been improved yet need to be further guaranteed for both domestic and foreign visitors. This really requires genuine commitment of not only Cambodia's government but also of all other stakeholders at all levels to make Cambodia a better tourist place.

Fourth, despite available and excessive loans from the Chinese government, there has been scepticism about Cambodia falling into what most economic analysts called a "debt trap" circumstance. According to Cambodia's Ministry of Finance and Economy last year, Cambodia's bilateral loans increased to US$5.3 billion, of which roughly US$3.9 billion was from China (Ministry of Economy and Finance 2017). The loans from China are four times more than those of Japan. Although the current debt level has not really been a grave concern for Cambodia in comparison to other countries, Cambodia should be more cautious not to have the same experience as Sri Lanka, unable to repay China's loans and interest.

Fifth, over the past decades, the level of educational attainment of the Cambodian population has so far increased significantly, as evidenced by a gradual increase in the enrolment rates at both public and private schools at all levels, especially at the primary level (Madhur 2014). However, both the quantity and quality of Cambodia's education remains low compared to that of other countries in the region. Most Cambodian labour is intensive and the labourers unskilled. Therefore, the Cambodian government needs to make a more political commitment to enhancing its educational system to promote more human resources and address current and future skill gaps to strengthen its economic competitiveness and promote economic growth.

Moreover, as to China's intentions, the BRI, a combination of huge development projects along more than 60 countries, has been viewed by some Western analysts and scholars as a "String of Chinese Pearls" to economically, strategically, and militarily encircle not only Southeast Asia, South Asia, Central Asia, and Africa but also the Middle East and Europe. For those analysts, these projects could also be posing huge strategic threats to security and defence of the encircled countries in the long run. Therefore, Cambodia should also be more cautious regarding China's security intention in the region, especially Southeast Asia, where China has increasingly projected its soft power influence.

Last but not least, China's generous aid and assistance to Cambodia has been described as "non-transparent" and "ineffective" to construct and rebuild physical infrastructure owing to Cambodia's systematic corruption and China's unaudited aid structure. Therefore, most aid and loans from China cannot effectively develop Cambodia's infrastructure to facilitate the BRI economic projects. In addition, it is argued that the growing dependency on China's aid and assistance will allow China to influence its foreign policy and decision making in ASEAN, as Cambodia is one of the member states.

The way ahead and recommendations

Over the last two decades, Cambodia and China have developed and upgraded their bilateral relationship into a Comprehensive Strategic Partnership of Cooperation, allowing China to become Cambodia's major aid donor and top investor. Due to this close bilateral relationship, since 2014, Cambodia has strongly supported the China-backed BRI, which has been the biggest infrastructure and economic development project in what Chinese President Xi Jinping called "new era" of development and cooperation. Cambodia's support of the BRI projects is mainly not only political-security but also economic and sociocultural, to promote Cambodia's national interests. In addition, it is clear that the BRI has served as a "push factor" for Cambodia to rehabilitate and construct its physical infrastructures conducive to its long-term economic competitiveness and growth according to Cambodia's National Strategic Development Plan and its IDP.

However, the potential challenges facing Cambodia are its lack of financial resources for infrastructure development, its ineffective ports, poor services and sanitation, low systematic production chain, patron-driven structure or complex bureaucratic system, rampant corruption, lack of skilled labourers, debt trap scenario, and other barriers limiting Cambodia's potential to take more advantage of the BRI.

Therefore, to ensure the success of the BRI projects, all relevant B&R actors, including Cambodia, China, and ASEAN, should continue their political commitment to carrying out their responsibilities, because the BRI will bring all countries along the route shared benefits and world peace.

Cambodia

As a small and low-middle income country in the region, Cambodia should continue: (1) supporting the BRI to achieve its long-term economic benefits while being more cautious about China's soft power influence, or the so-called China charm offensive; (2) improving the effectiveness of trade facilitation, investment, and the business environment; (3) further enhancing and strictly implementing legal and regulatory frameworks and investment procedures to ensure long-term investment in Cambodia; (4) enhancing Cambodia's aid effectiveness in and quality of physical infrastructure connectivity and logistics system; (5) continuing to develop human resources and enhancing skills orientation in response to the growing needs of the BRI market, including Cambodia's local market; (6) further encouraging and developing technological standards, innovation, and R&D to promote Cambodia's long-term economic competitiveness and development; (7) continuing to combat corruption; and (8) being more cautious about the debt trap scenario due to Cambodia's ongoing excessive loans with aggregated interests that would make the country unable or impossible to repay.

China

As a major and the most responsible stakeholder, China should continue: (1) assuring Cambodia and the other smaller and medium countries along the silk route of its peaceful rise and engagement, especially in Asia and the Pacific (including Southeast Asia); (2) genuinely convincing Cambodia and the other smaller and developing countries that China has much to offer the region, not only "the size of the money bag or its soft power" but also knowledge, experiences, modern technology, and expertise, especially infrastructure development; (3) promoting China's aid effectiveness and transparency for Cambodia's long-term benefits in order to build China's image and governance model for other developing countries; and (4) further enhancing the quality of China-funded infrastructure construction in Cambodia.

China and ASEAN

China and ASEAN should continue: (1) promoting China-ASEAN maritime cooperation inherent to China's 21st-Century Maritime Silk Road and promoting communication/cooperation in such areas as maritime environment, marine safety and security, culture, and people-to-people connectivity at sea; (2) further promoting people-to-people connectivity as a priority of its foreign policy, such as education, culture, tourism, youth exchanges, think tanks, and local governments; and (3) enhancing existing economic development frameworks such as ASEAN Comprehensive Investment Agree (ACIA), ASEAN–China Free Trade Agreement (ACFTA), and the Regional Comprehensive Economic Partnership (RCEP).

Bibliography

Asian Development Bank 2010, 'Financing Asia's infrastructure: modes of development and integration of Asian financial markets', ADBI Working Paper Series, No. 229.

Asian Development Bank 2015, 'ADB's GMS Economic Cooperation Program'. Available from: www.boi.go.th/tir/issue/200807_18_7/58.htm. [12 November 2017].

Asian Development Bank 2017, 'Asia infrastructure needs exceed $1.7 trillion per year, double previous estimate'. Available from: www.adb.org/news/asia-infrastructure-needs-exceed-17-trillion-year-double-previous-estimates. [18 November 2017].

'Assembly approves Cambodia's stake in AIIB' 2016. *Phnom Penh Post*, 14 January. Available from: www.phnompenhpost.com/business/assembly-approves-cambodias-stake-aiib. [12 November 2017].

Belford, A & Prak, CT 2015, 'Chinese influence in Cambodia grows with army school, aid'. Available from: www.reuters.com/article/us-cambodia-china-military/chinese-influence-in-cambodia-grows-with-army-school-aid-idUSKBN0MT0SW20150402. [18 November 2017].

Business Korea 2015, 'Chinese policy: One Belt One Road picking up speed'. Available from: www.businesskorea.co.kr/english/news/politics/10244-chinese-policy-one-road-one-belt-project-picking-speed. [12 November 2017].

Cambodia Airports 2017, 'Traffic at Cambodia airports grows double digits in January 2017'. Available from: www.cambodia-airports.aero/en/our-business/about-cambodia-airports/news/cambodia-airports-monthly-newsletter-jan-2017#anchor. [20 January 2018].

'Cambodia-China talk expressway' 2016. *Khmer Times*, 12 August. Available from: www.khmertimeskh.com/news/28412/cambodia-china-talk-expressway/. [12 November 2017].

Chandler, D & Harris, P 2007, *Zhou Daguan: a record of Cambodia*. Silkworm Books, Chiang Mai, Thailand.

Chap, S 2010. 'Trade, FDI, and ODA between Cambodia and China/Japan/Korea', in M Kagami (ed), *Economic relations of China, Japan and Korea with the Mekong River Basin countries*. BRC Research Report No. 3, Bangkok Research Center, IDE-JETRO, Bangkok, Thailand.

Chea, V 2016, 'City to airport rail link'. Available from: www.khmertimeskh.com/news/32780/city-to-airport-rail-link/. [12 January 2018].

China Ministry of Foreign Affairs 2014, 'Xi Jinping meets Prime Minister Hun Sen of Cambodia'. Available from: www.fmprc.gov.cn/mfa_eng/topics_665678/ytjhzzdrsrcldrfzshyjxghd/t1208728.shtml. [12 November 2017].

'China publishes Arctic policy, eyeing vision of "Polar Silk Road"' 2018, January 26. *Xinhua*. Available from: www.xinhuanet.com/english/2018-01/26/c_136926357.htm. [10 February 2018].

'Chronology of China's Belt and Road Initiative' 2015, April 22. *Xinhua*. Available from: www.businesskorea.co.kr/english/news/politics/10244-chinese-policy-one-road-one-belt-project-picking-speed. [12 November 2017].

The Council for the Development of Cambodia 2010, 'Cambodia: infrastructure'. Available from: www.cambodiainvestment.gov.kh/investors-information/infra structure.html. [12 November 2017].

The Council for the Development of Cambodia 2017, 'Investment trend'. Available from: www.cambodiainvestment.gov.kh/why-invest-in-cambodia/investment-enviro ment/investment-trend.html. [12 November 2017].

The Council for the Development of Cambodia n.d., 'Investment incentives'. Available from: www.cambodiainvestment.gov.kh/investment-scheme/investment-incen tives.html. [12 January 2018].

'Foreign Ministry Spokesperson Geng Shuang's Regular Press Conference' 2018, January 04. Available from: http://www.fmprc.gov.cn/mfa_eng/xwfw_665399/s2510_665401/t1523680.shtml. [08 August 2018].

Hofman, B 2015, 'China's One Belt One Road initiative: what we know thus far'. Available from: http://blogs.worldbank.org/eastasiapacific/china-one-belt-one-road-initiative-what-we-know-thus-far. [12 November 2017].

HKTDC Research 2017, 'Cambodia: SEZs in focus'. Available from: http://econo mists-pick-research.hktdc.com/business-news/article/Research-Articles/Cambo dia-SEZs-in-Focus/rp/en/1/1X000000/1X0A9P4T.htm. [12 November 2017].

Kawase, K 2018, 'Cambodia's biggest port sees China coveting Japan's dominant role'. Available from https://asia.nikkei.com/Business/Company-in-focus/Cambodia-s-biggest-port-sees-China-coveting-Japan-s-dominant-role. [03 August 2018].

'Lack of funds delays railway' 2014. *Phnom Penh Post*, 22 April. Available from: www.phnompenhpost.com/business/lack-funds-delays-railway. [12 November 2017].

Lim, WT, Chan, HLH, Tseng, HK & Lim, XW 2016, *China's One Belt One Road initiative*. World Scientific, Singapore.

Madhur, S 2014, 'Cambodia's skill gap: an anatomy of issues and policy options'. CDRI Working Paper Series No. 98. Cambodia Development Resource Institute, Phnom Penh.

Ministry of Economy and Finance 2017, 'Cambodia public debt statistical bulletin (No. 3)'. Available from: https://gdicdm.mef.gov.kh/en/2017/04/19/1539.html. [12 November 2017].

Nyiri, P & Tan, D 2017, *Chinese encounters in Southeast Asia: How people, money and ideas are changing the region*. The University of Washington Press, Seattle, WA.

Open Development Cambodia 2016, 'China's aids'. Available from: https://open developmentcambodia.net/topics/chinese-aid/. [10 February 2017].

Phnom Penh Declaration 2018, January 10. *The second Mekong-Lancang Cooperation (MLC) leaders' meeting 'Our River of Peace and Sustainable Development'*. Available from: http://pressocm.gov.kh/wp-content/uploads/2018/01/20180110_Phnom_Penh_Declaration_MLC_ENG.pdf [12 January 2018].

'Prime minister reiterates "One-China" policy' 2010, *Cambodia Daily*, 27 March. Available from: www.cambodiadaily.com/news/prime-minister-reiterates-one-china-policy-15932/. [20 April 2016].

Radio Free Asia 2014, 'China pledges multimillion-dollar development aid to Cambodia'. Available from: www.rfa.org/english/news/cambodia/chinese-develop ment-aid-11102014171429.html. [14 November 2017].

Rose, M 2017, 'Cambodian rail upgrading projects struggle on'. Available from: www.railjournal.com/index.php/asia/network-upgrade-projects-struggle-on. html. [12 November 2017].

The Royal Government of Cambodia 2014, 'Cambodia's national strategic development plan 2014–2018'. Available from: http://cdc-crdb.gov.kh/cdc/documents/ NSDP_2014-2018.pdf. [14 November 2017].

The Royal Government of Cambodia 2015, 'Cambodia's industrial development plan 2015–2025'. Available from: www.cambodiainvestment.gov.kh/content/ uploads/2015/09/IDP-English-Version-FINAL1.pdf. [Accessed 14 November 2017].

Suon, S 2016, *Enabling investment climate in Cambodia: leveraging regional and global production linkages*. The Council for Development in Cambodia (CDC), Phnom Penh.

Var, V 2016. 'China's influence in Cambodia'. Available from: www.khmertimeskh. com/news/26618/china – s-influence-in-cambodia/. [14 November 2017].

Verver M 2012. *Templates of Chineseness and trajectories of Chinese entrepreneurship in Phnom Penh*. The Vrije University, Amsterdam.

Winter, T 2018, 'One Belt, One Road, One Heritage: cultural diplomacy and the Silk Road'. Available from: https://thediplomat.com/2016/03/one-belt-one-road-one-heritage-cultural-diplomacy-and-the-silk-road/. [12 November 2017].

Xi, J 2013, 'Speech by Chinese President Xi Jinping to Indonesian Parliament'. Available from: www.asean-china-center.org/english/2013-10/03/c_133062675. htm. [12 November 2017].

Zhai, Q 2000. *China and the Vietnam Wars: 1950–1975*, pp. 187–189. The University of Carolina Press, Columbia, SC.

7 Economic cooperation and infrastructure linkage between Malaysia and China under the Belt and Road Initiative

Chow-bing Ngeow

In late 2013, Xi Jinping announced the boldly visionary Belt and Road Initiative (BRI). Neither "belt" nor "road" is new; it is a revival of ancient trade routes that once characterized China's economic openness to, and cultural exchanges with, the neighbouring and outside world. Now, most of the countries along the Belt and the Road are poor developing countries. China's plan to revive these routes would have to be underpinned by strong investment in connectivity infrastructure in these countries. Stretching over three continents and involving more than 60 countries, the BRI is indeed a very ambitious project, the success (or failure) of which will likely determine China's future status in the world.

In general, Malaysia has responded positively to this initiative (Ngeow 2016). Notwithstanding some sceptical voices (particularly among certain sectors of civil society and the political opposition), both government and the private sector see Malaysia's participation in the BRI and the anticipated greater Chinese economic presence in Malaysia as beneficial for Malaysia to upgrade its infrastructure and enhance its growth potential. This chapter will introduce China's participation in several major infrastructure projects and (briefly) some cultural ones in Malaysia, primarily Peninsular Malaysia,[1] in relation to the BRI. It will be mainly descriptive rather than theoretical. It highlights in detail the origins, timeframes, the actors involved, and the likely impact of these projects but does not seek to advance an analytical or a theoretical argument. Nevertheless, certain reflections and preliminary observations will be offered in the concluding section of the chapter.

One City Centre, Two Parks East and West, Three Rails North and South

In a press interview, former Chinese Ambassador to Malaysia Dr Huang Huikang positioned Malaysia as a "good neighbour, good friend, good partner" of China. ('Zhongma guanxi jin zuihao shiqi' 2017). Indeed, even during the recent geopolitical troubles in the South China Sea, Malaysia, and in particular its Prime Minister, Najib Tun Razak, has been determined to maintain a positive relationship with China. Since becoming the prime minister in 2009, Najib has undertaken three bilateral state visits (2009, 2014, and 2016) and numerous other working visits to China (mostly in conjunction with attendance at international fora such as the Asia Pacific Economic Cooperation [APEC] Forum, the China–ASEAN Expo, and more recently, the Belt and Road Summit in May 2017), making China one of his most frequently visited countries as a prime minister and underscoring the frequency of high-level political interaction between the leaders of China and Malaysia. Since 2008, China has become Malaysia's largest trading partner consecutively every year, which coincides roughly with the premiership of Najib (2009 – present). During his 2014 visit to Beijing, Najib signed a new joint communiqué with China, formalizing the Sino–Malaysian bilateral relationship as a "comprehensive strategic partnership".

In the same interview, Dr Huang also laid out several flagship Sino–Malaysian infrastructure projects that are being undertaken or considered: One City Centre (中心一城), Two Parks East and West (东西两园), and Three Rails North and South (南北三路) ('Zhongma guanxi jin zuihao shiqi' 2017). One City Centre refers to the Bandar Malaysia project. Two Parks East and West refers to the Malaysia–China Kuantan Industrial Park (MCKIP) and the related Kuantan Port, located on the east coast of Peninsular Malaysia, and the Malacca Gateway Project, which is located on the west coast. Three Rails North and South refers to the Gemas–Johor Baru Double Tracking Railway, East Coast Rail Link (ECRL), and Kuala Lumpur–Singapore High-Speed Rail (KLSHSR) (see Figure 7.1 and Table 7.4). Together, these are the major existing and potential Sino–Malaysian cooperative BRI-related projects.

Bandar Malaysia

Bandar Malaysia is an urban development project at the heart of the metropolitan city of Kuala Lumpur. The importance of Bandar Malaysia lies in its being planned as the master terminus of the future Kuala Lumpur–Singapore High-Speed Rail (KLSHSR) and the transportation hub in the Greater Kuala Lumpur area, servicing a number of public transport systems such as Mass Rapid Transport, KTM Komuter, Bus Rapid Transit, and Express Rail Link. In addition to being a transportation hub, it will include financial, commercial, property, and tourist elements. Reportedly, it will be a futuristic underground city modelled after Montreal, Canada's underground city (Tee 2017, p. B3). The whole project is to be developed for the next 20 to 25 years and is slated to be valued at more than RM200 billion/US$47 billion.[2] The government of Malaysia has offered a number of incentive policies to attract investments to the project, including exemptions from income tax for ten years, exemptions from stamp duty, real property gains tax and withholding tax for eight years, and exemptions from import duty selected construction materials ('Stake in Bandar Malaysia not for sale, says MOF' 2017).

Covering 200 hectares (486 acres), Bandar Malaysia was fully owned by the controversial sovereign wealth fund 1 Malaysia Development Berhad (1MDB)[3] until December 2015, when 1MDB sold 60 percent of its stake in Bandar Malaysia to a Sino–Malaysian joint venture called IWH–CREC for RM7.4 billion/US$1.75 billion (the total value was RM12.35 billion/US$3 billion). The

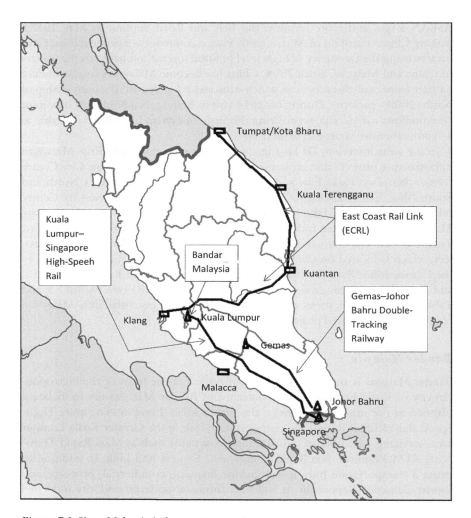

Figure 7.1 Sino–Malaysia infrastructure projects
Source: Author's compilation.

remaining stakes were sold to TRX City, which is owned by the Ministry of
Finance Incorporated, a holding company controlled by the government's Ministry of Finance. IWH–CREC is an entity formed by two parties: Iskandar Waterfront Holding (IWH), which owns 60 percent, and China Railway Engineering
Corp (CREC), which owns the remaining 40 percent. In addition, CREC agreed
to invest RM8 billion/US$1.9 billion to build an operations headquarters in
Bandar Malaysia as well as an integrated office complex which is to house multi-
national companies.

IWH[4] itself is also owned by different entities: Credence Resources, which is a private equity owned by ethnic Malaysian Chinese business tycoon Lim Kang Hoo, has 60 percent; the remaining 40 percent belongs to Kumpulan Prasarana Rakyat Johor Sdn Bhd (KPRJ),[5] the investment arm of the state government of Johor.[6] IWH therefore describes itself as a public-private partnership. Consequently, through both the federal government (Ministry of Finance Incorporated) and the Johor state government (KPRJ), Malaysia retained a 54 percent stake of Bandar Malaysia, CREC had 24 percent, and Credence Resources has the remaining 22 percent. A number of major banks had pledged financing support, including ones in China (Bank of China, Industrial and Commercial Bank of China, China Communications Bank) and Malaysia (CIMB Bank, Maybank, RHB Bank) ('Damacheng jiangcheng shijieji duhui' 2016; 'Stake in Bandar Malaysia not for sale, says MOF' 2017).

IWH–CREC's bid for the Bandar Malaysia project, however, suffered a serious and likely irreversible setback in early May 2017, when TRX City, owned by the Ministry of Finance of Malaysia, announced that the deal was terminated due to IWH–CREC's failure to meet conditions precedent (CP, implying the failure to pay on time) ('To kill a mega deal 2017; Damacheng shougu gaocui' 2017), which was almost immediately disputed by the consortium. Reportedly, 60 percent of the fund was already made, and Bank Negara Malaysia (the central bank of Malaysia) had already approved and confirmed the monetary transaction ('Bujieshou jiaoyi shixiao' 2017). This was a highly unusual event and the real story is still shrouded in mystery. *The Wall Street Journal* reported that the Chinese government has refused to financially back CREC (probably due to the government's policy of capital control), resulting in the failure of the latter to make payment (Hope & Wright 2017). Local daily *The Star* reported Malaysia was unwilling to fulfil certain Chinese conditions. The newspaper quoted a source inside Malaysian government, saying:

> "There were many differences in the detailed terms between the Chinese and MoF [Ministry of Finance Incorporated] officers. The Chinese side has come out with a shopping list for Malaysia to fulfil, but Malaysian officers cannot commit to many of the proposed terms due to national interest and social reasons", said the source.
>
> China said it had done its part in 2015 to help Malaysia overcome its financial problems during critical times. Now Malaysia must play its part to ensure the Chinese investment in Bandar Malaysia gets maximum returns.
>
> (Ho 2017)

One of the major items of "China's shopping list", is that Malaysia ensure China will win the KLSHSR project, which Malaysia, together with Singapore, has yet to decide. Quoting the same source, *The Star* also reported that China proposed that the HSR (high-speed rail) terminus within Bandar Malaysia would be owned and controlled by China, which goes against the national interests of Malaysia. Disagreeing with these conditions means the deal with IWH–CREC would have to be called off (Ho 2017). Others pointed out that the increased valuation of the land could be a factor (Shanmugam 2017).

All these theories, however, are not fully satisfactory in accounting for the exact reason why the deal was terminated. Although China's capital control policy is aimed at controlling capital outflow, it is unlikely that this policy will affect such a strategic investment by an important state-owned enterprise with symbolic political meaning, especially after the Chinese ambassador to Malaysia has elevated the project into a flagship project between Malaysia and China. Doing so would seriously jeopardize China's reputation at the time it is seeking to play a greater role through the BRI. Regarding China's attempt to link the HSR project with the Bandar Malaysia project, it is plausible; but if it is true, then it shows that China's strong-armed negotiation tactic has backfired. But this theory (cited from an unnamed source within the Malaysian government) could also be purposely used to shift blame to China and justify MoF's action. The third theory implies that Malaysia is willing to abrogate a signed agreement and risk jeopardizing its good relationship with China, just for the sake of additional profit of a few billion ringgit Malaysia.

The termination of the deal took place two weeks before Najib's visit to Beijing to attend the Belt and Road Summit. During the summit he met China's property tycoon, Wang Jianlin. Reportedly, Najib was seeking Wang's Wanda group to form another consortium with a Malaysian entity to replace IWH–CREC. However, this is unlikely to occur, given Wang's group has come under increased scrutiny from the Chinese government for its capital outflow activities. In July, the Second Minister of Finance of Malaysia, Johari Abdul Ghani, announced to the press that there are now eight new bidders for the Bandar Malaysia project, but other press reports suggested nine bidders, including seven enterprises from China and two from Japan. They are: China State Construction International, China Gezhouba Group, Greentown China, Vanke, China Communications Construction, China Resources Group, John Holland (an Australian-registered company fully owned by China Communications Construction), Daiwa House Industry Group, and Mitsui Fudosan ('8 gonsi jingbiao Damacheng' 2017).

Malaysia–China Kuantan Industrial Park (MCKIP) and Kuantan Port

Malaysia and China decided to develop and establish two joint industrial parks in 2011 and 2012. The China–Malaysia Qinzhou Industrial Park (CMQIP) was first proposed by then-Chinese Premier Wen Jiabao during his visit to Malaysia in 2011 and was accepted by his Malaysian counterpart, Najib Abdul Razak. Subsequently in October 2011, the official agreement was signed in Nanning, and CMQIP was officially launched in April 2012. It was during the launch of CMQIP that a sister industrial park, Malaysia–China Kuantan Industrial Park (MCKIP), was agreed by both prime ministers to be set up.

CMQIP is the third national-level government-to-government industrial park (after the Suzhou Industrial Park and Tianjian Eco-city projects, both jointly sponsored by the Chinese and Singaporean governments) to be established in China. Qinzhou is a mid-level city in Guangxi, but it occupies a strategic position facing the Beibu Gulf (the Gulf of Tonkin) region. Due to the provincial government of Guangxi pursuing the Beibu Gulf Economic Region programme (an ambitious regional developmental plan that features stronger economic cooperation between Guangxi and Southeast Asia), the importance of Qinzhou has increased significantly. CMQIP has a total planned area of 13,588 acres and will be jointly developed by a Sino–Malaysian joint venture between a Malaysian consortium known as Qinzhou Development (Malaysia) Consortium Sdn Bhd, and Qinzhou Jingwu Investment Co. Ltd. The Malaysian consortium holds 49 percent of the shares in the joint venture, the Chinese party holding the rest. The consortium in turn was formed by two Malaysian private enterprises: S. P. Setia and Rimbunan Hijau. The board of directors of this Sino–Malaysian joint venture is the former deputy mayor of Qinzhou city government; the CEO is a former official of the Malaysian Minister of International Trade and Industry.

MCKIP is located just outside Kuantan, the capital city of the state of Pahang, the state where Najib is from (and where he has a parliamentary seat). Pahang, together with two other states, Kelantan and Terengganu, form what is known as the East Coast Economic Region (ECER), a regional developmental plan that focuses on the poorer east coast states in Malaysia. ECER is directed by a statutory body, ECER Development Council, chaired by Prime Minister Najib as well. Kuantan is a port city and has been identified as the strategic integrated industrial and logistics hub for ECER ('Donghaian tiedao kong chongji shicheng' 2016).

Originally only allocated about 1,500 acres, MCKIP later expanded to about 3,000 acres, and now has three sections. The original 1,500-acre section is now called MCKIP1, and the newer sections are called MCKIP2 and MCKIP3. MCKIP1 and MCKIP2 are next to each other, but MCKIP3 is located further away, closer to Kuantan Port. Interestingly, the master developer of MCKIP (discussed later) only owns the land of MCKIP1; MCKIP2 and MCKIP3 are owned by different partners, such as Sime Darby and IJM, operator of the Kuantan Port. In the planning, MCKIP1 and MCKIP2 will feature heavy industries, but MCKIP3 is designed as a residential and logistics hub.[7] Sandwiched between these three sections of MCKIP and Kuantan Port are two other developmental parks: Kuantan Integrated Biopark and Gebeng integrated Petrochemical Complex. Together they form a large industrial zone, and Kuantan Port is the main outlet for export.

It was estimated that the cost of development of MCKIP would be around RM2.5 billion/US$600 million (Yap 2016, p. 60). MCKIP was not officially launched until February 2013, because it took some time for China and Malaysia to sort out the ownership stakes of the joint venture company (MCKIP Sdn Bhd) that would act as the master developer of MCKIP. A Chinese consortium (Guangxi Beibu Gulf ASEAN Investment) comprising firms affiliated with the Guangxi provincial government (Guangxi Beibu Gulf International Port Group, or GBGIPG,[8] with 95 percent share of the consortium) and Qinzhou city government (Qinzhou Investment Development, with 5 percent share of the consortium) was formed to hold 49 percent of the shares of MCKIP Sdn Bhd. A Malaysian consortium, Kuantan Pahang Holdings Sdn Bhd, originally consisted of S.P. Setia and Rimbunan Hijau. Pahang state government and Pahang's own investment arm has the remaining shares. Both S.P. Setia and Rimbunan Hijau, however, had by early 2014 withdrawn from the MCKIP project (but remain committed to CMQIP) and sold their stakes in the consortium to IJM, one of the largest Malaysian construction companies and owner of the Kuantan Port, and Sime Darby, a Malaysian government-linked company heavily involved in palm oil plantation and export.

The government of Malaysia has placed high hopes on MCKIP to especially hike Malaysia–China trade and China's investments in Malaysia (Khor 2013). According to government plan, MCKIP will be an integral part of ECER and has been given many preferential policies. These include a 15-year corporate tax exemption (which is the only case in Malaysia), 15 percent income tax rate for all qualified knowledge workers, import duty and sales tax exemption, stamp duty exemption, and a facilitation fund of up to RM200 million/US$47 million for investing companies to set up basic infrastructure (MCKIP n.d.). The industries that were identified as focal for MCKIP include oil, electrical products, plastic and metal, automobile components, steel plates, and renewable energy, among others. According to the latest media reports, MCKIP has from 2013 to 2016 attracted about RM19 billion in investment and is expected to draw in another RM8 billion to RM10 billion in 2017 ('MCKIP secures RM19b in investments, targets another RM10b this year' 2017).

The largest investment so far is Alliance Steel (M), a subsidiary of Guangxi Beibu Gulf Iron and Steel, which itself is formed by two enterprises: GBGIPG and Guangxi Shenglong Metallurgy Corporation, a private enterprise based in Guangxi.[9] Alliance steel has invested RM4.2 billion/US$1 billion in constructing a modern plant on a 710-acre site within MCKIP. Alliance Steel is reportedly one of the most advanced steelmakers in China and is investing a state-of-the-art steel plant, producing high-speed wire rods, bars, and an H-shaped beam, with an annual production of 3.5 million tons. The technology of producing an H-shaped beam reportedly is the first to be introduced into ASEAN.[10] Once completed, the steel plant has a strong economic potential to drive the developments in Kuantan and the east coast ('Huang Huikang: Guandan chanyeyuan Lianhe gangte qiye jiangcheng Dongmeng zui xianjin gangtiechang' 2017).

Kuantan's status as the major eastern coastal port of Malaysia also holds special attraction for the Chinese, who are in general interested in investing in port facilities and management. The development of MCKIP therefore is in tandem with China's investment in the development of Kuantan Port. Kuantan Port faces the Gulf of Thailand and the South China Sea and is the closest Malaysian port to both China and Vietnam geographically. To underline the close relationship between MCKIP and Kuantan Port, the chairman of MCKIP Sdn Bhd, Soam Heng Choon, is concurrently serving as the Chief Executive Officer and managing director of IJM. GBGIPG has bought 40 percent ownership of the Kuantan Port Consortium (KPC) from IJM, which has a 30-year concession starting in 1998 to manage, operate, and develop Kuantan Port. The purchase of the 40 percent stake reportedly was a Malaysia's first and needed special approval from the highest level of the Malaysian government.[11] In investing in KPC, GBGIPG has also injected the necessary capital for KPC to carry out a port expansion and upgrading project amounting to RM4 billion/US$950 million. The upgrading of Kuantan Port will double the existing capacity of the port to eventually accommodate 52 million freight weight tons (FWT) and 1.5 million 20-foot equivalent units (TEU) ('IJM: Kuantan Port upgrade crucial' 2016). China Harbour Engineering Corporation (CHEC), a fully owned subsidiary of China Communications Construction Corporation (CCCC), is the main contractor to carry out the upgrading job. A 12-kilometre conveyor belt is also being built to connect MCKIP1, MCKIP2, and Kuantan Port, so that manufactured products from the industrial park can be easily transferred to the port for export. In May 2016, the central government of Malaysia also approved the application by Kuantan Port to become a free port (free trade zone) ('Guandan gangkou cheng mianshuigang' 2016). Malaysia ambitiously hopes that the transformation of Kuantan Port will make it into a logistics hub in the Asia–Pacific and drive the development of ECER.

Overseeing the activities and progress of both industrial parks is the Joint Council of the Parks, which consists of delegates from the provincial government of Guangxi, the state government of Pahang, the Ministry of Commerce of China, and the Ministry of International Trade and Industry of Malaysia. Malaysia also appointed a special envoy, Ong Ka Ting, a former president of the Malaysian Chinese Association, one of the main component parties of the ruling Barisan Nasional government in Malaysia, to help implement the industrial parks. Ong is also the chairman of the Malaysia–China Business Council (MCBC), whose board members come almost exclusively from the Chinese business elite and selected retired politicians from the ruling parties (see Yap 2016).

Given the emphasis placed upon MCKIP and its symbolic status as manifestation of Malaysia–China friendship, one would have expected MCKIP to progress rapidly. Nevertheless, the fact is that it lags significantly behind not only its counterpart, CMQIP, in China but also in expectations from both Malaysian and Chinese governments. Information gathered from interviewing insiders reveals that, although the federal government has been enthusiastic about the project, the Pahang state government's attitude was originally lacklustre.[12] Although Najib played a role in deciding that the industrial park would be placed in Kuantan, it was the state government of Pahang that decided which particular area was to be allocated to house the industrial park. Not only was the size of MCKIP dwarfed by CMQIP, creating a significant disparity between the two, but the site selected for MCKIP also contained substandard soil. The site was originally marshy and in need of embankment, which increased the cost of investment and deterred prospective investors. It was only later that MCKIP expanded with the help of one its investors, Sime Darby, approving the transfer of more land from Sime Darby to MCKIP. Still, the size of MCKIP, even after expansion, remains limited. For instance, the investment from Alliance Steel already takes up close to half of the area of MCKIP1. The size limitation of MCKIP may affect the economic scale, and in order for Kuantan Port to fully utilize its future increased capacity, it must rely also on the planned East Coast Rail Link (ECRL).

With ECRL (discussed in a later subsection), Kuantan Port will be linked with the most advanced port (Port Klang) and city (Kuala Lumpur) on the west coast. In theory, once all these infrastructure projects are complete, ships can unload their goods at Port Klang, transport through ECRL to Kuantan Port, and from Kuantan ship to China and Vietnam, bypassing Singapore and the rest of the Straits of Malacca. The future potential of Kuantan has therefore attracted a number of China's port partners. Huizhou Port, in Guangdong Province, formed a "sister port relationship" with Kuantan in 2016 ('Guandan gangkou cheng mianshuigang' 2016). This is in addition to the Malaysia–China Port Alliance which was mooted in 2015 and finalized under an agreement in July 2016. Under the port alliance, ten Chinese ports will form a collaborative partnership – Dalian, Shanghai, Ningbo, Qinzhou, Guangzhou, Fuzhou, Xiamen, Shezhen, Hainan, and Taicang – with six Malaysian ports – Port Klang, Malacca (discussed later), Penang, Johor, Kuantan, and Bintulu.

Malacca gateway and Malacca–Guangdong Industrial Park

Unlike other projects, the origin of the Malacca Gateway project has nothing to do with governmental initiatives (either Malaysia or China); instead, it has been driven by a Malaysian private company, KAJ Development, which secured a concession from the Malacca state government to develop the project in 2009. It was only much later, around 2015–2016, that the China partnership came in and was included as part of BRI-related projects. Although the main driver remains a private enterprise with only limited financial involvement from the state government, the state government of Malacca has been quite supportive of the Malacca Gateway project. Its chief minister, Idris Haron, envisions that the port in Malacca will play a crucial role, and will become a "new landmark" in the huge market of China–ASEAN trade in the future. He said, "the Belt and Road Initiative of China has brought many investment opportunities and capital inflow into Malacca. We have to seize this opportunity, and port development is no exception" ('Jia gangkou liaocheng Dongmeng xin dibiao' 2017).

Malacca Gateway is an integrated project featuring tourism, commercial, property, oil and gas, container, and maritime developments on four islands (three reclaimed, one natural), off the coast of the city of Malacca, totalling about 1,366 acres. The total investment cost of the project amounts to about RM30 billion ('Return of Malacca's gory days 2016). Each island is earmarked for a different kind of development (see Table 7.1). Islands 1 and 2 will be the first to develop.

KAJ Development secured the investment by PowerChina International in the development of Malacca Gateway, and both sides signed an agreement in September 2016 under the witness of the Minister of International Trade and Industry of Malaysia. Two other agreements were signed between KAJ Development, PowerInternational, Shenzhen Yantian Port Group, and Rizhao Port Group in

Table 7.1 Malacca Gateway project

Island	Size	Developments	Parties
Island 1 (reclaimed)	218 acres	Cruise terminal, ferry terminal, hotel, health, education, residential, entertainment, tourism	KAJ, PowerChina International
Island 2 (reclaimed)	300 acres	Commercial, insurance, finance, corporate headquarters, residential, free trade zone	KAJ, PowerChina International
Island 3 (natural)	98 acres	Liquid cargo terminal, oil and gas	KAJ, PowerChina International, Shenzhen Yantian Port Group, Rizhao Port Group
Island 4 (reclaimed)	750 acres	Container terminal and port logistics, Maritime Industrial Park (shipbuilding and ship repair)	KAJ, Chief Minister Inc., PowerChina International, CCCC

Source: Author's compilation.

October 2015 and May 2017 respectively. In the development of Islands 1 and 2, PowerChina International and KAJ Development will be the sole developers. On Island 3, Shenzhen Yantian Port Group (from Guangdong Province) and Rizhao Port Group (from Shandong Province) will join the project. It has also been specifically mentioned that the development of Island 3 will cost RM8 billion/US$1.9 billion. Island 4 has been designated a government-to-government cooperative project (between Malacca state and Guangdong Province); hence, in addition to KAJ Development and PowerChina International, two state-backed entities become partners (Chief Minister Inc. is the investment arm of the state government of Malacca; CCCC is the nominated partner by the Guangdong provincial government). Reportedly, KAJ Development remains the majority stakeholder (51 percent) of the project. However, there are no further details about the share structure, and apparently the terms of the share structure of the four islands are still being negotiated.

PowerChina International is a large state-owned enterprise (SOE) under the direct administration of the State-owned Assets Supervision and Administration Commission of the State Council of China. It was formed by combining several large SOEs, including Sinohydro Group and HydroChina Group, in 2011. Sinohydro has previously been involved in several projects in Malaysia as well, most notably in several dam projects in the state of Sarawak. On the Malacca Gateway project, PowerChina International has basically delegated and appointed its own subsidiary, Sinohydro, as the main contractor to carry out the joint development with KAJ Development ('Huangjinggang zaixian gucheng huihuang' 2017).

Islands 3 and 4 are collectively termed "portopolis" by KAJ Development and are seen as the backbone of the Malacca Gateway project. Whereas Island 3 is designed as a liquid cargo terminal, which is to service the oil and gas tankers, Island 4 is projected to develop into a container and bulk terminal that can eventually handle up to 4 million TEU. In addition, a Maritime Industrial Park is to be built on Island 4, to mainly engage in shipbuilding and ship repair industries. Although in 2016–2017 the shipbuilding industry suffered a decline worldwide, KAJ Development believes that the Maritime Industrial Park can find a niche, as Malaysia still does not have a major shipyard along the Straits of Malacca.

The designation of Island 4 as a container port indicates that Malacca Gateway has ambitions to capture a greater cargo business market share from the Straits of Malacca, one of the busiest shipping lanes in the world, from perhaps two of its most likely competitors, Port Klang in Malaysia and Singapore. A KAJ Development company official, however, has revealed that, because of the close relationship between Malacca and Guangdong Province, the Guangdong government has promised to direct ships from the province to use Malacca Gateway in the future.[13] In addition, in conjunction with the development of Malacca Gateway is the development of a Malacca–Guangdong Industrial Park, a separate project that does not involve KAJ Development but rather the Malacca state government. It is envisioned that goods produced in this Malacca–Guangdong Industrial Park will utilize the services of Island 4 in the future.

Malacca–Guangdong Industrial Park is located in Jasin, a district about 30 kilometres northeast of Malacca Gateway. It is a state-province cooperative joint venture that was set up in 2016. Guangdong Province and Malacca state have entered into a strong partnership since both sides signed an agreement to have a "sister state-province relationship" in 2014.[14] The Malacca–Guangdong Industrial Park occupies about 2,500 acres. One of the first, and largest, investors in the park is China's Xinyi Glass, a modern glass manufacturer, which has invested about RM2.2 billion/US$500 million into the park ('Huang Huikang: yinru chuangxin jishu, Zhongzi lai Ma fei qiangfanwan' 2017).

Despite the optimism of both the Malacca state government and KAJ Development, one crucial deficiency of the Malacca Gateway project that could become a major flaw is the lack of infrastructure connectivity to the mainland-based transport systems within peninsular Malaysia. Malacca Gateway is now only accessible through road and not rail. To fully utilize the potential of Island 4 as a cargo port, a more efficient infrastructure network is needed to connect Malacca Gateway to other important cities and rail systems within peninsular Malaysia. KLSHSR has a designated station in Malacca, but the exact location of the station has not been determined. Malacca Gateway has come into the picture of KLSHSR planning officials, as it is designated by KLSHSR as the "feeder to Malaysia's central belt".[15] However, as of March 2017, the author had not confirmed if there is any plan to enhance the infrastructure connectivity between the station and Malacca Gateway.

Gemas–Johor Bahru Double-Tracking Railway Project

The Gemas–Johor Bahru Electrified Double-Tracking Railway Project connects Johor Bahru, the southern tip of Peninsular Malaysia (and the capital city of the state of Johor) to Johor's northern part. It is part of the wider electrified double-tracking railway project, which aims to improve and modernize the old and existing rail tracts that connect Peninsular Malaysia from north to south. The wider project is divided into different stretches, and all other stretches have already been awarded.[16] The Gemas–Johor Bahru stretch, about 200 kilometres and located within the state of Johor, is the last remaining stretch and is reportedly worth RM8.9 billion/US$2.11 billion.

The electrified double-tracking railway project has a complicated story. In 2002, the China Railway Engineering Corporation (CREC) was issued a letter of intent by the Malaysian government for this project. However, in 2003 the letter was scrapped by then-Prime Minister Mahathir, who awarded it to a local consortium (MMC–Gamuda). Then in 2003, Prime Minister Abdullah Badawi scrapped the whole deal. But it was revived in 2007, and CREC resubmitted its bid, this time for the Gemas–Johor Bahru stretch only. However, two other Chinese companies emerged to contend for this project: China Railway Construction Corporation (CRCC) and CCCC ('China railway builders hit by Malaysian politics' 2012). As required, all of them have to find a local partner to win the project. This apparently complicated the matter, as all the local partners selected by the three China competitors were backed by different political and business elite players in Malaysia.

During Najib's visit to China in 2009, he personally made a promise to Hu Jintao, then China's president, that the Gemas–Johor Bahru project would be awarded to a Chinese company. However, the identity of the company had not been decided. CREC was reportedly the frontrunner and was closely working with a prominent Malaysian Chinese entrepreneur in the bid for this project. But in December 2011, China Road and Bridge Construction (CRBC), now the subsidiary of CCCC, emerged as the likely contractor. Najib was alleged to have preferred CCCC, through the brokering of a golfing buddy (an ethnic Chinese) who happens to be the owner of a construction firm (George Kent) that has won many government projects (Barrock 2013). The participation of CRCC, in the meantime, was allegedly facilitated by Daim Zainuddin ('China railway builders hit by Malaysian politics' 2012), an influential former minister close to former Prime Minister Mahathir Mohammad, and CRCC's bid was supported by the Sultan of Johor and yet another prominent Malaysian Chinese entrepreneur. Its local partner was first reported to be Gamuda, a Malaysian infrastructure company with a close relationship with the who's who within the ruling circle, also partly owned by the Perak royal family and the partner in the MMC–Gamuda consortium that built another stretch of the electrified double-tracking railway project.

Due to the involvement of so many important political figures, it is unsurprising that the whole deal has dragged on unnecessarily for many years. Table 7.2 illustrates the different players involved in the competition in this project.

Table 7.2 Competition over Gemas–Johor Bahru Double-Tracking Railway project

Chinese Construction Company	Original Local Partner	Local Political Support
China Railway Engineering Corporation (CREC)	Malton	Najib
China Communications Construction (CCCC)	George Kent	Najib
China Railway Construction Corporation (CRCC)	Gamuda	Daim Zainuddin, Sultan of Johor

Source: Author's compilation.

In October 2016, the Ministry of Transport finally awarded the project to a consortium that was eventually formed by the three competitors. CRCC is the leading player, holding a 40 percent stake in the consortium; CREC and CCCC each have a 30 percent stake. The RM8.9 billion/US$2.11 billion project, other than constructing the electrified double-track rail, includes the building of nine new passage stations, two rolling stock depots, and three open stations next to the existing line. The project is expected to begin work in 2017 and will take four years to complete. Its local partner is identified as SIPP Railway, a private vehicle controlled by the Sultan of Johor. According to a CRCC manager in Malaysia, the role of SIPP has yet to be clarified, but it will help in the process of "land acquisition". In addition, the Chinese consortium, reportedly under the terms of the Ministry of Transport, has to subcontract at least 30 percent of the work to local companies ('RM8.9 bil Gemas – JB double – tracking project to spin off jobs for locals' 2017).

East Coast Rail Link (ECRL)

The three states on the east coast of Peninsular Malaysia (Pahang, which hosts MCKIP and Kuantan Port, Terengganu, and Kelantan) have long been among the poorest in Malaysia. A key factor contributing to such underdevelopment was the absence of an effective land-based infrastructure linkage between the metropolitan cities on the west coast and the less-developed and less-populated cities and towns on the east coast. East Coast Rail Link (ECRL) was therefore mooted in the 1980s, when Najib was serving as the MB (Menteri Besar, or Chief Minister) for the state of Pahang ('Naji: Donghaian xiejie tiedao jiahua luoshi youlai Mazhong youhao guanxi' 2016). ECRL was to link the east coast states of Kelantan, Terengganu, Pahang, and the west coast states and cities such as Selangor, Kuala Lumpur, and Klang. However, due to a shortage of funds, the government could not push for its implementation.

During Najib's visit to China in late 2016, the government finally secured the necessary funds from China to build the railway. Through direct negotiation, CCCC is the main contractor for this project. Main financing would come from a soft loan provided by China EximBank. The terms are set so that CCCC will have to find local partners and subcontractors to ensure adequate Malaysian participation in the project and to share the benefits ('Zhong dai dama 550yi' 2016). Many details of the project were not clarified until one year later, when ECRL was officially launched on 9 August 2017. The launching itself was attended by Najib and by Wang Yong, a State Councillor of China.

After completion, ECRL will be the longest railway project in Malaysia, about 688 kilometres.[17] There will be two main phases of the project: the first main phase will connect from Kota Bharu, the northernmost major city on the east coast, to the Integrated Transport Terminal in Gombak, within the state of Selangor and about 20 kilometres north of Kuala Lumpur. The second phase will be the extension from Gombak to the Port of Klang, the completion of which will link the most important Malaysian port on the west coast and facing the Malacca Strait, to the ports on the east coast, including Kuantan Port, hence creating a "land bridge" that bypasses the rest of the Malacca Strait. The whole project will take roughly seven years to complete (by 2024). Estimated to cost RM55 billion/US$13 billion, 85 percent of the whole project is to be financed by a soft loan provided by China EximBank. The terms of the soft loan accordingly are no requirement for payment in the first seven years, and the full loan is to be fully repaid within 20 years at an interest rate of 3.25 percent. The loan is also denominated in Malaysian ringgit, hence limiting any risk of Malaysian currency depreciation. The remaining 15 percent would be financed through *sukuk* (Islamic bonds) programmes by local banks. Although CCCC is the main contractor, it is required to subcontract up to 30 percent of its contract to Malaysian participants, which translates into about RM16 billion/US$3.8 billion (Ganeshwaran & Gurmeet 2017, p. 14). Several major local builders such as Gemuda, IJM, and Fajarbaru have already lined up to become the major subcontractors for ECRL ('Fajarbaru eyeing ECRL sub–contract jobs' 2017; 'Gamuda in strong position to secure ECRL jobs' 2017). ECRL will also serve both passengers and cargo transport. According to the government's own projection, by 2030 there will be 5.4 million passengers and 53 million tons of cargo utilizing the services of ECRL. Thirty percent of the profit of the project will come from passengers and 70 percent through freight ('ECRL project a mindset – changer' 2017).

Najib described the project as a game changer or "mindset-changer" and noted that "ECRL would promote development of industrial areas and boost the growing trend of transit-oriented development that nurtures compact residential districts and commercial centres along the 22 stations" ('ECRL project a mindset-changer' 2017), while citing an unknown survey that purportedly shows 96 percent of the people in the state of Pahang support the project ('Dongtie dailai gaibian, Naji: zhouzhao diqu shouyi' 2017). Wang Yong, China's State Councillor, also praised the project as a "flagship" project of BRI, a "model of China–Malaysia cooperation" that benefits the Malaysian people ('Dongtie shi zhongma qijian xiangmu' 2017).

Although the government has strongly promoted ECRL, the project has faced intense criticism. The most controversial part of the project is cost. Originally estimated at RM30 billion, it was announced to be RM55 billion when the MOU (memorandum of understanding) to construct ECRL was signed in Beijing in November 2016. The sudden jump in price created suspicion among the Malaysian opposition and civil society that part of the fund would be diverted for other purposes, primarily to help with the troubled 1MDB. Nevertheless, the government came up with the justification that the original pricing did not include the cost of all rolling stock, signalling systems, and supporting infrastructure. Jomo K.S., a well-known economist, also questions whether the government's projection of the volume of passengers and cargo, hence the viability of the ECRL project, is realistic or not. In his view, many "white elephant" projects have been created in the past based on wrong assumptions about their "multiplier" effect, and as a result the government accumulated significant debt. And since the main financer and contractor are Chinese companies, there are very likely few direct benefits to Malaysia, and at the same time Malaysia risks getting itself into a debt situation (Jomo 2017). This concern is shared by Nazir Abdul Razak, the younger brother of Najib and chairman of CIMB Group, the second-largest banking group in Malaysia. In a round table Nazir, although he agreed that ECRL would be beneficial, questioned the price tag, whether Malaysia will be capable of servicing the debt in the future, as well as its social and environmental impact ('Cu shencha dongtie jihua, Naxier: baokuo touzi guimo yu jiazhi' 2017). Another issue was the lack of transparency in appointing CCCC as the main contractor for this project. The government, despite demands from the opposition, has not released any feasibility study, and the detailed financial terms remain murky (Lim 2018). CCCC itself also has been questioned, since one of its subsidiaries, China Road and Bridge Construction, had been on the blacklist of the World Bank. Now, CCCC has come out with clarifications. Accordingly, CCCC's own estimation of the project amounted to RM46 billion, a difference of RM9 billion, as stated by the government of Malaysia. Astonishingly as well, a CCCC company official has acknowledged in a media interview that he has no idea why there is a "deviation in costs" between the Malaysian government and CCCC ('China's largest port construction firm to venture into property development in Malaysia' 2017).

Regardless of the controversies about the pricing, financing, and awarding of ECRL, there is little doubt that, once completed, it will be hugely beneficial in improving connectivity and in the economic development of the east coast of Malaysia. Linking up Klang (the largest and most important port of Malaysia, with the capacity to handle 12 million TEU annually) and Kuala Lumpur (the commercial hub) with Kuantan could potentially make Kuantan the future logistics hub for ASEAN–China trade. As mentioned, ECRL could help provide an alternative route to the traditional sea-based route that passes through the Straits of Malacca and Singapore. This has created certain anxieties in Singapore, as ECRL is seen as potentially threatening to Singapore's status as an international logistics hub ('Longxin gaotie jiao 2 qiye yingyun' 2016).

Hence, in conjunction with the construction of ECRL, there have been reports that Port Klang is planning for an expansion of its facilities. An offshore island,

Carey Island, reportedly has been earmarked by the Ministry of Transport to become a new development project that will expand Port Klang's handling capacity to 30 million TEU. The project will cost RM200 billion/US$47.36 billion and reportedly will involve, again, a China investor/partner ('2 qianyi jian Basheng disan gang' 2017). In addition, analysts in the corporate sector are estimating that the construction of ECRL itself may bring about an 8 percent growth in the construction sector in the three east coast states and contribute to the growth of other related sectors such as real estate ('Jianzu huodong liao meinian zeng 8%' 2017). Jebasingam Issace John, the chief executive officer of the ECER Development Council, estimated that the improved connectivity between Port Klang and Kuantan Port will contribute "an additional one to 1.5 percent of the GDP to the ECER" ('ECER attracts RM109b in investments' 2017).

Kuala Lumpur–Singapore High-Speed Rail (KLSHSR)

The Kuala Lumpur–Singapore High-Speed Rail (KLSHSR) Project was first proposed by Najib in 2010 as part of the government's Economic Transformation Program. In September 2013, Najib and Singapore Prime Minister Lee Hsien Long announced that both countries had agreed to jointly build KLSHSR, at a cost estimated to be at least RM40 billion. In 2014, Malaysia announced that KLSHSR would go through eight stations, seven of them within Malaysia. Originally planned to be completed by 2020, the deadline was postponed in 2015, after several rounds of bilateral negotiations of the project, which was more complex than originally thought. In addition, scepticism of the whole project emerged, regarding whether the ticket price (accordingly fixed at no more than RM400 per person per ride) could adequately cover the construction cost (originally estimated at RM40 billion/US$9.5 billion, later revised to RM60 billion/US$14.2 billion), whether there is sustainable ridership, how much time it actually saves compared to the Kuala Lumpur–Singapore flight, and whether KLSHSR competes with the ongoing double-tracking railway project (Jacob 2015).

Despite these concerns, both Malaysia and Singapore went ahead with the project. Finally, more concrete details about KLSHSR emerged in the second half of 2016. First, in July 2016, both countries signed an MOU on KLSHSR, and then, in December 2016, a formal agreement was signed. According to the July MOU and the December agreement, the call for open tender will begin before the end of 2017. The RM60-billion project is projected to take ten years to complete (in 2026). The length of KLSHSR is about 350 kilometres, of which 335 kilometres are located within Malaysia, and 15 kilometres in Singapore. There will be eight stops along KLSHSR, seven located in Malaysia (one, as mentioned, will be in Malacca). Three customs, immigration, and quarantine (CIQ) facilities will be installed in Singapore, Johor Baru, and Kuala Lumpur.

What is also notable is that the project will be divided into three parts: operations (OpCo), railway assets (AssetsCo), and infrastructure (InfraCo). Table 7.3 is an illustration of the role, functions, ownership, and tendering process of the three parts. According to the CEO of MyHSR Corporation Sdn Bhd (MyHSR

Table 7.3 Three-part structure of the Kuala Lumpur-Singapore High Speed Rail (KLSHSR) project

Types of Corporation	Countries	Responsibilities	Ownership	Tender
InfraCo	Malaysia	Stations and facilities in Malaysia	Government of Malaysia	Open tender called by Malaysian Government
	Singapore	Stations and facilities in Singapore	Government of Singapore	Open tender called by Singapore government
OpCo	International	Providing service to international travel	Private	Open tender jointly called by Singapore and Malaysia
	Domestic	Providing service to domestic travel (within Malaysia)	Private	Open tender called by Malaysia
AssestsCo		Rolling stock, rail assets, network operator	Private	Open tender jointly called by Singapore and Malaysia

Source: 'Longxin gaotie yiwei gongcun gongrong' 2016.

Corp, which is owned by the Ministry of Finance Incorporated and was set up to be the developer and asset owner of the KLSHSR on the Malaysian side), the biggest part of this three-part structure will be InfraCo, which involves the building of tunnels, viaducts, and stations and will be owned by the governments (of Malaysia and Singapore separately). "The maintenance and provision of the railway assets, the trains, the signalling, the tracks, the management of the network" ('HSR structure levels playing field for international bidders' 2016) has to be done by AssetsCo, which can be owned by private parties and subject to competitive open tender. Finally, two operators (OpCo), one handling the domestic connections within Malaysia and the other handling international travel between Malaysia and Singapore, will be responsible for customer service and increase of ridership ('HSR structure levels playing field for international bidders' 2016).

Since the announcement in 2013 that Malaysia and Singapore have agreed to build KLSHSR, there has been growing competition between China, Japan, and later, South Korea and France. The competition between China and Japan has been particularly intense. In May 2016, a major delegation led by Sheng Guangzu, then general manager of China Railway Corporation (and the last Minister of National Railways) visited Malaysia to lobby for a Chinese consortium to win the KLSHSR project. China Railway Corporation is the national railway operator of China (before 2013 it was the Ministry of National Railways under the State Council of China) and is not involved in the construction business, but it plays a leading and coordinating role in bringing together nine major Chinese companies to form a consortium to bid for KLSHSR. The nine-member consortium includes: China Railway Engineering Corp (CREC), China Investment Corp, China EximBank, China Railway Construction Corp (CRCC), China Communications Construction Corp (CCCC), China Railway Rolling Stock Corp (CRRC) and China Railway Signal and Communication Corp (CRSC), Third Railway Survey and Design Institute Group Corporation (TSDI), and China Railway First Survey and Design Institute Group Corp (FSDI) ('Sanguo lizheng gaotie zichan guanli' 2017).

The way KLSHSR is structured (as shown in Table 7.3), there are five tenders so Malaysia (and Singapore) does not have to award all tenders to the corporations of one country but to several countries, in a way diversifying to different partners. However, according to an exclusive with a Chinese-language business daily in Malaysia, China is not much interested in obtaining the contracts of InfraCo or OpCo but is most interested in the contract of AssetsCo, the part that can demonstrate the state of technology and management of China's high-speed rail achievement. However, this is also the tender that Japan and South Korea are focusing on, so China is facing serious competition. The announcement of the winner of the tender is likely to be either late 2017 or early 2018 ('Sanguo lizheng gaotie zichan guanli' 2017).

CCCC, CREC, CRCC, PowerChina International, GBGIPG

Table 7.4 summarizes the key facts about the infrastructure projects discussed earlier. From the previous discussion, it can be seen that a number of large China companies have been heavily involved in these projects: CCCC, CREC, CRCC, PowerChina International, and GBGIPG. Of these, only GBGIPG is owned by the government of Guangxi; the rest are owned by the central government in Beijing. Incidentally, many of them are also involved in many other projects outside the above-mentioned BRI-related projects. CCCC is perhaps the most active at the moment. CCCC itself was the result of a merger in 2005 between two entities, China Harbour Engineering Corporation (CHEC) and China Road and Bridge Construction (CRBC). Both CREC and CRBC were contenders for the Penang Second Bridge project in 2004–2006. CREC was the contractor that completed the construction of the Penang Second Bridge. Other major Malaysia-related projects of CCCC include Samalaju Port at Sarawak, a reclamation project at Seri Tanjung Pinang in the state of Penang, and a Mass Rapid Transit project in Kuala Lumpur–Putrajaya–Selangor (joint venture with local constructor George Kent). CREC became involved in property development, in both Kuala Lumpur and the state of Sabah (partnering with local developer Titijaya). CRCC is rather a latecomer compared to CCCC and CREC, but it has been involved in a massive undersea tunnel project in Penang. The subsidiary of PowerChina International, Sinohydro, is a familiar face in Malaysia, especially in Sarawak. It entered the Malaysian market in early 1996, where it was the contracting party to the huge (and controversial) Bakun dam project.

Table 7.4 China's BRI-Related infrastructure projects in Malaysia

Project		Parties (M = Malaysia C = China)	Value (ringgit Malaysia, billion)	Details
Bandar Malaysia		[Before May 2017] (M) MOF: 40 percent (M-C) IWH-CREC: 60 percent	12	• IWH itself is owned by two parties: 60 percent belongs to Lim Kang Hoo and 40 percent to Kumpulan Prasarana Rakyat Johor • Strong role of the Sultan of Johor • Eventual value estimated as RM200 billion • CREC investing in building a HQ in Bandar Malaysia (RM8.4billion) • Termination of agreement in May 2017
Kuantan	Kuantan Port	(M) IJM: 60 percent (C) GBGIPG: 40 percent	4 (port expansion project)	• GBGIPG investment into the Kuantan Port Consortium (KPC) crucial for construction of a deepwater terminal
	Malaysia–China Kuantan Industrial Park (MCKIP)	(M) Kuantan Pahang Holdings Sdn Bhd: 51 percent (C) Guangxi Beibu Gulf ASEAN Investment: 49 percent	2.5	• Originally 1,500 acres, now expanded to 3,000 acres • Malaysian Consortium (Kuantan Pahang Holdings Sdn Bhd): IJM 40 percent, Sime Darby 30 percent, Pahang 30 percent • Chinese Consourtium (Guangxi Beibu Gulf ASEAN Investment): GBGIP: 95 percent, Qinzhou Investment Development: 5 percent
Malacca	Malacca Gateway	(M) KAJ Development (51 percent by estimation) (M) Chief Minister Inc. (C) PowerChina International (C) Shenzhen Yantian Port (C) Rizhao Port (C) CCCC	30	• Four islands (three reclaimed and one natural), total about 1,366 acres • Islands 1 and 2: Commercial and tourist islands, free trade zone • Island 3: Liquid cargo Terminal • Island 4: Cargo and Maritime Industrial Park • Share structure still being negotiated

Project			
Malacca–Guangdong Industrial Park	??	??	• 2,500 acres, located in Jasin, about 30 kilometres northeast of Malacca Gateway • Jointly developed by Malacca state government and Guangdong provincial government
Gemas–Johor Baru Double-Tracking Railway	8.9	(C) CRCC: 40 percent (C) CREC: 30 percent (C) CCCC: 30 percent	• 200-kilometre project • Local partner with SIPP, a company linked with the Sultan of Johor
East Coast Rail Link (ECRL)	55	(C) CCCC: 70 percent (100 percent as main contractor, to sublet 30 percent of work to local partners) (M) ??: 30 percent	• Financing from EximBank of China (20-year loan and no repayment in the first seven years) • 688-kilometre project, linking Port Klang on the west coast to Kota Bharu on the east coast
Kuala Lumpur–Singapore High-Speed Rail (KLSHSR)	60–65	Not awarded yet	• 350 km project • Three-tiered structure of ownership (infrastructure, operations, assets) • Competition from China, Japan, South Korea, France • China's competition: The nine-member consortium comprises China Railway Engineering Corp (CREC), China Investment Corp, EximBank of China, China Railway Construction Corp (CRCC), China Communications Construction Corp (CCCC), China Railway Rolling Stock Corp (CRRC) and China Railway Signal & Communication Corp (CRSC), Third Railway Survey and Design Institute Group Corporation (TSDI), China Railway First Survey and Design Institute Group Corp (FSDI)

Source: Author's compilation

People-to-people projects: Xiamen University Malaysia and *Impression Malacca*

In addition to the six infrastructure projects discussed above (Bandar Malaysia, MCKIP/Kuantan Port, Malacca Gateway, Gemas–Johor Bahru Double-Tracking Railway, ECRL, and KLSHSR) are two projects that need to be briefly discussed here: Xiamen University Malaysia Campus (XMUMC) and *Impression Malacca*. These two projects are not infrastructure projects but are part of the BRI-related projects, in enhancing people-to-people connections, one of the five areas of cooperation under BRI (the other four being policy coordination, infrastructure connectivity, trade facilitation, and financial cooperation). Chinese Ambassador to Malaysia Dr Huang Huikang has particularly identified both projects as BRI-related ones that will contribute to people-to-people understanding between Malaysia and China.

Xiamen University Malaysia Campus

In a 2011 visit to Xiamen University, Ong Ka Ting (Malaysia's Special Envoy to China who played a key role in facilitating the cooperation between Malaysia–China Kuantan Industrial Park and China–Malaysia Qinzhou Industrial Park) and Hou Kok Chung (then the Deputy Minister of Higher Education in Malaysia, now serving as a vice president of the Malaysian Chinese Association) first came up with the idea of inviting Xiamen University to set up a branch campus in Malaysia. Xiamen University followed through and sent several delegations to Malaysia in the next few months to understand and study Malaysian higher education environment and policies and to inspect the site selected for the branch campus. The selected 150-acre site is in Sepang, which is close to both the administrative capital, Putrajaya, and metropolitan Kuala Lumpur. The original land was owned by Sime Darby, one of the largest government-linked conglomerates in Malaysia, which was sold to Xiamen University at a preferential price (Yap 2016, p. 97). Xiamen University's partner in developing the site was Sunsuria, whose executive chairman, Ter Leong Yap, is also the current president of the Associated Chinese Chamber of Commerce and Industry Malaysia (ACCCIM), the largest Malaysian Chinese business organization.[18] The construction of the campus would cost about RM1.3 billion/US$309 million. One of the major contractors to build the university's buildings was Sinohydro.

Xiamen University formally applied to the Ministry of Higher Education in Malaysia to set up a branch campus in Malaysia in August 2012, called Xiamen University Malaysia Campus (XMUMC). It was officially announced by Najib in January 2013. In February 2013, the then-chairman of the Chinese People's Political Consultative Conference (CPPCC) and one of the members of the Politburo Standing Committee of the Chinese Communist Party, Jia Qingling, visited Malaysia and witnessed the signing of the agreement to set up XMUMC This shows the endorsement of China's central government in this "first" overseas operation of a Chinese University. XMUMC was officially launched in July 2014 (Yap 2016, pp. 98–115).[19]

XMUMC has five schools (School of Ocean and Environment, School of Economics and Management, School of Chinese Language and Culture, School of Medicine, and School of Information Science and Technology), with 17 majors. XMUMC became operational in 2015, the first batch of student enrolment numbering 187 students. As of March 2017, it was estimated that the number of students will rise to about 3,000 ('Xiada fenxiao shoukai xianhe' 2017). XMUMC plans to enrol 5,000 students in 2020 and eventually to have student body of 10,000 students. The targeted sources of students include China, Malaysia, and ASEAN countries (*Xiamen University Malaysia Campus* n.d., p. 24). Although at the initial stage most teaching staff will be sent from the parent campus in China, eventually XMUMC is to employ mostly local staff.

Impression Malacca

The *Impression* series was mooted by three famed Chinese directors (Zhang Yimou, Wang Chaoge, and Fan Yue) that combine performing arts, dance, lights, and other stage technologies. The first *Impression* show was in Guilin, in 2003, called *Impression Liu Sanjie*, and has garnered critical acclaim and achieved commercial success. Since then, the *Impression* series has expanded to nine other localities in China, featuring different themes that fit the local cultures and history. The series has become an important brand name of Chinese cultural performance.

In 2013, one of the *Impression* directors, Wang Chaoge, was in Malacca to sign the agreement to bring *Impression* to Malacca, the first city to host the series outside China. Subsequently, a local developer, Yong Tai Group, won the concession to build Impression Theatre and the surrounding integrated development project called Impression City. Impression Theatre occupies a site of about 17 acres, and Impression City itself occupies 117 acres, including the theatre, to be built on reclaimed land not far from Malacca Gateway. Impression City is projected to have a gross development value of RM5.4 billion/US$1.28 billion and is to be completed within eight to ten years. Sino Haijing Holdings, a China company listed in Hong Kong, has invested in Yong Tai and holds 30 percent share of the company.[20] The theatre itself will be ready in 2017, and the first *Impression* show will be launched in early 2018.

Conclusion and reflections

This chapter highlights and discusses several major infrastructure (and cultural) projects that Malaysia and China are collaborating on under the BRI. Based on the previous discussion, broadly three observation points can be made here.

First, many of these projects predated Xi Jinping's announcement of the Belt and Road in late 2013, but now they are included as part of the initiative. Once the BRI was announced, these projects, originally planned separately and in isolation of one another perhaps, slowly came together and became more coherent, and it is now clear that they form an overall rational and strategic picture. MCKIP, Kuatan Port, Malacca Gateway, and ECRL all have the potential to enhance the "land bridge role" of the Malaya Peninsula. China has also shown interest in developing another west coast port, Bagan Datuk, located in the state of Perak, and in developing an oil pipeline from the port to Bachok, another port on the east coast. This will suggest another infrastructure connectivity project linking the east and west coasts. If all these projects are successfully implemented, this will be a huge transformation of Malaysian infrastructure and significantly elevate Malaysia's strategic potential in the trade between the Indian Ocean and the Pacific. In the process it will enhance significantly Malaysia's economic growth as well. Malaysia, for that matter, will continue to have a China-friendly foreign policy in the coming years. One could use a geopolitical lens in looking at the benefits China will accrue from these infrastructure projects, as they do seem to serve to reduce China's famous "Malacca Dilemma" to a certain extent; they will give China more options and can be seen as China's insurance policy should any geopolitical complications arise to affect China's access to the Malacca Strait. However, beyond geopolitical considerations, China may also be genuinely interested in upgrading Malaysia's infrastructure and enhancing Malaysia's trade potential, from which China can also benefit.

Second, the role of local stakeholders cannot be underestimated. Many of these projects involve local stakeholders, primarily state governments, political elite, and important decision makers in the civil service and government-lined companies. In the case of Bandar Malaysia, although the fallout is still shrouded in mystery, it can be sure that MoF officials (which ultimately answer to Prime Minister Najib) made the decision to terminate the deal, which affects China's interests. However, in other projects where local stakeholders give full support, in general there is a stronger foundation for these projects to proceed. Malaysia is a federal system, but some of the states also maintain a heredity constitutional monarch (like Johor). The monarchs are not to involve themselves in politics, but they are allowed to be involved in business, and some of them, such as the Sultan of Johor, have been quite active in pushing for many China-related business deals in Malaysia. Under the Malaysian federal system, the state governments enjoy autonomy, in particular policies related to land. Hence, securing the support of the state government will be crucial for the success of these projects. In Pahang, although originally the state government was not very enthusiastic about MCKIP and Kuantan Port, and the ECER authority had to play a major partnering role in the developments of these projects, lately the Pahang state government has shown more willingness and support, giving impetus to the faster development of these projects. In Malacca, the state government from the beginning has been very supportive of Malacca Gateway, Malacca–Guangdong Industrial Park, and *Impression Malacca*. The Sultan of Johor has been a strong presence, and his partnerships with the China investors ensure the latter's participation in projects such as Bandar Malaysia and Gemas–Johor Bahru Double-Tracking Railway project. The key roles played by these local state actors cannot be underestimated in understanding Sino–Malaysian collaboration under the BRI. It can therefore be hypothesized that the more local governments and local political/business elite are involved, the more stakeholders there are who wish to see the project succeed, and therefore the more likely it is to get the necessary support.

Third, China's growing economic presence, if not handled well, may create growing local anxieties. China's economic presence in Malaysia is getting larger year by year, owing in particular to the BRI that China is promoting at the moment. Despite the capital control that China imposed in early 2017, many of the infrastructure projects are government-to-government and are unlikely to be seriously affected. An increased Chinese economic presence in Malaysia, however, has also become a domestic political issue in Malaysia. Given that many Chinese companies work closely with the establishment elite, in particular Prime Minister Najib, many opposition leaders, including the newly formed Malay-based opposition party, Bersatu (led by former Prime Minister Mahathir and former Deputy Prime Minister Muhyiddin Yassin), have been accusing China's investment as facilitating the political survival (and corruption) of the present ruling government. Some critics have even linked Malaysia's economic deals with China with the South China Sea issue and see Najib's efforts as undermining national sovereignty for the sake of (personal) political and economic gains (see Ngeow 2017). The preference of these Chinese companies to work with the elite, their lack of experience in handling public relations issues, and lack of transparency in certain economic deals also have not helped. Hence, in order to make Sino–Malaysian infrastructure cooperation more sustainable, it is imperative that the Chinese companies adopt clean practices in their projects in Malaysia and learn to address local criticisms and concerns.

Notwithstanding some controversies generated by the increased economic presence of China, it can be expected that China's economic influence and presence in Malaysia will likely to grow in the coming years, especially under the BRI promoted by the Chinese government and supported by the Malaysian government. Malaysia stands to gain from this initiative but will have to balance its own interests (including those of the people and not just the elite) and China's interests well.

Postscript

The draft of this chapter was submitted before the historic 14th General Election of Malaysia in May 2018, which changed the government. The new Prime Minister Mahathir Mohammad has expressed that Malaysia will continue to support the BRI, but with stronger scrutiny to ensure Malaysia's interests are protected. Within months, ECRL and KLSHSR were suspended, together with some China-related oil and gas pipeline projects. More details about the financial irregularities regarding the ECRL were revealed as well.

Henceforth, out of the six projects mentioned, only Kuantan, Malacca, and the Gemas-Johor Bahru Double-Tracking Railway survived (Bandar Malaysia is still in limbo following the termination of the agreement in May 2017). However, there is the possibility that ECRL and KLSHSR will continue, perhaps under a very different format and design, with drastically reduced costs, or revived when the financial situation of Malaysia becomes better. The author still holds on to the views that these infrastructure projects are not inherently a bad thing to boost economic development, although unfortunately they are linked to the alleged corruption of the former Prime Minister Najib. The concluding observations made in the chapter also are still valid.

Notes

1 Two eastern Malaysian states, Sarawak and Sabah, are also witnessing the increasing economic presence of China, but the focus of this chapter is on Peninsular Malaysia only.
2 Malaysia's ringgit has devalued against the US dollar significantly since 2015 and hovered at RM1: US$0.24 in 2017. All conversion to US dollars in this article is based on the most recent exchange rate as of the writing.
3 1 Malaysia Development Berhad (IMDB) has been alleged to siphon off funds to benefit Najib while it is mired in debt. Two of China's SOEs (China General Nuclear Power Corp and China Railway Engineering Corp) stepped in to help out 1MDB by buying its assets in late 2015.
4 IWH itself also owns several subsidiaries, one of the most notable being Iskandar Waterfront City (IWC), which owns a vast stretch of land in southern Johor Bahru (called Danga Bay) and which partners with several notable China developers, including Country Garden and Greenland, in developing high-end real estate property on Danga Bay. In March 2017, IWH bought all the shares of IWC and merged the two entities ('IWH heping yihaicheng shangshi' 2017).
5 Lim Kang Hoo is said to have a close relationship with the Sultan of the southern state of Johor.
6 Some news reports, however, seem to suggest that KPRJ was acting in the interests of the Sultan of Johor.
7 Discussion notes from Author's field trip to headquarters of IJM in Kuala Lumpur, 1 April 2017.
8 GBGIPG also recently formed a joint venture with a Brunei government-linked company to run the largest container terminal of Brunei in Maura Port. See 'China–Brunei JV starts running Brunei's container terminal' 2017.
9 Discussion notes from Author's field trip to MCKIP, 17 April 2017.
10 Discussion notes from Author's field trip to MCKIP, 17 April 2017.
11 Discussion notes from Author's field trip to MCKIP, 17 April 2017.
12 Interview with an official from MCBC, 1 October 2013.
13 Discussion notes from Author's field trip to Malacca Gateway, 17 March 2017.
14 In addition to Malacca Gateway and Malacca–Guangdong Industrial Park, there is now a direct flight between Guangzhou (the capital city of Guangdong Province) and Malacca.
15 Discussion notes from Author's field trip to Malacca Gateway, 17 March 2017.
16 Including MMC–Germuda, YTL, UEM (all major Malaysian construction companies), and Ircon (an Indian company).
17 Originally estimated to be 600 kilometres. Because of the planned building of several bridges linking ECRL stations areas with the high risk of floods, the total length is now estimated to be 688 kilometres.
18 Disclosure: Since 2014, Sunsuria has funded several conferences organized by the Institute of China Studies, with which this author is affiliated.

19 Soochow University (in Jiangsu Province) set up an operation in Laos before Xiamen University came to Malaysia, but Soochow University's operation in Laos reportedly has not been very successful.
20 Discussion notes from Author's field trip to Impression Malacca, 17 March 2017.

Bibliography

'2qianyi jian Basheng disan gang' (RM200 billion to build the third port in Klang) 2017, *Nanyang Business Daily*, 30 January, p. A2.

'8 gonsi jingbiao Damacheng' (Eight companies competing for Bandar Malaysia) 2017, *Nanyang Business Daily*, 26 July, p. A2.

Barrock, J 2013, 'Warlords battling for RM8 bil bemas-JB rail job', *Kinibiz*, 11 March. Available from: www.kinibiz.com/story/corporate/8124/%E2%80%98 warlords%E2%80%99-battling-for-rm8-bil-gemas-jb-rail-job.html. [2 June 2016].

'Bujieshou jiaoyi shixiao' (Not to accept the termination of the deal) 2017, *Sinchew Daily*, 6 May, p. 1.

'China-Brunei JV starts running Brunei's container terminal' 2017, *Reuters*, 22 February. Available from: www.reuters.com/article/china-shipping/china-brunei-jv-starts-running-bruneis-container-terminal-xinhua-idUSL4N1G660Q [22 June 2017].

'China's largest port construction firm to venture into property development in Malaysia' 2017, *The Edge Malaysia*, 9 January, p. 20.

'China railway builders hit by Malaysian politics' 2012, *South China Morning Post*, 16 January, Business, p. 4.

'Cu shencha dongtie jihua, Naxier: baokuo touzi guimo yu jiazhi' (ECRL should be scrutinized, Nazir: including its scale and value) 2017, *Sinchew Daily*, 21 July, p. 12.

'Damacheng jiangcheng shijieji duhui' (Bandar Malaysia will be a world-class city) 2016, *Nanyang Business Daily*, 17 June, p. A2.

'Damacheng shougu gaocui' (The deal for Bandar Malaysia is off) 2017, *Sinchew Daily*, 4 May, p. 1.

'Donghaian tiedao kong chongji shicheng' (ECRL may threaten Singapore) 2016, *Nanyang Business Daily*, 23 December, p. A2.

'Dongtie dailai gaibian, Naji: zhouzhao diqu shouyi' (ECRL brings changes, Najib: Surrounding areas will benefit) 2017, *Sinchew Daily*, 23 April, p. 4.

'Dongtie shi zhongma qijian xiangmu' (ECRL is a China-Malaysia flagship project) 2017, *Sinchew Daily*, 10 August, p. 3.

'ECER attracts RM109b in investments' 2017, *New Straits Times*, 8 August, p. 6.

'ECRL project a mindset-changer' 2017, *New Straits Times*, 10 August, p. 2.

'Fajarbaru eyeing ECRL sub-contract jobs' 2017, *New Straits Times*, 18 August, p. B4.

'Gamuda in strong position to secure ECRL jobs' 2017, *The Star*, 11 August, p, B5.

Ganeshwaran, K & Gurmeet, K 2017, 'The rail economics of ECRL', *The Star*, 12 August, pp. 14–15.

'Guandan gangkou cheng mianshuigang' (Kuantan Port to be tax-free port) 2016, *Nanyang Business Daily*, 11 May, p. A3.

Ho, WF 2017, 'Rescue Bandar Malaysia or face fallout', *The Star*, 5 May. Available from: www.thestar.com.my/news/nation/2017/05/05/rescue-bandar-malaysia-or-face-fallout-buyers-of-project-failed-to-meet-payment-obligations-says-fin/ [Accessed 7 May 2017].

Hope, B & Wright, T 2017, 'China-backed plan to prop up scandal-plagued Malaysian fund 1MDB collapses', *The Wall Street Journal*, 3 May. Available from: www.wsj.com/articles/deal-to-prop-up-malaysias-1mdb-falls-apart-1493828337 [7 May 2017].

'HSR structure levels playing field for international bidders' 2016, *The Edge Malaysia*, 25 July, p. 16.

'Huang Huikang: Guandan chanyeyuan Lianhe gangte qiye jiangcheng Dongmeng zui xianjin gangtiechang' (Huang Huikang: Alliance Steel in Kuantan Industrial Park will become the most advanced steel plant in ASEAN) 2017, *Sinchew Daily*, 16 March, p. 8.

'Huang Huikang: yinru chuangxin jishu, Zhongzi lai Ma fei qiangfanwan' (Huang Huikang: Transferring innovative technology, China's investment in Malaysia is not taking away jobs) 2017, *Sinchew Daily*, 12 March, p. 6.

'Huangjinggang zaixian gucheng huihuang' (Malacca Gateway will rekindle the glory of an old city) 2017, *Nanyang Business Daily*, 12 March, p. A3.

'IJM: Kuantan Port upgrade crucial' 2016, *New Straits Times*, 6 April, p. B2.

'IWH heping yihaicheng shangshi' (IWH merges with IWC to be listed) 2017, *Nanyang Business Daily*, 9 March, p. A18.

Jacob, S 2015, 'Who needs RM40 billion HSR?' *Kinibiz*, 20 July, no. 7, pp. 66–69.

'Jia gangkou liaocheng Dongmeng xin dibiao' (Port in Malacca will become a new landmark in ASEAN) 2017, *Nanyang Business Daily*, 18 April, p. A2.

'Jianzu huodong liao meinian zeng 8%' (Construction activities estimated to increase 8%) 2017, *Nanyang Business Daily*, 24 January, p. A5.

Jomo, KS 2017, 'ECRL folly bound to fail and burden the nation', *Malaysiakini*, 11 August. Available from: www.malaysiakini.com/news/391563#pSXDCTBFGKW WRcFt.99. [12 August 2017].

Khor, YL 2013, 'The significance of China-Malaysia industrial parks', *ISEAS Perspective*, 17 June, 37.

Lim, Guanie 2018. "Resolving the Malacca Dilemma: Malaysia's Role in the Belt and Road Intiative." In Securing the Belt and Road Initiative: Risk Assessment, Private Security and Special Insurances Along the New Wave of Chinese Outbound Investments, edited by Alessandro Arduino and Xue Gong, 81–99. New York: Palgrave Macmillan.

'Longxin gaotie jiao 2 qiye yingyun' (KL-Singapore HSR to be operated by two entities) 2016, *Nanyang Business Daily*, 18 July, p. A3.

'Longxin gaotie yiwei gongcun gongrong' (KL-Singapore HSR meaning common prosperity) 2016, *Nanyang Business Daily*, 14 December, p. A3.

MCKIP n.d., 'MCKIP: Strategic gateway to ASEAN and Asia Pacific'. Promotional brochure.

'MCKIP secures RM19b in investments, targets another RM10b this year' 2017, *The Edge Property*, 24 January. Available from: http://news.theedgeproperty.com.my/content/1041295/mckip-secures-rm19b-investments-targets-another-rm10b-year [22 February 2017].

'Naji: Donghaian xiejie tiedao jiahua luoshi youlai Mazhong youhao guanxi' (Najib: Implementation of ECRL depends on friendly relations between China and Malaysia) 2016, *Sinchew Daily*, 18 December, p. 6.

Ngeow, CB 2016, 'Jingji gaoyu diyuan zhengzhi: Malaixiya dui 21shiji haishang sichou zhilu de guandian' (Economics over geopolitics: Malaysian views of the

21st century Maritime Silk Road), *Nanyang wenti yanjiu (Southeast Asian Affairs)*, 4, pp. 53–66.

Ngeow, CB 2017, 'The domestic frays in Sino – Malaysian ties', *East Asian Forum*, 26 January. Available from: www.eastasiaforum.org/2017/01/26/the-domestic-frays-in-sino-malaysian-ties/. [22 February 2017].

'Return of Malacca's gory days' 2016, *New Straits Times*, 2 September, p. B2.

'RM8.9 bil Gemas-JB double-tracking project to spin off jobs for locals' 2017, *The Edge Malaysia*, 13 February, p. 20.

'Sanguo lizheng gaotie zichan guanli' (Three countries in the fight for the high speed rail assets management) 2017, *Nanyang Business Daily*, 4 June, p. A1.

Shanmugam, M 2017, 'Who gains from Bandar Malaysia fallout?' *The Star*, Business Section, p. 12.

'Stake in Bandar Malaysia not for sale, says MOF' 2017, *The Malaysian Reserve*, 7 February, pp. 1, 4.

Tee, LS 2017, 'Framing a listing for Iskandar Waterfront', *The Star*, Business section, 25 February, p. 3.

'To kill a mega deal' 2017, *The Edge Malaysia*, 8 May, pp. 68–70.

'Xiada fenxiao shoukai xianhe' (Xiamen University Malaysia is a pioneer) 2017, *Sinchew Daily*, 11 March, p. 14.

Xiamen University Malaysia Campus n.d., Promotional brochure.

Yap, HL 2016, *Mazhong yuanmeng: Huang Jiading churen shouxiang duihua teshi wunianji* (Achieving the dreams of Malaysia and China: The five-year journey of Ong Ka Ting, Malaysia's special envoy to China). Malaysia-China Business Council, Kuala Lumpur.

'Zhong dai dama 550yi' (China to loan Malaysia RM55 billion) 2016, *Sinchew Daily*, 1 November, p. 3.

'Zhongma guanxi jin zuihao shiqi' (Sino–Malaysian relations to enter the best period) 2017, *Sinchew Daily*, 10 February, p. 11.

Part IV
e-Commerce and logistics

8 e-Commerce readiness from the Association of Southeast Asian Nations (ASEAN) to the Belt and Road Initiative

Kam-Fai Wong, Chun-Hung Cheng, and Waiman Cheung

Introduction

Effective realization of the Belt and Road Initiative (BRI) will heavily depend on interconnectivity and intercommunication among and between partner economies (countries) covered in the BRI. Due to the advancement of the Internet and the worldwide proliferation of social media applications, e-commerce has gradually become not only a viable but also an effective means for international trade, which covers cross-border e-commerce between economies along the belt and road. In addition to transportation and logistics, information and communication technology (ICT) infrastructures are critical success factors for BRI business development.

However, the huge economic disparity among partner economies and the digital divide problem is apparent and may seriously affect e-commerce development in these partner economies. China has a population of 1.4 billion and accounts for 44 percent of the world retail e-commerce market (see Figure 8.1). In contrast, South Asian countries together only account for 1.2 percent of the same market even though their population is about 300 million more than China's. This might be due to the low Internet penetration rate in the region, 23 percent of the population of 1.7 billion. This is in contrast with Central and Eastern Europe, whose Internet penetration rate is about 68 percent of its population.

"Five areas of connectivity" – policy coordination, facilities connectivity, unimpeded trade, financial integration, and people-to-people bond – aim to foster the concurrent development of the Belt and Road countries and strengthen cooperation on the political, economic, and cultural fronts. Of these areas, ICT connectivity is the most important part at this stage, as uneven development of the Internet and communication infrastructure among the BRI countries will inevitably hinder business development in the region. The digital divide will obstruct the interconnection and intercommunication between partner countries and hinder information flow and hence trade flows. Furthermore, it may even have further negative impacts on the essential condition of political mutual trust, economic integration, and culture tolerance in the BRI economic zone at large.

The Retail E-Commerce Market in the Six Major Regions along One Belt One Road

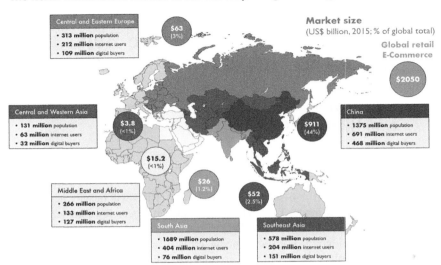

Figure 8.1 The retail e-commerce market size in the six major regions along BRI regions

Source: Klaus Schwab, "The Global Competitiveness Report 2016–2017", World Economic Forum (Map drawn by authors of this chapter according to cited source).

BRI and ASEAN regions

The Southeast Asian region is the first hub of "The 21st-Century Maritime Silk Road" when its route departs from the Chinese coastline (China and the World Program 2016). From 2009 to 2015, ASEAN (Association of Southeast Asian Nations), which comprises ten countries (Brunei, Myanmar, Cambodia, Indonesia, Laos, Malaysia, Philippines, Singapore, Thailand, and Vietnam) has become a major economic force in Asia as well as a driver of global economic growth. ASEAN has, since 2011, been China's third-largest trading partner, and the trading trends indicate that two-way trade will increase in the coming years (Cao & Gan 2012).

As strategic trading partners of China and ASEAN are included in the BRI, they are valuable study examples for the initiative. The BRI faces circumstances in the ASEAN region that are expected to be similar to the experience in Central Asia or even in Europe. Therefore, in order to discover the potential challenges, such as digital divide, when comprehensively implementing the BRI project in the future, it is worthwhile to study ASEAN countries first and attempt to find viable plans that are potentially applicable to other BRI countries.

Having a population of more than 600 million and a nominal GDP (gross domestic product) of US$2.31 trillion, ASEAN has rapidly become one of the largest economic zones in the world (J.P. Morgan 2015). In 2011, ASEAN expanded 7.4 percent, which was not only beyond expectation but also greatly exceeding the 1.3 percent growth in 2009. This growth was impressive, given that the world economy as a whole in the second half of 2011 was very unstable and that the spread of Europe's sovereign-debt crisis started to unfold. In 2012, ASEAN continued to record impressive growth despite global economic setbacks. This means that the countries of Southeast Asia presented a high tolerance to the complicated economic environment and a low dependence on commodity exports. Table 8.1 summarized the GDP ranking of ASEAN countries.

The economic growth of ASEAN countries did slow down overall in 2013. Indonesia, Thailand, and Malaysia performed the worst in comparison with their neighbouring peers. In 2014, the economies of ASEAN countries slowed down further, except for some individual countries. Indonesia, as the largest economy in ASEAN, had 5.0 percent economic growth in 2014, which was 0.6 percent below that of 2013 and which was the lowest growth seen since 2009. Thailand, with a growth rate of 0.7 percent in 2014, dropped 2.2 percent from the previous year. The economic growth for Malaysia increased from 1.2 percent to 6.0 percent in the same year. The growth rates of Laos, Cambodia, Philippines, and Singapore all decreased from the previous year. However, Vietnam saw acceleration in its growth rates, which was 6.0 percent in 2014 and 5.4 percent in 2015. Myanmar was the fastest-growing economy in the region, with an expansion of 7.7 percent in 2014, 0.6 percent lower than the year before. Myanmar's rapid growth was fuelled by the deepening of economic reforms, structure regulation, and the sustainable growth in the construction, manufacture, and service sectors.

The economic growth target for Southeast Asian countries in 2015 was set at 4.4 percent, lower than the 4.9 percent target in 2014 (Chen & Ni 2016).

Table 8.1 GDP ranking of Southeast Asian countries

Southeast Asian Countries GDP Ranking		
Rank	*Country*	*GDP (US$100 million)*
7	India	20,598.99
16	Indonesia	8,617.70
29	Thailand	3,735.36
33	Malaysia	3,134.79
35	Philippines	2,993.14
37	Singapore	2,939.59
45	Vietnam	1,988.05
67	Myanmar	657.75
105	Cambodia	177.14
116	Laos	125.48
120	Brunei	116.36

Source: International Monetary Fund(IMF), "World Economic Outlook", April 2016.

According to the 2014–2015 Annual report on the development of Southeast Asia blue book> (东南亚蓝皮书 – 东南亚地区发展报告 (2014～2015)), the International Monetary Fund (IMF) forecast that the economic growth in 2015 for Brunei is –1.2 percent, 7 percent for Cambodia, 4.7 percent for Indonesia, 7.3 percent for Laos, 4.7 percent for Malaysia, 8.4 percent for Myanmar, 6 percent for the Philippines, 2.2 percent for Singapore, 2.5 percent for Thailand, and 6.5 percent for Vietnam.

The same report attributed the low economic growth of Southeast Asian countries to the impact of a global economic slowdown. The global economic slump continued in 2016. However, the economy of ASEAN countries was still bright and was expected to remain flexible. The projected economic growth of ASEAN countries in 2016 was slightly higher than for 2015. The growth in 2016 for Indonesia was 5.2–5.6 percent, 4–5 percent for Malaysia, 7 percent for Philippines, 1–3 percent for Singapore, 3.5–4 percent for Thailand, and 6.7 percent for Vietnam.

The primary objective of both the formation of ASEAN and the BRI is the same, to connect partner economies to enhance regional competitiveness and support sustainable economic growth. To achieve these goals, the key regional stakeholders in different economies need to be closely interconnected through the Internet, which is also used as a channel to facilitate cross-border e-business. Nonetheless, the different capacities of the information highway in different economies may lead to a digital divide problem and in turn may seriously hinder regional business development. This common circumstance is shared by many major economic associations globally, including the BRI and ASEAN. The BRI can be viewed as a large cross-country project with 66 countries in Asia and Europe. ASEAN can be studied as a reflection example of the BRI for many reasons. First, there is high diversity in the human development level in both ASEAN and the BRI. According to the Human Development Report (2016), there are two very high human development countries, two high development countries, and six medium human development countries in ASEAN. Similarly, among the BRI countries, the human development level varies; most countries are at or above the moderate development level and only three in the low development group. In other words, ASEAN countries can be representative of most BRI countries in level human development. Second, the ranges of GDP per capita are $1,230–$52,961 in ASEAN and $565–$60,787 in BRI, indicating that economic development is quite similar. Third, the percentage of Internet users among the total population of ASEAN is very similar to that of BRI, 35.5 percent in ASEAN and 39.2 percent in BRI. The proportion of digital buyers is also quite similar in BRI and ASEAN, 26.1 percent in Southeast Asia and 22.1 percent in BRI. Thus, ASEAN could be studied as an example for the BRI, and it might be easier to overcome potential problems in ASEAN because there are only ten countries instead of the 66 in BRI. Furthermore, the methodology and experience of settling this global difficulty will be beneficial to all economic associations in the future, especially for the BRI.

ICT infrastructure is the fundamental element for e-business. Without a high-level IT infrastructure, there cannot be sustainable e-business. Although we know that China has put a lot of effort into assisting the development of IT infrastructure in ASEAN countries, we do not have a clear understanding of what capabilities and capacities these countries have. The development of information communication and ICT in the ASEAN region is dependent on many factors, such as economic development, telecommunications infrastructure, and social media usage. Even the language services development for each country is very important because Internet users will need to understand the user interfaces of their applications in their local languages.

Throughout the literature, there is a gap in providing a full picture on e-commerce development at country level. Many prior reports, such as *The Global Information Technology Report, Measuring the Information Society Report, Global Competitive Index*, and *Global Innovation Index*, only examine the ICT development of countries or the general environment for business, which are just parts of e-commerce development. However, there are other factors which may influence e-commerce promotion (e.g. social media usage, language services, online payment available, and ability to pay). In this report, we aim to develop an e-commerce readiness index, which holistically addresses general environment, ICT infrastructure, and e-commerce facilitation at country level. The e-commerce readiness index fills the above-mentioned gap by considering e-commerce facilitation factors (such as language services, social media usage, and payment) together with general environment and ICT infrastructure, to give a whole picture of e-commerce development in a particular country.

The aim of this chapter is to (1) investigate the level of ICT infrastructure of ASEAN countries, (2) find reasons (such as policy, population, hardware, or software) for the digital divide problem, (3) give a comprehensive description of the e-commerce developing stage of these countries, and (4) provide recommendations for Hong Kong as a super connector for what can be done to facilitate ASEAN countries resolving the digital divide problem and then for BRI countries. Due to the similarities of ASEAN countries with BRI countries, the e-commerce readiness index can be also used for other BRI countries to assess their e-commerce development. The contributions of this study are (1) developing an e-commerce readiness index to measure a particular country's e-commerce developing stage, (2) incorporating language as an important factor the index, and (3) discussing what Hong Kong can do as the super connector in BRI.

e-Commerce readiness

E-Commerce readiness refers to a country's current e-commerce development stage. Many factors influence a country's e-commerce development. The general environment, such as policy and regulatory environment, business environment, and innovation environment, affects e-commerce readiness. Without a favourable general environment, there will not be many commercial or business activities. IT infrastructure, which provides an essential basis for e-commerce, includes ease of access to the Internet, general usage of IT, and skills for IT. Social media acts as an information-sharing intermedia. Customers often share with each other their attitudes and opinions about products. A lower level of social media usage may result in a lack of information sharing about products, affecting a customer's intention to buy. Payment is another factor influencing e-commerce readiness. Customers cannot complete a purchase on the Internet if they do not have a way to pay online. Another important factor adversely affecting cross-border e-commerce is language. In summary, we have considered three aspects which will affect e-commerce development at the country level: general environment, IT infrastructure, and e-commerce facilitation. We show these factors in Figure 8.2.

General environment

General environment refers to the policy and regulatory environment, business environment, and innovation environment. The *Global Information Technology Report (2016)* (GITR) stressed that the success of a country in leveraging ICTs depends in part on the quality of the overall operating environment. Whether a country's policy is good for e-commerce development, and whether a country's regulatory environment is suitable for companies to survive reflect how a country's business environment supports entrepreneurship and business development.

It is important for governments to enable stakeholders in business to gain confidence in e-commerce solutions. This may not only be achieved through using security technologies (e.g. for preventing fraud, information leaks, and other forms of attacks) but also through strategic initiatives to change the users' trust in ICT for commercial activities and transactions. For this reason, legal and

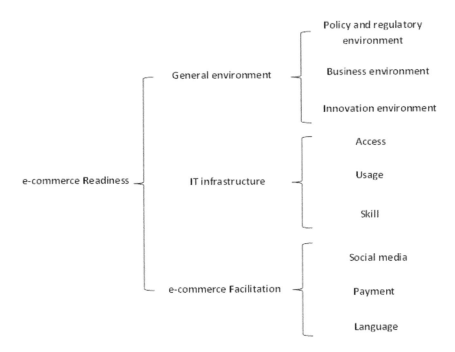

Figure 8.2 e-commerce readiness components

regulatory policies are crucial pre-conditions for the promotion of users' confidence (Almeida, Avila & Boncanoska 2007).

Generally, business activities usually rely on laws and regulations' validity conditions, enforcement, liability limitations, and resolution. Several problems emerge when conducting the shift from traditional commerce to e-commerce, such as whether the existing laws are applicable to the new digital trades, as well as whether new laws and regulations facilitate communications and transactions online. Particular attention has been directed to the issue of digital certification, a technical mechanism to ensure the validity and security of electronic transactions. In addition, as long as e-commerce is intrinsically international, alignment of laws and regulations with international practices is crucial.

As mentioned, commercial activities or business activities are also important for a country's e-commerce development. Without a good business environment, companies will not invest in e-commerce. Innovation environment is another important factor to consider. E-Commerce relies on innovative technology, which will enable more facilitation and functions for e-commerce, such as e-payment and e-signature. Having a more proficient innovative environment will give greater opportunities for businesses to thrive.

IT infrastructure

IT infrastructure refers to the composite of hardware, software, network resources, and services required for the existence, operation, and management of an enterprise IT environment. It allows an organization to deliver IT solutions and services to its employees, partners, and/or customers and is usually internal to an organization and deployed within owned facilities.

Electronic commerce, or e-commerce as it is more commonly known, is the buying and selling of goods or services over a computer network, e.g. the Internet. In this mode of business activity, viewing, selling, negotiation, and payment of the traditional shopping experience is conducted electronically. As all activities are done online, a complete IT infrastructure should be the basic requirement for e-commerce. We will measure the IT infrastructure development from three angles (access, usage, and skills), which are identical to the measurement done by the *Measuring the Information Society Report* (MISR).

e-Commerce facilitation

E-Commerce facilitation is different from IT infrastructure. It refers to e-commerce facilitation technology related to e-commerce, such as social media, e-payment, and language services. For example, in the 1990s, mainstream e-commerce took place by a buyer initiating a computer transaction over the Internet or a proprietary network (Wikibooks 2017). And, e-payment is "a precondition for the successful development of e-commerce" (Kurbalijia & Gelbstein 2005).

In general, if users feel comfortable making transactions online, they may save time and money. E-payment directly supports business growth and, according to some macroeconomic studies, annual savings of perhaps 1 percent of GDP can be realized if a country is able to shift from an all paper – based to an all – electronic-based payment system. However, due to the concerns about money and payment-related issues, the potential benefits of e-payment can be hard to achieve. Digital cash and a low technology penetration rate create problems in developing countries due to lack of trust in online transactions caused by a low-level of digital security. These are major obstacles to widespread acceptance of e-payment. Electronic money (also known as electronic cash, electronic currency, digital currency, and digital cash) refers to money exchanged by electronic means. Typically, this involves the use of a computer network of the Internet and a digital stored value system. Electronic funds transfer and direct deposit are examples of electronic money (Mansell & Steinmueller 2000).

Literature review

E-Commerce is the process of buying and selling, or exchanging products, services, and information using computer networks, including the Internet (Turban et al. 2002). The development of e-commerce in the ASEAN region depends on many factors, such as the environment, information technology infrastructure, and social media usage (Kurnia 2008).

Existing IT-related indexes

GITR focuses on ICT. It defines the Networked Readiness Index (NRI), containing 53 individual indicators to measure the drivers. Countries are assessed on four categories of indicators: (1) the overall environment for technology use and creation (political, regulatory, business, and innovation); (2) networked readiness in ICT infrastructure, affordability, and skills; (3) technology adoption/usage by the three groups of stakeholders (government, the private sector, and private individuals); and (4) the economic and social impact of new technologies.

The International Telecommunication Union (ITU) releases MISR (*Measuring the Information Society Report*) every year. This annual report presents a global and regional overview of the latest ICT developments. It aims to stimulate the ICT policy debate in ITU member-states by providing an objective assessment of how countries perform in ICT and by highlighting areas that need further improvement.

The ICT Development Index (IDI) introduced by MISR, which measures: (1) the level and evolution over time of ICT development within countries and their experience relative to other countries; (2) progress in ICT development in both developed and developing countries; (3) the digital divide, i.e. differences between countries in their levels of ICT development; and (4) the development potential of ICTs and the extent to which countries can make use of them to enhance growth and development in the context of available capabilities and skills.

General business environment

The GITR stresses that the success of a country in leveraging ICTs depends in part on the quality of the overall operating environment. Whether a country's policy is good for e-commerce development and whether a country's regulatory environment is suitable for companies to survive are important. This reflects how a country's business environment supports entrepreneurship through examining a government's efficiency and the ease of starting a business.

A study by Almeida, Avila and Boncanoska (2013) emphasized the importance of environment, indicating that, without a good environment, e-commerce cannot be developed well.

IT infrastructure

Because of the island terrain in many ASEAN countries, mobile-broadband service has become the focus of the telecommunication industry in these countries. In 2014, the coverage of mobile-broadband was 43 percent. This coverage has increased 25 times in Indonesia in recent years. Thailand became the fastest-growing mobile-broadband market, which has the second-highest coverage and users in ASEAN countries. The rapidly growing 3G service in Thailand has drawn the attention of *Groupe Spécial Mobile (GSMA)* GSMA, which predicts that the fixed and mobile-broadband coverage will reach 133 percent providing US\$23 billion growth of GDP by 2020. Also, the cost of fixed-line broadband in ASEAN countries is rapidly decreasing. The ratio of fixed-line broadband cost to GNI (Gross National Income) per capita for ASEAN countries fell on average from 37.16 percent in 2010 to 6.21 percent in 2013. For example, Cambodia's GNI decreased from 92.5 percent to 15 percent. The cost of mobile data for ASEAN countries dropped from 4.92 percent to 2.80 percent from 2010 to 2013. Laos, as an example, decreased this ratio from 8.6 percent to 5.9 percent (White Paper on China – ASEAN Information Technology Development and Cooperation 2016).

The number of Internet users in ASEAN countries is rapidly growing. In June 2016, the Internet user coverage and the population of Internet users in ASEAN countries reached 40.67 percent and 260 million, respectively, fourth in the world. The increasing rates of Internet users in Cambodia and Myanmar were the highest, 34.74 percent and 32.38 percent. ASEAN will soon become one of the world's fastest-growing Internet markets. In 2012, the Internet industry in the emerging market of Malaysia achieved 4.1 percent contribution to the GDP. Along with the explosion of e-commerce, online media, and online travel market, the size of the Internet economy for ASEAN countries will increase 6.5 times from year 2012 to 2025 (White Paper on China – ASEAN Information Technology Development and Cooperation 2016).

Gibbs and Kraemer (2004) conducted a ten-country case study in 2003 and concluded that e-commerce diffusion required a well-developed information infrastructure. Their framework posited that the availability and affordability of information infrastructure were important enablers for e-commerce diffusion. Items reflecting information infrastructure availability include penetration of telephone fixed lines and computers, the percentage of Internet subscribers, and broadband width. Affordability, such as the cost of Internet, also hinders e-commerce development. Jennex, Amoroso and Adelakun (2004) studied the success factors for small companies in developing countries. They listed three attributes for efficient technical infrastructure: telecommunications infrastructure, up-to-date PCs and other computer hardware and software available, and the technical skills of workers.

Moreover, other studies gave us useful guidance to assess the IT infrastructure for e-commerce promotion. Mukti (2000) surveyed 110 Malaysian companies and found that many companies were concerned about security. Dedrick and Kraemer (2001) examined e-commerce in China and identified additional supporting issues such as banking services, computer manufacturing, and IT services industries. The Electronic Commerce Infrastructure Info – Communications Development Authority of Singapore (E-commerce Infrastructure in Singapore 2002) provides several enabling infrastructure services for e-commerce. They are the network service for linking businesses, directory services for search and retrieval, security services for safe communication and transaction, and solution providers for creating e-commerce systems.

Mobile commerce has developed rapidly these years and become a critical part of e-commerce. Wireless information technology development cannot be ignored. Zhang and Prybutok (2005) compared the mobile commerce development in China, Europe, and the United States. Their research mainly concerned the issues of consumer demographics, short message service usage, and 3G technology. These wireless technologies should also be considered in the IT infrastructure for e-commerce.

e-Commerce facilitation

The development of ICT in the ASEAN region is dependent on many factors, such as economic development, social media usage, and even language services for interface design in each country.

Oxley and Yeung (2001) discuss credible payment channels. They concluded that different credible payment channels influence the success of e-commerce. If a country does not support online payment, there will be fewer transactions than with an online payment channel. Also, if the citizens can have more online payment types, it will be more convenient to buy products or services online.

Young and Srivastava (2007) discussed the impact of social influence in e-commerce decision making, and Swamynathan et al. (2006) examined social network's effect on e-commerce. As Internet-based social media has become popular, consumers who are searching for more information about a product or service often follow this new media for users' comments. It has become apparent that the customer decision process is influenced by information from trusted people, not from product manufacturers or from recommendation systems. The social influence of high-quality reviews written by previous consumers can have a direct, positive effect on the potential consumer's decision making, and this effect can propagate through a social network. E-Commerce companies are well positioned to take advantage of the social influence among consumers as a decision support tool by allowing a consumer to evaluate the appropriateness of recommendations and reviews.

e-Commerce readiness index

The e-commerce readiness index (ERI) is a composite index of three main categories (sub-indexes): general environment sub-index, IT infrastructure sub-index, and e-commerce facilitation sub-index; nine subcategories (pillars), and 52 individual indicators distributed across different pillars. The three pillars and 22 indicators for general environment sub-index are derived from GITR; three pillars and 15 indicators for IT infrastructure sub-index are derived from MISR; and the social media pillar containing four indicators for e-commerce facilitation is based on Swamynathan et al. (2006). The payment pillar containing six indicators is based on Oxley and Yeung (2001). We developed a language pillar containing five indicators. No previous study has linked language to e-commerce readiness. The full list of indicators, grouped by pillars and sub-indexes, is provided later.

The computation of the ERI is based on successive aggregations of scores, from the indicator level (the most disaggregated level) to the overall ERI score (the highest level). Scores for indicators are obtained from the two reports: GITR and MISR. In these two reports, scores are measured on a scale of 1 to 7, and therefore they do not need transformation prior to aggregation. Other indicators, obtained from other sources, are scaled differently. In order to align them with the survey's results, we apply min–max transformation to transform them into a 1-to-7 scale. We also use an arithmetic mean to aggregate individual indicators within each pillar and use the same method for higher aggregation levels (pillars and sub-indexes).

Environment sub-index

There are three equally weighed pillars to measure the environment sub-index: policy and regulation, business, and innovation. Each pillar is measured by several indicators. The policy and regulation environment pillar captures how the business is protected by local policy and regulation and includes these indicators (effectiveness of law-making bodies, laws relating to ICTs, judicial independence, efficiency of legal system in settling disputes, efficiency of legal system in challenging regulations, number of procedures to enforce a contract, number of days to enforce a contract, intellectual property protection, and property rights). The number of procedures to enforce a contract and number of days to enforce a contract are merged into one indicator by average to indicate the contract-enforcing effectiveness. Intellectual property protection and property rights are merged and averaged. They are shown in the 3P protection indicator.

The business environment pillar measures the difficulty of conducting business in each country. It includes seven indicators: GDP, venture capital availability, number of days required to start a business, number of procedures required to start a business, intensity of local competition, corporate income tax, and total tax rate. Number of days required to start a business and number of procedures required to start a business are merged into one indicator by average to measure the difficulty of starting a business. Corporate income tax and total tax rate are merged into one indicator to show the tax level.

The innovation pillar captures the investment on innovation and the innovation capability of each country. Six indicators are included: company spending on R&D (research and development), PCT patent applications, gross expenditure on R&D, quality of scientific research institutions, availability of latest technologies, and government procurement of advanced technology products.

IT infrastructure sub-index

There are three equally weighed pillars to measure the environment sub-index: access, usage, and skills. Each pillar is measured by several factors. The access pillar captures IT infrastructure readiness and includes six infrastructure and access indicators: fixed-telephone subscriptions, mobile-cellular telephone subscriptions, international Internet bandwidth per Internet user, households with a computer, households with Internet access, and mobile network coverage.

The usage pillar captures IT infrastructure intensity and includes five intensity and usage indicators: individuals using the Internet, fixed-broadband subscriptions, mobile-broadband subscriptions, prepaid mobile cellular tariffs, and fixed-broadband Internet tariffs.

The skill pillar seeks to capture capabilities or skills which are important for IT infrastructure. It includes four indicators: mean years of schooling, gross secondary enrolment, gross tertiary enrolment, and adult literacy rate.

e-Commerce facilitation sub-index

There are three equally weighed pillars to measure the e-commerce facilitation development: social media, payment, and language. The social media pillar indicates the popularity of social media in each country and includes four indicators: social media users, social media users by mobile, average daily use of social media, and social media users. Average daily use of social media and social media users are merged into one indicator to represent the intensity of social media usage (*Global Digital & Social Media Stats: 2015*; Criteo: Rise of Southeast Asia e-commerce' 2016).

The payment pillar captures the availability of payment for e-commerce and includes six indicators: credit card, electronic payments usage, mobile phone usage, commercial bank branch, GNI, and gross national savings. Credit cards, electronic payments used to make payments, and mobile phones used to pay bills are merged into one indicator to measure the popularity of the new payment.

GNI and gross national savings are merged into one indicator to measure people's affordability.

The language pillar captures the difficulty of conducting cross-board e-commerce business. We select the top five languages commonly used in connective websites: Chinese, English, Japanese, German, and Hindi. And of seven of the most popular free translation websites, we checked whether the translation between these five languages and the countries' official languages is supported.

Gap analysis

Data we need may not be all readily available. To deal with the missing data, we firstly test whether the missing data are crucial to our analysis. For each pillar, we rank countries with no missing data values by two ranking methods, averaging all indicators and averaging selected indicators by excluding the indicators for which other countries do not have data values. If the rankings in the two ranking methods do not vary more than one slot, indicators missing data values do not affect the actual ranking significantly. Therefore, we will use the average of an indicator with data values across different countries to approximate the corresponding indicator value for a country with missing data value. However, if the rankings in the two ranking methods differ by more than one slot, missing data will affect the actual rankings significantly. In this case, we have to drop countries from our consideration. Hence, we have eight countries excluding Brunei and Laos in the policy and regulatory environment, the business environment, the access, and the usage pillars. Nine countries except Brunei are ranked in the innovation environment and the payment pillars. All ten countries are ranked for other pillars. Finally, we have eight countries excluding Brunei and Laos for the environment sub-index and the ICT infrastructure sub-index, and nine countries excluding Brunei for the e-commerce facilitation sub-index. The total e-Commerce Readiness Index (eCRI) contains eight countries without Brunei and Laos (see Appendix, Tables 8.2–8.12). Moreover, we calculate ASEAN average scores for each pillar, which are shown as the light gray line in each of the spider graphs.

Brunei

The analysis of Brunei is severely affected by missing data values. Therefore, we cannot draw a conclusion for the eCRI of Brunei. Though parts of all three sub-index ranks are missing, we can find some minor information about Brunei. In innovation environment, Brunei ranks last of the ten countries, which indicates relative underdevelopment in e-commerce readiness. For ICT infrastructure, we find Brunei is a well-developed country in skill. Without data about mobile network coverage, prepaid mobile cellular tariffs, and fixed-broadband Internet tariffs, it is difficult to conclude how ICT infrastructure access and usage in Brunei fare. For e-commerce facilitation, we also find Brunei performs excellently in the social media and the language pillars. However, we need more information about credit cards, electronic payment usage, and mobile phone usage, to measure the payment development in Brunei.

As shown in Figure 8.3, compared with ASEAN average scores (indicated by a light gray line), Brunei is outstanding in skill, social media, and language. But the score of innovation environment in Brunei falls a little below the average score. We cannot compare other pillars due to lack of data for Brunei.

The scores of three indicators (GDP, company spending on R&D, and PCT (Patent Cooperation Treaty) patent applications) are very low compared with the scores of other indicators in the environment sub-index. The extremely underdeveloped indicators in ICT infrastructure sub-index are fixed-telephone subscriptions, international Internet bandwidth, fixed-broadband Internet subscriptions, and active mobile-broadband subscriptions.

Cambodia

Overall, Cambodia ranks seventh out of the eight countries. It falls behind in the environment sub-index, ranking seventh in the policy and regulation and the innovation pillars, and sixth in the business pillar among the eight countries, excluding Brunei and Laos. ICT infrastructure development in Cambodia is also not good by all measures, again ranking sixth out of the eight countries in the access and the usage pillars, and eighth out of the ten countries in the skill pillar. For the e-commerce facilitation sub-index, the social media score ranks eighth out of ten, the payment score ranks seventh out of nine, excluding Brunei, and the language score is the lowest in all the ASEAN countries.

Cambodia is an underdeveloped country, no single pillar score exceeding the cross-country average. Specifically, the scores of some pillars (skill, payment, and language) have a significant gap between the average scores. Other pillars are just moderately developed, the scores close to the average level.

Without comparing other countries, the scores for number of procedures to enforce a contract, number of days required to start a business, and PCT patent applications are extremely low in the environment sub-index. In the ICT infrastructure sub-index, the scores for fixed-telephone subscriptions, international Internet bandwidth, percentage of households with a computer, percentage of households with Internet access, percentage of individuals using the Internet, fixed-broadband Internet subscriptions, and all indicators in the skill pillar are very low. However, mobile-cellular telephone subscriptions and mobile network coverage are high. In the e-commerce facilitation sub-index, scores of social media users, social media users by mobile, all payment indicators, and machine translation for local language are low (Figure 8.4).

Indonesia

Indonesia ranks middle, which is fifth out of eight in according to eCRI. Indonesia is the third most developed country out of eight for e-commerce environment. But the gap between Indonesia and the top two countries is quite wide.

Brunei

	Rank	Value
E-commerce Readiness Index	N/A	N/A
Environment Sub-index	N/A	N/A
1st pillar: Policy and regulatory environment	N/A	N/A
2nd pillar: Business environment	N/A	N/A
3rd pillar: Innovation environment	10	2.58
IT infrastructure Sub-index	N/A	N/A
4th pillar: Access	N/A	N/A
5th pillar: Usage	N/A	N/A
6th pillar: Skill	2	5.63
E-commerce facilitation Sub-index	N/A	N/A
7th pillar: Social media	1	5.87
8th pillar: Payment	N/A	N/A
9th pillar: Language	1	6.8

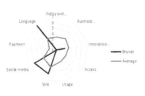

The E-commerce Readiness Index in detail

Indicator	Value
1st pillar Political and regulatory environment	
1.01 Effectiveness of law-making bodies	N/A
1.02 Laws relating to ICTs	N/A
1.03 Judicial independence	N/A
1.04 Efficiency of legal system in settling disputes	N/A
1.05 Efficiency of legal system in challenging regulations	N/A
1.06 Number of procedures to enforce a contract	N/A
1.07 Number of days to enforce a contract	N/A
1.08 Intellectual property protection	N/A
1.09 Property rights	3.8
2nd pillar Business environment	
2.01 GDP(100 million USD)	116.36
2.02 Venture capital availability	N/A
2.03 Number of days required to start a business	N/A
2.04 Number of procedures required to start a business	N/A
2.05 Intensity of local competition	N/A
2.06 Corporate Tax/Corporate income tax	18.5%
2.07 Total tax rate, % profits	8.7%
3rd pillar Innovation environment	
3.01 Company spending on R&D	2.9
3.02 PCT patent applications	3.3
3.03 Gross expenditure on R&D, % of GDP	N/A
3.04 Quality of scientific research institutions	, 3.4
3.05 Availability of latest technologies	N/A
3.06 Government procurement of advanced technology products	N/A
4th pillar Access	
4.01 Fixed-telephone subscriptions per 100 inhabitants	9
4.02 Mobile-cellular telephone subscriptions per 100 inhabitants	108.1
4.03 International Internet bandwidth per Internet user (Bit/s)	63090
4.04 Percentage of households with computer	93.4
4.05 Percentage of households with Internet access	81.7
4.06 Mobile network coverage per 100 population	N/A

Indicator	Value
5th pillar Usage	
5.01 Percentage of individuals using the Internet	71.2
5.02 Fixed-broadband Internet subscriptions per 100 inhabitants	8
5.03 Active mobile-broadband subscriptions per 100 inhabitants	4.5
5.04 Prepaid mobile cellular tariffs, PPP $/min	N/A
5.05 Fixed broadband Internet tariffs, PPP $/month	N/A
6th pillar Skill	
6.01 Mean years of schooling	8.8
6.02 Secondary gross enrolment ratio	99.1
6.03 Tertiary gross enrolment ratio	31.7
6.04 Adult literacy rate	79.9
7th pillar Social media	
7.01 social media users (in million)	0.37
7.02 social media users by Mobile (in million)	0.33
7.03 average daily use of social media (minutes)	N/A
7.04 social media users (percentage of using facebook everyday)	51%
8th pillar Payment	
8.01 credit card (% age 15+)	N/A
8.02 Electronic payments used to make payments (% age 15+)	N/A
8.03 Mobile phone used to pay bills (% age 15+)	N/A
8.04 commercial bank branch (per 100,000 persons)	19.828
8.05 GNI per capital	38010
8.06 Gross national savings % GDP	29%.
9th pillar Language	
9.01 Chinese	7
9.02 English	7
9.03 Japanese	7
9.04 German	7
9.05 Hindi	6

Figure 8.3 e-commerce readiness for Brunei

Cambodia

	Rank	Value
E-commerce Readiness Index	7	2.27
Environment Sub-index	7	3.1
1st pillar: Policy and regulatory environment	7	2.93
2nd pillar: Business environment	6	3.59
3rd pillar: Innovation environment	7	2.78
IT infrastructure Sub-index	7	2.39
4th pillar: Access	6	3.04
5th pillar: Usage	6	2.97
6th pillar: Skill	10	1.15
E-commerce facilitation Sub-index	7	1.33
7th pillar: Social media	7	2.78
8th pillar: Payment	7	1.40
9th pillar: Language	8	1

The E-commerce Readiness Index in detail

Indicator	Value	Indicator	Value
1st pillar Political and regulatory environment		**5th pillar Usage**	
1.01 Effectiveness of law-making bodies	2.9	5.01 Percentage of individuals using the Internet	19
1.02 Laws relating to ICTs	3.1	5.02 Fixed-broadband Internet subscriptions per 100 inhabitants	0.5
1.03 Judicial independence	2.5	5.03 Active mobile-broadband subscriptions per 100 inhabitants	42.8
1.04 Efficiency of legal system in settling disputes	2.8	5.04 Prepaid mobile cellular tariffs, PPP $/min	0.23
1.05 Efficiency of legal system in challenging regulations	2.6	5.05 Fixed broadband Internet tariffs, PPP $/month	29.81
1.06 Number of procedures to enforce a contract	44	**6th pillar Skill**	
1.07 Number of days to enforce a contract	483	6.01 Mean years of schooling	4.4
1.08 Intellectual property protection	2.8	6.02 Secondary gross enrolment ratio	45
1.09 Property rights	3.8	6.03 Tertiary gross enrolment ratio	15.8
2nd pillar Business environment		6.04 Adult literacy rate	77.2
2.01 GDP(100 million USD)	177.14	**7th pillar Social media**	
2.02 Venture capital availability	2.7	7.01 social media users (in million)	4.9
2.03 Number of days required to start a business	87	7.02 social media users by Mobile (in million)	4.4
2.04 Number of procedures required to start a business	7	7.03 average daily use of social media (minutes)	N/A
2.05 Intensity of local competition	4.7	7.04 social media users (percentage of using Facebook everyday)	57%
2.06 Corporate Tax/Corporate income tax	20%	**8th pillar Payment**	
2.07 Total tax rate, % profits	21%	8.01 credit card (% age 15+)	2.89%
3rd pillar Innovation environment		8.02 Electronic payments used to make payments (% age 15+)	0.49%.
3.01 Company spending on R&D	3.1	8.03 Mobile phone used to pay bills (% age 15+)	0.08%
3.02 PCT patent applications	0	8.04 commercial bank branch (per 100,000 persons)	5.58
3.03 Gross expenditure on R&D, % of GDP	N/A	8.05 GNI per capital	1070
3.04 Quality of scientific research institutions	2.8	8.06 Gross national savings % GDP	11.3%
3.05 Availability of latest technologies	4.2	**9th pillar Language**	
3.06 Government procurement of advanced technology products	2.8	9.01 Chinese	1
4th pillar Access		9.02 English	1
4.01 Fixed-telephone subscriptions per 100 inhabitants	1.6	9.03 Japanese	1
4.02 Mobile-cellular telephone subscriptions per 100 inhabitants	133	9.04 German	1
4.03 International Internet bandwidth per Internet user (Bit/s)	17792	9.05 Hindi	1
4.04 Percentage of households with computer	16		
4.05 Percentage of households with Internet access	21		
4.06 Mobile network coverage per 100 population	99		

Figure 8.4 e-commerce readiness for Cambodia

For ICT infrastructure, Indonesia ranks fourth out of eight in the access pillar, and fifth out of eight in the usage and the skill pillars. Moreover, Indonesia is unbalanced in the development of e-commerce facilitation, ranking eighth out of ten in the social media pillar, and ranking fourth out of nine in the payment pillar. At the same time, the language service for the local population is at the medium level among ten countries.

Compared with ASEAN averages scores, all pillars in Indonesia except social media are around the middle level. In other words, Indonesia is moderately developed in most aspects of e-readiness. For social media development, the score in Indonesia is about 1.5 points less than the average score. Thus, the government should make more effort to encourage the citizens to engage in social media activities.

The scores for procedures to enforce a contract, number of procedures required to start a business, PCT patent applications, and gross expenditure on R&D are significantly low, which shows that the country requires more effort to improve the e-commerce environment. ICT infrastructure, percentage of households with a computer, percentage of individuals using the Internet, and fixed-broadband Internet subscriptions could be the bottleneck hindering e-commerce development. In the e-commerce facilitation sub-index, social media users (percentage Facebook every day), credit cards, electronic payments used to make payments, mobile phones used to pay bills, and GNI get relatively low scores compared with other indicators in Indonesia (Figure 8.5).

Laos

In the case of Laos, missing data is a problem for more rigorous analysis. Thus, it is hard to draw a conclusion for the overall e-commerce readiness of that country. But we can see that Laos is underdeveloped in the innovation environment. For ICT infrastructure, we find that Laos falls behind in skill, the second last among ASEAN countries. Due to missing data on mobile network coverage, prepaid mobile cellular tariff, and fixed-broadband Internet tariffs, we cannot conclude on the state of ICT infrastructure for access and usage in Laos. Considering e-commerce facilitation, the development in Laos ranks last in the social media pillar and ninth in the payment pillar. Also, the language pillar gets the lowest score of all the countries.

Compared with ASEAN average scores, the scores of Laos are behind in all aspects. The only pillar close to the average is innovation environment, which is one point less than the average. The other four pillars (skill, social media, payment, and language) fall heavily behind the average. And because of lack of data, we cannot draw a conclusion about the other pillars.

The scores for GDP and PCT patent applications are extremely low in the environment sub-index. In the ICT infrastructure sub-index, Laos only shows an acceptable score in the indicator for fixed-telephone subscriptions and gets very low scores in all other indicators. For e-commerce facilitation, only the indicator for social media users (percentage using Facebook every day) gets a relatively high score; other indicators are all still underdeveloped (Figure 8.6).

Indonesia

	Rank	Value
E-commerce Readiness Index	5	3.54
Environment Sub-index	4	3.71
1st pillar: Policy and regulatory environment	3	3.92
2nd pillar: Business environment	4	3.89
3rd pillar: Innovation environment	3	3.30
IT infrastructure Sub-index	4	3.82
4th pillar: Access	4	3.52
5th pillar: Usage	5	3.22
6th pillar: Skill	6	4.72
E-commerce facilitation Sub-index	5	3.08
7th pillar: Social media	8	2.53
8th pillar: Payment	4	2.72
9th pillar: Language	5	3.2

The E-commerce Readiness Index in detail

Indicator	Value
1st pillar Political and regulatory environment	
1.01 Effectiveness of law-making bodies	3.8
1.02 Laws relating to ICTs	4.1
1.03 Judicial independence	4.0
1.04 Efficiency of legal system in settling disputes	3.9
1.05 Efficiency of legal system in challenging regulations	3.9
1.06 Number of procedures to enforce a contract	40
1.07 Number of days to enforce a contract	471
1.08 Intellectual property protection	4.3
1.09 Property rights	4.4
2nd pillar Business environment	
2.01 GDP(100 million USD)	8617.7
2.02 Venture capital availability	3.8
2.03 Number of days required to start a business	48
2.04 Number of procedures required to start a business	13
2.05 Intensity of local competition	5.1
2.06 Corporate Tax/Corporate income tax	25%
2.07 Total tax rate, % profits	29.7%
3rd pillar Innovation environment	
3.01 Company spending on R&D	4.4
3.02 PCT patent applications	0.1
3.03 Gross expenditure on R&D, % of GDP	0.1
3.04 Quality of scientific research institutions	4.4
3.05 Availability of latest technologies	4.8
3.06 Government procurement of advanced technology products	4.2
4th pillar Access	
4.01 Fixed-telephone subscriptions per 100 inhabitants	8.9
4.02 Mobile-cellular telephone subscriptions per 100 inhabitants	132.3
4.03 International Internet bandwidth per Internet user (Bit/s)	6584
4.04 Percentage of households with computer	18.7
4.05 Percentage of households with Internet access	38.4
4.06 Mobile network coverage per 100 population	100

Indicator	Value
5th pillar Usage	
5.01 Percentage of individuals using the Internet	22
5.02 Fixed-broadband Internet subscriptions per 100 inhabitants	1.1
5.03 Active mobile-broadband subscriptions per 100 inhabitants	42
5.04 Prepaid mobile cellular tariffs, PPP $/min	0.19
5.05 Fixed broadband Internet tariffs, PPP $/month	27.92
6th pillar Skill	
6.01 Mean years of schooling	7.6
6.02 Secondary gross enrolment ratio	82.5
6.03 Tertiary gross enrolment ratio	31.3
6.04 Adult literacy rate	93.9
7th pillar Social media	
7.01 social media users (in million)	106
7.02 social media users by Mobile (in million)	92
7.03 average daily use of social media (minutes)	198
7.04 social media users (percentage of using facebook everyday)	41%
8th pillar Payment	
8.01 credit card (% age 15+)	1.59%
8.02 Electronic payments used to make payments (% age 15+)	3.09%
8.03 Mobile phone used to pay bills (% age 15+)	0.23%
8.04 commercial bank branch (per 100,000 persons)	10.98
8.05 GNI per capital	3440
8.06 Gross national savings % GDP	32.5%
9th pillar Language	
9.01 Chinese	3
9.02 English	4
9.03 Japanese	3
9.04 German	3
9.05 Hindi	3

Figure 8.5 e-commerce readiness for Indonesia

Laos

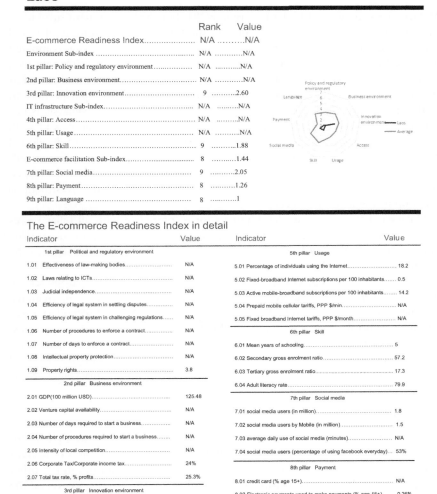

	Rank	Value
E-commerce Readiness Index	N/A	N/A
Environment Sub-index	N/A	N/A
1st pillar: Policy and regulatory environment	N/A	N/A
2nd pillar: Business environment	N/A	N/A
3rd pillar: Innovation environment	9	2.60
IT infrastructure Sub-index	N/A	N/A
4th pillar: Access	N/A	N/A
5th pillar: Usage	N/A	N/A
6th pillar: Skill	9	1.88
E-commerce facilitation Sub-index	8	1.44
7th pillar: Social media	9	2.05
8th pillar: Payment	8	1.26
9th pillar: Language	8	1

The E-commerce Readiness Index in detail

Indicator	Value
1st pillar Political and regulatory environment	
1.01 Effectiveness of law-making bodies	N/A
1.02 Laws relating to ICTs	N/A
1.03 Judicial independence	N/A
1.04 Efficiency of legal system in settling disputes	N/A
1.05 Efficiency of legal system in challenging regulations	N/A
1.06 Number of procedures to enforce a contract	N/A
1.07 Number of days to enforce a contract	N/A
1.08 Intellectual property protection	N/A
1.09 Property rights	3.8
2nd pillar Business environment	
2.01 GDP(100 million USD)	125.48
2.02 Venture capital availability	N/A
2.03 Number of days required to start a business	N/A
2.04 Number of procedures required to start a business	N/A
2.05 Intensity of local competition	N/A
2.06 Corporate Tax/Corporate income tax	24%
2.07 Total tax rate, % profits	25.3%
3rd pillar Innovation environment	
3.01 Company spending on R&D	3.4
3.02 PCT patent applications	0.2
3.03 Gross expenditure on R&D, % of GDP	N/A
3.04 Quality of scientific research institutions	3.4
3.05 Availability of latest technologies	N/A
3.06 Government procurement of advanced technology products	N/A
4th pillar Access	
4.01 Fixed-telephone subscriptions per 100 inhabitants	13.7
4.02 Mobile-cellular telephone subscriptions per 100 inhabitants	53.1
4.03 International Internet bandwidth per Internet user (Bit/s)	16795
4.04 Percentage of households with computer	11.4
4.05 Percentage of households with Internet access	11.4
4.06 Mobile network coverage per 100 population	N/A

Indicator	Value
5th pillar Usage	
5.01 Percentage of individuals using the Internet	18.2
5.02 Fixed-broadband Internet subscriptions per 100 inhabitants	0.5
5.03 Active mobile-broadband subscriptions per 100 inhabitants	14.2
5.04 Prepaid mobile cellular tariffs, PPP $/min	N/A
5.05 Fixed broadband Internet tariffs, PPP $/month	N/A
6th pillar Skill	
6.01 Mean years of schooling	5
6.02 Secondary gross enrolment ratio	57.2
6.03 Tertiary gross enrolment ratio	17.3
6.04 Adult literacy rate	79.9
7th pillar Social media	
7.01 social media users (in million)	1.8
7.02 social media users by Mobile (in million)	1.5
7.03 average daily use of social media (minutes)	N/A
7.04 social media users (percentage of using facebook everyday)	53%
8th pillar Payment	
8.01 credit card (% age 15+)	N/A
8.02 Electronic payments used to make payments (% age 15+)	0.26%
8.03 Mobile phone used to pay bills (% age 15+)	0.00%
8.04 commercial bank branch (per 100,000 persons)	2.67
8.05 GNI per capital	1740
8.06 Gross national savings % GDP	19.9%
9th pillar Language	
9.01 Chinese	1
9.02 English	1
9.03 Japanese	1
9.04 German	1
9.05 Hindi	1

Figure 8.6 e-commerce readiness for Laos

Malaysia

Malaysia gets the second-highest score in eCRI. For the environment sub-index, Malaysia is second in policy and regulation and third in the innovation pillar and the business pillar, indicative of good e-commerce readiness. However, compared with the best-performing country, Singapore, there is still a considerable gap. That is to say, Malaysia still has room to improve in e-commerce readiness. For ICT infrastructure, Malaysia ranks second in the access and usage pillars and fifth in the skill pillar. Therefore, ICT infrastructure development in Malaysia is not very balanced, and more effort needs to be made in improving people's IT skill. For the e-commerce facilitation sub-index, Malaysia is the fourth most developed country in the social media pillar, the third most developed in the payment pillar, and the fifth in the language pillar. So, Malaysia is a moderately developed country in e-commerce facilitation. It still requires more time and investment to catch up to the level of Singapore.

Malaysia shows satisfying development for e-commerce with all pillar scores except for language, exceeding the average scores. The scores of these nine pillars have one or two more points than the respective average scores. The score of the language pillar falls a little behind the average.

GDP, tax, and PCT patent applications are the three indicators that hinder the development environment in Malaysia. Fixed-telephone subscriptions, international Internet bandwidth, fixed-broadband Internet subscriptions, and secondary gross enrolment ratio are the factors that fall behind in the ICT infrastructure sub-index. e-Commerce issues, low scores of electronic payments used to make payments, mobile phone used to pay bills, commercial bank branch, GNI, and gross national savings show that payment development in Malaysia is unsatisfactory (Figure 8.7).

Myanmar

Myanmar is an underdeveloped country with the lowest eCRI of the eight countries. It is behind in e-commerce environment and ranks seventh out of the eight countries in the business pillar. It is last among the eight countries in the other two pillars. For ICT infrastructure, Myanmar also ranks last in the access and the usage pillars and eighth in the skill pillar. Furthermore, Myanmar gets the lowest scores in all three pillars in the e-commerce facilitation sub-index, which are extremely underdeveloped.

Myanmar is not well developed according to e-readiness; no pillar exceeds the average score. Business environment is the only pillar which gets an average level score. Other pillars perform worse than the average level. Social media and language are each two points less than the average.

In environment sub-index, the scores of the number of procedures to enforce a contract, number of days to enforce a contract, GDP, venture capital availability, and PCT patent applications are significantly lower than are the other indicator scores. And in the ICT infrastructure sub-index, only prepaid mobile cellular tariffs, fixed-broadband Internet tariffs, and adult literacy rate are relatively

Malaysia

	Rank	Value
E-commerce Readiness Index	2	4.68
Environment Sub-index	2	5.12
1st pillar: Policy and regulatory environment	2	5.23
2nd pillar: Business environment	3	5.62
3rd pillar: Innovation environment	2	4.52
IT infrastructure Sub-index	2	4.78
4th pillar: Access	2	4.68
5th pillar: Usage	2	4.70
6th pillar: Skill	5	5.23
E-commerce facilitation Sub-index	4	4.05
7th pillar: Social media	2	5.62
8th pillar: Payment	2	3.35
9th pillar: Language	5	3.2

The E-commerce Readiness Index in detail

Indicator	Value
1st pillar Political and regulatory environment	
1.01 Effectiveness of law-making bodies	5.3
1.02 Laws relating to ICTs	5.4
1.03 Judicial independence	5.0
1.04 Efficiency of legal system in settling disputes	5.3
1.05 Efficiency of legal system in challenging regulations	5.0
1.06 Number of procedures to enforce a contract	29
1.07 Number of days to enforce a contract	425
1.08 Intellectual property protection	5.4
1.09 Property rights	5.3
2nd pillar Business environment	
2.01 GDP(100 million USD)	3134.79
2.02 Venture capital availability	4.8
2.03 Number of days required to start a business	4.0
2.04 Number of procedures required to start a business	3.0
2.05 Intensity of local competition	5.4
2.06 Corporate Tax/Corporate income tax	24%
2.07 Total tax rate, % profits	40%
3rd pillar Innovation environment	
3.01 Company spending on R&D	5.2
3.02 PCT patent applications	11.3
3.03 Gross expenditure on R&D, % of GDP	1.1
3.04 Quality of scientific research institutions	5.3
3.05 Availability of latest technologies	5.7
3.06 Government procurement of advanced technology products	5.3
4th pillar Access	
4.01 Fixed-telephone subscriptions per 100 inhabitants	14.3
4.02 Mobile-cellular telephone subscriptions per 100 inhabitants	143.9
4.03 International Internet bandwidth per Internet user (Bit/s)	34119
4.04 Percentage of households with computer	67.6
4.05 Percentage of households with Internet access	70.1
4.06 Mobile network coverage per 100 population	95.4

Indicator	Value
5th pillar Usage	
5.01 Percentage of individuals using the Internet	71.1
5.02 Fixed-broadband Internet subscriptions per 100 inhabitants	9.0
5.03 Active mobile-broadband subscriptions per 100 inhabitants	89.9
5.04 Prepaid mobile cellular tariffs, PPP $/min	0.17
5.05 Fixed broadband Internet tariffs, PPP $/month	60.97
6th pillar Skill	
6.01 Mean years of schooling	10
6.02 Secondary gross enrolment ratio	71.1
6.03 Tertiary gross enrolment ratio	38.5
6.04 Adult literacy rate	94.6
7th pillar Social media	
7.01 social media users (in million)	22
7.02 social media users by Mobile (in million)	20
7.03 average daily use of social media (minutes)	199
7.04 social media users (percentage of using Facebook everyday)	64%
8th pillar Payment	
8.01 credit card (% age 15+)	20.16%
8.02 Electronic payments used to make payments (% age 15+)	12.65%
8.03 Mobile phone used to pay bills (% age 15+)	2.36%
8.04 commercial bank branch (per 100,000 persons)	10.71
8.05 GNI per capital	10570
8.06 Gross national savings % GDP	28%
9th pillar Language	
9.01 Chinese	3
9.02 English	4
9.03 Japanese	3
9.04 German	3
9.05 Hindi	3

Figure 8.7 e-commerce readiness for Malaysia

satisfactory compared with the other very low score indicators in Myanmar. For e-commerce facilitation issues, only the indicator of social media users (percentage using Facebook every day) shows a good score, whereas all other indicators perform poorly (Figure 8.8).

Philippines

E-Commerce readiness is moderate in Philippines, ranking fourth out of the eight countries. E-Commerce development in Philippines falls behind most countries, ranking sixth out of the eight countries in the policy and regulation pillar as well as the innovation pillar and last in the business pillar. For ICT infrastructure, Philippines ranks fifth and seventh out of eight countries respectively in the access and the usage pillars. However, its performance in the skill pillar is slightly better, ranking fourth out of the ten countries. For e-commerce facilitation, the rank of Philippines is fifth out of the ten countries in the social media pillar and fifth out of nine in the payment pillar. English is one of the official languages in Philippines, so the country gets a high score in the language pillar.

Five pillars (policy and regulatory environment, innovation environment, access, social media, and payment) are very close to the average level. However, the business environment and usage pillars falls a little bit behind. The skill pillar performs well and exceeds the average score. Moreover, the language pillar is outstanding, three points higher than the average score. The reason is Philippines uses English as one of the official languages.

Number of procedures required to start a business, tax, PCT patent applications, and gross expenditure on R&D could be the bottleneck in the environment sub-index. In ICT infrastructure sub-index, the indicators with extremely low scores are fixed-telephone subscriptions, international Internet bandwidth, fixed-broadband Internet subscriptions, and prepaid mobile cellular tariff. In the e-commerce facilitation sub-index, social media users (percentage using Facebook every day), credit card, electronic payments used to make payments, and GNI all fall behind the average of other indicators (Figure 8.9)

Singapore

Singapore is the best-prepared country for e-commerce, according to the eCRI in our analysis. For the environment, Singapore shows excellent performance in all pillars. In other words, Singapore provides a very good policy and regulation, business, and innovation environment for conducting e-commerce. In ICT infrastructure, Singapore ranks first again in all pillars, which means its ICT infrastructure development is mature in three aspects: access, usage, and skill. For e-commerce facilitation, Singapore is well developed, ranking first in the payment and the language pillar. But it falls a little behind in the social media pillar, ranking second among the ten ASEAN countries.

Singapore is the most developed ASEAN country, exceeding the average scores in all pillars. The gap between Singapore and the average is quite significant for

Myanmar

	Rank	Value
E-commerce Readiness Index	8	2.08
Environment Sub-index	8	2.87
1st pillar: Policy and regulatory environment	8	2.28
2nd pillar: Business environment	7	3.58
3rd pillar: Innovation environment	8	2.75
IT infrastructure Sub-index	8	2.08
4th pillar: Access	8	1.43
5th pillar: Usage	8	2.41
6th pillar: Skill	8	2.39
E-commerce facilitation Sub-index	9	1.28
7th pillar: Social media	10	1.78
8th pillar: Payment	8	1.06
9th pillar: Language	8	1

The E-commerce Readiness Index in detail

Indicator	Value
1st pillar Political and regulatory environment	
1.10 Effectiveness of law-making bodies	3.0
1.11 Laws relating to ICTs	2.5
1.12 Judicial independence	2.6
1.13 Efficiency of legal system in settling disputes	2.7
1.14 Efficiency of legal system in challenging regulations	2.6
1.15 Number of procedures to enforce a contract	45
1.16 Number of days to enforce a contract	1160
1.17 Intellectual property protection	2.8
1.18 Property rights	N/A
2nd pillar Business environment	
2.01 GDP(100 million USD)	657.75
2.02 Venture capital availability	1.8
2.03 Number of days required to start a business	13
2.04 Number of procedures required to start a business	11
2.05 Intensity of local competition	4.4
2.06 Corporate Tax/Corporate income tax	25%
2.07 Total tax rate, % profits	N/A
3rd pillar Innovation environment	
3.01 Company spending on R&D	N/A
3.02 PCT patent applications	N/A
3.03 Gross expenditure on R&D, % of GDP	N/A
3.04 Quality of scientific research institutions	N/A
3.05 Availability of latest technologies	2.7
3.06 Government procurement of advanced technology products	2.8
4th pillar Access	
4.01 Fixed-telephone subscriptions per 100 inhabitants	1
4.02 Mobile-cellular telephone subscriptions per 100 inhabitants	76.7
4.03 International Internet bandwidth per Internet user (Bit/s)	3676
4.04 Percentage of households with computer	14
4.05 Percentage of households with Internet access	15
4.06 Mobile network coverage per 100 population	73

Indicator	Value
5th pillar Usage	
5.01 Percentage of individuals using the Internet	21.8
5.02 Fixed-broadband Internet subscriptions per 100 inhabitants	0.6
5.03 Active mobile-broadband subscriptions per 100 inhabitants	29.5
5.04 Prepaid mobile cellular tariffs, PPP $/min	0.11
5.05 Fixed broadband Internet tariffs, PPP $/month	136.43
6th pillar Skill	
6.01 Mean years of schooling	4.1
6.02 Secondary gross enrolment ratio	51.3
6.03 Tertiary gross enrolment ratio	13.4
6.04 Adult literacy rate	93.1
7th pillar Social media	
7.01 social media users (in million)	14
7.02 social media users by Mobile (in million)	13
7.03 average daily use of social media (minutes)	N/A
7.04 social media users (percentage of using Facebook everyday)	49%
8th pillar Payment	
8.01 credit card (% age 15+)	0%
8.02 Electronic payments used to make payments (% age 15+)	N/A
8.03 Mobile phone used to pay bills (% age 15+)	N/A
8.04 commercial bank branch (per 100,000 persons)	3.14
8.05 GNI per capital	1160
8.06 Gross national savings % GDP	N/A
9th pillar Language	
9.01 Chinese	1
9.02 English	1
9.03 Japanese	1
9.04 German	1
9.05 Hindi	1

Figure 8.8 e-commerce readiness for Myanmar

Philippines

	Rank	Value
E-commerce Readiness Index	4	3.81
Environment Sub-index	6	3.18
1st pillar: Policy and regulatory environment	6	3.49
2nd pillar: Business environment	8	2.78
3rd pillar: Innovation environment	6	2.94
IT infrastructure Sub-index	6	3.77
4th pillar: Access	5	3.18
5th pillar: Usage	7	2.62
6th pillar: Skill	4	5.51
E-commerce facilitation Sub-index	2	4.47
7th pillar: Social media	5	4.24
8th pillar: Payment	5	2.36
9th pillar: Language	1	6.8

The E-commerce Readiness Index in detail

Indicator	Value	Indicator	Value
1st pillar Political and regulatory environment		**5th pillar Usage**	
1.01 Effectiveness of law-making bodies	3.5	5.01 Percentage of individuals using the Internet	40.7
1.02 Laws relating to ICTs	3.7	5.02 Fixed-broadband Internet subscriptions per 100 inhabitants	3.4
1.03 Judicial independence	3.7	5.03 Active mobile-broadband subscriptions per 100 inhabitants	41.6
1.04 Efficiency of legal system in settling disputes	3.3	5.04 Prepaid mobile cellular tariffs, PPP $/min	0.4
1.05 Efficiency of legal system in challenging regulations	3.3	5.05 Fixed broadband Internet tariffs, PPP $/month	54.59
1.06 Number of procedures to enforce a contract	37	**6th pillar Skill**	
1.07 Number of days to enforce a contract	842	6.01 Mean years of schooling	8.9
1.08 Intellectual property protection	3.9	6.02 Secondary gross enrolment ratio	88.4
1.09 Property rights	4.1	6.03 Tertiary gross enrolment ratio	35.8
2nd pillar Business environment		6.04 Adult literacy rate	96.3
2.01 GDP(100 million USD)	2993.14	**7th pillar Social media**	
2.02 Venture capital availability	3.1	7.01 social media users (in million)	60
2.03 Number of days required to start a business	29	7.02 social media users by Mobile (in million)	54
2.04 Number of procedures required to start a business	16	7.03 average daily use of social media (minutes)	257
2.05 Intensity of local competition	5.2	7.04 social media users (percentage of using facebook everyday)	42%
2.06 Corporate Tax/Corporate income tax	30%	**8th pillar Payment**	
2.07 Total tax rate, % profits	42.9%	8.01 credit card (% age 15+)	3.2%
3rd pillar Innovation environment		8.02 Electronic payments used to make payments (% age 15+)	2.1%
3.01 Company spending on R&D	3.7	8.03 Mobile phone used to pay bills (% age 15+)	2.12%
3.02 PCT patent applications	0.3	8.04 commercial bank branch (per 100,000 persons)	8.81
3.03 Gross expenditure on R&D, % of GDP	0.1	8.05 GNI per capital	3550
3.04 Quality of scientific research institutions	3.8	8.06 Gross national savings % GDP	23.7%
3.05 Availability of latest technologies	4.6	**9th pillar Language**	
3.06 Government procurement of advanced technology products	3.5	9.01 Chinese	7
4th pillar Access		9.02 English	7
4.01 Fixed-telephone subscriptions per 100 inhabitants	3	9.03 Japanese	7
4.02 Mobile-cellular telephone subscriptions per 100 inhabitants	118.1	9.04 German	7
4.03 International Internet bandwidth per Internet user (Bit/s)	37409	9.05 Hindi	6
4.04 Percentage of households with computer	27		
4.05 Percentage of households with Internet access	28.3		
4.06 Mobile network coverage per 100 population	99		

Figure 8.9 e-commerce readiness for Philippines

all pillars except social media. Social media in Singapore was only about 1.5 point higher than the average.

Although Singapore performs well in all pillars, there is room for improvement. For environment, more effort should be put into the efficiency of the legal system in challenging regulations, GDP, company spending on R&D, and government procurement of advanced technology products. For ICT infrastructure, prepaid mobile cellular tariffs, and fixed-broadband Internet tariffs in Singapore are relatively high, and the tertiary gross enrolment ratio is relatively low. In e-commerce facilitation issues, average daily use of social media in Singapore is lowest among ASEAN countries, and there are not enough commercial bank branches. Therefore, it would be better if the government can put more effort into these issues to strengthen the country's e-commerce readiness (Figure 8.10).

Thailand

Generally speaking, Thailand is medium in e-commerce readiness, ranking third among the eight countries. The development for the three sub-indexes is balanced in Thailand. Considering the environment sub-index, Thailand ranks fifth out of eight in the policy and regulation pillar as well as the innovation pillar, and third out of eight in the business pillar. Thailand provides an average level environment for conducting e-commerce. Thailand also is moderately well performing in the ICT infrastructure sub-index but is well performing in the skill pillar. The rank of Thailand is third out of eight in the access pillar, fourth out of eight in the usage pillar, and second out of ten in the skill pillar. For the e-commerce facilitation sub-index, Thailand is third out of ten in the social media pillar and third out of nine in the payment pillar, which shows moderate development. The second highest score for the language pillar indicates relatively good machine translation technology for Thailand.

Thailand is moderately developed comparatively, having average scores among ASEAN countries. The only pillar that falls behind is innovation environment; however, the gap is minor. The scores of other pillars all exceed the average. But the gap between Thailand and the average is not significant, no more than two points difference.

PCT patent applications and gross expenditure on R&D are the two lowest indicators in the environment sub-index. In other words, Thailand needs more investment in innovation development. In the ICT infrastructure sub-index, the relatively low-scoring indicators are fixed-telephone subscriptions, international Internet bandwidth, percentage of households with a computer, and percentage of individuals using the Internet. For e-commerce facilitation, the indicators of average daily use of social media, credit card, electronic payments used to make payments, mobile phone used to pay bills, and GNI are worse than the average (Figure 8.11).

Vietnam

Vietnam falls a little behind relative to the other ASEAN countries, according to the eCRI. It ranks sixth out of eight. For this reason, Vietnam is not quite

Singapore

	Rank	Value
E-commerce Readiness Index	1	6.23
Environment Sub-index	1	6.1
1st pillar: Policy and regulatory environment	1	6.14
2nd pillar: Business environment	1	6.16
3rd pillar: Innovation environment	1	6.0
IT infrastructure Sub-index	1	6.6
4th pillar: Access	1	6.93
5th pillar: Usage	1	6.22
6th pillar: Skill	1	6.65
E-commerce facilitation Sub-index	1	6.0
7th pillar: Social media	2	5.43
8th pillar: Payment	1	5.78
9th pillar: Language	1	6.8

The E-commerce Readiness Index in detail

Indicator	Value
1st pillar Political and regulatory environment	
1.01 Effectiveness of law-making bodies	6.3
1.02 Laws relating to ICTs	5.7
1.03 Judicial independence	5.5
1.04 Efficiency of legal system in settling disputes	6.2
1.05 Efficiency of legal system in challenging regulations	5.2
1.06 Number of procedures to enforce a contract	21
1.07 Number of days to enforce a contract	150
1.08 Intellectual property protection	6.2
1.09 Property rights	6.3
2nd pillar Business environment	
2.01 GDP(100 million USD)	2939.59
2.02 Venture capital availability	4.6
2.03 Number of days required to start a business	3
2.04 Number of procedures required to start a business	3
2.05 Intensity of local competition	5.6
2.06 Corporate Tax/Corporate income tax	17%
2.07 Total tax rate, % profits	18.4%
3rd pillar Innovation environment	
3.01 Company spending on R&D	5
3.02 PCT patent applications	139.5
3.03 Gross expenditure on R&D, % of GDP	2
3.04 Quality of scientific research institutions	5.8
3.05 Availability of latest technologies	6.2
3.06 Government procurement of advanced technology products	.5
4th pillar Access	
4.01 Fixed-telephone subscriptions per 100 inhabitants	36
4.02 Mobile-cellular telephone subscriptions per 100 inhabitants	146.1
4.03 International Internet bandwidth per Internet user (Bit/s)	737006
4.04 Percentage of households with computer	87.5
4.05 Percentage of households with Internet access	89.5
4.06 Mobile network coverage per 100 population	100

Indicator	Value
5th pillar Usage	
5.01 Percentage of individuals using the Internet	82.1
5.02 Fixed-broadband Internet subscriptions per 100 inhabitants	26.5
5.03 Active mobile-broadband subscriptions per 100 inhabitants	142.2
5.04 Prepaid mobile cellular tariffs, PPP $/min	0.19
5.05 Fixed broadband Internet tariffs, PPP $/month	46.31
6th pillar Skill	
6.01 Mean years of schooling	11.6
6.02 Secondary gross enrolment ratio	97.2
6.03 Tertiary gross enrolment ratio	43.8
6.04 Adult literacy rate	96.8
7th pillar Social media	
7.01 social media users (in million)	4.4
7.02 social media users by Mobile (in million)	4.0
7.03 average daily use of social media (minutes)	127
7.04 social media users (percentage of using Facebook everyday)	64%
8th pillar Payment	
8.01 credit card (% age 15+)	35.42%
8.02 Electronic payments used to make payments (% age 15+)	41.50%
8.03 Mobile phone used to pay bills (% age 15+)	9.77%
8.04 commercial bank branch (per 100,000 persons)	9.37
8.05 GNI per capital	52090
8.06 Gross national savings % GDP	46%
9th pillar Language	
9.01 Chinese	7
9.02 English	7
9.03 Japanese	7
9.04 German	7
9.05 Hindi	6

Figure 8.10 e-commerce readiness for Singapore

Thailand

	Rank	Value
E-commerce Readiness Index	3	4.15
Environment Sub-index	3	3.88
1st pillar: Policy and regulatory environment	5	3.85
2nd pillar: Business environment	3	4.70
3rd pillar: Innovation environment	5	3.08
IT infrastructure Sub-index	3	4.65
4th pillar: Access	3	3.71
5th pillar: Usage	4	4.46
6th pillar: Skill	2	5.77
E-commerce facilitation Sub-index	3	4.15
7th pillar: Social media	3	5.11
8th pillar: Payment	3	3.15
9th pillar: Language	4	4.2

The E-commerce Readiness Index in detail

Indicator	Value
//1st pillar Political and regulatory environment	
1.01 Effectiveness of law-making bodies	3.4
1.02 Laws relating to ICTs	3.6
1.03 Judicial independence	4.1
1.04 Efficiency of legal system in settling disputes	3.9
1.05 Efficiency of legal system in challenging regulations	3.7
1.06 Number of procedures to enforce a contract	36
1.07 Number of days to enforce a contract	440
1.08 Intellectual property protection	3.2
1.09 Property rights	4.0
/2nd pillar Business environment	
2.01 GDP(100 million USD)	3735.36
2.02 Venture capital availability	3.3
2.03 Number of days required to start a business	28
2.04 Number of procedures required to start a business	6
2.05 Intensity of local competition	5.4
2.06 Corporate Tax/Corporate income tax	20%
2.07 Total tax rate, % profits	27.5%
/3rd pillar Innovation environment	
3.01 Company spending on R&D	3.6
3.02 PCT patent applications	1.4
3.03 Gross expenditure on R&D, % of GDP	0.4
3.04 Quality of scientific research institutions	4.1
3.05 Availability of latest technologies	4.7
3.06 Government procurement of advanced technology products	3.1
4th pillar Access	
4.01 Fixed-telephone subscriptions per 100 inhabitants	7.9
4.02 Mobile-cellular telephone subscriptions per 100 inhabitants	125.8
4.03 International Internet bandwidth per Internet user (Bit/s)	64907
4.04 Percentage of households with computer	29.5
4.05 Percentage of households with Internet access	52.2
4.06 Mobile network coverage per 100 population	97

Indicator	Value
/5th pillar Usage	
5.01 Percentage of individuals using the Internet	39.3
5.02 Fixed-broadband Internet subscriptions per 100 inhabitants	9.2
5.03 Active mobile-broadband subscriptions per 100 inhabitants	75.3
5.04 Prepaid mobile cellular tariffs, PPP $/min	0.09
5.05 Fixed broadband Internet tariffs, PPP $/month	42.47
/6th pillar Skill	
6.01 Mean years of schooling	7.3
6.02 Secondary gross enrolment ratio	86.2
6.03 Tertiary gross enrolment ratio	51.4
6.04 Adult literacy rate	96.7
/7th pillar Social media	
7.01 social media users (in million)	46
7.02 social media users by Mobile (in million)	42
7.03 average daily use of social media (minutes)	168
7.04 social media users (percentage of using Facebook everyday)	63%
8th pillar Payment	
8.01 credit card (% age 15+)	5.69%
8.02 Electronic payments used to make payments (% age 15+)	8.56%
8.03 Mobile phone used to pay bills (% age 15+)	0.47%
8.04 commercial bank branch (per 100,000 persons)	12.68
8.05 GNI per capital	5720
8.06 Gross national savings % GDP	32.9%
9th pillar Language	
9.01 Chinese	4
9.02 English	5
9.03 Japanese	4
9.04 German	4
9.05 Hindi	4

Figure 8.11 e-commerce readiness for Thailand

ready for e-commerce. Vietnam falls a little behind in all aspects and ranks fifth, fifth, and sixth in the environment sub-index, ICT infrastructure sub-index, and e-commerce facilitation sub-index respectively. And in all three pillars, Vietnam is mostly within fourth to sixth. The only outstanding pillar is usage, which shows wide usage of ICT infrastructure. However, the lowest ranking exists in the access pillar and the skill pillar.

Vietnam is very close to the average level in most pillars except the usage pillar. The difference between Vietnam and the average is not more than one point, whereas three pillars (policy and regulatory environment, business environment, and skill) exceed slightly, and five pillars (innovation environment, access, social media, payment, and language) fall a little behind. Vietnam is outstanding in usage, exceeding the average by approximately 1.5 points.

In self-comparison, the score of PCT patent applications is the lowest in the environment sub-index. All indicators in the access pillar are extremely low, except mobile-cellular telephone subscriptions. For e-commerce facilitation, the low scores in credit card, electronic payments used to make payments, commercial bank branches, and GNI heavily hinder the country's payment development (Figure 8.12).

Key findings

1   Singapore is in the leading position in e-commerce readiness among the ASEAN according to our eCRI. It shows a mature status for e-commerce development. It is relatively behind in the social media pillar, ranking second among the ten ASEAN countries. Our conjecture is that the high pressure of work and long working hours in Singapore prevent people from spending too much time on social media.

2   e-Commerce is relatively ready in Malaysia. The scores for most measurement pillars are mostly second or third among the ASEAN countries. Online payment and language are two main weaknesses for Malaysia.

3   e-Commerce developments in Thailand, Indonesia, Philippines, and Vietnam are all considered at a modest level. These countries have achieved moderate performance at most pillars. However, one can still observe different development characteristics in the different countries, for instance Indonesia has a more balanced development. Philippines is particularly strong in language, and Thailand shows strong achievement in Internet and related skills. There is still room for improvement in different aspects before e-commerce can take off in these countries.

4   Myanmar and Cambodia are classified in the below-average group among ASEAN. Their scores on most pillars are ranked below average, a clear indication that e-commerce in these two countries is underdeveloped. In other words, people conducting e-commerce in these countries will face great difficulties. Scores on the language pillar are particularly weak in Myanmar and Cambodia. Myanmar is also weak in Internet skills, and Cambodia has more problems in accessing the Internet. The respective governments will need to

Vietnam

	Rank	Value
E-commerce Readiness Index	6	3.47
Environment Sub-index	5	3.70
1st pillar: Policy and regulatory environment	4	3.86
2nd pillar: Business environment	5	3.87
3rd pillar: Innovation environment	4	3.16
IT infrastructure Sub-index	5	3.78
4th pillar: Access	7	2.30
5th pillar: Usage	3	4.47
6th pillar: Skill	7	4.57
E-commerce facilitation Sub-index	6	2.92
7th pillar: Social media	6	3.57
8th pillar: Payment	6	1.98
9th pillar: Language	5	3.2

The E-commerce Readiness Index in detail

Indicator	Value
1st pillar Political and regulatory environment	
1.01 Effectiveness of law-making bodies	3.8
1.02 Laws relating to ICTs	3.9
1.03 Judicial independence	3.5
1.04 Efficiency of legal system in settling disputes	3.7
1.05 Efficiency of legal system in challenging regulations	3.4
1.06 Number of procedures to enforce a contract	36
1.07 Number of days to enforce a contract	400
1.08 Intellectual property protection	3.6
1.09 Property rights	4.0
2nd pillar Business environment	
2.01 GDP(100 million USD)	1988.05
2.02 Venture capital availability	3.0
2.03 Number of days required to start a business	20
2.04 Number of procedures required to start a business	10
2.05 Intensity of local competition	5
2.06 Corporate Tax/Corporate income tax	20%
2.07 Total tax rate, % profits	21%
3rd pillar Innovation environment	
3.01 Company spending on R&D	3.5
3.02 PCT patent applications	0.2
3.03 Gross expenditure on R&D, % of GDP	N/A
3.04 Quality of scientific research institutions	3.4
3.05 Availability of latest technologies	4.0
3.06 Government procurement of advanced technology products	3.9
4th pillar Access	
4.01 Fixed-telephone subscriptions per 100 inhabitants	6.3
4.02 Mobile-cellular telephone subscriptions per 100 inhabitants	130.6
4.03 International Internet bandwidth per Internet user (Bit/s)	24374
4.04 Percentage of households with computer	22
4.05 Percentage of households with Internet access	24.1
4.06 Mobile network coverage per 100 population	7

Indicator	Value
5th pillar Usage	
5.01 Percentage of individuals using the Internet	52.7
5.02 Fixed-broadband Internet subscriptions per 100 inhabitants	8.1
5.03 Active mobile-broadband subscriptions per 100 inhabitants	39
5.04 Prepaid mobile cellular tariffs, PPP $/min	0.15
5.05 Fixed broadband Internet tariffs, PPP $/month	2.59
6th pillar Skill	
6.01 Mean years of schooling	7.5
6.02 Secondary gross enrolment ratio	77.2
6.03 Tertiary gross enrolment ratio	30.5
6.04 Adult literacy rate	94.5
7th pillar Social media	
7.01 social media users (in million)	46
7.02 social media users by Mobile (in million)	41
7.03 average daily use of social media (minutes)	159
7.04 social media users (percentage of using Facebook everyday)	59%
8th pillar Payment	
8.01 credit card (% age 15+)	1.93%
8.02 Electronic payments used to make payments (% age 15+)	2.53%
8.03 Mobile phone used to pay bills (% age 15+)	3.58%
8.04 commercial bank branch (per 100,000 persons)	3.831
8.05 GNI per capital	1990
8.06 Gross national savings % GDP	29%
9th pillar Language	
9.01 Chinese	3
9.02 English	4
9.03 Japanese	3
9.04 German	3
9.05 Hindi	3

Figure 8.12 e-commerce readiness for Vietnam

invest significant efforts and may need external help in training and putting an Internet infrastructure in place.

5   Due to lack of data, we are not able to draw overall conclusions on the e-commerce readiness of Brunei and Laos. However, with limited data we can still observe and see differences between the two countries. Although it falls behind in the innovation pillar, Brunei shows good achievement in possessing Internet-related skills, using social media, and language pillars. This may be explained by the fact the population is small and relatively wealthy. As for Laos, its scores on all measurement pillars are low, indicating e-commerce is underdeveloped.

6   In general, overall access to the Internet among ASEAN countries is low. This means better Internet infrastructure is needed throughout ASEAN, except for Singapore. The same is true for online payment availability. However, the difference between Internet infrastructure and online payment may be that the former has to be developed locally, whereas the later can be served by overseas payment platforms.

As a result, we can roughly classify the ten countries into three categories. Malaysia and Singapore are the two e-commerce-ready countries, but Malaysia still has room to improve its online payment and language facilitation. Indonesia, Philippines, Thailand, and Vietnam are countries in the middle rank. They have different strengths and shortcomings, but they mostly fall behind in online payment. The remaining the countries still have much to improve.

Discussion and recommendations

We provide a way to measure e-commerce readiness. ASEAN is one of the economies in the BRI. The primary objective of both the BRI and ASEAN is to connect their partner economies to enhance regional competitiveness and sustainable economic growth. To achieve these goals, the key regional stakeholders in different economies need to be closely interconnected through the Internet, also used as a channel to facilitate cross-border e-business. Nonetheless, different development in the information highway might lead to a digital divide problem and in turn will seriously hinder regional business development. This common circumstance is shared by many economic associations globally including the BRI and ASEAN. ASEAN is just used as an example here; the method can apply to the BRI.

Moreover, we provide a formative measurement for all IT-related business. The first two general sub-indexes (environment and ICT infrastructure) can apply to other IT-related business assessments. The only modification is to substitute another facilitation sub-index for the e-commerce facilitation sub-index.

However, we humbly admit some shortcomings. For example, when calculating the index scores, all pillars and sub-indices are equally weighted, which may not provide a whole view of the country's development. More experts' opinions will be needed to justify the index weight. Moreover, the project is only desktop research.

Some of the unavailable data results in the loss of ranking of two countries. The results will be more comprehensive if we try other studies and collect more data.

This chapter sheds light on the e-commerce readiness of each country in ASEAN. The results show that the development for e-commerce is unbalanced in ASEAN countries, and each country has its own strengths and weaknesses. Based on the results, we have three recommendations.

Self-improvement: As the previous sections discuss, the development in different aspects is uneven for most countries. The most underdeveloped factors can be obstacles that hinder e-commerce development. Our report helps figure out the weaknesses and strengths of each country. Each country can then focus on overcoming its weaknesses according to eCRI in the e-commerce development plan.

Technology cooperation: Countries, especially those in the middle, have unbalanced development in ICT infrastructure. Each has its own strengths and weaknesses. They can cooperate by providing their strengths to help others and get assistance from others to overcome their weaknesses.

Market merge: Since the populations in ASEAN countries are small, we suggest countries with same language or that are geographically close countries create a shared e-commerce market. A bigger market will give entrepreneurs more incentives to conduct e-commerce business and allow the market to be more competitive in the world. For countries with a language barrier, we suggest more investment on machine translation for local languages to English and to Chinese.

Acknowledgements

The work described in this paper is partially funded by the Global China Research Programme, The Chinese University of Hong Kong.

Bibliography

Almeida, G.A.A., Avila, A., Boncanoska, V. (2007). Promoting E-commerce in Developing Countries, Internet Governance and Policy Discussions Paper, Retrieved on November, 15, 2014 from http://archive1.diplomacy.edu/pool/fileInline.php?IDPool=454

Almeida, A & Boncanoska, D 2013, 'Online grocery retailing in Jordan: future perspective', *European, Mediterranean & Middle Eastern Conference on Information Systems.* 17–18 October, 2013.

Cao, Y & Gan, Y 2012, 'Regional outlook: Southeast Asia in 2012', 31 August (东南亚地区形势: 2012年). Available from: http://d.g.wanfangdata.com.cn/Periodical_dnyyj201202001.aspx. [31 August 2012].

Chen, X & Ni, W 2016, 'Economic situation analysis of Southeast Asia in 2015' (2015年东南亚地区经济形势: 表现及展望). Available from: http://d.g.wanfangdata.com.cn/Periodical_dny201601005.aspx. [27 April 2016].

China and the World Program 2016, 'The One Belt One Road project and China's foreign relations', 13 April. Available from: https://cwp.princeton.edu/news/one-belt-one-road-project-and-chinas-foreign-relations. [13 April 2016].

'Criteo: rise of Southeast Asia e-commerce' (东南亚移动电子商务正在崛起). Available from: www.199it.com/archives/459853.html. [12 May 2016].

Dedrick, J & Kraemer, KL 2001, 'China IT report', *Electronic Journal on Information Systems in Developing Countries*, vol. 6, no. 2, pp. 1–10. Available from: www.ejisdc.org, [1 February 2018]

E-Commerce and E-Business/E-Commerce in Developing Countries. (2017, August 1). Wikibooks, The Free Textbook Project. Retrieved 08:27, August 9, 2018 from https://en.wikibooks.org/w/index.php?title=E-Commerce_and_E-Business/E-Commerce_in_Developing_Countries&oldid=3253625.

The Electronic Commerce Infrastructure Info-Communications Development Authority of Singapore 2002, 'E-commerce infrastructure in Singapore'. Available from: http://unpan1.un.org/intradoc/groups/public/documents/APCITY/UNPAN003003.pdf. [17 March 2002].

Gibbs, JL & Kraemer, KL 2004, 'A cross-country investigation of the determinants of scope of e-commerce use: an institutional approach', *Electronic Markets*, vol. 14, no. 2, pp. 124–137.

Global Digital & Social Media Stats 2015, Available from: www.socialmediatoday.com/content/global-digital-social-media-stats-2015. [22 January 2015].

Global Information Technology Report 2016, Available from: www.weforum.org/reports/the-global-information-technology-report-2016. [6 July 2016].

Human Development Report 2016, Available from: http://hdr.undp.org/en/2016-report, 27 March, 2017.

International Monetary Fund (IMF) 2016, "World Economic Outlook", April.

Jennex, ME, Amoroso, D & Adelakun, O 2004, 'E-commerce infrastructure success factors for small companies in developing economies', *Electronic Commerce Research*, vol. 4, no. 3, pp. 263–286.

Morgan, JP 2015, 'ASEAN's bright future: growth opportunities for corporates in the ASEAN region', July. Available from: www.jpmorgan.com/country/US/EN/cib/investment-banking/trade-asean-future. [1 July 2015].

Kurbalija, J & Gelbstein, E 2005, *Internet governance: issues, actors and divides*. DiploFoundation, Valletta, Malta.

Kurnia, S 2008, 'Exploring e-commerce readiness in China: the case of the grocery industry', *Proceedings of the 41st Hawaii International Conference on System Sciences*, 7–10 January 2008.

Mansell, R, & Steinmueller, WE 2000, *Mobilizing the information society: strategies for growth and opportunity*. Oxford University Press, Oxford.

Mukti, NA 2000, 'Barriers to putting businesses on the Internet in Malaysia', *The Electronic Journal of Information Systems in Developing Countries*, vol. 2, no. 1, pp. 1–6.

Oxley, JE & Yeung, B 2001, 'E-commerce readiness: institutional environment and international competitiveness', *Journal of International Business Studies*, vol. 32, no. 4, pp. 705–723.

Schwab, Klaus 2016, "The Global Competitiveness Report 2016–2017", *World Economic Forum*.

Swamynathan, G, Wilson, C, Boe, B, Almeroth, K & Zhao, BY 2006, 'Do social networks improve e-commerce? A study on social marketplaces'. *Proceedings of the First Workshop on Online Social Networks*, 17–22, August 2006.

Turban, E, King, D, Lee, J, Warkentin, M & Chung, HM 2002, *Electronic commerce; a managerial perspective*, International Edition, Pearson Education, NJ.

White Paper on China-ASEAN Information Technology Development and Cooperation 2016 (2016年中国-东盟信息化发展与合作白皮书). Available from: www.catr.cn/kxyj/qwfb/bps/201609/P020160911662398099416.pdf. [2 September 2016].

Young, AK & Srivastava, J 2007, 'Impact of social influence in e-commerce decision making'. *Proceedings of the Ninth International Conference on Electronic Commerce*. 19–22 August 2007.

Zhang, X & Prybutok, VR 2005. 'How the mobile communication markets differ in China, the US, and Europe', *Communications of the ACM*, vol. 48, no. 3, pp. 111–114.

Appendix

Detailed e-Commerce readiness scores for ASEAN

Table 8.2 Detailed e-commerce readiness scores for Brunei

Indicator	Value
1st pillar: Political and regulatory environment	
1.01 Effectiveness of law-making bodies	N/A
1.02 Laws relating to ICTs	N/A
1.03 Judicial independence	N/A
1.04 Efficiency of legal system in settling disputes	N/A
1.05 Efficiency of legal system in challenging regulations	N/A
1.06 Number of procedures to enforce a contract	N/A
1.07 Number of days to enforce a contract	N/A
1.08 Intellectual property protection	N/A
1.09 Property rights	3.8
2nd pillar: Business environment	
2.01 GDP (US$100 million)	116.36
2.02 Venture capital availability	N/A
2.03 Number of days required to start a business	N/A
2.04 Number of procedures required to start a business	N/A
2.05 Intensity of local competition	N/A
2.06 Corporate tax/Corporate income tax	18.5%
2.07 Total tax rate, % profits	8.7%
3rd pillar: Innovation environment	
3.01 Company spending on R&D	2.9
3.02 PCT patent applications	3.3
3.03 Gross expenditure on R&D, % of GDP	N/A
3.04 Quality of scientific research institutions	3.4
3.05 Availability of latest technologies	N/A
3.06 Government procurement of advanced technology products	N/A
4th pillar: Access	
4.01 Fixed-telephone subscriptions per 100 inhabitants	9
4.02 Mobile-cellular telephone subscriptions per 100 inhabitants	108.1
4.03 International Internet bandwidth per Internet user (Bit/s)	63090
4.04 Percentage of households with a computer	93.4
4.05 Percentage of households with Internet access	81.7
4.06 Mobile network coverage per 100 population	N/A

Indicator	Value
5th pillar: Usage	
5.01 Percentage of individuals using the Internet	71.2
5.02 Fixed-broadband Internet subscriptions per 100 inhabitants	8
5.03 Active mobile-broadband subscriptions per 100 inhabitants	4.5
5.04 Prepaid mobile cellular tariffs, PPP $/min	N/A
5.05 Fixed broadband Internet tariffs, PPP $/month	N/A
6th pillar: Skill	
6.01 Mean years of schooling	8.8
6.02 Secondary gross enrolment ratio	99.1
6.03 Tertiary gross enrolment ratio	31.7
6.04 Adult literacy rate	79.9
7th pillar: Social media	
7.01 Social media users (in millions)	0.37
7.02 Social media users by mobile (in millions)	0.33
7.03 Average daily use of social media (minutes)	N/A
7.04 Social media users (percentage using Facebook every day)	51%
8th pillar: Payment	
8.01 Credit card (% age 15+)	N/A
8.02 Electronic payments used to make payments (% age 15+)	N/A
8.03 Mobile phone used to pay bills (% age 15+)	N/A
8.04 Commercial bank branch (per 100,000 persons)	19.828
8.05 GNI per capital	38010
8.06 Gross national savings % GDP	29%
9th pillar: Language	
9.01 Chinese	7
9.02 English	7
9.03 Japanese	7
9.04 German	7
9.05 Hindi	6

Table 8.3 Detailed e-commerce readiness scores for Cambodia

Indicator	Value
1st pillar: Political and regulatory environment	
1.01 Effectiveness of law-making bodies	2.9
1.02 Laws relating to ICTs	3.1
1.03 Judicial independence	2.5
1.04 Efficiency of legal system in settling disputes	2.8
1.05 Efficiency of legal system in challenging regulations	2.6
1.06 Number of procedures to enforce a contract	44
1.07 Number of days to enforce a contract	483
1.08 Intellectual property protection	2.8
1.09 Property rights	3.8
2nd pillar: Business environment	
2.01 GDP (US$100 million)	177.14
2.02 Venture capital availability	2.7
2.03 Number of days required to start a business	87

(*Continued*)

Table 8.3 (Continued)

Indicator	Value
2.04 Number of procedures required to start a business	7
2.05 Intensity of local competition	4.7
2.06 Corporate tax/Corporate income tax	20%
2.07 Total tax rate, % profits	21%
3rd pillar: Innovation environment	
3.01 Company spending on R&D	3.1
3.02 PCT patent applications	0
3.03 Gross expenditure on R&D, % of GDP	N/A
3.04 Quality of scientific research institutions	2.8
3.05 Availability of latest technologies	4.2
3.06 Government procurement of advanced technology products.	2.8
4th pillar: Access	
4.01 Fixed-telephone subscriptions per 100 inhabitants	1.6
4.02 Mobile-cellular telephone subscriptions per 100 inhabitants	133
4.03 International Internet bandwidth per Internet user (Bit/s)	17792
4.04 Percentage of households with a computer	16
4.05 Percentage of households with Internet access	21
4.06 Mobile network coverage per 100 population	99
5th pillar: Usage	
5.01 Percentage of individuals using the Internet	19
5.02 Fixed-broadband Internet subscriptions per 100 inhabitants	0.5
5.03 Active mobile-broadband subscriptions per 100 inhabitants	42.8
5.04 Prepaid mobile cellular tariffs, PPP $/min	0.23
5.05 Fixed broadband Internet tariffs, PPP $/month	29.81
6th pillar: Skill	
6.01 Mean years of schooling	4.4
6.02 Secondary gross enrolment ratio	45
6.03 Tertiary gross enrolment ratio.	15.8
6.04 Adult literacy rate	77.2
7th pillar: Social media	
7.01 Social media users (in million)	4.9
7.02 Social media users by mobile (in million)	4.4
7.03 Average daily use of social media (minutes)	N/A
7.04 Social media users (percentage using Facebook everyday)	57%
8th pillar: Payment	
8.01 Credit card (% age 15+)	2.89%
8.02 Electronic payments used to make payments (% age 15+)	0.49%.
8.03 Mobile phone used to pay bills (% age 15+)	0.08%
8.04 Commercial bank branch (per 100,000 persons)	5.58
8.05 GNI per capital	1070
8.06 Gross national savings % GDP	11.3%
9th pillar: Language	
9.01 Chinese	1
9.02 English	1
9.03 Japanese	1
9.04 German	1
9.05 Hindi	1

Table 8.4 Detailed e-commerce readiness scores for Indonesia

Indicator	Value
1st pillar: Political and regulatory environment	
1.01 Effectiveness of law-making bodies	3.8
1.02 Laws relating to ICTs	4.1
1.03 Judicial independence	4.0
1.04 Efficiency of legal system in settling disputes	3.9
1.05 Efficiency of legal system in challenging regulations	3.9
1.06 Number of procedures to enforce a contract	40
1.07 Number of days to enforce a contract	471
1.08 Intellectual property protection	4.3
1.09 Property rights	4.4
2nd pillar: Business environment	
2.01 GDP (US$100 million)	8617.7
2.02 Venture capital availability	3.8
2.03 Number of days required to start a business	48
2.04 Number of procedures required to start a business	13
2.05 Intensity of local competition	5.1
2.06 Corporate Tax/Corporate income tax	25%
2.07 Total tax rate, % profits	29.7%
3rd pillar: Innovation environment	
3.01 Company spending on R&D	4.4
3.02 PCT patent applications	0.1
3.03 Gross expenditure on R&D, % of GDP	0.1
3.04 Quality of scientific research institutions	4.4
3.05 Availability of latest technologies	4.8
3.06 Government procurement of advanced technology products.	4.2
4th pillar: Access	
4.01 Fixed-telephone subscriptions per 100 inhabitants	8.9
4.02 Mobile-cellular telephone subscriptions per 100 inhabitants	132.3
4.03 International Internet bandwidth per Internet user (Bit/s)	6584
4.04 Percentage of households with a computer	18.7
4.05 Percentage of households with Internet access	38.4
4.06 Mobile network coverage per 100 population	100
5th pillar: Usage	
5.01 Percentage of individuals using the Internet	22
5.02 Fixed-broadband Internet subscriptions per 100 inhabitants	1.1
5.03 Active mobile-broadband subscriptions per 100 inhabitants	42
5.04 Prepaid mobile cellular tariffs, PPP $/min	0.19
5.05 Fixed broadband Internet tariffs, PPP $/month	27.92
6th pillar: Skill	
6.01 Mean years of schooling	7.6
6.02 Secondary gross enrolment ratio	82.5
6.03 Tertiary gross enrolment ratio	31.3
6.04 Adult literacy rate	93.9
7th pillar: Social media	
7.01 Social media users (in million)	106
7.02 Social media users by Mobile (in million)	92
7.03 Average daily use of social media (minutes)	198
7.04 Social media users (percentage using Facebook every day)	41%

(*Continued*)

Table 8.4 (Continued)

Indicator	Value
8th pillar: Payment	
8.01 Credit card (% age 15+)	1.59%
8.02 Electronic payments used to make payments (% age 15+)	3.09%
8.03 Mobile phone used to pay bills (% age 15+)	0.23%
8.04 Commercial bank branch (per 100,000 persons)	10.98
8.05 GNI per capital	3440
8.06 Gross national savings % GDP	32.5%
9th pillar: Language	
9.01 Chinese	3
9.02 English	4
9.03 Japanese	3
9.04 German	3
9.05 Hindi	3

Table 8.5 Detailed e-commerce readiness scores for Laos

Indicator	Value
1st pillar: Political and regulatory environment	
1.01 Effectiveness of law-making bodies	N/A
1.02 Laws relating to ICTs	N/A
1.03 Judicial independence	N/A
1.04 Efficiency of legal system in settling disputes.	N/A
1.05 Efficiency of legal system in challenging regulations.	N/A
1.06 Number of procedures to enforce a contract.	N/A
1.07 Number of days to enforce a contract.	N/A
1.08 Intellectual property protection.	N/A
1.09 Property rights	3.8
2nd pillar: Business environment	
2.01 GDP (US$100 million)	125.48
2.02 Venture capital availability	N/A
2.03 Number of days required to start a business.	N/A
2.04 Number of procedures required to start a business.	N/A
2.05 Intensity of local competition	N/A
2.06 Corporate tax/Corporate income tax	24%
2.07 Total tax rate, % profits	25.3%
3rd pillar: Innovation environment	
3.01 Company spending on R&D	3.4
3.02 PCT patent applications	0.2
3.03 Gross expenditure on R&D, % of GDP	N/A
3.04 Quality of scientific research institutions	3.4
3.05 Availability of latest technologies	N/A
3.06 Government procurement of advanced technology products	N/A
4th pillar: Access	
4.01 Fixed-telephone subscriptions per 100 inhabitants.	13.7
4.02 Mobile-cellular telephone subscriptions per 100 inhabitants.	53.1
4.03 International Internet bandwidth per Internet user (Bit/s)	16795
4.04 Percentage of households with a computer	11.4
4.05 Percentage of households with Internet access	11.4
4.06 Mobile network coverage per 100 population	N/A

Indicator	Value
5th pillar: Usage	
5.01 Percentage of individuals using the Internet	18.2
5.02 Fixed-broadband Internet subscriptions per 100 inhabitants	0.5
5.03 Active mobile-broadband subscriptions per 100 inhabitants	14.2
5.04 Prepaid mobile cellular tariffs, PPP $/min	N/A
5.05 Fixed broadband Internet tariffs, PPP $/month	N/A
6th pillar: Skill	
6.01 Mean years of schooling	5
6.02 Secondary gross enrolment ratio	57.2
6.03 Tertiary gross enrolment ratio	17.3
6.04 Adult literacy rate	79.9
7th pillar: Social media	
7.01 Social media users (in million)	1.8
7.02 Social media users by Mobile (in million)	1.5
7.03 Average daily use of social media (minutes)	N/A
7.04 Social media users (percentage using Facebook everyday)	53%
8th pillar: Payment	
8.01 Credit card (% age 15+)	N/A
8.02 Electronic payments used to make payments (% age 15+)	0.26%
8.03 Mobile phone used to pay bills (% age 15+)	0.00%
8.04 Commercial bank branch (per 100,000 persons)	2.67
8.05 GNI per capital	1740
8.06 Gross national savings % GDP	19.9%
9th pillar: Language	
9.01 Chinese	1
9.02 English	1
9.03 Japanese	1
9.04 German	1
9.05 Hindi	1

Table 8.6 Detailed e-commerce readiness scores for Malaysia

Indicator	Value
1st pillar: Political and regulatory environment	
1.01 Effectiveness of law-making bodies	5.3
1.02 Laws relating to ICTs	5.4
1.03 Judicial independence	5.0
1.04 Efficiency of legal system in settling disputes	5.3
1.05 Efficiency of legal system in challenging regulations	5.0
1.06 Number of procedures to enforce a contract	29
1.07 Number of days to enforce a contract	425
1.08 Intellectual property protection	5.4
1.09 Property rights	5.3
2nd pillar: Business environment	
2.01 GDP (US$100 million)	3134.79
2.02 Venture capital availability	4.8
2.03 Number of days required to start a business	4.0

(*Continued*)

Table 8.6 (Continued)

Indicator	Value
2.04 Number of procedures required to start a business	3.0
2.05 Intensity of local competition	5.4
2.06 Corporate tax/Corporate income tax	24%
2.07 Total tax rate, % profits	40%
3rd pillar: Innovation environment	
3.01 Company spending on R&D	5.2
3.02 PCT patent applications	11.3
3.03 Gross expenditure on R&D, % of GDP	1.1
3.04 Quality of scientific research institutions	5.3
3.05 Availability of latest technologies	5.7
3.06 Government procurement of advanced technology products	5.3
4th pillar: Access	
4.01 Fixed-telephone subscriptions per 100 inhabitants	14.3
4.02 Mobile-cellular telephone subscriptions per 100 inhabitants	143.9
4.03 International Internet bandwidth per Internet user (Bit/s)	34119
4.04 Percentage of households with a computer	67.6
4.05 Percentage of households with Internet access	70.1
4.06 Mobile network coverage per 100 population	95.4
5th pillar: Usage	
5.01 Percentage of individuals using the Internet	71.1
5.02 Fixed-broadband Internet subscriptions per 100 inhabitants	9.0
5.03 Active mobile-broadband subscriptions per 100 inhabitants	89.9
5.04 Prepaid mobile cellular tariffs, PPP $/min	0.17
5.05 Fixed broadband Internet tariffs, PPP $/month	60.97
6th pillar: Skill	
6.01 Mean years of schooling	10
6.02 Secondary gross enrolment ratio	71.1
6.03 Tertiary gross enrolment ratio	38.5
6.04 Adult literacy rate	94.6
7th pillar: Social media	
7.01 Social media users (in million)	22
7.02 Social media users by Mobile (in million)	20
7.03 Average daily use of social media (minutes)	199
7.04 Social media users (percentage using Facebook everyday)	64%
8th pillar: Payment	
8.01 Credit card (% age 15+)	20.16%
8.02 Electronic payments used to make payments (% age 15+)	12.65%
8.03 Mobile phone used to pay bills (% age 15+)	2.36%
8.04 Commercial bank branch (per 100,000 persons)	10.71
8.05 GNI per capital	10570
8.06 Gross national savings % GDP	28%
9th pillar: Language	
9.01 Chinese	3
9.02 English	4
9.03 Japanese	3
9.04 German	3
9.05 Hindi	3

Table 8.7 Detailed e-commerce readiness scores for Myanmar

Indicator	Value
1st pillar: Political and regulatory environment	
1.01 Effectiveness of law-making bodies	3.0
1.02 Laws relating to ICTs	2.5
1.03 Judicial independence	2.6
1.04 Efficiency of legal system in settling disputes	2.7
1.05 Efficiency of legal system in challenging regulations	2.6
1.06 Number of procedures to enforce a contract	45
1.07 Number of days to enforce a contract	1160
1.08 Intellectual property protection	2.8
1.09 Property rights.	N/A
2nd pillar: Business environment	
2.01 GDP (US$100 million)	657.75
2.02 Venture capital availability	1.8
2.03 Number of days required to start a business	13
2.04 Number of procedures required to start a business	11
2.05 Intensity of local competition	4.4
2.06 Corporate Tax/Corporate income tax	25%
2.07 Total tax rate, % profits	N/A
3rd pillar: Innovation environment	
3.01 Company spending on R&D	N/A
3.02 PCT patent applications	N/A
3.03 Gross expenditure on R&D, % of GDP	N/A
3.04 Quality of scientific research institutions	N/A
3.05 Availability of latest technologies	2.7
3.06 Government procurement of advanced technology products	2.8
4th pillar: Access	
4.01 Fixed-telephone subscriptions per 100 inhabitants	1
4.02 Mobile-cellular telephone subscriptions per 100 inhabitants	76.7
4.03 International Internet bandwidth per Internet user (Bit/s)	3676
4.04 Percentage of households with a computer	14
4.05 Percentage of households with Internet access	15
4.06 Mobile network coverage per 100 population	73
5th pillar: Usage	
5.01 Percentage of individuals using the Internet.	21.8
5.02 Fixed-broadband Internet subscriptions per 100 inhabitants	0.6
5.03 Active mobile-broadband subscriptions per 100 inhabitants	29.5
5.04 Prepaid mobile cellular tariffs, PPP $/min	0.11
5.05 Fixed broadband Internet tariffs, PPP $/month	136.43
6th pillar: Skill	
6.01 Mean years of schooling	4.1
6.02 Secondary gross enrolment ratio	51.3
6.03 Tertiary gross enrolment ratio	13.4
6.04 Adult literacy rate	93.1
7th pillar: Social media	
7.01 Social media users (in million)	14
7.02 Social media users by Mobile (in million)	13
7.03 Average daily use of social media (minutes)	N/A
7.04 Social media users (percentage using Facebook everyday)	49%

(*Continued*)

Table 8.7 (Continued)

Indicator	Value
8th pillar: Payment	
8.01 Credit card (% age 15+)	0%
8.02 Electronic payments used to make payments (% age 15+)	N/A
8.03 Mobile phone used to pay bills (% age 15+)	N/A
8.04 Commercial bank branch (per 100,000 persons)	3.14
8.05 GNI per capital	1160
8.06 Gross national savings % GDP	N/A
9th pillar: Language	
9.01 Chinese	1
9.02 English	1
9.03 Japanese	1
9.04 German	1
9.05 Hindi	1

Table 8.8 Detailed e-commerce readiness scores for Philippines

Indicator	Value
1st pillar: Political and regulatory environment	
1.01 Effectiveness of law-making bodies	3.5
1.02 Laws relating to ICTs	3.7
1.03 Judicial independence	3.7
1.04 Efficiency of legal system in settling disputes	3.3
1.05 Efficiency of legal system in challenging regulations	3.3
1.06 Number of procedures to enforce a contract	37
1.07 Number of days to enforce a contract	842
1.08 Intellectual property protection	3.9
1.09 Property rights	4.1
2nd pillar: Business environment	
2.01 GDP (US$100 million)	2993.14
2.02 Venture capital availability	3.1
2.03 Number of days required to start a business	29
2.04 Number of procedures required to start a business	16
2.05 Intensity of local competition	5.2
2.06 Corporate Tax/Corporate income tax	30%
2.07 Total tax rate, % profits	42.9%
3rd pillar: Innovation environment	
3.01 Company spending on R&D	3.7
3.02 PCT patent applications	0.3
3.03 Gross expenditure on R&D, % of GDP	0.1
3.04 Quality of scientific research institutions	3.8
3.05 Availability of latest technologies	4.6
3.06 Government procurement of advanced technology products	3.5
4th pillar: Access	
4.01 Fixed-telephone subscriptions per 100 inhabitants	3
4.02 Mobile-cellular telephone subscriptions per 100 inhabitants	118.1
4.03 International Internet bandwidth per Internet user (Bit/s)	37409

Indicator	Value
4.04 Percentage of households with a computer	27
4.05 Percentage of households with Internet access	28.3
4.06 Mobile network coverage per 100 population	99
5th pillar: Usage	
5.01 Percentage of individuals using the Internet	40.7
5.02 Fixed-broadband Internet subscriptions per 100 inhabitants	3.4
5.03 Active mobile-broadband subscriptions per 100 inhabitants	41.6
5.04 Prepaid mobile cellular tariffs, PPP $/min	0.4
5.05 Fixed broadband Internet tariffs, PPP $/month	54.59
6th pillar: Skill	
6.01 Mean years of schooling	8.9
6.02 Secondary gross enrolment ratio	88.4
6.03 Tertiary gross enrolment ratio	35.8
6.04 Adult literacy rate	6.3
7th pillar: Social media	
7.01 Social media users (in million)	60
7.02 Social media users by Mobile (in million)	54
7.03 Average daily use of social media (minutes)	257
7.04 Social media users (percentage using Facebook everyday)	42%
8th pillar: Payment	
8.01 Credit card (% age 15+)	3.2%
8.02 Electronic payments used to make payments (% age 15+)	2.1%
8.03 Mobile phone used to pay bills (% age 15+)	2.12%
8.04 Commercial bank branch (per 100,000 persons)	8.81
8.05 GNI per capital	3550
8.06 Gross national savings %GDP	23.7%
9th pillar: Language	
9.01 Chinese	7
9.02 English	7
9.03 Japanese	7
9.04 German	7
9.05 Hindi	6

Table 8.9 Detailed e-commerce readiness scores for Singapore

Indicator	Value
1st pillar: Political and regulatory environment	
1.01 Effectiveness of law-making bodies	6.3
1.02 Laws relating to ICTs	5.7
1.03 Judicial independence	5.5
1.04 Efficiency of legal system in settling disputes	6.2
1.05 Efficiency of legal system in challenging regulations	5.2
1.06 Number of procedures to enforce a contract	21
1.07 Number of days to enforce a contract	150
1.08 Intellectual property protection	6.2
1.09 Property rights	6.3

(Continued)

Table 8.9 (Continued)

Indicator	Value
2nd pillar: Business environment	
2.01 GDP (US$100 million)	2939.59
2.02 Venture capital availability	4.6
2.03 Number of days required to start a business	3
2.04 Number of procedures required to start a business	3
2.05 Intensity of local competition	5.6
2.06 Corporate Tax/Corporate income tax	17%
2.07 Total tax rate, % profits	18.4%
3rd pillar: Innovation environment	
3.01 Company spending on R&D	5
3.02 PCT patent applications	139.5
3.03 Gross expenditure on R&D, % of GDP	2
3.04 Quality of scientific research institutions	5.8
3.05 Availability of latest technologies	6.2
3.06 Government procurement of advanced technology products	5
4th pillar: Access	
4.01 Fixed-telephone subscriptions per 100 inhabitants	36
4.02 Mobile-cellular telephone subscriptions per 100 inhabitants	146.1
4.03 International Internet bandwidth per Internet user (Bit/s)	737006
4.04 Percentage of households with a computer	87.5
4.05 Percentage of households with Internet access	89.5
4.06 Mobile network coverage per 100 population	100
5th pillar: Usage	
5.01 Percentage of individuals using the Internet	82.1
5.02 Fixed-broadband Internet subscriptions per 100 inhabitants	26.5
5.03 Active mobile-broadband subscriptions per 100 inhabitants	142.2
5.04 Prepaid mobile cellular tariffs, PPP $/min	0.19
5.05 Fixed broadband Internet tariffs, PPP $/month	46.31
6th pillar: Skill	
6.01 Mean years of schooling	11.6
6.02 Secondary gross enrolment ratio	97.2
6.03 Tertiary gross enrolment ratio	43.8
6.04 Adult literacy rate	96.8
7th pillar Social media	
7.01 Social media users (in million)	4
7.02 Social media users by Mobile (in million)	4.0
7.03 Average daily use of social media (minutes)	127
7.04 Social media users (percentage using Facebook everyday)	64%
8th pillar: Payment	
8.01 Credit card (% age 15+)	35.42%
8.02 Electronic payments used to make payments (% age 15+)	41.50%
8.03 Mobile phone used to pay bills (% age 15+)	9.77%
8.04 Commercial bank branch (per 100,000 persons)	9.37
8.05 GNI per capital	52090
8.06 Gross national savings % GDP	46%
9th pillar: Language	
9.01 Chinese	7
9.02 English	7
9.03 Japanese	7
9.04 German	7
9.05 Hindi	6

Table 8.10 Detailed e-commerce readiness scores for Thailand

Indicator	Value
1st pillar: Political and regulatory environment	
1.01 Effectiveness of law-making bodies	34
1.02 Laws relating to ICTs	36
1.03 Judicial independence	41
1.04 Efficiency of legal system in settling disputes	39
1.05 Efficiency of legal system in challenging regulations	37
1.06 Number of procedures to enforce a contract	36
1.07 Number of days to enforce a contract	440
1.08 Intellectual property protection	32
1.09 Property rights	40
2nd pillar: Business environment	
2.01 GDP (US$100 million)	373536
2.02 Venture capital availability	33
2.03 Number of days required to start a business	28
2.04 Number of procedures required to start a business	6
2.05 Intensity of local competition	54
2.06 Corporate Tax/Corporate income tax	20%
2.07 Total tax rate, % profits	275%
3rd pillar: Innovation environment	
3.01 Company spending on R&D	36
3.02 PCT patent applications	14
3.03 Gross expenditure on R&D, % of GDP	04
3.04 Quality of scientific research institutions	41
3.05 Availability of latest technologies	47
3.06 Government procurement of advanced technology products	31
4th pillar: Access	
4.01 Fixed-telephone subscriptions per 100 inhabitants	79
4.02 Mobile-cellular telephone subscriptions per 100 inhabitants	1258
4.03 International Internet bandwidth per Internet user (Bit/s)	64907
4.04 Percentage of households with a computer	295
4.05 Percentage of households with Internet access	522
4.06 Mobile network coverage per 100 population	97
5th pillar: Usage	
5.01 Percentage of individuals using the Internet	393
5.02 Fixed-broadband Internet subscriptions per 100 inhabitants	92
5.03 Active mobile-broadband subscriptions per 100 inhabitants	753
5.04 Prepaid mobile cellular tariffs, PPP $/min	009
5.05 Fixed broadband Internet tariffs, PPP $/month	4247
6th pillar Skill	
6.01 Mean years of schooling	73
6.02 Secondary gross enrolment ratio	862
6.03 Tertiary gross enrolment ratio	514
6.04 Adult literacy rate	967
7th pillar: Social media	
7.01 Social media users (in million)	46
7.02 Social media users by Mobile (in million)	42
7.03 Average daily use of social media (minutes)	168
7.04 Social media users (percentage using Facebook everyday)	63%

(*Continued*)

Table 8.10 (Continued)

Indicator	Value
8th pillar: Payment	
8.01 Credit card (% age 15+)	569%
8.02 Electronic payments used to make payments (% age 15+)	856%
8.03 Mobile phone used to pay bills (% age 15+)	047%
8.04 commercial bank branch (per 100,000 persons)	1268
8.05 GNI per capital	5720
8.06 Gross national savings % GDP	329%
9thpillar Language	
9.01 Chinese	4
9.02 English	5
9.03 Japanese	4
9.04 German	4
9.05 Hindi	4

Table 8.11 Detailed e-commerce readiness scores for Vietnam

Indicator	Value
1st pillar: Political and regulatory environment	
1.01 Effectiveness of law-making bodies	38
1.02 Laws relating to ICTs	39
1.03 Judicial independence	35
1.04 Efficiency of legal system in settling disputes	37
1.05 Efficiency of legal system in challenging regulations	34
1.06 Number of procedures to enforce a contract	36
1.07 Number of days to enforce a contract	400
1.08 Intellectual property protection	36
1.09 Property rights	40
2nd pillar: Business environment	
2.01 GDP (US$100 million)	198805
2.02 Venture capital availability	30
2.03 Number of days required to start a business	20
2.04 Number of procedures required to start a business	10
2.05 Intensity of local competition	5
2.06 Corporate Tax/Corporate income tax	20%
2.07 Total tax rate, % profits	21%
3rd pillar: Innovation environment	
3.01 Company spending on R&D	35
3.02 PCT patent applications	02
3.03 Gross expenditure on R&D, % of GDP	N/A
3.04 Quality of scientific research institutions	34
3.05 Availability of latest technologies	40
3.06 Government procurement of advanced technology products	39
4th pillar: Access	
4.01 Fixed-telephone subscriptions per 100 inhabitants	63
4.02 Mobile-cellular telephone subscriptions per 100 inhabitants	1306
4.03 International Internet bandwidth per Internet user (Bit/s)	24374
4.04 Percentage of households with a computer	22
4.05 Percentage of households with Internet access	241
4.06 Mobile network coverage per 100 population	7

Indicator	Value
5th pillar: Usage	
5.01 Percentage of individuals using the Internet	527
5.02 Fixed-broadband Internet subscriptions per 100 inhabitants	81
5.03 Active mobile-broadband subscriptions per 100 inhabitants	39
5.04 Prepaid mobile cellular tariffs, PPP $/min	015
5.05 Fixed broadband Internet tariffs, PPP $/month	259
6th pillar: Skill	
6.01 Mean years of schooling	75
6.02 Secondary gross enrolment ratio	772
6.03 Tertiary gross enrolment ratio	305
6.04 Adult literacy rate	945
7th pillar: Social media	
7.01 Social media users (in million)	46
7.02 Social media users by Mobile (in million)	41
7.03 Average daily use of social media (minutes)	159
7.04 Social media users (percentage using Facebook everyday)	59%
8th pillar: Payment	
8.01 Credit card (% age 15+)	193%
8.02 Electronic payments used to make payments (% age 15+)	253%
8.03 Mobile phone used to pay bills (% age 15+)	358%
8.04 Commercial bank branch (per 100,000 persons)	3831
8.05 GNI per capital	1990
8.06 Gross national savings % GDP	29%
9th pillar: Language	
9.01 Chinese	3
9.02 English	4
9.03 Japanese	3
9.04 German	3
9.05 Hindi	3

Table 8.12 Detailed e-commerce readiness scores for Hong Kong

Indicator	Value
1st pillar: Political and regulatory environment	
1.01 Effectiveness of law-making bodies	4.2
1.02 Laws relating to ICTs	5.1
1.03 Judicial independence	6.3
1.04 Efficiency of legal system in settling disputes	6.0
1.05 Efficiency of legal system in challenging regulations	5.6
1.06 Number of procedures to enforce a contract	26
1.07 Number of days to enforce a contract	360
1.08 Intellectual property protection	6.0
1.09 Property rights	6.2
2nd pillar: Business environment	
2.01 GDP (US$100 million)	414.6
2.02 Venture capital availability	4.3
2.03 Number of days required to start a business	2
2.04 Number of procedures required to start a business	2

(*Continued*)

Table 8.12 (Continued)

Indicator	Value
2.05 Intensity of local competition	6.2
2.06 Corporate Tax/Corporate income tax	16.5%
2.07 Total tax rate, % profits	22.8%
3rd pillar: Innovation environment	
3.01 Company spending on R&D	4.0
3.02 PCT patent applications	N/A
3.03 Gross expenditure on R&D, % of GDP	0.7
3.04 Quality of scientific research institutions	4.8
3.05 Availability of latest technologies	6.0
3.06 Government procurement of advanced technology products	3.8
4th pillar: Access	
4.01 Fixed-telephone subscriptions per 100 inhabitants	59.2
4.02 Mobile-cellular telephone subscriptions per 100 inhabitants	228.8
4.03 International Internet bandwidth per Internet user (Bit/s)	4155651
4.04 Percentage of households with a computer	80.4
4.05 Percentage of households with Internet access	79.0
4.06 Mobile network coverage per 100 population	100
5th pillar: Usage	
5.01 Percentage of individuals using the Internet	84.9
5.02 Fixed-broadband Internet subscriptions per 100 inhabitants	31.9
5.03 Active mobile-broadband subscriptions per 100 inhabitants	107.0
5.04 Prepaid mobile cellular tariffs, PPP $/min	0.02
5.05 Fixed broadband Internet tariffs, PPP $/month	29.71
6th pillar: Skill	
6.01 Mean years of schooling	11.2
6.02 Secondary gross enrolment ratio	100.6
6.03 Tertiary gross enrolment ratio	68.8
6.04 Adult literacy rate	99
7th pillar: Social media	
7.01 Social media users (in million)	5.5
7.02 Social media users by Mobile (in million)	4.9
7.03 Average daily use of social media (minutes)	101
7.04 Social media users (percentage using Facebook everyday)	58%
8th pillar: Payment	
8.01 Credit card (% age 15+)	64.26
8.02 Electronic payments used to make payments (% age 15+)	16.91
8.03 Mobile phone used to pay bills (% age 15+)	N/A
8.04 Commercial bank branch (per 100,000 persons)	22.3
8.05 GNI per capital	41000
8.06 Gross national savings % GDP	24.8%.
9th pillar: Language	
9.01 Chinese	7
9.02 English	7
9.03 Japanese	7
9.04 German	7
9.05 Hindi	6

9 Maritime logistics

Challenges and opportunities in Asia Pacific region in the perspective of the Belt and Road Initiative

Jai Acharya

Introduction

Maritime transport is the backbone of international trade and the global economy. About 80 percent of global trade by volume and over 70 percent of global trade by value are carried by sea and are handled by ports worldwide (Review of Marine Transport - UNCTAD 2015). These shares are even higher in most developing countries.

Over the last decade, China, Hong Kong SAR, the Republic of Korea, and Singapore have moved up in the rankings of the largest ship-owning countries. As ships become bigger and companies strive to achieve economies of scale, fewer companies remain in individual markets. Experts from the *Review of Maritime Transport* (UNCTAD 2015) say that it will be a challenge for policymakers to support technological advances and cost savings through economies of scale yet at the same time ensure a sufficiently competitive environment so that cost savings are effectively passed on to the clients, that is, importers and exporters. Currently, the maritime logistics and supply chain system is going through quite a challenging phase, in which a cyclical crisis of supply and demand has coincided with a depression in the oil and gas sector. Most of the world's tonnage moves within and through Asia, particularly the Asia Pacific region. The majority of ship managers are based in this region, and most seafarers (officers and ratings) are from Asian countries. Shipbuilding facilities, technical expertise, and commercial decisions are effectively controlled by the market players and stakeholders of this region.

Global trade slowdown and the trade-gross domestic product relationship

Long-term trade-GDP elasticity was estimated at 1.3 in 1970–85, 2.2 in 1986–2000, 1.3 in the 2000s, and 0.7 in 2008–2013. The estimates suggest that the contribution of cyclical factors to trade slowdown is more pronounced during crises and recession periods. However, reduced elasticities outside times of crises point to other potential factors. An oft-cited potential structural factor in the observed reduced elasticity is the recent limited growth in vertical specialization and the global fragmentation of production, reflecting a maturation of value chains (in China and the United States) (Review of Marine Transport – UNCTAD 2016; Constantinescu, Mattoo & Ruta 2015).

Whereas the decline in trade elasticities of primary goods and investment goods relates in particular to cyclical factors, lower trade elasticity for intermediate goods mainly reflects structural causes, such as a shift in production and trade patterns in global value chains. Overall decline in the vertical specialization process is evident when considering trade in intermediate goods, especially in East Asia.

China's share of intermediate imports as a proportion of its exports of manufacturing goods, which measures the reliance of the manufacturing sector on imported inputs, has declined constantly over the last decade, from almost 60 percent in 2002 to less than 40 percent in 2014. Another measure, the share of China's intermediate goods in its total imports, fell from 33 percent in 2001 to about 18 percent in 2014 (Review of Marine Transport – UNCTAD 2016).

Although still substantially high, vertical specialization in other countries in East Asia has also declined in recent years. These trends are also indicative of a potential re-shoring or near-shoring process (that is, moving manufacturing activity home or closer to home) and of the consolidation of production processes into geographical clusters of production that, together, result in relatively lower levels of trade per unit of output. Other potential explanatory factors are changes in the composition of global demand, with slow recovery in investment goods that are more trade intensive than is government and consumer spending, as well as a shift in the composition of consumer demand away from manufactured goods to services.

Globally, the share of capital goods in total imports dropped from 35 percent in 2000 to 30 percent in 2014. In the same period, consumer goods, which tend to have lower import content relative to investment goods, maintained their share of about 30 percent. Another view is that the decline in the global wage share and related negative impact on domestic demand growth may have also contributed to slower trade growth (Review of Marine Transport – UNCTAD 2016).

The global wage share continued to decline due to continued efforts to raise competitiveness, such as by delocalizing production to low-cost sites. Greater access to global markets has often been associated with deterioration in national wage income compared with the global level. Although boosting global aggregate demand remains a key point in stimulating global trade growth, various non-cyclical factors suggest that, even if trade recovers gradually, trade elasticities may not return to the high levels of the late 1990s and early 2000s.

Challenges

The commercial shipping market is of significant scale and complexity, every shipment usually involving a chain of ship owners, ship managers, and operators, often registered as limited liability companies in low-disclosure jurisdictions. Almost all held through offshore-registered special-purpose setup companies.

As an efficient mode of transportation and liberalization of world economy, shipping industry has potential for further growth. More than 50,000 merchant ships transport cargo in the world. The world fleet is registered in over 150 nations and has over a million seafarers. As high value assets, an estimated annual income in freight rates from operating merchant ships could be over half a trillion US dollars (International Chamber of Shipping Annual Review – ICS 2017).

Maritime assets are mobile and all these assets (vessels) are under the regulatory framework of the International Maritime Organization (IMO) and national regulations of the country where registered. At the same time, some specific regulations are imposed in trading area and the vessels' port/country of call. The ship owners/managers have to monitor vessel trade patterns very closely and ensure and current regulatory compliance.

Ships being mobile assets, the financial stakes are very high. Increasingly, complex corporate structures and financing methods, particularly in the emerging/high-growth markets, where the financial/banking regulations and IMO regulatory framework compliance along with suppliers services, port authorities, and local maritime laws become intermingled in a complex way and stakeholders are vulnerable to strange/unknown liabilities. A requirement to make rapid decisions on high-value transactions based on what is often limited data and business intelligence/large databases on right and relevant information play a great part in secured business. The acceptance and use of open credit terms to facilitate transactions, often millions of dollars, makes a more vulnerable situation for ship owners/operators.

The emergence of sanctions and anti-bribery legislation is increasing reputational risk and compliance requirements. Environmental compliance challenges across the oceans and special areas are a great challenge and financial burden on the ship owners/managers/operators. The Ship Emissions Control and Relevant Regulatory Compliance are non-negotiable in most cases. There are high penalties for on non-compliance. Only in special cases interim dispensation is granted by the regulatory administration bodies. Economic viability for ship owners to comply with environmental codes is a matter of great concern today. Above all, the challenging international/regional political scenario on ocean governance, piracy, and exclusive economic zones is a matter of concern for safe and secure international shipping.

Opportunities

Even considering the above-mentioned challenges, there are proven track records on success and profitability in maritime business. Operational excellence is achieved due to the induction of innovative technology and modern application of artificial intelligence. The induction of new-generation vessels with green technology and smart ship technology applications are providing environmentally friendly and cost-effective operation of the vessels. The rise of new superpowers in Asia Pacific with a new approach on ocean transportation and innovative ideas on global connectivity through the Belt and Road Initiative (BRI), originating in China, will play an important role in the future success of shipping and in the offshore (oil and gas) industry.

The concept and endorsement for a blue economy by many countries will enable us to protect our oceans from pollution and keep biodiversity intact. The blue economy concept, initiated by Dr Awni Benham, president of the International Ocean Institute (IOI), has been well received and recognized globally

It was endorsed in the Rio+20 Global Conference by many countries and will be playing a promising role in the overall improvement of coastal states and inhabitants. Broader cooperation and consent on freedom of navigation and the United Nations Convention on the Law of the Sea (UNCLOS) for safe and secure international trade through oceans is the call of today and the future (Behnam 2012, 2014).

Maritime transportation business: current scenario

The IMO theme for the year 2016 is "Shipping is indispensable to the world". In the true sense, it has been a proven fact for millennia. Although trade and economic slowdown in China is bad news for shipping, other countries have the potential to drive further growth. South–South trade is gaining momentum, and planned initiatives of China such as the BRI and the Partnership for Quality Infrastructure, as well as the expanded Panama Canal and Suez Canal, have the potential to affect seaborne trade, reshape world shipping networks, and generate business opportunities. In parallel, trends such as the fourth industrial revolution, big data, and electronic commerce are unfolding and entail both challenges and opportunities for countries and maritime transport.

Maritime businesses: 2016

Prediction, it is often said, is very difficult, especially if it is about the future. The year 2016 was a very difficult year for shipping. However, policymakers may not always fully appreciate the very challenging economic conditions in which shipping companies are operating. Crisis is a word that can easily be overused in the context of shipping markets which have always been highly cyclical and subject to extreme freight rate volatility. But with the exception of oil tankers (benefitting from the dramatic fall in oil prices since the end of 2014, as governments and traders stockpile cheap crude), most shipping sectors are facing the worst trading conditions seen in living memory, even including the deep shipping recession of the 1980s. Whereas a cape-size bulk carrier in 2008 might have enjoyed a day rate of US$200,000, an identical ship of the same age in 2016 might be earning as little as below US$5,000, in many cases insufficient to cover operating costs or the interest payments on mortgages (Review of Marine Transport – UNCTAD 2017). Shipping has never fully recovered from the impact of the 2008 financial crisis. Nevertheless, sluggish growth in OECD (Organisation for Economic Cooperation and Development) economies was partly compensated by the impressive growth in demand for shipping from China and other emerging nations. But in 2016 the industry was confronted with the double whammy of falling growth in demand for maritime transport combined with serious over-capacity (Review of Marine Transport – UNCTAD 2016).

To put it simply, there are just far too many ships, many of them much bigger than ever before, chasing far too few cargoes. The problem is complicated by the understandable reluctance of many lenders to accept the dramatic impact on their balance sheets of uneconomic ships being sent for recycling before their loans have been repaid. The world fleet grew by 3.5 percent in the 12 months to 1 January 2016 (in dead-weight tons (DWT)). This is the lowest growth rate since 2003 yet still higher than the 2.1 percent growth in demand, leading to a continued situation of global overcapacity. The position of countries within global container shipping networks is reflected in the United Nations Conference on Trade and Development (UNCTAD) liner shipping connectivity index. Even though the medium-sized container vessels have been demolished on very large scale, the new fleet of large-capacity vessels (12,000 TEUs and above) and smaller/feeder vessels are still in demand (Review of Marine Transport – UNCTAD 2016, 2017).

Global seaborne trade

Maritime transport is the backbone of globalization and lies at the heart of cross-border transport networks that support supply chains and enable international trade.

An economic sector in its own right that generates employment, income and revenue, transport, including maritime transport, is cross-cutting and permeates other sectors and activities. Maritime transport enables industrial development by supporting manufacturing growth, bringing together consumers and intermediate and capital goods industries, and promoting regional economic and trade integration.

The importance of transport has been recognized in the Sustainable Development Goals, which have integrated infrastructure and transport as an important consideration. Although none of the goals is exclusively dedicated to transport or maritime transport in particular, transport is considered a critical factor for the effective realization of eight goals and 11 targets, both directly and indirectly.

In May 2016, the best-connected countries were:

1 Morocco, Egypt, and South Africa in Africa;
2 China and the Republic of Korea in Eastern Asia;
3 Panama and Colombia in Latin America and the Caribbean
4 Sri Lanka and India in South Asia; and
5 Singapore and Malaysia in Southeast Asia.

The Belt and Road Initiative

The Belt and Road initiative aims to promote connectivity and cooperation among countries primarily in Eurasia through the 21st-Century Maritime Silk Route (Maritime Silk Road) and the land-based Silk Road Economic Belt.

According to the action plan, the belt will have three routes and the road will have two:

The Silk Road Economic Belt covers:

1   China ➔ Central Asia ➔ Russia ➔ Europe (the Baltic)
2   China ➔ Central Asia ➔ West Asia ➔ Persian Gulf ➔ Mediterranean Sea
3   China ➔ Southeast Asia ➔ South Asia ➔ Indian Ocean

The 21st-Century Maritime Silk Road covers:

1   Coastal China ➔ South China Sea ➔ Indian Ocean ➔ Europe
2   Coastal China ➔ South China Sea ➔ South Pacific

Positioning of regions and provinces of China in the BRI

Coastal regions of China and Hong Kong SAR, Macau, and Taiwan have unique characteristics of a high level of openness, robust economic strengths with fully developed coastal ports and international hub airports. These are also the key players in building the Maritime Silk Road.

The strategic proposal formally referred as the BRI is also part of China's strategy to secure its status and influence as one of the world's most powerful economies. Although the BRI is not short of detractors and sceptics, it is difficult to ignore the general support and enthusiasm generated in both public and private sectors and the general consensus that the BRI has built impressive momentum.

The initiative envisages the construction of a trade and transport infrastructure network involving 60 countries accounting for 60 percent of the world's population and representing a collective GDP equivalent to 33 percent of the world's total. The surface transport component focuses on linking China to Europe through Central Asia and the Russian Federation; China with Western Asia through Central Asia; and China with Southeast Asia, South Asia, and the Indian Ocean. The maritime transport component focuses on linking China with Europe through the Indian Ocean, and China with the southern Pacific Ocean (Hong Kong China Trade Development Council 2016).

In China, the initiative is expected to help revitalize domestic industries; bring higher returns for Chinese capital and higher demand for Chinese goods and services; absorb China's labour; and use China's excess industrial capacity, such as cement and steel for infrastructure industries – ports, roads, rail, and trains. Greater energy security for China may also be achieved by making use of alternative routes to the Straits of Malacca through Myanmar, Bangladesh, Pakistan, Sri Lanka, and other countries en route. Beyond China, the initiative may help reduce transport costs, increase trade flows, promote the development of emerging industries, and open new markets to all involved countries.

Another important expected contribution is to close the persistent infrastructure gap in developing regions, especially in transport. Infrastructure investment needs for Asia are estimated at US$50 billion per year through 2020, and for Africa they are estimated to exceed US$93 billion (*Bloomberg Brief* 2015). Beyond the initiative, China has already committed over US$10 billion in investment to develop the Bagamoyo port in the United Republic of Tanzania and has contracts to build railways connecting the ports of Dar-es-Salaam and Mombasa with inland countries (Bohlund & Orlik 2015; Review of Marine Transport – UNCTAD 2015). Such investments may stimulate trade in Africa, where a tripling of China's investment value in 2008–2013 was associated with a doubling of exports, from US$55 billion in 2008 to US$116 billion in 2014 (Bohlund & Orlik 2015).

Maritime connections linking China to the Port of Piraeus, Greece, through the Indian Ocean and Suez Canal are expected to provide an alternative to ports such as Antwerp, Belgium; Hamburg, Germany; and Rotterdam, the Netherlands, while cutting ten days off the journey to Central or Eastern Europe. From the Asia-Pacific perspective, the success of the BRI rests heavily on the optimization of the transport infrastructure and services, including shipping and logistics, required to support connectivity in China, Asia Pacific, South–Southeast Asia, and beyond. In turn, the transport sector may benefit from the trade growth opportunities generated by the initiative and growth in volumes stemming from reduced transport costs, greater market access and connectivity, infrastructure, and industrial development. With regard to maritime transport, infrastructure and services may provide an additional boost to lift volumes and reverse the recent trends of weak demand and slowly growing trade and help bring balance to the market, which currently faces a mismatch between supply and demand, as well as continued excess capacity.

Sustainable and resilient maritime transport systems

The year 2015 was a milestone for sustainable development. Because the international community is currently elaborating a post-2015 development agenda, there is a renewed opportunity to strengthen the international commitment to sustainable development and consider how best to mainstream sustainability principles across all economic sectors, including maritime transport. Over 80 percent of world merchandise trade is carried by sea, so maritime transport remains the backbone of international trade and globalization. Equally, the sector is a key enabling factor for other sectors and economic activities such as marine equipment manufacturing, maritime auxiliary services (e.g. insurance, banking, brokering, classification, and consultancy), fisheries, tourism, and the offshore energy sector, as well as other marine-based industries such as shipbuilding and ship demolition. In this context, sustainable maritime transport systems entail, among other factors, transport infrastructure and services that are safe, socially acceptable, universally accessible, reliable, affordable, fuel efficient, environmentally friendly, low carbon, and climate-resilient.

Achieving greater sustainability in transport, including maritime transport, has long been recognized as a key development objective, including in the context of the 1992 Earth Summit, the UN Conference on Sustainable Development (UNCTAD XIII – 2012), and the Third International Conference on Small Island Developing States (SIDS). Established with a view to providing recommendations on sustainable transport that are actionable at global, national, and local, and sectoral levels, the High-Level Advisory Group from UNCTAD is expected to publish a report on the global transport outlook and convene the first international conference on sustainable development in 2016.

A structural change in the relationship between demand for shipping and global economic growth may not be insurmountable as long as the industry can manage capacity. But shipping's recent record in this respect has not been impressive. To restore equilibrium in the market, a large number of vessels are being recycled before the end of their normal 25-year life. Early recycling might be good for the collective but may not always be in the best interests of many individual shipping companies, especially if their ships are debt free, well maintained, and still operate efficiently and profitably. However, the concept of keeping a maximum age for ships is to be discouraged due to difficulties in regulatory compliance, maintenance of ageing vessels, and safety and pollution-prevention reasons. If ships are routinely demolished around the age of 15 years (instead of 25 years), it helps environmental sustainability.

Possible impact on Singapore's new growth track

Singapore was one of the earliest supporters of the BRI, recognizing its magnitude and enormous potential. The benefits of China's initiative are clear for the ASEAN region. As economic growth slows in the Southeast Asian region and a clear need for infrastructure development is evident, governments across Asia have the opportunity to boost infrastructure spending and improve reputations through the BRI. However, as a nation-state with some of the world's most advanced infrastructure and an already sophisticated port and transportation system linking to its neighbours, there could be ample of opportunities for Singapore due to built-in ingredients such as strong basic fundamentals of economics, well-trained and professional human resources, and excellent records on governance. As Deng Xiaoping said, "Learn from all countries in the world and most of all learn from Singapore" (Freiman 2016).

Being strategically located along the Maritime Silk Road, the BRI is expected to unlock untapped regions – Central Asia – creating new trade and investment for Singapore companies. In particular, Singapore's well-established logistics and infrastructure sectors are expected to reap benefits from the BRI. Singapore has a strong pool of local companies with wide-ranging infrastructure capabilities, from power, water, to transport management. These companies' familiarity with doing business in Asia also makes them excellent partners for Chinese companies to explore infrastructure projects and market opportunities in the region. The establishment of the ASEAN Economic Community in December 2015 is also expected to multiply the benefits of the BRI even further. Singapore is playing a key role as country coordinator for ASEAN–China dialogue relations and had a remit to hold this role for the next three years. This will enhance Singapore's super-connector role, particularly as the Belt and Road links China with its Southeast Asian neighbours.

In addition, as one of the region's leading financial and professional services hubs, there are many areas for Singapore to capitalize on. For instance, Singapore is a world leader for offshore RMB (renminbi) exchange, alongside Hong Kong SAR, and this creates natural synergies for a financial collaborative role in international and regional monetary affairs.

It can be seen from Singapore signing an MOU (memorandum of understanding) with banks such as ICBC Limited, China Construction Bank, and Bank of China to bring S$90 billion worth of financing for Belt and Road projects to the table. Professional services firms are also poised to capitalize on the significant opportunities in advising both Singapore-based and foreign enterprises as they expand into the region. However, the BRI is not without its challenges.

To succeed, it requires a combination of jigsaw of financial capabilities, the latest technology, special skills acumen, and the capability to implement mega projects in a region with diverse cultures, religions, languages, and political systems. Singapore has much more to offer China in this regard, and the BRI will certainly lead to deeper ties between these two countries.

Possible impact on Hong Kong's new growth track

Hong Kong should be able to find a considerable spectrum of opportunities in infrastructure and real estate services, financing, project risk/quality assessment/management, and several other related fields. The launch of the BRI will increase people-to-people exchanges between China and the countries concerned, as well as boost demand for international logistics. Hong Kong has a leading edge in global logistics links and operation. In addition to freight services, Hong Kong can give further leverage to its functions as a maritime services centre. In view of new upcoming free trade zones in mainland China and the need of developing maritime and infrastructure services there, Hong Kong may explore possibilities of collaboration with these developing free trade zones.

Hong Kong would be in position to play a key role is financial services. It can provide value-added services, including fundraising, financing, bonds, asset management, insurance, and offshore RMB business. Hong Kong can also play an important role in the Asian Infrastructure Investment Bank, BRICS Bank, and Silk Road (Land and Sea) Fund, including encouraging these institutions to set up their headquarters and branches in the territory and make optimum use of Hong Kong's international talent, as well as inviting the Land and Maritime Silk Road Fund to set up sub-funds in Hong Kong. In addition, passenger and freight transport, aircraft leasing, and other aviation-related financial services represent a considerable number of opportunities.

In the industry sector, infrastructure may be the first stage in the development of the BRI. It requires investment and project contracting and will drive demand for relevant services.

Due to its strategic location and proximity to mainland China, Hong Kong will be in position to play a more proactive role in the Belt and Road cooperation platform by hosting international events, conferences, and summits/fora in the relevant sectors such as infrastructure development, finance/fundraising techniques, investments, and maritime and aviation industries. An established pool of intellectuals, think tanks, and globally reputed educational institutions will place Hong Kong in a unique position in the perspective of the BRI among the other participating countries by conducting research, training, and the exchange of knowledge and expertise. Hong Kong could be the right platform for the training of human resources in relevant fields, such as maritime and aviation logistics, and infrastructure development.

In industrial cooperation, China's overseas economic and trade cooperation zones will become platforms for overseas investment and cooperation for Chinese enterprises, as well as platforms for the clustering of industries. Southeast Asia, South Asia, and Central Asia may further develop into a more extensive network of bases for industrial relocation and even open up as consumer markets. The demand for logistics, supply chain management, consumer products and services may increase with the growth of these regions. Following the opening of logistics hubs in Central Asia, there will be railways linking China with the region. For example, Hong Kong businesses may consider using the Chongqing–Xinjiang–Europe railway to transport goods directly from Chongqing to the Central Asian market, thus saving time and money.

With regard to regional development, apart from Southeast Asia, South Asia, and even Central Asia, Central and Eastern Europe, the demand of mainland provinces for infrastructure investment and logistics services in support of the BRI will generate business opportunities for the relevant industries.

Legal and regulatory framework

In 2014, important regulatory developments in the field of transport and trade facilitation included the adoption of the International Code for Ships Operating in Polar Waters (Polar Code), entered in to force on 1 January 2017, as well as a range of regulatory developments relating to maritime and supply chain security and environmental issues.

To further strengthen the legal framework relating to ship-source air pollution and the reduction of GHG (greenhouse gas) emissions from international shipping, several regulatory measures were adopted at the IMO, and the Third IMO Greenhouse Gas Study 2014 was finalized. Also, guidelines for the development of the Inventory of Hazardous Materials (HAZMAT) required under the 2010 International Convention on Liability and Compensation for Damage in Connection with the Carriage of Hazardous and Noxious Substances by Sea (but not yet in force) were adopted, and further progress was made with respect to technical matters related to ballast water management, ship recycling, and measures helping to prevent and combat pollution of the sea from oil and other harmful substances. Continued enhancements were made to regulatory measures in the field of maritime and supply chain security and their implementation, including the issuance of a new version of the World Customs Organization Framework of Standards to Secure and Facilitate Global Trade in June 2015, which includes a new pillar, "Customs to other Government and inter-government agencies". In the suppression of maritime piracy and armed robbery, positive developments were noted in the waters off the coast of Somalia and the wider western Indian Ocean. Concern remains, however, about the seafarers still being held hostage. A downward trend of attacks in the Gulf of Guinea was also observed, indicating that international, regional, and national efforts are beginning to take effect.

Access, connectivity, and infrastructure

The strategic importance of maritime transport infrastructure and services for market access, globalized production, trade competitiveness, employment, income generation, poverty reduction, and social progress cannot be overemphasized. Consequently, for many developing countries, addressing the physical and non-physical barriers such as infrastructure issues, missing links, and interoperability of tools, equipment, technologies, and standards are prime concerns. The transport infrastructure gap remains a significant challenge in many developing regions.

As maritime transport infrastructure such as ports have long life cycles, not accounting for the long-term sustainability and resilience, including climate-resilience requirements, costly retrofitting of equipment and infrastructure and adjustment of operations and services may be involved. A well-articulated transport infrastructure vision and a long-term plan that also seeks to close the infrastructure gap in maritime transport should be pursued as matters of priority. Such efforts should be based on a careful coordination of the social, economic, and physical development of maritime transport systems. The BRI could be a step towards addressing such issues (see Table 9.1).

Energy and transport costs

The heavy reliance of maritime transport on fossil fuels for propulsion enhances the exposure of freight rates and transport costs to high oil price volatility. Although the mid-2014 drop in oil and bunker fuel prices were a welcome development, the effect is likely to be uncertain, given the projected growth in the global energy demand and the risk of rapid cuts in oil production due to reduced investment in the oil extractive and refining industries. An assessment of the effect of oil prices on maritime freight rates, including for containerized goods, bulk cargo/ore/minerals and crude oil, reveals that rates and therefore transport costs in all three market segments were sensitive to a rise in oil prices, albeit to different degrees (Review of Marine Transport – UNCTAD 2015).

Global growth and massive employability potential

The BRI is a drive to build infrastructure connecting China and the other 64 Silk Road countries of ASEAN, South and Central Asia, and the Middle East.

Table 9.1 Belt and Road Initiative (BRI) projected infrastructure investments in maritime sector by China

Country	Infrastructure Projects
Bangladesh	Studies for Bangladesh–China–India–Myanmar corridor; deepwater port, Payra
Indonesia	Road and Port Infrastructure, Kalimantan (US$1.1 billion)
Malaysia	Malaysia–China Kuantan Industrial Park, including deepwater container port, steel and aluminium plants and palm oil refinery ($3.4 billion)
Myanmar	Bangladesh–China–India–Myanmar transport network, including roads, railways, waterways and airports; Kyaukphyu–Kunming oil and gas pipelines; Myanmar–Yunnan optical cable
Pakistan	China–Pakistan Economic Corridor (CPEC), Highway; port upgrades, including airport, power plant and roads; Port of Gwadar
Sri Lanka	Deepwater port in Hambantota ($600 million); China Merchants Holdings International investment in Port of Colombo ($500 million)
Vietnam	Port upgrades, Haiphong; Lang Son–Hanoi highway
Africa	Agreement with African Union to help build railways, roads, and airports; coastal road, Nigeria ($13 billion); Nairobi–Mombasa railway, Kenya ($3.8 billion); Addis Ababa – Djibouti railway ($4 billion)
Europe	Upgrade of Port of Piraeus, Greece ($260 million); Hungary–Serbia high-speed railway ($3 billion); China–Spain cargo
Georgia	International economic zone, Tbilisi ($150 million); deepwater port, Anaklia ($5 billion)
Lithuania	Encouraging investment in joint railway and Port projects; China Merchants Group letter of intent with port of Klaipeda
Central and South America	Pledged investment to region (US$250 billion); proposed transcontinental railway between coasts of Brazil and Peru ($10 billion); natural gas development, pipelines, power generation facilities, highways, ports and telecommunications

Source: UNCTAD Reports 2015

The initiative is well recognized as a welcome stimulus to global growth, helping countries face the challenges of poor physical and social infrastructure.

What is less discussed but equally important is the BRI's necessity to address the massive and urgent need to create hundreds of millions of jobs across the region to absorb a dramatic surge in the working population, especially the young adult population. If this problem is unaddressed, a growing jobs gap could lead to political fragility, the rise of new fanatical movements, and new economic and conflict-driven refugee crises that would dwarf what the world, especially Europe, has faced recently.

In poor and emerging countries, joblessness, particularly among rapidly growing young working populations, can contribute to instability. In 2010, just before the Arab Spring, surveys found that, of 11 issues such as political, social, and religious controversy, employment ranked first in importance in all six Arab countries.

Nowhere will the job creation challenge be more acute than in the 39 Silk Road countries whose workforces are expanding. Those countries (across ASEAN, South Asia, and the Middle East) face perhaps the greatest short-term job creation challenge in world history. Whereas China and many European countries face ageing demographics, between 2015 and 2030 the working population of the growing 39 Silk Road countries will increase by a startling 382 million. To employ 382 million new workers requires creating more new jobs than the total working population of the EU 28 (or two times the current working population in the United States) in 15 years (Eastspring Investments-Donald Kanak 2017).

The job creation potential in infrastructure has been well established. Studies in the United States suggest that every US$1 billion investment in infrastructure will result in 13,000–22,000 jobs created. The job creation potential will be even greater in developing countries, and many jobs can be created while simultaneously greening the economy. The renewable energy sector in China employs 1 million people, and India expects to generate 900,000 jobs by 2025 in biomass gasification. In Brazil, biofuels have produced about 1.3 million jobs in rural areas, and recycling and waste management employs an estimated 500,000 people. Research has also shown that investment in social infrastructure (e.g. education, health) yields substantially more employment than investment limited to physical infrastructure and can provide vital contributions to the process of productivity change, income growth, and specialization of the economy (Table 9.2).

Together, the countries along the Belt and Road will create an "economic cooperation area" that stretches from the Western Pacific to the Baltic Sea. According to computation, these 65 countries jointly account for 62.3 percent, 30.0 percent, and 24.0 percent of the world's population, GDP and household

Table 9.2 Outlook on global working population

Countries	POP Working in Millions (2015)	Increase in Millions (2015–30)
China	929	−49
European Silk Road	209	−30
India	737	175
Growing South Asia, Excluding India (five countries)	211	68
Growing ASEAN (nine countries)	328	61
Growing Central Asia and Middle East, Excl. India (24 countries)	283	78
Growing 39 Silk Road Countries	1559	382

Source: Donald Kanak, 2017

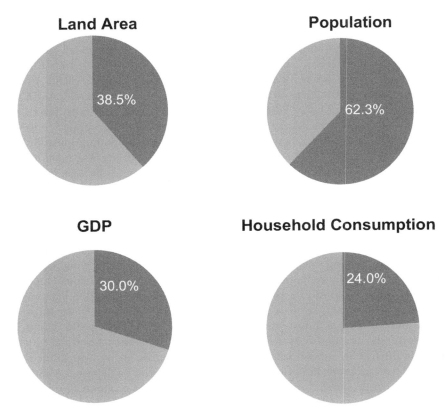

Figure 9.1 Economic Significance of the Belt and Road Countries

Source: Chin & He (2016).

Note: % as share in world total.

consumption, respectively, today (Figure 9.1). For details of the computation, please refer to Exhibit 3 (Table 9.3).

Cyber risk management

Cyber security is crucial for merchant ships' security, safety and insurance. Ship management relies on information technology, for example, Electronic Chart Display and Information Systems (ECDIS). IMO maritime safety committee recommended some guidelines on maritime cyber risk management in May 2016. The guidelines provided directions to be taken by shipping industry to protect vessels in operation (International Chamber of Shipping – ICS 2017).

Table 9.3 Countries along the Belt and Road (Exhibit 3)

Region	Country	Land area (sq. km) thousand, 2014)	Population (million, 2014)	GDP (current US$ billion, 2014)	Household consumption (current US$ billion, 2013)
East Asia	China	9,388.2	1,364.3	10,354.8	3,424.7
	Mongolia	1,553.6	2.9	12.0	7.0
Southeast Asia	Brunei	5.3	0.4	17.1	3.6
	Cambodia	176.5	15.3	16.8	12.0
	Indonesia	1,811.6	254.5	888.5	521.6
	Laos	230.8	6.7	12.0	7.3
	Malaysia	328.6	29.9	338.1	167.5
	Myanmar	653.1	53.4	64.3	N/A
	Philippines	298.2	99.1	284.8	199.4
	Singapore	0.7	5.5	307.9	110.8
	Timor-Leste	14.9	1.2	1.4	1.1
	Thailand	510.9	67.7	404.8	218.7
	Vietnam	310.1	90.7	186.2	112.1
South Asia	Afghanistan	652.9	31.6	20.0	16.4
	Bangladesh	130.2	159.1	172.9	109.3
	Bhutan	38.1	0.8	2.0	1.1
	India	2,973.2	1,295.3	2,048.5	1,111.3
	Maldives	0.3	0.4	3.1	N/A
	Nepal	143.4	28.2	19.8	15.1
	Pakistan	770.9	185.0	243.6	186.7
	Sri Lanka	62.7	20.6	78.8	N/A
Central Asia	Kazakhstan	2,699.7	17.3	217.9	117.5
	Kyrgyzstan	191.8	5.8	7.4	7.1
	Tajikistan	140.0	8.3	9.2	9.5
	Turkmenistan	469.9	5.3	47.9	N/A
	Uzbekistan	425.4	30.8	62.6	21.6
Middle East and North Africa	Bahrain	0.8	1.4	33.9	13.3
	Egypt	995.5	89.6	286.5	219.9
	Iran	1,628.6	78.1	425.3	254.7
	Iraq	434.3	34.8	223.5	N/A
	Israel	21.6	8.2	305.7	162.4
	Jordan	88.8	6.6	35.8	27.5
	Kuwait	17.8	3.8	163.6	43.8
	Lebanon	10.2	4.5	45.7	37.5
	Oman	309.5	4.2	81.8	23.7
	Palestine	6.0	4.3	12.7	11.1
	Qatar	11.6	2.2	210.1	28.0
	Saudi Arabia	2,149.7	30.9	746.2	223.7
	Syria	183.6	22.2	N/A	N/A
	United Arab Emirates	83.6	9.1	399.5	176.0
	Yemen	528.0	26.2	N/A	N/A

(*Continued*)

Table 9.3 (Continued)

Region	Country	Land area (sq. km thousand, 2014)	Population (million, 2014)	GDP (current US$ billion, 2014)	Household consumption (current US$ billion, 2013)
Europe	Albania	27.4	2.9	13.2	10.0
	Armenia	28.5	3.0	11.6	9.7
	Azerbaijan	82.7	9.5	75.2	30.8
	Belarus	202.9	9.5	76.1	36.3
	Bosnia and Herzegovina	51.2	3.8	18.3	15.3
	Bulgaria	108.6	7.2	56.7	34.8
	Czech	77.2	10.5	205.3	103.7
	Croatia	56.0	4.2	57.1	34.9
	Estonia	42.4	1.3	26.5	12.9
	Georgia	69.5	4.5	16.5	11.5
	Hungary	90.5	9.9	138.3	70.3
	Latvia	62.2	2.0	31.3	18.6
	Lithuania	62.7	2.9	48.4	29.2
	Macedonia	25.2	2.1	11.3	7.7
	Moldova	32.9	3.6	8.0	7.4
	Montenegro	13.5	0.6	4.6	3.6
	Poland	306.2	38.0	545.0	319.1
	Romania	230.0	19.9	199.0	118.7
	Russia	16,376.9	143.8	1,860.6	1,097.4
	Serbia	87.5	7.1	43.9	34.3
	Slovakia	48.1	5.4	100.2	55.5
	Slovenia	20.1	2.1	49.5	26.2
	Turkey	769.6	75.9	798.4	582.9
	Ukraine	579.3	45.4	131.8	130.6
B&R countries total		49,901.2	4,521.4	23,319.9	10,404.0
Share of B&R countries in world total		38.5%	62.3%	30.0%	24.0%

Source: Helen Chin, Winnie He 2016 (Global Sourcing, Fung Business Intelligence Centre)

Conclusion

Integrated global collaboration on the BRI could be a driving force to make a great change in the lifestyle of current and future generations if it goes with an inclusive and trust-building spirit.

The BRI can play a key role in the optimization of connectivity for land and sea transportation through the Maritime Silk Road as low transport connectivity remains a major hurdle for developing countries to connect to global markets. In particular, landlocked developing countries, small island developing states, and other smaller and weak economies face considerable challenges in benefitting from trade opportunities, as they have access to fewer, less frequent, less reliable, and more costly transport connections. As maritime transport continues to be the main mode of transport for the imports and exports of most developing countries, it is important to identify policies that help improve maritime transport connectivity.

Maritime transport is facing the dual challenge of climate mitigation and adaptation. Transport networks and seaports in particular are likely to be highly affected by climate change factors, given port location and vulnerability. Building the climate resilience of maritime transport systems is therefore a precondition for sustainability. Climatic factors such as rising water levels, floods, storms, precipitation, extreme weather events, and associated risks such as coastal erosion, inundation, and deterioration of hinterland connections have implications for shipping volumes and costs, cargo loading and capacity, sailing and/or loading schedules, storage, and warehousing. International trade being increasingly multimodal and requiring the use of rail, road, and waterway transport, these problems will also affect the transport corridors above and beyond the ports acting as gateways. It will have to have global collaboration/intergovernmental cooperation to make it happen in reality.

Bibliography

Behnam, A 2012, 'Sustainable human settlements in coastal cities associated with events of Rio+20', In *Global forum on electric mobility and conference on sustainable human settlements.* Available from: www.un.org/esa/dsd/susdevtopics/sdt_pdfs/meetings2012/statements/behnam.pdf. [15 September 2016].

Behnam, A 2014, *Tracing the blue economy.* The Fondation de Malta, Malta.

Bloomberg Brief 2015, *One Belt, One Road: Assessing the economic impact of China's New Silk Road.* 2 July.

Bohlund, M & Orlik, T 2015, *China's road to Africa lifts investment, adds debt risk.* Bloomberg Intelligence. 18 June.

Chin, H & He, W 2016, *The Belt and Road initiative: 65 countries and beyond.* Global Sourcing, Fung Business Intelligence Centre, Hong Kong.

China-Britain Business Council 2015, 'One Belt One Road: a role for United Kingdom companies in developing China's new initiative-new opportunities in China and beyond'. [Online] Available from: www.cbbc.org/sectors/one-belt,-oneroad/. [15 September 2016].

Constantinescu, C, Mattoo, A & Ruta, M 2015, 'The global trade slowdown: cyclical or structural?' International Monetary Fund Working Paper No. 15/6.

European Central Bank 2015, 'Understanding the weakness of world trade', *Economic Bulletin*, vol. 3.

Freiman, I 2016, 'Belt and Road: Singapore's new growth track?'. [Online] Available from http://www.blplaw.com/expert-legal-insights/articles/belt-and-road-singapores-new-growth-track, [28 September 2016].

Hong Kong Trade Development Council (HKTDC) 2016, 'The Belt and Road initiative'. [Online] Available from: http://china-trade-research.hktdc.com/business-news/article/One-Belt-One-Road/The-Belt-and-Road-Initiative/obor/en/1/1X000000/1X0A36B7. [15 September 2016].

The International Chamber of Shipping (ICS) 2016, *International chamber of shipping 2016 annual review.* International Chamber of Shipping, London.

The International Chamber of Shipping (ICS) 2017a, *International chamber of shipping 2017 annual review*. International Chamber of Shipping, London.

The International Chamber of Shipping (ICS) 2017b, 'Shipping and world trade'. Available from: www.ics-shipping.org/shipping-facts/shipping-and-world-trade. [15 September 2016].

International Maritime Organization (IMO) 2016, 'International code for ships operating in Polar Waters (Polar Code)'. [Online] Available from: www.imo.org/en/MediaCentre/HotTopics/polar/Documents/POLAR%20CODE%20TEXT%20AS%20ADOPTED.pdf. [20 July 2016].

Kanak, D 2017, *Belt & Road and international cooperation: key to global growth and reducing long-term risks*. Eastspring Investments, Hong Kong.

United Nations Conference on Trade and Development (UNCTAD) 2015, *Review of maritime transport 2015*. United Nations Publication, Geneva.

United Nations Conference on Trade and Development (UNCTAD) 2016, *Review of maritime transport 2016*. United Nations Publication, Geneva.

United Nations Conference on Trade and Development (UNCTAD) 2017, *Review of maritime transport 2017*. United Nations Publication, Geneva.

United Nations Conference on Trade and Development (UNCTAS) 2015a, *The world's commercial shipping fleet grew at lowest rate in 10 years in 2014-new UNCTAD data*.

United Nations Conference on Trade and Development (UNCTAS) 2015b, *Maritime transport and climate policy at a critical juncture*, UNCTAS Report Says.

United Nations Department of Economic and Social Affairs 2016, 'Jointly building the "Belt and Road" towards the sustainable development goals'. Available from: www.un.org/development/desa/en/news/policy/building-belt-road-towards-sdgs.html. [15 September 2016].

World Bank 2016, 'Global Economic Prospects: Divergences and Risks'. World Bank Group. [Online] Available from: http://pubdocs.worldbank.org/en/84286146 3605615468/Global-Economic-Prospects-June-2016-Divergences-and-risks.pdf. [15 September 2016].

Part V
Prospect and challenges

10 Plotting the future of the Belt and Road Initiative

Connections, opportunities, and challenges

Peter Frankopan

Belt and Road Initiative in a time of global change

The study of history involves studying connections in the past. Being willing and able to look at the ways in which societies interacted with each other, found common ground, and managed to cooperate can produce insights that are as interesting and doubtless more useful than the usual interests of historians and those who read history books – where attention is usually focused on war and conflict, on struggles for power and on the deeds (or incompetence) of individual leaders.

Sometimes it is the study of institutions and stability that can prove most interesting, although this means sacrificing the thrills and excitement of battles for the sort of historical study that looks at the past in terms of continuity and connections, rather than the more usual story of dislocation and breakdown.

The 21st century is a time when we can see many countries actively looking for ways to work together and achieve mutual benefits of socio-economic development, poverty alleviation, and improvements not only in the quality of life, but the raising of ambitions and expectations for the future. Investing for the long-term requires the belief and confidence that the local and regional conditions will improve. Fear and doubts can be closely linked to highly defensive decisions economically, politically and even militarily: countless examples can be given from the past of cases where states felt that they had no option other than take drastic steps, either against their neighbours or in some cases even against their own populations.

Understanding the rhythms of history is particularly important at a time of global change. In 1990, Asia's share of world GDP, measured in real US$ purchasing power parity (PPP) was 23.2%. Over the next 25 years, it rose to 38.8 percent – an astonishing transformation that is still ongoing. By 2040, some estimates believe that Asia's share will account for almost half of all global GDP.[1] The National Intelligence Council in the United States put this into perspective: "By 2030 Asia will have surpassed North America and Europe combined in terms of global power, based upon GDP, population size, military spending and technological investment".[2]

In the context of why those changes are taking place and the ways in which they can be accelerated, it is striking to note the existence of many national, state-backed plans for how to take advantage of current conditions and develop a strategy to take them forward. These include the "Vision 2030" of Saudi Arabia, India's "Look East" and "Look West" proposals and Kazakhstan's "Bright Future" plans. All seek to prepare for the future and either suggest pathways towards innovation, to mutually beneficial international cooperation that often includes major infrastructure improvements, or both. All involve thought being given to large-scale investments into road building, train lines, smart cities – as well to the legal and administrative architecture required to put them into practice.

The most significant and wide-ranging of such plans is the Belt and Road Initiative that is China's signature economic and foreign policy. It was first announced in September 2013 when President XI Jinping of China gave a speech in Astana in Kazakhstan at Nazarbayev University. It was a foreign policy priority for China, he said, to develop friendly cooperative relations with the central Asian countries. The peoples and countries of the Silk Roads, he went on, had seen thousands of years of cooperation, despite "differences in race, belief and cultural background".[3]

The Belt and Road now dominates narratives across Asia, as well as in Europe and Africa. While it is tempting to create maps that show the geographical boundaries of the new Silk Roads, there is limited point in doing so. The Silk Roads of the present and future are abstract because in fact there are many different roads and different corridors – just as there were in the past. The Silk Roads in history were a plural, abstract, and vague network, rather than a series of fixed points: a web of connections, rather than an exclusive and enclosed set of towns and cities that were defined by their interactions.

Since President Xi made his speech, just under one trillion dollars have been committed into around 960 projects, including highways, railway lines, deepwater ports, airports, pipelines and large-scale infrastructure projects ranging across just over 60 countries which include about 65 percent of the world's population living in the so-called Belt and Road countries. Membership of this network is in the eye of the beholder – or rather, the eye of the borrower as most of China's Silk Roads investments have been made in the form of loans.[4]

There is no clear definition or rule as to which countries, peoples, or locations can be included or excluded from these networks – just as with the Silk Roads of the past. In the past, trade did not slow down or take account of language, race, or ethnicity. What mattered were trade networks and matching supply with demand. In today's world too, therefore, barriers are artificial when it comes to the primary targets of Chinese investments – namely minerals, energy resources, food and water, and major infrastructure projects including railways, highways, deepwater ports, and airports.

The significance of the Belt and Road Initiative lies partly in the financial resources being expended on a series of major projects across a wide range of countries in South, Southeastern, Central, and Western Asia. However, it also matters because of the basic demographics of global population distribution and the associated factors of consumption that go hand in hand with meeting the day to day requirement of nearly two thirds of the world's population.[5] Some believe that the sums so far committed to projects will rise further still in the future, perhaps running to 4 and perhaps even as high as 8 trillion dollars.[6]

In May 2017, when the Belt and Road Forum was held in Beijing, the achievements of the Belt and Road initiative were celebrated alongside a future setting out of the pathways under which the Belt and Road would intensify and continue to tie the countries of Asia and Africa and of some parts of Europe together, funnelled and fuelled by Chinese investment and Chinese money. "Exchange will replace estrangement", said President Xi, "mutual learning will replace clashes, and coexistence will replace a sense of superiority'.[7]

Lessons from history of the Silk Roads

One of the key elements of Belt and Road is the referencing back to the past, to the Silk Roads of antiquity and to centuries gone by. Spanning thousands of miles and years, the ancient silk roads embodied the spirit of peace and cooperation, openness, inclusiveness, mutual learning, and mutual benefit. This is the fundamental part of the message coming from Beijing which is that the Belt and Road Initiative is about creating a climate for mutual gain and for a "win-win" scenario where social, economic, and political development go hand-in-hand.

The initiative was referred to by President Xi as the "project of the century", the dawning of a new era where Belt and Road will allow partnerships and dialogues with no confrontation, and friendships rather than enmities.[8] The narrative of playing up the benefits of stability and the benefits of cooperation – without explicitly mentioning the down sides and the dangers of fragilities and breakdowns in relationships – is extremely important. As we often read in the press, we live in a globalized world, one that is highly interconnected, and where travel, the way we communicate, and the way we exchange ideas keeps accelerating thanks to the technology that allows us to work and move quicker, cheaper, and more efficiently than at any point in human history.

It is important, however, to place globalization within a suitable context. Although we think inter-continental exchange, long-distance trade, and interconnections that cover hundreds and indeed thousands of miles are new phenomena, our ancestors in the distant past were deeply interested in how people lived on the other side of the world, how they lived and what they thought. Blending materials from sources like the *Shi Ji*, written in Han Dynasty China in the third century BC, and surveys commissioned by the emperor Augustus in Rome 2,000 years ago allows us to create maps that resemble those of the new Silk Roads – presenting ways in which cities, peoples, and communities were linked by land and sea two millennia ago.

Materials written at that time in Rome and in China set out who lived where across the spine of Asia, how long it took to get from one place to the next, and explained what opportunities and challenges were raised by the people who lived there. They explained what resources and commodities were available and at what price, and what could be gained from building long-term relationships.

These were the Silk Roads of the past, roads, highways, and connections that facilitated the spread of goods and ideas – and helped create the world in which we live today.[9]

The name of the Silk Roads was coined in the 1870s by a German geographer, Ferdinand von Richthofen. He was trying to explain the trade between Han dynasty China, with the rest of Asia. Although he chose to focus on silk, a high-value elite luxury product that actually was traded in relatively small volumes, von Richthofen could equally have chosen spices, ceramics, other textiles, or even information, knowledge, or technology to describe the networks.[10]

Nevertheless, the Silk Roads label stuck and soon became popular. In the 20th century, it became synonymous with long-distance trade and travel – even though most of the trade that passed through these networks was much more limited in scale, range, and nature. Most of our interconnections today, as they were in the past, are local: our most frequent interactions are with people who live nearby, in our apartment block, in our neighbourhood, in our city, in our country. Interactions with people living a long way away may be memorable, but they are much rarer than everyday exchanges.

What drives more memorable, higher-value and noteworthy trade, then, is the availability and demand for goods and resources that are most in demand. Naturally, these change over time because of technology, fashion, and variations in supply. In today's world, for example, spices, ceramics, and textiles are perhaps less important than access to rare earths – like beryillium and dysprosium that are essential components for laptops, batteries, and hi-tech products – or even control of digital networks, data harvesting, and gathering of personal information.

Nevertheless, there are dangers in reducing human interaction to trade and commercial exchange. When we travel we also bring ideas about food, about music, about language, about faith, and about dreams. And of course, we also bring pathogens with us and diseases too: in the 14th century, the Black Death was spread along the mainland and sea routes linking Asia, Africa, and Europe together; today, the same can be done by international airline routes. People who fall ill get on planes and spread disease to their fellow passengers, enabling avian and swine flu, as well as other deadly and potentially deadly diseases to spread from one side of the planet to the other in 24 hours – more or less the furthest two corners of the globe are located from each other by flights.

Interactions in the past occasionally took place on a massive scale. We find shipwrecks off the coast of Southeast Asia and Indonesia with 70,000 items on a single shipment being taken from China to the Gulf. So much was being shipped over long-distance a thousand years ago that anything that fell overboard from a cargo ship had to be salvaged by divers: it was not worth the while of the ship's captain and crew to stop, turn round, and try to receive whatever had been lost. Such was the scale of shipping – and the speed, regularity, and importance of moving goods from one location to another.[11] In the old days, time was money too.[12]

Just as the Silk Roads stimulated local trade as well as long distance trade, helped circulate high value items, and brought together all sorts of other ideas, so too did they enable the transmission of technology which in the past was just as important as it is today. Investment produces new ways of doing business, new ways of living, and technological changes and advantages. For example, demand for goods in the Gulf spurred innovation in kiln technology in China, leading to a dramatic rise in the numbers of ceramic pieces that could be fired up in one setting.[13]

Exchange of technology included military hardware, tactics, and ideas – which were also studied eagerly and adopted, modified, and improved. During the Ming dynasty, there was great awareness of the sophistication and reliability of Western weapons, inspiring many to study them carefully. Some even wrote poems extolling the brilliance of cannon and guns made in Europe, while others worked out how to copy the technology and make it better "with modifications".[14]

Of course, one of the most fundamental aspects of enabling exchange of all kinds, cultural, commercial, economic, linguistic, and so on is stability and security. These issues were as important in the past as they are today. When we read Ibn Battuta writing in the 14th century, one of the most striking observations he makes about travelling in Asia and specifically in China is the security of the road systems. "China is the safest country and best country for the traveller", he wrote. Checks were made on outsiders on a daily basis, which in turn meant that "a man travels for nine months alone with great wealth and has nothing to fear".[15]

Stability and security are very closely linked with prosperity and with conditions that enable and encourage people to trade together. Francesco Pegolotti wrote an important compendium that gathered together lists, reports, and accounts of what could be found where in Asia. Pegolotti was less worried about writing about life and death dangers and threats to physical security, but in being overcharged for goods. Do not shave and grow a beard, he advised; and above all, hire the best local guide you could find and afford to deal with merchants, dealers, and brokers who were some of the most experienced – if not *the* most experienced – on earth.

In this sense, it is important to look at the history of Asia both in terms of its role in global history, but also to see the connections, exchanges, and rivalries between the peoples living between the Pacific and the Mediterranean and Atlantic Ocean and how the different cultures, languages, different faiths, and ethnicities competed and borrowed from each other. As is to be expected, some periods were much more stable than others, usually when the interests of the leaders have been closely aligned, or when one successful leader, or group of leaders, have been able to create a set of circumstances enabling long-distance trade to flourish following a period of turbulence.

From ancient Persia to the Mongols to the modern world, it has been clear that society flourishes and does best when that talent rises to the top and creates a meritocracy. This was the secret of success in China, India, Persia, and elsewhere: despite the vagaries and proclivities of the emperors, rulers, and shahs themselves, all sat at the stop of mighty empires because they could rely on administrators who put their decisions into practice – and maintained order and justice to the best of their abilities. In understanding such stability, a key area to pay attention to is the efforts made in pre-industrial states to stamping out corruption and inefficiency to ensure good governance.

In the past, successful states and political entities have had functioning bureaucracies that have created the right circumstances for investments – for of course, one of the most important elements in planning for the future is investing in the infrastructure that enables growth and opens up more opportunities. These include building basic transport networks that include roads, bridges, and places to stay; but also provision of clean water which is vital for sanitation and to keep cities healthy, attention paid to agriculture to enable urban populations to live sustainably, and of course public buildings such as bathhouses, places of worship, and spaces that celebrate and create common identities.[16]

These observations have a resonance today; but they are common themes that run back more than two millennia when it comes to looking at the history of the Silk Roads. There is a value and an importance in looking back to see how different rulers, different neighbours have managed to create successful relationships with their neighbours through high-level diplomatic exchanges, through low-level border exchanges, through dialogue, and through the ability to try to enable passage of individuals and goods across borders. The Silk Roads in the past were successful and played such an important role in the history of the world because these flows did not just take place but structures and systems were put in place to help them take place.

This is not to say that the history of the Silk Roads was always peaceful, or even that exchange is always positive. The networks of the past – and of the present and future – could transmit bad ideas, as well as good; they could enable the spread of disease as well as knowledge; they could create tensions and rivalries as well as common interests. What mattered most, however, was the ability to adapt. As I write at the start of my book on The Silk Roads, one of my favourite quotes is by the King of Zhao in northwestern China in the 4th century BC who said that "a talent for following the ways of yesterday is not sufficient to improve the world of today".[17]

This strikes me as particularly appropriate in the world of the early 21st century, a time when the process of change feels rapid to all of us – whether because of the new technologies that connect us more intensively and rapidly than ever before, or because of major geopolitical change. These are times when it is difficult to assess the intentions and likely decisions of the United States administration under President Trump that flatters one minute and threatens the next; which talks of trade barriers and literal walls going up, but at the same time expects and demands that others do their share, rather than leave the United States to shoulder the burden alone.

A complex and changing situation in North Korea, a problematic picture of a Middle East that is riddled – again – with violence and uncertainty, are just two of the major issues demanding global attention today. So too does the continued dislocation in Afghanistan, where Taliban and ISIS-K threaten not only the daily lives of the population, but also that in neighbouring countries in Central Asia which are themselves anxious about the contagion of ideas about fundamentalism spilling over and taking hold.

We can see division elsewhere too, not least in Europe, where Britain's vision for the future involves its exit from the European Union following a public referendum in 2016. The rise of far-right parties and the turbulence in countries like Hungary and Poland, but also in Spain where rallies regarding the independence of Catalonia draw hundreds of thousands on to the streets shows the degree of angst and disagreement about the direction of the European Union, individual member-states and even about European values are at a time of rising immigration and concern about integration of new arrivals. The pattern is similar in the United States, where a nation seems divided between competing views about what the United States does and should represent both at home and abroad, less welcoming and less tolerant towards others.

The sense of being at cross-roads is not confined to Europe and the United States. Pakistan has to face decisions about massive investment by China, about normalizing its relationship with India, and about how to best manage its relationship with Iran. Russia too is clearly trying to work out its role in the new world order, where its cultural impact currently outweighs its resources – but where it also maintains significant influence around the world. Military involvement in Syria lies at one end of Russia's willingness to intervene in a way that it has not done since the days of the Soviet Union; while its promotion of the Eurasian Economic Union as a means of facilitating cooperation with Belarus, Kazakhstan, Armenia, and Kyrgyzstan lies at the other.

This is mirrored by the rising geopolitical visions of others, which also include military interventions – such as Saudi Arabia's expensive engagement in Yemen and its freezing of relations with Qatar, or Iran's spreading tentacles throughout the Middle East, most notably in Syria and Iraq, but also in Yemen. There are a lot of moving pieces in the complex jigsaw of global geopolitics at the moment.

The role of the Belt and Road Initiative

The world is changing all around us. The reality, though, is that change has been a constant in world history. We only need to look back three decades to see this clearly. From late 1980s alone, as well as the fall of the Berlin Wall, the collapse of the Soviet Union, Apartheid ended in South Africa, South America changed fundamentally, the Middle East was transformed by military intervention, state breakdown and civil war, North Africa caught fire with the promise of an Arab spring giving way to chaos, while economic growth in India, China, and elsewhere in Asia helped shift the centre of global political and economic gravity to the east. The world is changing, because the world has always been changing – and always will.

This makes it hard to both evaluate phenomena like the Belt and Road Initiative as they develop – and harder still to anticipate the consequences that they may (or may not) have. Nevertheless, what is clear is that investments that have manageable levels of risk require stability – something that is not always simple or easy if the sands are always shifting. And while that flux can of course be about rivalry between states, it can also be impacted by the character of individual leaders and even that of high-ranking officials, and it can be impacted too by unforeseen or unusual events. In the spring of 2018, for example, the outbreak of widespread street protests in Iran was closely linked to a period of drought that served to put pressure on the rural economy, drove prices up, and prompted a popular backlash against the elites.

One of the key lessons in history is that national, regional, and supra-regional stability benefits everyone, creating a win-win scenario – even if that does not mean that benefits and fruits of cooperation are equally shared. Nevertheless, it compares sharply with the alternative – dislocation and instability, which can lead to tariffs, trade wars, and in the worst cases conflict. Warfare has an impact that can have global consequences – as was the case during the Arab-Israeli war of 1973. As a result of conflict in the Middle East, oil prices around the world more than quadrupled, in turn placing considerable strain on financial systems, government budgets, and leading to sky-rocketing inflation that was itself enormously destabilising.[18]

It is clear, therefore, that the Belt and Road can potentially bring benefits not only commercially and economically, but also by providing a platform to allow better communication between neighbouring states. As such, it is one of a series of initiatives that has helped facilitate the building of close ties across Asia – alongside groups like the Shanghai Cooperation Organisation, the Central Asia Cooperation Organisation, the Eurasian Economic Union, and the Heads of Caspian States summits, all of which aim to improve ties across some or all of the regions that make up the Silk Roads.

Nevertheless, its impact is potentially enormous, as the case of the China Pakistan Economic Corridor, one of the six so-called economic corridors spanning Asia, Europe, and Africa shows. This corridor, known as CPEC, includes road upgrades to link the southern coast of the country with western China, a raft of power plants, and optical cable to improve communication across a country that has a population approaching 200 million people. The investment into infrastructure has the opportunity to dramatically transform Pakistan's economy and society over a relatively short period of time. Pakistan is expected to see US$60 billion of investment from China, mainly in the form of loans

One of the problems in Pakistan today is electricity outages which affects industrial productivity. It also affects family life – determining when meal times are (and impacting dietary choices), playing a role in how children are taught at school and how they do their homework in the evenings. Economists believe that the upside to Pakistan's GDP will be significant, with the only difference of opinion centred on how great the growth will be as a result of the injection of capital and expertise – assuming, of course, that the various projects have been correctly evaluated, do not run over budget, and perform as expected.[19]

It should be stressed that the importance of these assumptions and the consequences of them not being realized – can and will have consequences that may not be so much as significant as dramatic. A project to build a deepwater port at Hambantota in Sri Lanka that failed on these metrics ended in acrimony and more specifically, with a Chinese operating company taking control of the port on a 99-year lease in exchange for the debt that had been built up and could not be repaid. There have been other similar cases too where debt levels have either spiralled out of control already, or threaten to do so in the future – causing some commentators to warn of a dislocation between the vision and reality, and also of the potential negative consequences where the financing risks behind projects are either poorly understood or overlooked altogether.

With 65 percent of the world's population living along countries that are part of the Belt and Road Initiative, however, there is the possibility that successful implementation of individual projects and groups of projects will affect not hundreds of millions but billions of people's lives positively if the plans are carried out carefully, efficiently, and diligently. In that sense the scale of the investment of the Belt and Roads, put by some in the trillions of dollars, as well as its over-arching vision, is mind boggling, because the process of these intensifications allow for more, quicker, better, faster, and safer levels of exchange.

There are multiple motivations for China's development and championing of the BRI, ranging from identifying and securing resources necessary for its own social and economic development in the coming decade, notably in the energy sector, to exporting excess capacity as the country moves from a period of rapid urbanization and construction into a services economy. There are security issues too behind the growing role China seeks to play internationally, both over the land and maritime routes where activities in the South China Sea to build and militarise a series of islands might be seen to point to a defensive mind-set, rather than aggressive expansion of power.

And then of course the BRI is an important demonstration of China showing leadership on the international stage. The significance is enhanced by the apparent problems elsewhere in the world. China is talking of helping, uniting, and intensifying relations at a time when others are talking about disengagement. The timing may be fortuitous, but it is striking that there is a vacuum that can be exploited, especially if it is done in a way that includes rather than excludes others. The establishment of the Asian Infrastructure Investment Bank (AIIB) is one sign of the willingness of China to work with others to fund some of the projects that form part of the BRI.

These four motivations – needs, excess capacity, security, and international leadership – seem a useful prism through which to try to understand the BRI, with the caveat that the Initiative is still in its early states, having only been announced in 2013. But each of these elements seems logical in its own way, eminently plausible, understandable, and almost exactly what one might expect smart policymakers in Beijing to be proposing.

The difficulty is that they while logical they are not necessarily complementary. Each one of them can contrast and conflict with another, which can in turn mean that they can undermine each other. So in the first instance, there is the reality of expectation and reality inside China itself. One question will revolve around how BRI is seen as and when individual projects run into difficulty, become unviable, or present thorny issues of resolution – especially if they raise tensions and are reputationally damaging. Another question will revolve around how Chinese investments abroad are perceived and understood within China, whether they prove successful or otherwise. Putting money into the infrastructure of other states is not always straightforward and can become hard to justify if, as, and when there are hiccups closer to home. Helping neighbours and potential rivals at a time of plenty is different to doing so when conditions deteriorate. And then of course there are forces outside control that can prove reputationally damaging – such as in Macedonia where unsustainable costs have led to the cancellation of a motorway project mid-construction, and has led to bitter recriminations. Examples like this will do little to encourage support for the BRI domestically.

Tests to the initiative

There is the challenge too of seeing how well China is able to make BRI be a "win-win" scenario for all involved. Some of the countries that are seeing investments or proposals are complicated and what is more have complex and difficult regional relations. It is hard, for example, to navigate the Middle East without being drawn into taking sides between Saudi Arabia and Iran, whose leaders threatened military action against each other in 2017. It is difficult to play cards carefully when dealing with complex local political rivalries and disputes – such as in the Gulf where Qatar has been marginalized and isolated by its regional rivals. Giving assurances that investment is only driven by economic principles, and can be kept distinct from politics, masks the reality of complicated decisions in complex regions. Much will depend on the skill of Chinese diplomats and officials in being able to soothe tensions and being able to win friends in the coming years. That starts, in my opinion, with education, learning, and mutual respect.

Perhaps the most obvious test case for that will come with India, a country with which China has long enjoyed a cultural, political, and military rivalry. In the summer of 2017, that rivalry spilled over into a stand-off at the Doklam plateau in the Himalayas where the countries have a long-standing border dispute. This escalated to soldiers from both countries engaging each other – mercifully only with hand-to-hand combat. A real challenge for Beijing (as well as for Delhi) will be working out how to de-escalate these and other problems, and either work together or not be threatened by each other's actions.

So while the Silk Roads of the past provide a context and a model for cooperation and of people getting on with each other despite "differences in race, belief and cultural background", it is not enough to rely on past history and the memory of that collaboration. It needs to be reinforced on a regular basis alongside the realization that just working together may be a good idea in theory, it does not work unless thought goes into how that plays out in practice. It is one thing too to talk of tolerating different races, faiths, and backgrounds – and another to do so in practice. As the Assistant Secretary General of the United Nations warned recently, human rights activists – and human rights themselves – are coming under intense pressure across Asia.[20]

So the coming years will be all about the hard-work, the "nitty gritty", of how relationships are forged, how they are maintained, and how well they fare during the inevitable ups and downs during a time of change. Much depends, then, on how well all sides can adapt. Learning from mistakes is not easy or pleasant. But as it becomes clear which parts of the BRI are most effective and most efficient – and which are the most problematic and difficult – the motivations and aims of the initiative will change by necessity; how they do so will determine the long-term success of the BRI as a whole.

Another major challenge presented by the BRI is its asymmetry. As the Minister of Commerce in Pakistan put it in 2017, his great worry was that quote "China will sell us cheap goods because we can't compete". That does not sound like win-win. But, as the minister added, there was little choice. Infrastructure projects are very expensive and without BRI support, they would not be undertaken in Pakistan. "China", he conceded "is the only game in town".[21]

The scale of money and investment coming from China alone means that countries are faced with difficult choices about which projects to accept and how financially and economically viable they are. The International Monetary Fund has warned about the dangers of less well-developed economies taking on excessive or unsupportable levels of debt – and the risks this poses.[22] A new high-speed railway across Laos will account for nearly 50 percent of the country's entire GDP, or an new railway line has been built linking Mombasa to Nairobi that is part of a series of railway networks to be built by China in Africa and which represents the largest single infrastructure project built since Kenyan independence 50 years ago. Few observers doubt that here will be more cases like the Hambantota port fiasco in Sri Lanka – which not surprisingly creates ill-will locally and raises alarms further afield.

So too does the sense that while China is keen to make inroads in other markets, the same level of openness is not being reciprocated. As President Kenyatta of Kenya put it when he opened the railway, while he welcomed participating in the Belt and Road and looked forward to reaping its fruits, it was also important that China open up its own markets in return.[23] It is all very well asking for access to other people's infrastructure and to other people's markets to sell Chinese goods, in other words, but having barriers in place that prevent reciprocal arrangements is not helpful.

Asymmetry and frustrations can be extremely damaging to long-term views about China and to its wider strategic aims. It is striking, for example, that since the opening of the Chinese-financed (and Chinese built) rail line, President Kenyatta has taken to calling for closer cooperation with other East African nations – explicitly urging them to do in order to compete with China.[24] Some Chinese projects in Africa and elsewhere have already been nicknamed "red elephants" – a reference not to the popularity of this magnificent animal, but to its cumbersome size and limited usefulness.

There are bound to be ups and downs. At the end of 2017, a new Nepalese Prime Minister cancelled the Budhi Gandaki Hydro Electric Plant that was worth US$2.5 billion on the basis that the loan terms were too expensive and made the project too risky – although a few months later there was talk of reviving the proposal. The Diamer-Bhasha dam project in Pakistan worth US$14 billion was cancelled around the same time over the lack of competitive tendering that has become a feature – and a consistent complaint about projects that are not just financed with Chinese loans, but then awarded to Chinese contractors. Only a quarter of contracts that have been awarded since 2013 have gone to local businesses, which means that the benefits to the country in question are not as immediate as they otherwise could be.

Across the Silk Roads, celebrating the past and talk of working together do not just go hand in hand; they are all but ubiquitous. China has certainly played a major role in stimulating this new trend. The BRI represents a real opportunity to help spur change, to upgrade national infrastructures, and to help with poverty alleviation. But it can also dovetail with the concerns that some have about over-dependence on China and Chinese capital will produce debt burdens that will lead to a state being crushed rather than blossoming. As history teaches so clearly, steering away from unintentional colonization is not easy – but like so many lessons from the past, it needs to be constantly repeated.

There are other emerging responses to the BRI that may in time turn out to be complementary rather than alternatives. India has a series of formal and semi-formal policies that have similar aims as the BRI, as do Kazakhstan, Vietnam, Japan, and Russia, while sovereign wealth funds and multilateral financial organizations like the AIIB, the Asian Development Bank, and the European Bank for Reconstruction and Development all have investment strategies closely linked to economic, industrial, and social development in individual countries along the Silk Roads that form part of a wider approach to the region generally. Ironically, one of the early and unexpected achievements of the BRI has been to prompt new collaborations outside the BRI framework – such as that proposed by the President of Kenya in Africa.

That cannot be a bad thing – for two reasons. First, the more cooperation the better the chances of long-term geopolitical and economic stability. Bur second, of course, more participants means more competition, which in turn both provides options in countries seeking investment, but also helps drives costs down. The conclusion, then, is a positive one. For Asia to flourish, it is important to satisfy almost insatiable demand for investment in transport networks, energy plants, sustainable agriculture, and smart cities. If BRI is part of that bigger picture – then that is good news for everyone regionally and beyond.

Conclusion

It is always worth looking at the past, present, and future by trying to see how different ideas feed into each other, by assessing how connections produce expected and unexpected consequences, and above all to see how the process of change itself manifests itself. The Silk Roads have always been highly responsive to global change – and in many cases, have been responsible for provoking that change. Shifting patterns of supply and demand for goods, control over transport networks, and the introduction of new technologies have played important roles in shaping and reshaping what happens along the Silk Roads – but it is not hard to understand that this in turn is part of a bigger picture too.

We are living through a period of particular turbulence and potential fragilities. It is clear that the Belt and Road has the ability to transform the lives of billions. The most important thing, as BRI goes forward, is to understand what constitutes success and failure in Beijing and but also in Silk Roads countries and to be able measure expectations and realities in a meaningful way. The ability to learn from mistakes is an important one – which is one reason we have universities to help us learn this skill. Without knowledge we can achieve nothing.

Notes

1 Deloitte Insights, 'Packing a mightier punch: Asia's economic growth among global markets continues' (London, 2016), p. 24; Oxford Economics, *Global infrastructure outlook. Infrastructure investment needs. 50 countries, 7 sectors to 2040* (2017), p. 13.
2 National Intelligence Council, *Global trends 2030 – alternative worlds* (2012), p. 4.
3 Xinhua, Speech by Xi Jinping, 'Promote people-to-people friendship and create a better future', 7 September 2013.
4 State Council Information Office, 'Six major economic corridors form the "Belt and Road" framework. China Development Bank invests \$890bn', 2 May 2015.
5 HSBC, 'Reshaping the Future World Economy', 11 May 2017.
6 South China Morning Post, 'Cost of funding "Belt and Road Initiative" is a daunting task', 27 September 2017.
7 Xinhua, 'Full text of President Xi's speech at opening of Belt and Road forum', 14 May 2017.
8 Xinhua, 'Full text of President Xi Jinping's speech at opening of Belt and Road forum', 14 May 2017.
9 P. Frankopan, *The Silk Roads: a new history of the world* (London, 2015), pp. 1–26.
10 F. von Richthofen, 'Über die zentralasiatischen Seidenstrassen bis zum 2. Jahrhundert. n. Chr.', *Verhandlungen der Gesellschaft für Erdkunde zu Berlin* 4 (1877), 96–122.
11 Frankopan, *Silk Roads*, p. 96.
12 H. Khalileh, *Admiralty and Maritime laws in the Mediterranean Sea (ca. 800–1050): the Kitāb Akriyat al Sufun vis-à-vis the Nomos Rhodion Nautikos* (Leiden, 2006), pp. 212–214.
13 J. Stargardt, 'Indian Ocean trade in the ninth and tenth centuries: demand, distance, and profit', *South Asian Studies* 30.1 (2014), 35–55.
14 T. Andrade, *The Gunpowder Age* (Princeton, 2016), pp. 135–143.
15 Ibn Battuta, *al-Riwla*, tr. H. Gibb, *The Travels of Ibn Battuta*, 4 vols (Cambridge, 1994), 4, 22, pp. 893–894.
16 See for example, P. Frankopan, 'Geschichte des globalen Stadt', in A. Birken (ed) *ZukunftsWerte. Verantwortug für die Welt von Morgen* (Göttingen, 2018), pp. 230–237.
17 Frankopan, *Silk Roads*, p. xviii.
18 E. Bini & G. Garavini, *Oil shock: the 1973 crisis and its economic legacy* (London, 2018).
19 For a useful appraisal here, see the summary produced by Deloitte, 'How will CPEC boos Pakistan economy?', https://www2.deloitte.com/content/dam/Deloitte/pk/Documents/risk/pak-china-eco-corridor-deloittepk-noexp.pdf.

20 Andrew Gilmour, 'Imprisoned, threatened, silence: human rights workers across Asia are in danger' *Guardian*, 18 May 2018.
21 Quoted in *Financial Times*, 'China takes "project of the century" to Pakistan', 17 May 2017.
22 Financial Times, 'IMF's Lagarde warns China on Belt and Road debt', 12 April 2018.
23 'Kenya president urges rebalance of China-Africa trade,' *Financial Times*, 14 May 2017.
24 'Kenyatta urges regional cooperation to compete with China', *Observer Uganda*, 27 February 2018.

Index

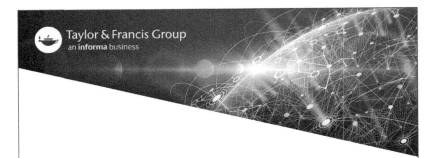

For Product Safety Concerns and Information please contact our EU representative GPSR@taylorandfrancis.com Taylor & Francis Verlag GmbH, Kaufingerstraße 24, 80331 München, Germany

Printed and bound by CPI Group (UK) Ltd, Croydon, CR0 4YY

01/05/2025

01858446-0002